LORD BYRON

The Complete
Poetical Works

37. XLIII

Wandering in Youth I traced the path of him
+ The Woman friend of Rome's last mortal Maid,
The friend of Tully; as my Bark did skim
The bright blue waters with a fanning Wind,
Came Megara before me, and behind
Aegina lay, Piraeus on the right,
And Corinth on the left; I lay reclined
Along the prow, & saw all these, unite
In ruin, even as he had seen the desolate
                                        Sight; —

Note

The celebrated Letter of Servius Sulpicius to Cicero
on the death of his daughter describes as it then
was & now is a path which I often traced in Greece
both by sea & land in different journeys & voyages.

"On my return from Asia, as I was sailing from
Aegina towards Megara, I began to contemplate the prospect of the
countries around me: Aegina was behind, Megara before me, Piraeus
on the right, Corinth on the left; all which towns once famous and
flourishing now lie overturned & buried in their ruins: upon this
sight I could not but think presently within myself, Alas! how do we poor
mortals fret & vex ourselves if any of our friends happen to die
or be killed, whose life is yet so short, when the carcasses of so
many noble cities lie here exposed before me in one view?" &c.
                                                        &c.

Childe Harold's Pilgrimage, Canto IV, stanza 44, with
Byron's note

*Reproduced with permission from the holograph MS. in the collection of
John Murray Ltd.*

LORD BYRON

The Complete Poetical Works

EDITED BY
JEROME J. McGANN

VOLUME II

Childe Harold's Pilgrimage

OXFORD
AT THE CLARENDON PRESS
1980

Oxford University Press, Walton Street, Oxford OX2 6DP

OXFORD LONDON GLASGOW
NEW YORK TORONTO MELBOURNE WELLINGTON
KUALA LUMPUR SINGAPORE HONG KONG TOKYO
DELHI BOMBAY CALCUTTA MADRAS KARACHI
NAIROBI DAR ES SALAAM CAPE TOWN

*Published in the United States by
Oxford University Press, New York*

British Library Cataloguing in Publication Data
Byron, George Gordon, *Baron Byron*
    Lord Byron, the complete poetical works. –
    (Oxford English texts)
    Vol. 2
    I. McGann, Jerome John   II. Series
    821'.7   PR4350   78–41111
    ISBN 0–19–812754–5
    ISBN 0–19–812764–2 Pbk.

*Printed in Great Britain
at the University Press, Oxford
by Eric Buckley
Printer to the University*

PREFACE TO VOLUME II

THE text of *Childe Harold's Pilgrimage* is one of the most reliable in the Byron canon. Consequently, the present edition has made relatively few alterations in the received work. In Cantos I–II the only significant error transmitted through the previous printings involves some garbled punctuation in the final stanza of Canto II.

Because Byron did not correct the proofs of Canto III, its text has suffered the greatest damage, though even here the problems are not major ones. A few unauthorized textual changes were printed in the first edition which have not heretofore been corrected (see, for example, stanzas 2, 22, 25). Most important, however, are Byron's political notes for Canto III, which his publisher removed from the poem, much to Byron's annoyance. These notes are restored to the poem here for the first time.

The received Canto IV is a good clear text for the most part. The most important correction here is not made in the poetical text but in Byron's prose Dedication to Hobhouse. Byron's corrected copy of Canto IV, previously known to editors, carries a number of textual emendations which have already been incorporated into the poem in earlier editions. But this important passage in the Dedication—where Byron discusses the conflict between Classic and Romantic poetry—has not previously been emended according to Byron's directions.

The mass of new manuscript material which bears upon *Childe Harold's Pilgrimage* has had a significant impact upon the preparation of the editor's notes and commentaries. This large body of primary evidence has enabled a sharper and more detailed presentation of the poem's origins and context, and hence it ought to strengthen the reader's critical grasp of Byron's great work.

Finally, I owe a special word of thanks to Professor Diskin Clay, who gave me some timely advice and instruction on Byron's Romaic extracts printed with Cantos I–II.

Childe Harold's Pilgrimage,
A Romaunt

L'univers est une espèce de livre, dont on n'a lu que la première page quand on n'a vu que son pays. J'en ai feuilleté un assez grand nombre, que j'ai trouvé également mauvaises. Cet examen ne m'a point été infructueux. Je haïssais ma patrie. Toutes les impertinences des peuples divers, parmi lesquels j'ai vécu, m'ont réconcilié avec elle. Quand je n'aurais tiré d'autre bénéfice de mes voyages que celui-là, je n'en regretterais ni les frais, ni les fatigues.   LE COSMOPOLITE.

PREFACE

[to Cantos I–II]

The following poem was written, for the most part, amidst the scenes which it attempts to describe. It was begun in Albania; and the parts relative to Spain and Portugal were composed from the author's observations in those countries. Thus much it may be necessary to state for the correctness of the descriptions. The ⁵ scenes attempted to be sketched are in Spain, Portugal, Epirus, Acarnania, and Greece. There for the present the poem stops: its reception will determine whether the author may venture to conduct his readers to the capital of the East, through Ionia and Phrygia: these two cantos are merely experimental.   10

174. Copy text: *CHP*(*7*), collated with *MSS. M, D, MI, MA, MB, MC, MDa, MDb, MDc, DA, NL, T, Υ, H, L, G, O; Proofs H* and *M; B's MS.* corrections in various letters; *CHP(1)–CHP(6), CHP(8)–CHP(10), 1831, 1832, C, More*

Title   Childe ⟨Burun's⟩ Pilgrimage *M*; Childe Harold's Pilgrimage. A Romaunt. *all separate editions of Cantos I–II*
epigraph   *no MS.*
Preface   Advertisement *Da; cor. in Dc*

1 amidst] ⟨on⟩ *Da*   2 attempts] professes Υ, *Da, marked for correction Dc* 4–5 Portugal . . . countries] Portugal ⟨worked up⟩ from the Author's notes made in those countries Υ   4–5 Thus . . . descriptions] Thus much is necessary to be stated in a descriptive poem.— Υ; A fictitious character is introduced for the sake of giving some connection to the piece, which ⟨aspires / pretends to no plan⟩ makes no pretension to regularity. Υ, *Da without cancellations*; ⟨The Ariosto is so far taken as a model, that the author is grave or gay high or low as suited him at the moment without considering how far his composition be injured by such a mixture⟩ Υ   6 scenes . . . in] countries sketched are Υ   7–8 stops . . . will] stops; ⟨if the public should be kind enough to wish to accompany the author still further East, he could take them as far as Constantinople⟩ its reception must Υ   stops; ⟨the⟩ its reception ⟨in its present state⟩ will *Da*   9 through] by way of Υ

A fictitious character is introduced for the sake of giving some connexion to the piece; which, however, makes no pretension to regularity. It has been suggested to me by friends, on whose opinions I set a high value, that in this fictitious character, 'Childe
15 Harold', I may incur the suspicion of having intended some real personage: this I beg leave, once for all, to disclaim—Harold is the child of imagination, for the purpose I have stated. In some very trivial particulars, and those merely local, there might be grounds for such a notion; but in the main points, I should hope, none
20 whatever.

It is almost superfluous to mention that the appellation 'Childe', as 'Childe Waters', 'Childe Childers', &c. is used as more consonant with the old structure of versification which I have adopted. The 'Good Night', in the beginning of the first canto, was suggested
25 by 'Lord Maxwell's Good Night', in the Border Minstrelsy, edited by Mr. Scott.

With the different poems which have been published on Spanish subjects, there may be found some slight coincidence in the first part, which treats of the Peninsula, but it can only be casual; as,
30 with the exception of a few concluding stanzas, the whole of this poem was written in the Levant.

The stanza of Spenser, according to one of our most successful poets, admits of every variety. Dr. Beattie makes the following observation: 'Not long ago I began a poem in the style and stanza of
35 Spenser, in which I propose to give full scope to my inclination, and be either droll or pathetic, descriptive or sentimental, tender or satirical, as the humour strikes me; for, if I mistake not, the measure which I have adopted admits equally of all these kinds of composi-

11–26 *Not in* Υ, *Da*   12 connexion to] connection ⟨and action⟩ to *Dc*   15–20 intended . . . whatever] drawn 'from myself'. *Db*, *cor. in Dc*; This I beg leave once for all to disclaim. I wanted a character to give some connection to the poem, and ⟨I⟩ the one adopted suited my purpose as well as any other.—In some very trivial particulars, and those merely local there might be grounds for such an idea but in the main points I should hope none whatever. *Db*; My reader will observe that where the author speaks in his own person he assumes a very different tone from that of 'The cheerless thing, the man without a friend'— *Db*, *cor. in Dc*; at least till death had deprived him of his ⟨dearest⟩ nearest connections. ⟨I crave pardon for the egotism in a note which proceeds from my wish to dismiss / discard the / any probable imputation of it to the *text*.⟩ *Db*   22 used] ⟨taken⟩ *Db*   23 adopted] endeavored to adopt *Db*   25–6 edited by] ⟨of⟩ *Db*   27–9 poems . . . treats] poems published on Spanish subjects and perhaps with Mr. Scott's ⟨celebrated satire⟩ 'the Vision of Don Roderick' there may be some casual coincidence in that part of the poem which treats Υ 32 Spenser, according] Spenser ⟨if one of its most successful poets be not mistaken⟩ Υ 33 variety. Dr.] variety of manners. ⟨I shall⟩ Dr. Υ 33–4 variety . . . observation] variety of manners. ⟨I shall⟩ Dr. Beattie observes Υ 37 measure] *Dc*, *all edns.* manner Υ, *Da*

tion.'—Strengthened in my opinion by such authority, and by the example of some in the highest order of Italian poets, I shall make 40 no apology for attempts at similar variations in the following composition; satisfied that, if they are unsuccessful, their failure must be in the execution, rather than in the design sanctioned by the practice of Ariosto, Thomson, and Beattie.

ADDITION TO THE PREFACE

I have now waited till almost all our periodical journals have dis- 45 tributed their usual portion of criticism. To the justice of the generality of their criticisms I have nothing to object; it would ill become me to quarrel with their very slight degree of censure, when, perhaps, if they had been less kind they had been more candid. Returning, therefore, to all and each my best thanks for 50 their liberality, on one point alone shall I venture an observation. Amongst the many objections justly urged to the very indifferent character of the 'vagrant Childe', (whom, notwithstanding many hints to the contrary, I still maintain to be a fictitious personage), it has been stated, that besides the anachronism, he is very *un-* 55 *knightly*, as the times of the Knights were times of love, honour, and so forth. Now it so happens that the good old times, when 'l'amour du bon vieux tems, l'ámour antique' flourished, were the most profligate of all possible centuries. Those who have any doubts on this subject may consult St. Palaye, *passim*, and more particularly 60 vol. ii. page 69. The vows of chivalry were no better kept than any other vows whatsoever, and the songs of the Troubadours were not more decent, and certainly were much less refined, than those of Ovid.—The 'Cours d'amour, parlemens d'amour ou de courtesie et de gentilesse' had much more of love than of courtesy or gentleness. 65 —See Rolland on the same subject with St. Palaye.—Whatever other objection may be urged to that most unamiable personage Childe Harold, he was so far perfectly knightly in his attributes— 'No waiter, but a knight templar.'—By the by, I fear that Sir Tristram and Sir Lancelot were no better than they should be, 70 although very poetical personages and true knights 'sans peur', though not 'sans reproche'.—If the story of the institution of the

39 in] ⟨of⟩ *Da*   41 attempts at] the *Υ*   42 that . . . their] that the *Υ*; that their *Da*   42 composition] ⟨composition⟩ design *Υ*   44 the practice] the ⟨practices of the first celebrated⟩ *Υ*

'Garter' be not a fable, the knights of that order have for several centuries borne the badge of a Countess of Salisbury, of indifferent
75 memory. So much for chivalry. Burke need not have regretted that its days are over, though Maria Antoinette was quite as chaste as most of those in whose honours lances were shivered, and knights unhorsed.

Before the days of Bayard, and down to those of Sir Joseph
80 Banks (the most chaste and celebrated of ancient and modern times), few exceptions will be found to this statement, and I fear a little investigation will teach us not to regret these monstrous mummeries of the middle ages.

I now leave 'Childe Harold' to live his day, such as he is; it had
85 been more agreeable, and certainly more easy, to have drawn an amiable character. It had been easy to varnish over his faults, to make him do more and express less, but he never was intended as an example, further than to show that early perversion of mind and morals leads to satiety of past pleasures and disappointment in new
90 ones, and that even the beauties of nature, and the stimulus of travel (except ambition, the most powerful of all excitements) are lost on a soul so constituted, or rather misdirected. Had I proceeded with the Poem, this character would have deepened as he drew to the close; for the outline which I once meant to fill up for him was,
95 with some exceptions, the sketch of a modern Timon, perhaps a poetical Zeluco.

To Ianthe

Not in those climes where I have late been straying,
Though Beauty long hath there been matchless deem'd;
Not in those visions to the heart displaying
Forms which it sighs but to have only dream'd,
Hath aught like thee in truth or fancy seem'd: 5
Nor, having seen thee, shall I vainly seek
To paint those charms which varied as they beam'd—

To Ianthe   *untitled in L*; To the Lady Charlotte Harley *MI and proof*; To Ianthe *H; cor. in MI proof*

1 Not in] ⟨Dear as⟩ *L*   have late] have ⟨been⟩ just *L*   3 Not. . .to] Nor in those visions ⟨where⟩ to *L*   4 Forms which] Such forms *L*   5 Hath] ⟨To me⟩ Hath *L*
6 seen] found *L*   7 those . . . varied] the . . . ⟨dazzled⟩ varied *L*

To such as see thee not my words were weak;
To those who gaze on thee what language could they speak?

Ah! may'st thou ever be what now thou art,   10
Nor unbeseem the promise of thy spring,
As fair in form, as warm yet pure in heart,
Love's image upon earth without his wing,
And guileless beyond Hope's imagining!
And surely she who now so fondly rears   15
Thy youth, in thee, thus hourly brightening,
Beholds the rainbow of her future years,
Before whose heavenly hues all sorrow disappears.

Young Peri of the West!—'tis well for me
My years already doubly number thine;   20
My loveless eye unmov'd may gaze on thee,
And safely view thy ripening beauties shine;
Happy, I ne'er shall see them in decline,
Happier, that while all younger hearts shall bleed,
Mine shall escape the doom thine eyes assign   25
To those whose admiration shall succeed,
But mixed with pangs to Love's even loveliest hours decreed.

Oh! let that eye, which, wild as the Gazelle's,
Now brightly bold or beautifully shy,
Wins as it wanders, dazzles where it dwells,   30
Glance o'er this page; nor to my verse deny
That smile for which my breast might vainly sigh,
Could I to thee be ever more than friend:
This much, dear maid, accord; nor question why
To one so young my strain I would commend,   35
But bid me with my wreath one matchless lily blend.

8 To such . . .] ⟨Few I have gazed⟩ *L*; To ⟨those⟩ such *MI*   9 To those] To such *L*
19 West] ⟨North/West⟩ North *L*   20 My] Mine *L*, *MI and proof*, *H*   21 My
loveless . . .] ⟨Too late to love yet may⟩ *L*   gaze] look *L*   22 view] mark *L*
23 Happy . . . see] Happy ⟨that⟩ I . . . view *L*   24 while . . . bleed] ⟨while they conquer
other hearts⟩ *L*   25 shall . . . eyes] will . . . thou shalt *L*   27 with pangs] with ⟨all
the⟩ pangs *L*   even loveliest] ⟨deceitful⟩ *MI proof*   29 ⟨In guiltless ? or brighten to
? ⟩ *L*   brightly] wildly *L*   30 Wins . . .] ⟨Wounds as it wins⟩ *L*   wanders] ⟨changes /
shifts and⟩ *L*   32 That . . . breast] The . . . heart *L*   33 to] for *L*   34 maid]
girl *L*   35 my] this *L*   36 bid . . . lily] ⟨let . . . flower⟩ *L*

Such is thy name with this my verse entwin'd;
And long as kinder eyes a look shall cast
On Harold's page, Ianthe's here enshrin'd
Shall thus be first beheld, forgotten last: 40
My days once number'd, should this homage past
Attract thy fairy fingers near the lyre
Of him who hail'd thee, loveliest as thou wast,
Such is the most my memory may desire;
Though more than Hope can claim, could Friendship less
    require?   45

CANTO I

I.

Oh, thou! in Hellas deem'd of heav'nly birth,
Muse! form'd or fabled at the minstrel's will!
Since sham'd full oft by later lyres on earth,
Mine dares not call thee from thy sacred hill:
Yet there I've wander'd by thy vaunted rill;   5
Yes! sigh'd o'er Delphi's long-deserted shrine,
Where, save that feeble fountain, all is still;
Nor mote my shell awake the weary Nine
To grace so plain a tale—this lowly lay of mine.

37 ⟨Such shall thy name entwined with verse like⟩ L   this my verse] verse like mine L
38 kinder . . . cast] ⟨such may dare pretend to live⟩ L   a look shall] shall deign to L, H,
MI; a glance shall cor. in MI proof   39 One look along my page—thy name
enshrined L; A look . . . that name MI, H; Along my page, Ianthe's there enshrined cor.
in MI proof   40 thus] there L, MI, H; still cor. in MI proof   beheld] ⟨recalled⟩ L
41 ⟨And when my days are numbered and thy past⟩ L   homage] offering L
42–4   Present these dim Remembrances of him
                  Who saw and hailed thee loveliest when thou wast
                  ⟨With this world⟩ Amidst its ⟨frail⟩ varying shadows
                  bright or dim L cancelled
44 most . . . desire] ⟨safe memorial I desire / most Remembrance shall desire⟩ L   may]
⟨shall⟩ MI   45 can . . . require] may dare—ah less could I require L can claim—ah!
less could I require MI

1 in Hellas deem'd] of yore esteemed D   ⟨by men miscalled⟩ NL   2 Muse, ⟨God-
dess, Inspiration, what they will⟩ NL   3 ⟨Since human strains must always / still
bear the stamp of Earth⟩ NL   sham'd . . . lyres] later lyres are only strung NL, D
4 ⟨Sleep if it please then on thy native Hill⟩ NL   sacred] ⟨feeble⟩ glorious NL; glorious D
5 wander'd . . . vaunted] wooed thee—heard thy ⟨native⟩ / vaunted NL; wooed thee,
drank thy vaunted D   6 long-] now NL   7 Where ⟨all is deathlike, desolate and⟩
still NL   8 ⟨Then can / Ah could I dare to wake⟩ NL   mote] ⟨might⟩ NL

2.

Whilome in Albion's isle there dwelt a youth,   10
Who ne in virtue's ways did take delight;
But spent his days in riot most uncouth,
And vex'd with mirth the drowsy ear of Night.
Ah, me! in sooth he was a shameless wight,
Sore given to revel and ungodly glee;   15
Few earthly things found favour in his sight
Save concubines and carnal companie,
And flaunting wassailers of high and low degree.

3.

Childe Harold was he hight:—but whence his name
And lineage long, it suits me not to say;   20
Suffice it, that perchance they were of fame,
And had been glorious in another day:
But one sad losel soils a name for aye,
However mighty in the olden time;
Nor all that heralds rake from coffin'd clay,   25
Nor florid prose, nor honied lies of rhyme
Can blazon evil deeds, or consecrate a crime.

4.

Childe Harold bask'd him in the noon-tide sun,
Disporting there like any other fly;
Nor deem'd before his little day was done   30
One blast might chill him into misery.
But long ere scarce a third of his pass'd by,
Worse than adversity the Childe befell;
He felt the fulness of satiety:
Then loath'd he in his native land to dwell,   35
Which seem'd to him more lone than Eremite's sad cell.

5.

For he through Sin's long labyrinth had run,
Nor made atonement when he did amiss,

12 most uncouth] ⟨and in ruth⟩ M   15 ungodly glee] ⟨to Pageantry⟩ D
16–17 Few . . . save] He chused the bad and did the good afright With M; cor. in D
16 Few] No D   19 Harold] ⟨Burun⟩ M   26 honied] ⟨oily⟩ M   lies] glose D
alternate reading   27 or . . . a] nor . . . one M   28 Harold] ⟨Burun⟩ M
30 before his little] ⟨like others ere the⟩ D   35 Then] ⟨And⟩ M   37 through . . .
had] ⟨had oer the course too swiftly⟩ M

Had sigh'd to many though he lov'd but one,
And that lov'd one, alas! could ne'er be his.   40
Ah, happy she! to 'scape from him whose kiss
Had been pollution unto aught so chaste;
Who soon had left her charms for vulgar bliss,
And spoil'd her goodly lands to gild his waste,
Nor calm domestic peace had ever deign'd to taste.   45

6.

And now Childe Harold was sore sick at heart,
And from his fellow bacchanals would flee;
'Tis said, at times the sullen tear would start,
But Pride congeal'd the drop within his ee:
Apart he stalk'd in joyless reverie,   50
And from his native land resolv'd to go,
And visit scorching climes beyond the sea;
With pleasure drugg'd he almost long'd for woe,
And e'en for change of scene would seek the shades below.

7.

The Childe departed from his father's hall: 55
It was a vast and venerable pile;
So old, it seemed only not to fall,
Yet strength was pillar'd in each massy aisle.
Monastic dome! condemn'd to uses vile!
Where Superstition once had made her den   60
Now Paphian girls were known to sing and smile;
And monks might deem their time was come agen,
If ancient tales say true, nor wrong these holy men.

8.

Yet oft-times in his maddest mirthful mood
Strange pangs would flash along Childe Harold's brow, 65

39 sigh'd to] ⟨courted⟩ M   41 him] ⟨one⟩ M   46 And . . . Harold] ⟨But . . .
Burun⟩ M   50 ⟨And strait he fell into a reverie⟩ M, D   joyless] sullen D   speechless
/ silent / wayward / downcast / gloomy / wrinkling / joyless *alternate readings* O   53 With]
⟨Oh⟩ M   54 scene would] scene ⟨had⟩ M   57 seemed only] ⟨only⟩ seemed M
59 Monastic dome! condemn'd] ⟨Strange fate! devoted still⟩ M   61 girls were known]
⟨jades were heard⟩ M; nymphs were known D *alternate reading*

64–81   Of all his train there was a ⟨guilty⟩ henchman page
          A ⟨dark-eyed⟩ peasant boy who ⟨loved⟩ served his master well
          And often would his pranksome prate engage
          Childe ⟨Burun's⟩ Harold's ear when his proud heart did swell

CHILDE HAROLD.

THE CHILDE DEPARTED FROM HIS FATHERS HALL :

IT WAS A VAST AND VENERABLE PILE ;

Canto I Stanza 7

PUBLISHED BY JOHN MURRAY, ALBEMARLE STREET, DEC.ʳ 1, 1814.

Childe Harold's Pilgrimage, Canto I, stanza 7
(*Reproduced with the permission of the British Library*)

As if the memory of some deadly feud
Or disappointed passion lurk'd below:
But this none knew, nor haply car'd to know;
For his was not that open, artless soul
That feels relief by bidding sorrow flow,   70
Nor sought he friend to counsel or condole,
Whate'er his grief mote be, which he could not control.

9.

And none did love him—though to hall and bower
He gather'd revellers from far and near,
He knew them flatt'rers of the festal hour;   75
The heartless parasites of present cheer.
Yea! none did love him—not his lemans dear—
But pomp and power alone are woman's care,
And where these are light Eros finds a feere;
Maidens, like moths, are ever caught by glare,   80
And Mammon wins his way where Seraphs might despair.

10.

Childe Harold had a mother—not forgot,
Though parting from that mother he did shun;

With sable thoughts that he disdained to tell
Then would he smile on him ⟨and⟩ as ⟨Robin / Rupert⟩ Alwin smiled
When aught that from his young lips archly fell
The gloomy film ⟨of⟩ from ⟨Burun's⟩ Harold's eye beguiled
⟨And pleased the Childe appeared nor eer the boy reviled⟩

Him and one yeoman only did he take
To travel Eastward to a far countree
And though the boy was grieved to leave the lake
On whose fair banks he grew from Infancy
⟨Yet now / Albeit⟩ Eftsoons his little heart ⟨ ? high with glee⟩ beat merrily
⟨And⟩ With hope of foreign nations to behold
And many things right marvellous to see
Of which our ⟨lying⟩ vaunting voyagers have told
⟨From Mandeville's ? and men / scribes of monkish mold⟩
⟨In tomes prickt out with prints to monied ? / men of money sold⟩
⟨In many a tome as true as Mandeville's of old⟩ M

68 nor] or M   73 none did] ⟨few could⟩ M
74–7   ⟨An evil smile just bordering on a sneer
                              Curled on his lip een in the festal hour
                              As if he deemed no mortal wight his peer
                              To gentle dames still less could he be dear⟩ M

74 He] ⟨Haughty⟩ He M   77 Yea] No D alternate reading   78 ⟨Were aught⟩
But M   79 And . . . light Eros finds a feere] ⟨But⟩ And . . . let no Possessor fear M
80 ⟨The sex are slaves / Love shrinks outshone by Mammon's dazzling glare⟩ M
81 And Mammon] ⟨That demon⟩ M   Seraphs] Angels M; cor. in D   82 Harold]
⟨Burun⟩ M

A sister whom he lov'd, but saw her not
Before his weary pilgrimage begun: 85
If friends he had, he bade adieu to none.
Yet deem not thence his breast a breast of steel;
Ye, who have known what 'tis to doat upon
A few dear objects, will in sadness feel
Such partings break the heart they fondly hope to heal. 90

11.

His house, his home, his heritage, his lands,
The laughing dames in whom he did delight,
Whose large blue eyes, fair locks, and snowy hands
Might shake the saintship of an anchorite,
And long had fed his youthful appetite;   95
His goblets brimm'd with every costly wine,
And all that mote to luxury invite,
Without a sigh he left, to cross the brine,
And traverse Paynim shores, and pass Earth's central line.

12.

The sails were fill'd, and fair the light winds blew,   100
As glad to waft him from his native home;
And fast the white rocks faded from his view,
And soon were lost in circumambient foam:
And then, it may be, of his wish to roam
Repented he, but in his bosom slept   105
The silent thought, nor from his lips did come
One word of wail, whilst others sate and wept,
And to the reckless gales unmanly moaning kept.

13.

But when the sun was sinking in the sea
He seiz'd his harp, which he at times could string,   110
And strike, albeit with untaught melody,
When deem'd he no strange ear was listening:

86 ⟨Of friends he had but few embracing none⟩ *M*   If friends he had] ⟨Of faithful
friends⟩ *M*   87 not . . . a] him not from this with *M, D*   89 in sadness] ⟨most
surely⟩ *M*   91 heritage] vassals and *M*   92 The laughing dames] ⟨His damsels
all⟩ His Dalilahs *M*   99 and . . . line] ⟨where brighter sunbeams shine⟩ *M*
100 were] are *M*   103 were . . . foam] ⟨he lost them in surrounding foam⟩ *M*   Song
titled Childe Harold's Good Night *in M; title cancelled in D*

And now his fingers o'er it he did fling,
And tun'd his farewell in the dim twilight.
While flew the vessel on her snowy wing,   115
And fleeting shores receded from his sight,
Thus to the elements he pour'd his last 'Good night'.

1.

'Adieu, adieu! my native shore
    Fades o'er the waters blue;
The Night-winds sigh, the breakers roar,   120
    And shrieks the wild seamew.
Yon Sun that sets upon the sea
    We follow in his flight;
Farewell awhile to him and thee,
    My native Land—Good Night.   125

2.

'A few short hours and He will rise
    To give the Morrow birth;
And I shall hail the main and skies,
    But not my mother Earth.
Deserted is my own good hall,   130
    Its hearth is desolate;
Wild weeds are gathering on the wall;
    My dog howls at the gate.

3.

'Come hither, hither, my little page!
    Why dost thou weep and wail?   135
Or dost thou dread the billows' rage,
    Or tremble at the gale?
But dash the tear-drop from thine eye;
    Our ship is swift and strong:
Our fleetest falcon scarce can fly   140
    More merrily along.'

4.

'Let winds be shrill, let waves roll high,
    I fear not wave nor wind;

121 wild] ⟨sad⟩ *M*   127 the Morrow] tomorrow *M*; *cor. in D*   128 main]
waves *M*; *cor. in D*   140 Our best goss-hawk can hardly fly *M*   141 More]
So *M*; *cor. in D*   142–3 'Oh master dear I do not cry | From fear of wave or wind *M*

Yet marvel not, Sir Childe, that I
    Am sorrowful in mind;   145
For I have from my father gone,
    A mother whom I love,
And have no friend, save these alone,
    But thee—and one above.

5.

'My father bless'd me fervently,   150
    Yet did not much complain;
But sorely will my mother sigh
    Till I come back again.'—
'Enough, enough, my little lad!
    Such tears become thine eye;   155
If I thy guileless bosom had
    Mine own would not be dry.

6.

'Come hither, hither, my staunch yeoman,
    Why dost thou look so pale?
Or dost thou dread a French foeman?   160
    Or shiver at the gale?'—
'Deem'st thou I tremble for my life?
    Sir Childe, I'm not so weak;
But thinking on an absent wife
    Will blanch a faithful cheek.   165

7.

'My spouse and boys dwell near thy hall,
    Along the bordering lake,
And when they on their father call,
    What answer shall she make?'—

147 ⟨Brethren⟩ A mother ⟨and brethren seven⟩ M   149 But you and ⟨him in
one in heaven⟩ M   151 Yet] But M
158–65   ⟨My mother is a highborn dame
                                  And much misliketh me
                                  She saith my riot bringeth shame
                                  On all my ancestry
                                  I had a sister once I ween
                                  Whose tears perhaps will flow
                                  But her fair face I have not seen
                                  For three long years and moe⟩ M
161 shiver] shiv'rest M, D, edns. 1–6   162 Deem'st] ⟨Thinkst⟩ M   164 on
⟨of⟩ M   166 boys] ⟨babes⟩ M   167 Along] ⟨Upon⟩ M

'Enough, enough, my yeoman good,   170
    Thy grief let none gainsay;
But I, who am of lighter mood,
    Will laugh to flee away.

8.

'For who would trust the seeming sighs
    Of wife or paramour?   175
Fresh feres will dry the bright blue eyes
    We late saw streaming o'er.
For pleasures past I do not grieve,
    Nor perils gathering near;
My greatest grief is that I leave   180
    No thing that claims a tear.

9.

'And now I'm in the world alone,
    Upon the wide, wide sea:
But why should I for others groan,
    When none will sigh for me?   185
Perchance my dog will whine in vain,
    Till fed by stranger hands;
But long ere I come back again,
    He'd tear me where he stands.

10.

'With thee, my bark, I'll swiftly go   190
    Athwart the foaming brine;
Nor care what land thou bear'st me to,
    So not again to mine.

171–3 ⟨All this is well to say | But if I in thy sandals stood | I'd laugh to get away⟩ *M*
173 flee] get *M*   174–6 ⟨I have a ? of gentle ? | All / Each young and passing fair |
But which for my departure pined⟩ *M*
174–7   For who would trust a paramour
                              Or even a wedded feere
                              Though her blue eyes were streaming oer
                              And torn her yellow hair *M*
174–81   ⟨Methinks it would my bosom glad
                              To change my proud estate
                              And be again a laughing lad
                              With one beloved playmate
                              Since youth I scarce have passed an hour
                              Without disgust or pain
                              Except sometimes in Lady's bower
                              Or when the bowl I drain⟩ *M*
181 that claims] that's worth *M*; *cor. in D*   186 Perchance] ⟨Oh yes !⟩ *M*

Welcome, welcome, ye dark-blue waves!
  And when you fail my sight,   195
Welcome, ye deserts, and ye caves!
  My native Land—Good Night!'

14.

On, on the vessel flies, the land is gone,
And winds are rude in Biscay's sleepless bay.
Four days are sped, but with the fifth, anon,   200
New shores descried make every bosom gay;
And Cintra's mountain greets them on their way,
And Tagus dashing onward to the deep,
His fabled golden tribute bent to pay;
And soon on board the Lusian pilots leap,   205
And steer 'twixt fertile shores where yet few rustics reap.

15.

Oh, Christ! it is a goodly sight to see
What heaven hath done for this delicious land!
What fruits of fragrance blush on every tree!
What goodly prospects o'er the hills expand!   210
But man would mar them with an impious hand:
And when the Almighty lifts his fiercest scourge
'Gainst those who most transgress his high command,
With treble vengeance will his hot shafts urge
Gaul's locust host, and earth from fellest foemen   215
    purge.

16.

What beauties doth Lisboa first unfold!
Her image floating on that noble tide,
Which poets vainly pave with sands of gold,
But now whereon a thousand keels did ride
Of mighty strength, since Albion was allied,   220
And to the Lusians did her aid afford:
A nation swoln with ignorance and pride,

---

206 yet few] ⟨thronging⟩ M   208 heaven] God M; cor. in D   211 would mar]
⟨has marred⟩ M   212 lifts] ⟨wields⟩ M   215 These Lusian brutes, and earth
from worst of wretches purge M; cor. in D   217 Her image floating] ⟨So nobly shines
she⟩ M   218 vainly . . . of] ⟨prone to lie⟩ have paved with M; sprinkle oer with sands
of M, D; pave in vain with sands of O   221 Lusians] ⟨meanest⟩ M

Who lick yet loath the hand that waves the sword
To save them from the wrath of Gaul's unsparing lord.

17.

But whoso entereth within this town,   225
That, sheening far, celestial seems to be,
Disconsolate will wander up and down,
'Mid many things unsightly to strange ee;
For hut and palace show like filthily:
The dingy denizens are rear'd in dirt;   230
Ne personage of high or mean degree
Doth care for cleanness of surtout or shirt,
Though shent with Egypt's plague, unkempt, un-
   wash'd, unhurt.

18.

Poor, paltry slaves! yet born 'midst noblest scenes—
Why, Nature, waste thy wonders on such men?   235
Lo! Cintra's glorious Eden intervenes
In variegated maze of mount and glen.
Ah, me! what hand can pencil guide, or pen,
To follow half on which the eye dilates
Through views more dazzling unto mortal ken   240
Than those whereof such things the bard relates,
Who to the awe-struck world unlock'd Elysium's gates?

19.

The horrid crags, by toppling convent crown'd,
The cork-trees hoar that clothe the shaggy steep,
The mountain-moss by scorching skies imbrown'd,   245
The sunken glen, whose sunless shrubs must weep,
The tender azure of the unruffled deep,
The orange tints that gild the greenest bough,
The torrents that from cliff to valley leap,

---

223 lick yet loath] ⟨hate the very⟩ M   224 save] guard / shield M   225 whoso]
⟨he that⟩ M   226 That from the air ⟨seems so / seems daintily to be⟩ sheeneth daintily
M cancelled   celestial] ⟨dainty⟩ M   228 unsightly . . . ee] that grieve both nose and ee
M, D   229 hut and] ⟨every⟩ M   show like] smelleth M, D   230 The dingy] ⟨And
every⟩ M   rear'd in] ⟨clammed with⟩ M   238 hand . . . pen] ⟨feeble hand can guide
the pen⟩ M   240 more dazzling unto] ⟨too sweet and vast for⟩ M   241 Than
those . . .] ⟨Bounteous / Dazzling as those of which⟩ M   243 toppling] ⟨tottering⟩ M
249 ⟨The murmur of the sparkling torrents keep⟩ M

The vine on high, the willow branch below,   250
Mix'd in one mighty scene, with varied beauty glow.

20.

Then slowly climb the many-winding way,
And frequent turn to linger as you go,
From loftier rocks new loveliness survey,
And rest ye at our 'Lady's house of woe';   255
Where frugal monks their little relics show,
And sundry legends to the stranger tell:
Here impious men have punish'd been, and lo!
Deep in yon cave Honorius long did dwell,
In hope to merit Heaven by making earth a Hell.   260

21.

And here and there, as up the crags you spring,
Mark many rude-carv'd crosses near the path:
Yet deem not these devotion's offering—
These are memorials frail of murderous wrath:
For wheresoe'er the shrieking victim hath   265
Pour'd forth his blood beneath the assassin's knife
Some hand erects a cross of mouldering lath;
And grove and glen with thousand such are rife
Throughout this purple land, where law secures not
        life.

22.

On sloping mounds, or in the vale beneath,   270
Are domes where whilome kings did make repair;
But now the wild flowers round them only breathe;
Yet ruin'd splendour still is lingering there.

251 Mix'd . . . varied] ⟨In one eternal / united / gigantic scene of sovereign⟩ M
257 sundry] divers M; cor. in D   259 yon] the M   260 In hope] ⟨And soug⟩ M
264 memorials frail] ⟨the monuments⟩ M
270–8   Unhappy Vathek! in an evil hour
        ⟨By one fair form⟩ Gainst Nature's voice seduced to deed accurst,
        Once Fortune's minion, now thou feel'st her Power!
        Wrath's vials on thy lofty head have burst,
        In ⟨mind, in science⟩ wit, in ⟨talents⟩ genius, as in wealth the first
        How wondrous bright thy blooming morn arose
        But thou wert smitten with unhallowed thirst
        Of nameless crime, and ⟨round thee twining close⟩ thy sad day must close
        ⟨Scorn, Exile,⟩ To scorn, and Solitude unsought—the worst of woes. M
273 ruin'd splendour] ⟨splendid ruin⟩ M

And yonder towers the Prince's palace fair:
There thou too, Vathek! England's wealthiest son, 275
Once form'd thy Paradise, as not aware
When wanton Wealth her mightiest deeds hath done,
Meek Peace voluptuous lures was ever wont to shun.

23.

Here didst thou dwell, here schemes of pleasure plan,
Beneath yon mountain's ever beauteous brow: 280
But now, as if a thing unblest by Man,
Thy fairy dwelling is as lone as thou!
Here giant weeds a passage scarce allow
To halls deserted, portals gaping wide:
Fresh lessons to the thinking bosom, how   285
Vain are the pleasaunces on earth supplied,
Swept into wrecks anon by Time's ungentle tide!

24.

Behold the hall where chiefs were late conven'd!
Oh! dome displeasing unto British eye!
With diadem hight foolscap, lo! a fiend,   290
A little fiend that scoffs incessantly,
There sits in parchment robe array'd, and by
His side is hung a seal and sable scroll,
Where blazon'd glare names known to chivalry,
And sundry signatures adorn the roll,   295
Whereat the Urchin points and laughs with all his soul.

274 towers] ⟨near⟩ M
275-8   There too proud Vathek, England's wealthiest son
         Had formed his Paradise, as not aware
         When Wealth and ⟨Wit / Vice⟩ Taste their worst and best have done
         Meek Peace pollution's lure voluptuous still must shun M; *cor. in* D
279 here schemes of pleasure] ⟨amidst a servile⟩ M   281 as . . . by] thou blasted ⟨monu-
ment of⟩ Beacon unto M; thou Beacon unto erring D   283 a] the M, D
286 on earth] by ⟨wealth⟩ art M, D   288 ⟨To Marialva's mansion shall we wend?⟩ M
292 robe array'd] ⟨jerkin / robe yclad⟩ M   294 glare . . . chivalry] glares a name
spelt 'Wellesley' M, D   295 adorn] ⟨are on⟩ M
288-96   a In golden characters right well designed
               First on the list appeareth one 'Junot,'
               Then certain other glorious names we find,
               ⟨Which rhyme compelleth me to place below⟩
               Dull Victors! baffled by a vanquished foe,
               ⟨Beings to⟩ Wheedled by conynge tongues ⟨their⟩ of laurels due,
               ⟨And⟩ Stand, worthy of each other in a row—
               Sirs Arthur, Harry, and the dizzard Hew
               Dalrymple, seely wight, sore dupe of t'other ⟨two⟩ tew.

25.

Convention is the dwarfish demon styl'd
That foil'd the knights in Marialva's dome:
Of brains (if brains they had) he them beguil'd,
And turn'd a nation's shallow joy to gloom.   300
Here Folly dash'd to earth the victor's plume,
And Policy regain'd what arms had lost:
For chiefs like ours in vain may laurels bloom!
Woe to the conqu'ring, not the conquer'd host,
Since baffled Triumph droops on Lusitania's coast!   305

26.

And ever since that martial synod met,
    Britannia sickens, Cintra! at thy name;
And folks in office at the mention fret,
    And fain would blush, if blush they could, for
        shame.

b Convention is the dwarfy demon ⟨called⟩ styled
    That foiled the knights in Marialva's dome:
    ⟨Their⟩ Of brains (if brains they had) he ⟨there enthralled⟩ them beguiled,
    And turned a nation's shallow joy to gloom.
    For well I wot, when first the news did come
    That Vimiera's field by Gaul was lost,
    For paragraph ne paper scarce had room,
    Such ⟨tri⟩ Paeans teemed for our triumphant host,
    In Courier, Chronicle, and eke in Morning Post.

c But when Convention sent his handy work
    Pens, tongues, feet, hands, combined in wild uproar;
    Mayor, Aldermen, laid down the uplifted fork,
    The Bench of Bishops half forgot to snore;
    Stern Cobbett, who for one whole week forbore
    To question aught, ⟨and sate like reckless lamb / withouten word⟩ once more
        with transport leap't,
    ⟨Now⟩ And bit his devilish quill agen, and swore
    ⟨Ne foes such treaty down our throats should cram⟩
    With foes such treaty never should be kept,
    ⟨While roared / yelled the Blatant Beast, in one immense 'God damn' / and
        thundering yelled 'God damn'!⟩
    Then burst the Blatant Beast, and roared, and raged and—slept!

d Thus unto Heaven appealed the people: Heaven
    Which loves the lieges of our gracious King,
    Decreed that ere our Generals were forgiven,
    Enquiry should be held about the thing.
    But Mercy cloaked the babes beneath her wing,
    And as they spared our foes so spared we them
    (Where was the pity of our sires for Byng?)
    Yet knaves, not idiots should the law condemn;
    Then live ye gallant Knights! and bless your Judges' phlegm! *M, D*
306 And] But *D*   308 fret] sweat *M, D*

How will posterity the deed proclaim!   310
Will not our own and fellow-nations sneer,
To view these champions cheated of their fame,
By foes in fight o'erthrown, yet victors here,
Where Scorn her fingers points through many a
        coming year?

27.

So deem'd the Childe, as o'er the mountains he   315
Did take his way in solitary guise:
Sweet was the scene, yet soon he thought to flee,
More restless than the swallow in the skies:
Though here awhile he learn'd to moralize,
For Meditation fix'd at times on him;   320
And conscious Reason whisper'd to despise
His early youth, mispent in maddest whim;
But as he gaz'd on truth his aching eyes grew dim.

28.

To horse! to horse! he quits, for ever quits
A scene of peace, though soothing to his soul: 325
Again he rouses from his moping fits,
But seeks not now the harlot and the bowl.
Onward he flies, nor fix'd as yet the goal
Where he shall rest him on his pilgrimage;
And o'er him many changing scenes must roll   330
Ere toil his thirst for travel can assuage,
Or he shall calm his breast, or learn experience sage.

29.

Yet Mafra shall one moment claim delay,
Where dwelt of yore the Lusian's luckless queen;
And church and court did mingle their array,   335
And mass and revel were alternate seen;
Lordling and freres—ill sorted fry I ween!

315 So deem'd] Thus thought *M*; *cor. in D*   318 swallow . . . skies] ⟨Falcon as he
flies⟩ *M*   325 though soothing] ⟨long foreign⟩ *M*   327 harlot] strumpet *M, D*
331 ⟨And countries more remote his hopes engage⟩ *M*   332 Or] ⟨Ere⟩ *M*   334 the
. . . luckless] ⟨Lusiana's crazy⟩ *D*; the Lusians' crazy *M, D*; ⟨the mind-perturbed⟩ *M*
336 mass] ⟨prayer⟩ *M*

But here the Babylonian whore hath built
A dome where flaunts she in such glorious sheen,
That men forget the blood which she hath spilt,   340
And bow the knee to Pomp that loves to varnish guilt.

30.

O'er vales that teem with fruits, romantic hills,
(Oh, that such hills upheld a freeborn race!)
Whereon to gaze the eye with joyaunce fills,
Childe Harold wends through many a pleasant
    place.   345
Though sluggards deem it but a foolish chase,
And marvel men should quit their easy chair,
The toilsome way, and long, long league to trace,
Oh! there is sweetness in the mountain air,
And life, that bloated Ease can never hope to   350
    share.

31.

More bleak to view the hills at length recede,
And, less luxuriant, smoother vales extend:
Immense horizon-bounded plains succeed!
Far as the eye discerns, withouten end,
Spain's realms appear whereon her shepherds tend   355
Flocks whose rich fleece right well the trader knows
Now must the pastor's arms his lambs defend:
For Spain is compass'd by unyielding foes,
And all must shield their all, or share Subjection's
    woes.

32.

Where Lusitania and her sister meet,   360
Deem ye what bounds the rival realms divide?
Or ere the jealous queens of nations greet,
Doth Tayo interpose his mighty tide?
Or dark Sierras rise in craggy pride?

339 dome] house *M, D*   341 loves to] ⟨aye can⟩ *M*   345 Harold] ⟨Burun⟩ *M*
351 ⟨And less sick / swoln with culture soon the vales extend⟩ *M*   353 ⟨And
long⟩ horizon-bounded ⟨realms appear⟩ *M*   354 withouten] ⟨without an⟩ *D*
355 whereon her] ⟨on there the / where flocks her⟩ *M*   356 Flocks . . . trader] ⟨These
flocks whose fleece the wily trader⟩ *M*   357 lambs] ⟨flock⟩ *M*   359 their all]
their ⟨home⟩ *M*   361 Deem ye] ⟨Say Muse⟩ *M*

Or fence of art, like China's vasty wall?—   365
Ne barrier wall, ne river deep and wide,
Ne horrid crags, nor mountains dark and tall,
Rise like the rocks that part Hispania's land from Gaul:

33.

But these between a silver streamlet glides,
And scarce a name distinguisheth the brook,   370
Though rival kingdoms press its verdant sides.
Here leans the idle shepherd on his crook,
And vacant on the rippling waves doth look,
That peaceful still 'twixt bitterest foeman flow;
For proud each peasant as the noblest duke: 375
Well doth the Spanish hind the difference know
'Twixt him and Lusian slave, the lowest of the low.

34.

But ere the mingling bounds have far been pass'd
Dark Guadiana rolls his power along
In sullen billows, murmuring and vast,   380
So noted ancient roundelays among.
Whilome upon his banks did legions throng
Of Moor and knight, in mailed splendour drest:
Here ceas'd the swift their race, here sunk the
    strong;
The Paynim turban and the Christian crest   385
Mix'd on the bleeding stream, by floating hosts
    oppress'd.

35.

Oh, lovely Spain! renown'd, romantic land!
Where is that standard which Pelagio bore,
When Cava's traitor-sire first call'd the band
That dy'd thy mountain streams with Gothic gore?   390
Where are those bloody banners which of yore
Wav'd o'er thy sons, victorious to the gale,
And drove at last the spoilers to their shore?

365 fence of art] ⟨works of art / art's vain fence⟩ M   372 Here] ⟨Where / There⟩ M
374 'twixt] ⟨tween⟩ M   378 ere . . . bounds] ere the bounds of Spain M, D   far]
⟨long⟩ M   381 ⟨For ever famed in many a native song⟩ M   noted] noted ⟨forsooth⟩ M
382 Whilome . . . did] ⟨For on his banks of yore did⟩ M   388 Pelagio] Pelagius M, D

Red gleam'd the cross, and wan'd the crescent pale,
While Afric's echoes thrill'd with Moorish matrons'
wail.   395

36.

Teems not each ditty with the glorious tale?
Ah! such, alas! the hero's amplest fate!
When granite moulders and when records fail,
A peasant's plaint prolongs his dubious date.
Pride! bend thine eye from heaven to thine estate;   400
See how the Mighty shrink into a song!
Can Volume, Pillar, Pile preserve thee great?
Or must thou trust Tradition's simple tongue,
When Flattery sleeps with thee, and History does thee
wrong?

37.

Awake, ye sons of Spain! awake! advance!   405
Lo! Chivalry, your ancient goddess, cries,
But wields not, as of old, her thirsty lance,
Nor shakes her crimson plumage in the skies:
Now on the smoke of blazing bolts she flies,
And speaks in thunder through yon engine's roar: 410
In every peal she calls—'Awake! arise!'
Say, is her voice more feeble than of yore,
When her war-song was heard on Andalusia's shore?

38.

Hark!—heard you not those hoofs of dreadful note?
Sounds not the clang of conflict on the heath?   415
Saw ye not whom the reeking sabre smote;
Nor sav'd your brethren ere they sank beneath
Tyrants and tyrants' slaves?—the fires of death,
The bale-fires flash on high:—from rock to rock
Each volley tells that thousands cease to breathe;   420
Death rides upon the sulphury Siroc,
Red Battle stamps his foot, and nations feel the shock.

---

394 wan'd] ⟨waxed⟩ M   395 matrons'] ⟨nations'⟩ D   399 his . . . date] ⟨thy little date⟩
M   407 old] ⟨yore⟩ M   415 Sounds] ⟨Heard⟩ M   420–1 ⟨Blue columns
soaring loft in sulphury wreathe | Fragments on fragments in contention knock⟩ M

39.

Lo! where the Giant on the mountain stands,
His blood-red tresses deep'ning in the sun,
With death-shot glowing in his fiery hands,   425
And eye that scorcheth all it glares upon;
Restless it rolls, now fix'd, and now anon
Flashing afar,—and at his iron feet
Destruction cowers to mark what deeds are done;
For on this morn three potent nations meet,   430
To shed before his shrine the blood he deems most
    sweet.

40.

By Heaven! it is a splendid sight to see
(For one who hath no friend, no brother there)
Their rival scarfs of mix'd embroidery,
Their various arms that glitter in the air!   435
What gallant war-hounds rouse them from their lair,
And gnash their fangs, loud yelling for the prey!
All join the chase, but few the triumph share;
The Grave shall bear the chiefest prize away,
And Havoc scarce for joy can number their array.   440

41.

Three hosts combine to offer sacrifice;
Three tongues prefer strange orisons on high;
Three gaudy standards flout the pale blue skies;
The shouts are France, Spain, Albion, Victory!
The foe, the victim, and the fond ally   445
That fights for all, but ever fights in vain,
Are met—as if at home they could not die—
To feed the crow on Talavera's plain,
And fertilize the field that each pretends to gain.

42.

There shall they rot—Ambition's honour'd fools!   450
Yes, Honour decks the turf that wraps their clay!
Vain Sophistry! in these behold the tools,

---

434 of . . . embroidery] ⟨that shine so gloriously⟩ *D*   rival] ⟨rural⟩ *D*   436 rouse them]
⟨glitter in⟩ *M*   450–2 There shall they rot—while rhymers tell the fools | How Honour
decks the turf that wraps their clay | Liars avaunt! *M; cor. in D*   shall they] ⟨let them⟩
while] ⟨and⟩   How] ⟨That⟩,   decks] ⟨wraps⟩ *M*   452 Vain . . . behold] But Reason's
eye in these beholds *D*

The broken tools, that tyrants cast away
By myriads, when they dare to pave their way
With human hearts—to what?—a dream alone.   455
Can despots compass aught that hails their sway?
Or call with truth one span of earth their own,
Save that wherein at last they crumble bone by bone?

43.

Oh, Albuera! glorious field of grief!
As o'er thy plain the Pilgrim prick'd his steed,   460
Who could foresee thee, in a space so brief,
A scene where mingling foes should boast and bleed!
Peace to the perish'd! may the warrior's meed
And tears of triumph their reward prolong!
Till others fall where other chieftains lead   465
Thy name shall circle round the gaping throng,
And shine in worthless lays, the theme of transient
      song!

44.

Enough of Battle's minions! let them play
Their game of lives, and barter breath for fame:
Fame that will scarce reanimate their clay,   470
Though thousands fall to deck some single name.
In sooth 'twere sad to thwart their noble aim
Who strike, blest hirelings! for their country's good,
And die, that living might have prov'd her shame;
Perish'd, perchance, in some domestic feud,   475
Or in a narrower sphere wild Rapine's path pursu'd.

45.

Full swiftly Harold wends his lonely way
Where proud Sevilla triumphs unsubdued:
Yet is she free—the spoiler's wish'd-for prey!
Soon, soon shall Conquest's fiery foot intrude,   480

---

454 myriads] ⟨thousands⟩ M   455–6 a dream . . . aught] ⟨a fancied throne—As if
they compassed half⟩ M   457 call . . . span] ⟨called⟩ . . . pace M   459 field]
⟨sound⟩ D   462 where . . . should] for . . . to D   463 Peace to the] ⟨Yet peace be with
the⟩ D   464 their . . . prolong] ⟨make their memory long⟩ D   467 And . . . lays]
⟨There sink with other woes⟩ D   worthless] ⟨later⟩ D   473 Who . . . for ⟨Who
perish truly for / Who sinks in darkness for / Who like the dust to sink⟩ M   475 Perish'd]
⟨Falling⟩ M   perchance] perhaps M, D   476 wild] swift M, D   477 Full . . .
Harold] ⟨To Harold turn we as he⟩ M   479 free—]free? edns. 1–8, C

Blackening her lovely domes with traces rude.
Inevitable hour! 'Gainst fate to strive
Where Desolation plants her famish'd brood
Is vain, or Ilion, Tyre might yet survive,
And Virtue vanquish all, and Murder cease to thrive.   485

46.

But all unconscious of the coming doom,
The feast, the song, the revel here abounds;
Strange modes of merriment the hours consume,
Nor bleed these patriots with their country's
    wounds:
Not here War's clarion, but Love's rebeck sounds;   490
Here Folly still his votaries enthralls;
And young-eyed Lewdness walks her midnight
    rounds:
Girt with the silent crimes of Capitals,
Still to the last kind Vice clings to the tott'ring walls

47.

Not so the rustic—with his trembling mate   495
He lurks, nor casts his heavy eye afar,
Lest he should view his vineyard desolate,
Blasted below the dun hot breath of war.
No more beneath soft Eve's consenting star
Fandango twirls his jocund castanet: 500
Ah, monarchs! could ye taste the mirth ye mar,
Not in the toils of Glory would ye fret;
The hoarse dull drum would sleep, and Man be happy
    yet!

48.

How carols now the lusty muleteer?
Of love, romance, devotion is his lay,   505
As whilome he was wont the leagues to cheer,
His quick bells wildly jingling on the way?

482 'Gainst] ⟨with⟩ M   490 War's . . . rebeck] ⟨the trumpet, but the rebeck⟩ M
492 young-eyed] ⟨dark-eyed⟩ M   494 Still to] Still till M   495 rustic] ⟨peasant⟩
M   496 casts] ⟨lifts⟩ M   498 below] ⟨beneath⟩ M, D   502 fret] ⟨sweat⟩
M, D

No! as he speeds, he chaunts; 'Vivā el Rey!'
And checks his song to execrate Godoy,
The royal wittol Charles, and curse the day   510
When first Spain's queen beheld the black-ey'd boy,
And gore-fac'd Treason sprung from her adulterate joy.

49.

On yon long, level plain, at distance crown'd
With crags, whereon those Moorish turrets rest,
Wide scatter'd hoof-marks dint the wounded
    ground;   515
And, scath'd by fire, the green sward's darken'd vest
Tells that the foe was Andalusia's guest:
Here was the camp, the watch-flame, and the host,
Here the bold peasant storm'd the dragon's nest;
Still does he mark it with triumphant boast,   520
And points to yonder cliffs, which oft were won and
    lost.

50.

And whomsoe'er along the path you meet
Bears in his cap the badge of crimson hue,
Which tells you whom to shun and whom to
    greet:
Woe to the man that walks in public view   525
Without of loyalty this token true:
Sharp is the knife, and sudden is the stroke;
And sorely would the Gallic foeman rue,
If subtle poniards, wrapt beneath the cloke,
Could blunt the sabre's edge, or clear the cannon's
    smoke.   530

51.

At every turn Morena's dusky height
Sustains aloft the battery's iron load;
And, far as mortal eye can compass sight,
The mountain-howitzer, the broken road,

---

508 No] ⟨Now⟩ M   510 royal wittol Charles] ⟨aged wittol king⟩ M   514 With]
By M, D   517 that] ⟨when⟩ M   was . . .] ⟨has known the Spain⟩ M   519 Here
. . . storm'd] ⟨But . . . sacked⟩ M   520 Still does he] Yet ⟨do they⟩ M   530 blunt
. . . clear] ⟨match . . . pierce⟩ M   533 compass] ⟨take its⟩ M

The bristling palisade, the fosse o'er-flow'd,   535
The station'd bands, the never-vacant watch,
The magazine in rocky durance stow'd,
The holster'd steed beneath the shed of thatch,
The ball-pil'd pyramid, the ever-blazing match,

52.

Portend the deeds to come:—but he whose nod   540
Has tumbled feebler despots from their sway
A moment pauseth ere he lifts the rod;
A little moment deigneth to delay:
Soon will his legions sweep through these their way;
The West must own the Scourger of the world.   545
Ah! Spain! how sad will be thy reckoning-day,
When soars Gaul's Vulture, with his wings unfurl'd,
And thou shalt view thy sons in crowds to Hades hurl'd.

53.

And must they fall? the young, the proud, the brave,
To swell one bloated Chief's unwholesome reign?   550
No step between submission and a grave?
The rise of rapine and the fall of Spain?
And doth the Power that man adores ordain
Their doom, nor heed the suppliant's appeal?
Is all that desperate Valour acts in vain?   555
And Counsel sage, and patriotic Zeal,
The Veteran's skill, Youth's fire, and Manhood's
        heart of steel?

54.

Is it for this the Spanish maid, arous'd,
Hangs on the willow her unstrung guitar,
And, all unsex'd, the Anlace hath espous'd,   560
Sung the loud song, and dar'd the deed of war?
And she, whom once the semblance of a scar
Appall'd, an owlet's 'larum chill'd with dread,
Now views the column-scattering bay'net jar,

535 bristling] ⟨ready / point⟩ fosse] ⟨ditch⟩ M   536 never-vacant] never changing M,
D   538 holster'd] ⟨saddled⟩ M   539 ball-pil'd] Ball's piled M   545 West]
South M, D   547 Vulture] Eagle M, D   563 'larum] ⟨night shriek⟩ M
564 bay'net jar] ⟨bolt afar⟩ M

The falchion flash, and o'er the yet warm dead   565
Stalks with Minerva's step where Mars might quake
   to tread.

55.

Ye who shall marvel when you hear her tale,
Oh! had you known her in her softer hour,
Mark'd her black eye that mocks her coal-black
   veil,
Heard her light, lively tones in Lady's bower,   570
Seen her long locks that foil the painter's power,
Her fairy form, with more than female grace,
Scarce would you deem that Saragoza's tower
Beheld her smile in Danger's Gorgon face,
Thin the clos'd ranks, and lead in Glory's fearful
   chase.   575

56.

Her lover sinks—she sheds no ill-tim'd tear;
Her chief is slain—she fills his fatal post;
Her fellows flee—she checks their base career;
The foe retires—she heads the sallying host:
Who can appease like her a lover's ghost?   580
Who can avenge so well a leader's fall?
What maid retrieve when man's flush'd hope is lost?
Who hang so fiercely on the flying Gaul,
Foil'd by a woman's hand, before a batter'd wall?

57.

Yet are Spain's maids no race of Amazons,   585
But form'd for all the witching arts of love:
Though thus in arms they emulate her sons,
And in the horrid phalanx dare to move,
'Tis but the tender fierceness of the dove
Pecking the hand that hovers o'er her mate: 590
In softness as in firmness far above
Remoter females, fam'd for sickening prate;
Her mind is nobler sure, her charms perchance as great.

---

565 falchion] falchion's *D*   568 Oh!...known] Ah! had you seen *M*
575 fearful] ⟨hideous⟩ *M*   576 sinks] ⟨falls⟩ *M*   577 fatal] ⟨venturous⟩ *M*
581 avenge] ⟨appease⟩ *M*

58.

The seal Love's dimpling finger hath impress'd
Denotes how soft that chin which bears his touch: 595
Her lips, whose kisses pout to leave their nest,
Bid man be valiant ere he merit such:
Her glance how wildly beautiful! how much
Hath Phoebus woo'd in vain to spoil her cheek,
Which glows yet smoother from his amorous
    clutch!   600
Who round the North for paler dames would seek?
How poor their forms appear! how languid, wan, and
    weak!

59.

Match me, ye climes! which poets love to laud;
Match me, ye harams of the land! where now
I strike my strain, far distant, to applaud   605
Beauties that ev'n a cynic must avow;
Match me those Houries, whom ye scarce allow
To taste the gale lest Love should ride the wind,
With Spain's dark-glancing daughters—deign to
    know,
There your wise Prophet's paradise we find,   610
His black-eyed maids of Heaven, angelically kind.

60.

Oh, thou Parnassus! whom I now survey,
Not in the phrenzy of a dreamer's eye,
Not in the fabled landscape of a lay,
But soaring snow-clad through thy native sky,   615
In the wild pomp of mountain majesty!
What marvel if I thus essay to sing?
The humblest of thy pilgrims passing by
Would gladly woo thine Echoes with his string,
Though from thy heights no more one Muse will wave
    her wing.   620

594–6 ⟨The seal Love's rosy finger has imprest | On her fair chin denotes how soft his touch— | Her lips where kisses make voluptuous nest⟩ M   603 climes] ⟨lands⟩ M 604 land] ⟨East⟩ M   606 ev'n ... avow] ⟨need not fear a broken vow⟩ M 610 There your wise] ⟨That there your true⟩ M   614 fabled ... a] landscape of a fabled M, D   617 thus] ⟨now⟩ M

61.

Oft have I dream'd of Thee! whose glorious name
Who knows not, knows not man's divinest lore:
And now I view thee, 'tis, alas! with shame
That I in feeblest accents must adore.
When I recount thy worshippers of yore   625
I tremble, and can only bend the knee;
Nor raise my voice, nor vainly dare to soar,
But gaze beneath thy cloudy canopy
In silent joy to think at last I look on Thee!

62.

Happier in this than mightiest bards have been,   630
Whose fate to distant homes confin'd their lot,
Shall I unmov'd behold the hallow'd scene,
Which others rave of, though they know it not?
Though here no more Apollo haunts his grot,
And thou, the Muses' seat, art now their grave,   635
Some gentle Spirit still pervades the spot,
Sighs in the gale, keeps silence in the cave,
And glides with glassy foot o'er yon melodious Wave.

63.

Of thee hereafter.—Ev'n amidst my strain
I turn'd aside to pay my homage here;   640
Forgot the land, the sons, the maids of Spain;
Her fate, to every freeborn bosom dear,
And hail'd thee, not perchance without a tear.
Now to my theme—but from thy holy haunt
Let me some remnant, some memorial bear;   645
Yield me one leaf of Daphne's deathless plant,
Nor let thy votary's hope be deem'd an idle vaunt.

625 thy ⟨tuneful⟩ worshippers *M*   628 beneath] ⟨upon⟩ *M*   629 think ⟨I have⟩
at *M*   635 seat] ⟨Mount⟩ *M*   638 ⟨And walks with glassy steps oer Delphi's
sloping / Aganippe's wave⟩ *M*   glides] ⟨skims / prints⟩ *M*   642 bosom] ⟨Spirit⟩ *M*
643 perchance] perhaps *M; cor. in D*   645–6 ⟨Let me some remnant of thy Spirit
bear | Some glorious thought to my petition grant⟩ *M*

64.

But ne'er didst thou, fair Mount! when Greece was
    young,
See round thy giant base a brighter choir,
Nor e'er did Delphi, when her priestess sung   650
The Pythian hymn with more than mortal fire,
Behold a train more fitting to inspire
The song of love, than Andalusia's maids,
Nurst in the glowing lap of soft desire:
Ah! that to these were given such peaceful shades   655
As Greece can still bestow, though Glory fly her glades.

65.

Fair is proud Seville; let her country boast
Her strength, her wealth, her site of ancient days;
But Cadiz, rising on the distant coast,
Calls forth a sweeter, though ignoble praise.   660
Ah, Vice! how soft are thy voluptuous ways!
While boyish blood is mantling who can 'scape
The fascination of thy magic gaze?
A Cherub-hydra round us dost thou gape,
And mould to every taste thy dear delusive shape.   665

66.

When Paphos fell by Time—accursed Time!
The queen who conquers all must yield to thee—
The Pleasures fled, but sought as warm a clime;
And Venus, constant to her native sea,
To nought else constant, hither deign'd to flee;   670
And fix'd her shrine within these walls of white:
Though not to one dome circumscribeth she
Her worship, but, devoted to her rite,
A thousand altars rise, for ever blazing bright.

67.

From morn till night, from night till startled Morn
Peeps blushing on the Revel's laughing crew,   676

648 ne'er didst] ⟨not ever⟩ M   649 See] ⟨Saw⟩ M   651 The] Her M
660 though ignoble] ⟨but less noble⟩ M   662 is mantling] ⟨boils gaily⟩ M
663 The ⟨lurking lures of thy enchanting maze⟩ M   664 dost] doth *1st edn.*
667 who] that M   672 Though] ⟨But⟩ M   674 blazing] ⟨burning⟩ M

The song is heard, the rosy garland worn,
Devices quaint, and frolicks ever new,
Tread on each other's kibes. A long adieu
He bids to sober joy that here sojourns: 680
Nought interrupts the riot, though in lieu
Of true devotion monkish incense burns,
And Love and Prayer unite, or rule the hour by turns.

68.

The Sabbath comes, a day of blessed rest;
What hallows it upon this Christian shore?   685
Lo! it is sacred to a solemn feast:
Hark! heard you not the forest-monarch's roar?
Crashing the lance, he snuffs the spouting gore
Of man and steed, o'erthrown beneath his horn;
The throng'd Arena shakes with shouts for more;
Yells the mad crowd o'er entrails freshly torn,   691
Nor shrinks the female eye, nor ev'n affects to mourn.

69.

The seventh day this; the jubilee of man.
London! right well thou know'st the day of prayer:
Then thy spruce citizen, wash'd artizan,   695
And smug apprentice gulp their weekly air:
Thy coach of Hackney, whiskey, one-horse chair,
And humblest gig through sundry suburbs whirl,
To Hampstead, Brentford, Harrow make repair;
Till the tir'd jade the wheel forgets to hurl,   700
Provoking envious gibe from each pedestrian Churl.

70.

Some o'er thy Thamis row the ribbon'd fair,
Others along the safer Turnpike fly;
Some Richmond-hill ascend, some scud to Ware,
And many to the steep of Highgate hie.   705

---

677 worn,] worn; *1831, 1832, C, More*   680 here sojourns] ⟨sojourns there⟩ *M*
682–3 incense . . . turns] ⟨temples share / The hours misspent and all in turns in love or
prayer⟩ *M*   by turns] in turns *M, edns. 1–6*   689 steed] horse *M, D*   690 throng'd
Arena] ⟨shouting men⟩ *M*   691 o'er . . . torn] ⟨to see their entrails torn⟩ *M*
692 affects] appears *M*   698 humblest] humbler *M*   701 And droughty
man alights and roars for 'Roman Purl' *M; cor. in D*   702 Thamis row] Thames
convoy *M; cor. in D*

Ask ye, Boeotian shades! the reason why?
'Tis to the worship of the solemn Horn,
Grasp'd in the holy hand of Mystery,
In whose dread name both men and maids are
    sworn,
And consecrate the oath with draught, and dance till
    morn.   710

71.

All have their fooleries—not alike are thine,
Fair Cadiz, rising o'er the dark blue sea!
Soon as the matin bell proclaimeth nine,
Thy saint adorers count the rosary:
Much is the VIRGIN teaz'd to shrive them free   715
(Well do I ween the only virgin there)
From crimes as numerous as her beadsmen be;
Then to the crowded circus forth they fare,
Young, old, high, low, at once the same diversion share.

72.

The lists are op'd, the spacious area clear'd,   720
Thousands on thousands pil'd are seated round;
Long ere the first loud trumpet's note is heard,
Ne vacant space for lated wight is found:
Here dons, grandees, but chiefly dames abound,
Skill'd in the ogle of a roguish eye,   725
Yet ever well inclin'd to heal the wound;
None through their cold disdain are doom'd to die,
As moon-struck bards complain, by Love's sad archery.

73.

Hush'd is the din of tongues—on gallant steeds,
With milk-white crest, gold spur, and light-pois'd
    lance,   730
Four cavaliers prepare for venturous deeds,
And lowly bending to the lists advance;
Rich are their scarfs, their chargers featly prance:
If in the dangerous game they shine to-day,
The crowds loud shout and ladies lovely glance,   735
Best prize of better acts, they bear away,
And all that kings or chiefs e'er gain their toils repay.

708 holy] hoary M   727 through] ⟨by⟩ M

74.

In costly sheen and gaudy cloak array'd,
But all afoot, the light-limb'd Matadore
Stands in the centre, eager to invade   740
The lord of lowing herds; but not before
The ground, with cautious tread, is travers'd o'er,
Lest aught unseen should lurk to thwart his speed:
His arms a dart, he fights aloof, nor more
Can man achieve without the friendly steed,   745
Alas! too oft condemn'd for him to bear and bleed.

75.

Thrice sounds the clarion; lo! the signal falls,
The den expands, and Expectation mute
Gapes round the silent Circle's peopled walls.
Bounds with one lashing spring the mighty brute,
And, wildly staring, spurns, with sounding foot,   751
The sand, nor blindly rushes on his foe:
Here, there, he points his threatening front, to suit
His first attack, wide waving to and fro
His angry tail; red rolls his eye's dilated glow.   755

76.

Sudden he stops; his eye is fix'd: away,
Away, thou heedless boy! prepare the spear:
Now is thy time, to perish, or display
The skill that yet may check his mad career.
With well-tim'd croupe the nimble coursers veer;
On foams the bull, but not unscath'd he goes;   761
Streams from his flank the crimson torrent clear:
He flies, he wheels, distracted with his throes;
Dart follows dart; lance, lance; loud bellowings speak
     his woes.

77.

Again he comes; nor dart nor lance avail,   765
Nor the wild plunging of the tortur'd horse;
Though man and man's avenging arms assail,
Vain are his weapons, vainer is his force.

749 peopled] loaded *M, D, edns. 1–8*   766 horse] ⟨steed⟩ *M*

One gallant steed is stretch'd a mangled corse;
Another, hideous sight! unseam'd appears,   770
His gory chest unveils life's panting source,
Tho' death-struck still his feeble frame he rears,
Staggering, but stemming all, his lord unharm'd he
      bears.

78.

Foil'd, bleeding, breathless, furious to the last,
Full in the centre stands the bull at bay,   775
Mid wounds, and clinging darts, and lances brast,
And foes disabled in the brutal fray:
And now the Matadores around him play,
Shake the red cloak, and poise the ready brand:
Once more through all he burst his thundering
      way—   780
Vain rage! the mantle quits the conynge hand,
Wraps his fierce eye—'tis past—he sinks upon the
      sand!

79.

Where his vast neck just mingles with the spine,
Sheath'd in his form the deadly weapon lies.
He stops—he starts—disdaining to decline: 785
Slowly he falls, amidst triumphant cries,
Without a groan, without a struggle dies.
The decorated car appears—on high
The corse is pil'd—sweet sight for vulgar eyes—
Four steeds that spurn the rein, as swift as shy,   790
Hurl the dark bulk along, scarce seen in dashing by.

80.

Such the ungentle sport that oft invites
The Spanish maid, and cheers the Spanish swain.
Nurtur'd in blood betimes, his heart delights
In vengeance, gloating on another's pain.   795

769 mangled] ⟨breathless⟩ M   772 Tho'] Yet M   775 stands the bull] ⟨still
he stands⟩ M   776 clinging] ⟨scattered⟩ M   782 sinks upon] ⟨lies along⟩ M
789 ⟨The corse is reared—sparkling the chariot flies / The trophy corse is reared—
disgusting prize⟩ M   791 bulk . . . dashing] ⟨lord . . . foaming⟩ M

What private feuds the troubled village stain!
Though now one phalanx'd host should meet the
    foe,
Enough, alas! in humble homes remain,
To meditate 'gainst friends the secret blow,
For some slight cause of wrath, whence life's warm
    stream must flow.   800

81.

But Jealousy has fled: his bars, his bolts,
His wither'd centinel, Duenna sage!
And all whereat the generous soul revolts,
Which the stern dotard deem'd he could encage,
Have pass'd to darkness with the vanish'd age.   805
Who late so free as Spanish girls were seen,
(Ere War uprose in his volcanic rage),
With braided tresses bounding o'er the green,
While on the gay dance shone Night's lover-loving
    Queen?

82.

Oh! many a time, and oft, had Harold lov'd,   810
Or dream'd he lov'd, since Rapture is a dream;
But now his wayward bosom was unmov'd,
For not yet had he drunk of Lethe's stream;
And lately had he learn'd with truth to deem
Love has no gift so grateful as his wings: 815
How fair, how young, how soft soe'er he seem,
Full from the fount of Joy's delicious springs
Some bitter o'er the flowers its bubbling venom flings.

83.

Yet to the beauteous form he was not blind,
Though now it mov'd him as it moves the wise;   820
Not that Philosophy on such a mind
E'er deign'd to bend her chastely-awful eyes:

799 friends] friend *M*   800 warm] 〈dark〉 *M*   803 generous] 〈wondering〉 *M*
804 Which!. . .] 〈The which that〉 *M*   807 uprose in his] 〈streamed forward with〉 *M*
811 since] 〈for〉 *M*   817 Full] 〈Still〉 *M*   818 Some bitter bubbles up and even
on roses stings *M*; *cor. in D, O*   822 E'er] 〈Once〉 *M*

Painted by Tho.ˢ Stothard R.A.   Engraved by F. Engleheart.

CHILDE HAROLD.

WHO LATE SO FREE AS SPANISH GIRLS WERE SEEN,

(ERE WAR UPROSE IN HIS VOLCANIC RAGE,)

WITH BRAIDED TRESSES BOUNDING O'ER THE GREEN.

Canto I. Stanza 81.

PUBLISHED BY JOHN MURRAY, ALBEMARLE STREET, DEC.ᴿ 1, 1814.

Childe Harold's Pilgrimage, Canto I, stanza 81

(Reproduced with the permission of the British Library)

But Passion raves herself to rest, or flies;
And Vice, that digs her own voluptuous tomb,
Had buried long his hopes, no more to rise: 825
Pleasure's pall'd victim! life-abhorring gloom
Wrote on his faded brow curst Cain's unresting doom.

84.

Still he beheld, nor mingled with the throng;
But view'd them not with misanthropic hate:
Fain would he now have join'd the dance, the song;
But who may smile that sinks beneath his fate?   831
Nought that he saw his sadness could abate:
Yet once he struggled 'gainst the demon's sway,
And as in Beauty's bower he pensive sate,
Pour'd forth this unpremeditated lay,   835
To charms as fair as those that sooth'd his happier day.

To Inez

1.

Nay, smile not at my sullen brow,
    Alas! I cannot smile again;
Yet heaven avert that ever thou
    Shouldst weep, and haply weep in vain.   840

2.

And dost thou ask, what secret woe
    I bear, corroding joy and youth?
And wilt thou vainly seek to know
    A pang, ev'n thou must fail to soothe?

3.

It is not love, it is not hate,   845
    Nor low Ambition's honours lost,
That bids me loathe my present state,
    And fly from all I priz'd the most:

825 long] there *M, D*   826 Pleasure's . . . victim] ⟨Drugged with dull pleasures⟩ *M*
827 unresting] ⟨wandering⟩ *M*   834 Beauty's] ⟨his⟩ *M*
To Inez *untitled in M*
839 Yet] ⟨And⟩ *M*

4.

It is that weariness which springs
   From all I meet, or hear, or see: 850
To me no pleasure Beauty brings;
   Thine eyes have scarce a charm for me.

5.

It is that settled, ceaseless gloom
   The fabled Hebrew wanderer bore;
That will not look beyond the tomb,   855
   But cannot hope for rest before.

6.

What Exile from himself can flee?
   To Zones, though more and more remote,
Still, still pursues, where-e'er I be,
   The blight of life—the demon, Thought.   860

7.

Yet others rapt in pleasure seem,
   And taste of all that I forsake;
Oh! may they still of transport dream,
   And ne'er, at least like me, awake!

8.

Through many a clime 'tis mine to go,   865
   With many a retrospection curst;
And all my solace is to know,
   Whate'er betides, I've known the worst.

9.

What is that worst? Nay do not ask—
   In pity from the search forbear: 870
Smile on—nor venture to unmask
   Man's heart, and view the Hell that's there.

858–9 ⟨To other zones howe'er remote | Still, still pursuing clings to me⟩ *M*
870 In pity] ⟨Or asking⟩ *M*

85.

Adieu, fair Cadiz! yea, a long adieu!
Who may forget how well thy walls have stood?
When all were changing thou alone wert true,   875
First to be free and last to be subdued:
And if amidst a scene, a shock so rude,
Some native blood was seen thy streets to die;
A traitor only fell beneath the feud:
Here all were noble, save Nobility;   880
None hugg'd a Conqueror's chain, save fallen Chivalry!

86.

Such be the sons of Spain, and strange her fate!
They fight for freedom who were never free,
A Kingless people for a nerveless state;
Her vassals combat when their chieftains flee,   885
True to the veriest slaves of Treachery:
Fond of a land which gave them nought but life,
Pride points the path that leads to Liberty;
Back to the struggle, baffled in the strife,
War, war is still the cry, 'War even to the knife!'   890

87.

Ye, who would more of Spain and Spaniards know,
Go, read whate'er is writ of bloodiest strife:
Whate'er keen Vengeance urg'd on foreign foe
Can act, is acting there against man's life:
From flashing scimitar to secret knife,   895
War mouldeth there each weapon to his need—
So may he guard the sister and the wife,
So may he make each curst oppressor bleed,
So may such foes deserve the most remorseless deed!

883–4 free, . . . state; *1831, 1832, C, More*; free; . . . state *all early edns.*
891–9   *a* Ye! who would more of Spain and Spaniards know
                   Sights, Saints, antiques, arts, anecdotes, and War,
                   Go hie ye hence to Paternoster Row,
                   Are they not written in the Boke of Carr,
                   Green Erin's knight! and Europe's wandering star!
                   Then listen, readers, to the man of ink,
                   Hear what he did, and sought, and wrote afar
                   All these are cooped within one Quarto's brink,
                   This borrow, steal (*don't* buy) and tell us what you think.

var. *a9 don't*] or *D*   [*App. Crit. 891-9 cont. on p. 42*

88.

Flows there a tear of pity for the dead?   900
Look o'er the ravage of the reeking plain;
Look on the hands with female slaughter red;
Then to the dogs resign the unburied slain,
Then to the vulture let each corse remain;
Albeit unworthy of the prey-bird's maw,   905
Let their bleach'd bones, and blood's unbleaching
    stain,
Long mark the battle-field with hideous awe:
Thus only may our sons conceive the scenes we saw!

89.

Nor yet, alas! the dreadful work is done,
Fresh legions pour adown the Pyrenees;   910
It deepens still, the work is scarce begun,
Nor mortal eye the distant end foresees.

b There may you read with spectacles or eyes,
   How many Wellesleys did embark for Spain,
As if therein they meant to colonize,
   How many troops ycrossed the laughing main
That neer beheld the same return again
   How many buildings are in such a place,
How many leagues from this to yonder plain,
   How many relics each Cathedral grace,
And where Giralda stands on her gigantic base.

c There may you read (Oh Phoebus save Sir John
   That these my words prophetic may not err)
All that was said or sung, and lost or won
   By vaunting Wellesley or by blundering Frere
(He that wrote half the Needy Knife Grinder)
   Thus Poesy the way to grandeur paves
(Who would not such diplomatists prefer?)
   But cease, my Muse, thy speed some respite craves
Leave legates to the House, and Princes to their graves.

d Yet here of Vulpes mention may be made
   Who for the Junta modelled sapient laws,
Taught them to govern ere they were obeyed—
   Certes fit teacher to command, because
His soul Socratic no Xantippe awes,
   Blest with a dame in Virtue's bosom nurst,
With her let silent admiration pause!
   True to her second husband and her first
On such unshaken fame let Satire do its worst. *M; cor. in D*

var. *b*3 therein] ⟨that land⟩ *M*   var. *c*4 vaunting] ⟨shrivelled⟩ *M*   var. *c*6–7 ⟨None better known for doing things by halves | As many in our Senate did aver⟩ *M*   var. *d*3 Taught them] ⟨And taught⟩ *M*   var. *d*4 ⟨Yet surely Vulpes merits some applause⟩ *M* var. *d*5 His] ⟨Whose⟩ *M*   var. *d*6 dame ⟨by early⟩ in *M*   var. *d*8 and] ⟨as⟩ *M* var. *d*9 such] ⟨her⟩ *M*

Fall'n nations gaze on Spain; if freed, she frees
More than her fell Pizarros once enchain'd:
Strange retribution! now Columbia's ease   915
Repairs the wrongs that Quito's sons sustain'd,
While o'er the parent clime prowls Murder unrestrain'd.

90.

Not all the blood at Talavera shed,
Not all the marvels of Barossa's fight,
Not Albuera lavish of the dead,   920
Have won for Spain her well asserted right.
When shall her Olive-Branch be free from blight?
When shall she breathe her from the blushing toil?
How many a doubtful day shall sink in night,
Ere the Frank robber turn him from his spoil,   925
And Freedom's stranger-tree grow native of the soil!

91.

And thou, my friend!—since unavailing woe
Bursts from my heart, and mingles with the strain—
Had the sword laid thee with the mighty low,
Pride might forbid ev'n Friendship to complain: 930
But thus unlaurel'd to descend in vain,
By all forgotten, save the lonely breast,
And mix unbleeding with the boasted slain,
While Glory crowns so many a meaner crest!
What hadst thou done to sink so peacefully to rest?   935

92.

Oh, known the earliest, and esteem'd the most!
Dear to a heart where nought was left so dear!
Though to my hopeless days for ever lost,
In dreams deny me not to see thee here!
And Morn in secret shall renew the tear   940
Of Consciousness awaking to her woes,
And Fancy hover o'er thy bloodless bier,
Till my frail frame return to whence it rose,
And mourn'd and mourner lie united in repose.

927 unavailing woe] thus my selfish woe D   928 and . . . strain] to weaken in my / however light my / for ever light the strain D alternate readings   930 Pride had forbade me of thy fall to plain D   936 esteem'd] belov'd D; cor. in O   937 nought was left so] none so long was D   942 hover o'er] follow to D

93.

Here is one fytte of Harold's pilgrimage: 945
Ye who of him may further seek to know,
Shall find some tidings in a future page,
If he that rhymeth now may scribble moe.
Is this too much? stern Critic! say not so:
Patience! and ye shall hear what he beheld   950
In other lands, where he was doom'd to go:
Lands that contain the monuments of Eld,
Ere Greece and Grecian arts by barbarous hands were
    quell'd.

CANTO II

1.

Come, blue-eyed maid of heaven!—but thou, alas!
Didst never yet one mortal song inspire—
Goddess of Wisdom! here thy temple was,
And is, despite of war and wasting fire,
And years, that bade thy worship to expire: 5
But worse than steel, and flame, and ages slow,
Is the dread sceptre and dominion dire
Of men who never felt the sacred glow
That thoughts of thee and thine on polish'd breasts bestow.

2.

Ancient of days! august Athena! where,   10
Where are thy men of might? thy grand in soul?
Gone—glimmering through the dream of things that were:
First in the race that led to Glory's goal,
They won, and pass'd away—is this the whole?
A school-boy's tale, the wonder of an hour!   15
The warrior's weapon and the sophist's stole
Are sought in vain, and o'er each mouldering tower,
Dim with the mist of years, grey flits the shade of power.

3.

Son of the morning, rise! approach you here!
Come—but molest not yon defenceless urn: 20
Look on this spot—a nation's sepulchre!
Abode of gods, whose shrines no longer burn.
Even gods must yield—religions take their turn:
'Twas Jove's—'tis Mahomet's—and other creeds
Will rise with other years, till man shall learn   25
Vainly his incense soars, his victim bleeds;
Poor child of Doubt and Death, whose hope is built on reeds.

4.

Bound to the earth, he lifts his eye to heaven—
Is't not enough, unhappy thing! to know
Thou art? Is this a boon so kindly given,   30
That being, thou wouldst be again, and go,
Thou know'st not, reck'st not to what region, so
On earth no more, but mingled with the skies?
Still wilt thou dream on future joy and woe?
Regard and weigh yon dust before it flies: 35
That little urn saith more than thousand homilies.

5.

Or burst the vanish'd Hero's lofty mound;
Far on the solitary shore he sleeps:
He fell, and falling nations mourn'd around;
But now not one of saddening thousands weeps,   40
Nor warlike-worshipper his vigil keeps
Where demi-gods appear'd, as records tell.
Remove yon skull from out the scatter'd heaps:
Is that a temple where a God may dwell?
Why ev'n the worm at last disdains her shatter'd cell!   45

19 morning, rise] ⟨winged days / morning! Man⟩ M   22 shrines no longer] altars
cease to M   27 hope] Faith M; cor. in D   29–30 Is't not enough, Unhappy
thing! to know? | Thou art!—is this a boon so kindly given? M   33 mingled]
mingle M, D   34 dream . . . joy] harp . . . joys M   36 saith] ⟨tells⟩ M
38 sleeps] ⟨lies⟩ M   39 falling] falling, 1st edn.   42 ⟨Though twas a god as
graven⟩ records tell M   43 yon] ⟨that⟩ M

6.

Look on its broken arch, its ruin'd wall,
Its chambers desolate, and portals foul:
Yes, this was once Ambition's airy hall,
The dome of Thought, the palace of the Soul:
Behold through each lack-lustre, eyeless hole,   50
The gay recess of Wisdom and of Wit
And Passion's host, that never brook'd control:
Can all, saint, sage, or sophist ever writ,
People this lonely tower, this tenement refit?

7.

Well didst thou speak, Athena's wisest son!   55
'All that we know is, nothing can be known.'
Why should we shrink from what we cannot shun?
Each has his pang, but feeble sufferers groan
With brain-born dreams of evil all their own.
Pursue what Chance or Fate proclaimeth best;   60
Peace waits us on the shores of Acheron:
There no forc'd banquet claims the sated guest,
But Silence spreads the couch of ever welcome rest.

8.

Yet if, as holiest men have deem'd, there be
A land of souls beyond that sable shore,   65
To shame the doctrine of the Sadducee
And sophists, madly vain of dubious lore;
How sweet it were in concert to adore

57 what we] what ⟨ye⟩ M   58 has his M, D, all early edns.; hath his 1832, More;
hath its C
64–72   Frown not upon me, churlish Priest! that I
                          Look not for Life, where life may never be,
                          I am no sneerer at thy phantasy—
                          Thou pitiest me, alas! I envy thee,
                          Thou bold Discoverer in an unknown sea
                          Of happy isles and happier tenants there—
                          I ask thee not to prove a Sadduccee;
                          Still dream of Paradise thou know'st not where,
                          Which if it be thy sins will never let thee share. M; cor. in D

var. 2 Look not for] ⟨Dream not of⟩ M   var. 8–9 ⟨But look upon a scene that once
was fair | Zion's holy hill where thou woud'st fain repair⟩ M   var. 9 ⟨As those which
thou delight'st to rear in upper air / Yet lov'st too well to bid thine erring brother share⟩ M
64 Yet] ⟨But⟩ D   65 that] ⟨the⟩ D

With those who made our mortal labours light!
To hear each voice we fear'd to hear no more!   70
Behold each mighty shade reveal'd to sight,
The Bactrian, Samian sage, and all who taught the right!

9.

There, thou!—whose love and life together fled,
Have left me here to love and live in vain—
Twin'd with my heart, and can I deem thee dead,   75
When busy Memory flashes on my brain?
Well—I will dream that we may meet again,
And woo the vision to my vacant breast:
If aught of young Remembrance then remain,
Be as it may Futurity's behest,   80
For me 'twere bliss enough to know thy spirit blest!

10.

Here let me sit upon this massy stone,
The marble column's yet unshaken base;
Here, son of Saturn! was thy fav'rite throne:
Mightiest of many such! Hence let me trace   85
The latent grandeur of thy dwelling place.
It may not be: nor ev'n can Fancy's eye
Restore what Time hath labour'd to deface.
Yet these proud pillars claim no passing sigh,
Unmov'd the Moslem sits, the light Greek carols by.   90

11.

But who, of all the plunderers of yon fane
On high, where Pallas linger'd, loth to flee
The latest relic of her ancient reign;
The last, the worst, dull spoiler, who was he?
Blush, Caledonia! such thy son could be!   95
England! I joy no child he was of thine:
Thy free-born men should spare what once was free;
Yet they could violate each saddening shrine,
And bear these altars o'er the long-reluctant brine.

76 on] oer T   80 Be as it may] ⟨Whateer beside⟩ Howeer may be T   81 ⟨Or
seeing thee no more to sink in sullen rest⟩ D   For . . . know] To . . . see T   94 spoiler]
Robber M; cor. in D   95 Caledonia! such] Scotland such a slave M; cor. in D
97 should spare] revere M; cor. in D   98-9 Nor tear the sculpture from its saddening
shrine | Nor bear the spoil away athwart the weeping brine. M; cor. in D

12.

But most the modern Pict's ignoble boast,   100
To rive what Goth, and Turk, and Time hath spar'd:
Cold as the crags upon his native coast,
His mind as barren and his heart as hard,
Is he whose head conceiv'd, whose hand prepar'd,
Aught to displace Athena's poor remains: 105
Her sons too weak the sacred shrine to guard,
Yet felt some portion of their mother's pains,
And never knew, till then, the weight of Despot's chains.

13.

What! shall it e'er be said by British tongue,
Albion was happy in Athena's tears?   110
Though in thy name the slaves her bosom wrung,
Tell not the deed to blushing Europe's ears;
The ocean queen, the free Britannia bears
The last poor plunder from a bleeding land:
Yes, she, whose gen'rous aid her name endears,   115
Tore down those remnants with a Harpy's hand,
Which envious Eld forbore, and tyrants left to stand.

14.

Where was thine Aegis, Pallas! that appall'd
Stern Alaric and Havoc on their way?

---

100 But . . . Pict's] This be the wittol Pict's *M; cor. in D*   102 as the crags
upon] and accursed as *M; cor. in D*   110 in . . . tears] while Athena mourned *M;
cor. in D*   111 slaves] slave *M, D*
112–17   Albion! I would not see thee thus adorned
                         With gains thy generous spirit should have scorned,
                         From Man distinguished by some monstrous sign,
                         Like Attila the Hun was surely horned
                         Who wrought this ravage amid works divine
                         Oh that Minerva's voice lent its keen aid to mine. *M; cor. in D*
112 Let it not vibrate in pale Europe's ears *D*   113 bears] wears *D*   114 from]
of *D*   115 Yes,] That *D*   117 envious Eld forbore] ⟨centuries forgot⟩ *D*
118 Pallas] Goddess *M; cor. in D*
118–26   *a* Come then, ye classic Thieves of each degree,
                 Dark Hamilton and sullen Aberdeen,
                 Come pilfer all the Pilgrim loves to see,
                 All that yet consecrates the fading scene—
                 Ah! better were it ye had never been,
                 Nor ye, nor Elgin, nor that lesser wight,
                 The victim sad of vase-collecting spleen,
                 House-furnisher withal, one Thomas hight,
                 Than ye should bear one stone from wronged Athena's sight.

Where Peleus' son? whom Hell in vain enthrall'd,   120
His shade from Hades upon that dread day,
Bursting to light in terrible array!
What? could not Pluto spare the chief once more,
To scare a second robber from his prey?
Idly he wander'd on the Stygian shore,   125
Nor now preserv'd the walls he lov'd to shield before.

15.

Cold is the heart, fair Greece! that looks on thee,
Nor feels as lovers o'er the dust they lov'd;
Dull is the eye that will not weep to see
Thy walls defac'd, thy mouldering shrines remov'd   130
By British hands, which it had best behov'd
To guard those relics ne'er to be restor'd.
Curst be the hour when from their isle they rov'd,
And once again thy hapless bosom gor'd,
And snatch'd thy shrinking Gods to northern climes
abhorr'd!   135

16.

But where is Harold? shall I then forget
To urge the gloomy wanderer o'er the wave?
Little reck'd he of all that men regret;
No lov'd-one now in feign'd lament could rave;
No friend the parting hand extended gave,   140
Ere the cold stranger pass'd to other climes:
Hard is his heart whom charms may not enslave;
But Harold felt not as in other times,
And left without a sigh the land of war and crimes.

17.

He that has sail'd upon the dark blue sea,   145
Has view'd at times, I ween, a full fair sight;

b Or will the gentle Dilettanti crew
Now delegate the task to digging Gell,
That mighty limner of a bird's eye view,
How like to Nature let his volumes tell—
Who can with him the folio's limit swell
With all the author saw, or said he saw?
Who can topographize or delve so well?
No boaster he, nor impudent and raw,
His pencil, pen, and spade alike without a flaw. *M; cor. in D*

131 best] well *D*   139 feign'd] ⟨bored⟩ *M*

When the fresh breeze is fair as breeze may be,
The white sail set, the gallant frigate tight;
Masts, spires, and strand retiring to the right,
The glorious main expanding o'er the bow,   150
The convoy spread like wild swans in their flight,
The dullest sailer wearing bravely now,
So gaily curl the waves before each dashing prow.

18.

And oh, the little warlike world within!
The well-reev'd guns, the netted canopy,   155
The hoarse command, the busy humming din,
When, at a word, the tops are mann'd on high:
Hark to the Boatswain's call, the cheering cry!
While through the seaman's hand the tackle glides;
Or school-boy Midshipman that, standing by,   160
Strains his shrill pipe as good or ill betides,
And well the docile crew that skilful urchin guides.

19.

White is the glassy deck, without a stain,
Where on the watch the staid Lieutenant walks:
Look on that part which sacred doth remain   165
For the lone chieftain, who majestic stalks,
Silent and fear'd by all—not oft he talks
With aught beneath him, if he would preserve
That strict restraint, which broken, ever balks
Conquest and Fame: but Britons rarely swerve   170
From Law, however stern, which tends their strength to
    nerve.

20.

Blow! swiftly blow, thou keel-compelling gale!
Till the broad sun withdraws his lessening ray;
Then must the pennant-bearer slacken sail,
That lagging barks may make their lazy way.   175
Ah! grievance sore, and listless dull delay,
To waste on sluggish hulks the sweetest breeze!

152 wearing] ⟨wears right⟩ M   153 gaily] ⟨fairly⟩ M   157 When, at a word]
⟨'All hands aloft'⟩ M   162 skilful] rosy M   165 Look] ⟨Save⟩ M   171 From
. . stern] From Discipline's keen law M   177 waste on] lose for M, D

What leagues are lost before the dawn of day,
Thus loitering pensive on the willing seas,
The flapping sail haul'd down to halt for logs like these! 180

21.

The moon is up; by Heaven a lovely eve!
Long streams of light o'er dancing waves expand;
Now lads on shore may sigh, and maids believe:
Such be our fate when we return to land!
Meantime some rude Arion's restless hand   185
Wakes the brisk harmony that sailors love;
A circle there of merry listeners stand,
Or to some well-known measure featly move,
Thoughtless, as if on shore they still were free to rove.

22.

Through Calpe's straits survey the steepy shore;   190
Europe and Afric on each other gaze!
Lands of the dark-ey'd Maid and dusky Moor
Alike beheld beneath pale Hecate's blaze:
How softly on the Spanish shore she plays,
Disclosing rock, and slope, and forest brown,   195
Distinct, though darkening with her waning phase;
But Mauritania's giant-shadows frown,
From mountain-cliff to coast descending sombre down.

23.

'Tis night, when Meditation bids us feel
We once have lov'd, though love is at an end: 200
The heart, lone mourner of its baffled zeal,
Though friendless now, will dream it had a friend.
Who with the weight of years would wish to bend,
When Youth itself survives young Love and Joy?
Alas! when mingling souls forget to blend,   205

183 may . . . believe] ⟨their melting girls deceive⟩ M   185–6 Arion's . . . Wakes . . .
harmony] ⟨musician's . . . Plys . . . instrument⟩ M   190 Through . . . survey] ⟨Each
side the straits / Through well-known straits behold⟩ M   Calpe's] ⟨Calypso's⟩ D
193 Hecate's blaze] Dian's rays D alternate reading   198 mountain-cliff] mountain
crag M; cor. in D   201 ⟨Divided far by fortune, wave, or steel⟩ / ⟨Far from Affection's
chilled or changing Zeal⟩ / Bleeds the lone heart once boundless in its zeal M   202 ⟨Though
friendless now we once have had a friend⟩ M   Though . . . will dream] And . . . yet
dreams M   204 survives young] surviveth M, D

Death hath but little left him to destroy!
Ah! happy years! once more who would not be a boy?

24.

Thus bending o'er the vessel's laving side,
To gaze on Dian's wave-reflected sphere;
The soul forgets her schemes of Hope and Pride,   210
And flies unconscious o'er each backward year.
None are so desolate but something dear,
Dearer than self, possesses or possess'd
A thought, and claims the homage of a tear;
A flashing pang! of which the weary breast   215
Would still, albeit in vain, the heavy heart divest.

25.

To sit on rocks, to muse o'er flood and fell,
To slowly trace the forest's shady scene,
Where things that own not man's dominion dwell,
And mortal foot hath ne'er, or rarely been;   220
To climb the trackless mountain all unseen,
With the wild flock that never needs a fold;
Alone o'er steeps and foaming falls to lean;
This is not solitude; 'tis but to hold
Converse with Nature's charms, and view her stores
          unroll'd.   225

26.

But midst the crowd, the hum, the shock of men,
To hear, to see, to feel, and to possess,
And roam along, the world's tir'd denizen,
With none who bless us, none whom we can bless;
Minions of splendour shrinking from distress!   230
None that, with kindred consciousness endued,
If we were not, would seem to smile the less
Of all that flatter'd, follow'd, sought and sued;
This is to be alone; this, this is solitude!

207 once . . . boy] I would I were once more a boy *M, D*   209 To . . .] ⟨Or
gazing upwards on⟩ *M*   wave-reflected] wan reflected *M, D*   210 schemes]
⟨dreams⟩ *M*   212 desolate but] wretched but that *M, D alternate reading*   217 muse]
⟨gaze⟩ *M*   223 falls] linns *M; cor. in D*   225 view] see *M, D, edns. 1–6*
228 tir'd] ⟨free / wide⟩ *M*   229 who . . . whom] that . . . that *M, D*   234 be] live
M, D

27.

More blest the life of godly Eremite,   235
Such as on lonely Athos may be seen,
Watching at Eve upon the giant height,
That looks o'er waves so blue, skies so serene,
That he who there at such an hour hath been
Will wistful linger on that hallow'd spot;   240
Then slowly tear him from the 'witching scene,
Sigh forth one wish that such had been his lot,
Then turn to hate a world he had almost forgot.

28.

Pass we the long, unvarying course, the track
Oft trod, that never leaves a trace behind;   245
Pass we the calm, the gale, the change, the tack,
And each well known caprice of wave and wind;
Pass we the joys and sorrows sailors find,
Coop'd in their winged sea-girt citadel;
The foul, the fair, the contrary, the kind,   250
As breezes rise and fall and billows swell,
Till on some jocund morn—lo, land! and all is well.

29.

But not in silence pass Calypso's isles,
The sister tenants of the middle deep;
There for the weary still a haven smiles,   255
Though the fair goddess long hath ceas'd to weep,
And o'er her cliffs a fruitless watch to keep
For him who dar'd prefer a mortal bride:
Here, too, his boy essay'd the dreadful leap
Stern Mentor urg'd from high to yonder tide;   260
While thus of both bereft, the nymph-queen doubly sigh'd.

30.

Her reign is past, her gentle glories gone:
But trust not this; too easy youth, beware!

235 life] ⟨lot⟩ MA   236 may be] I have MA   237 Eve upon] even on MA
238 That MA, all early edns. Which 1832, More, C   240 linger] ⟨gaze⟩ MA
244 course] voyage M   250 the contrary, the kind] the adverse and the kind D
alternate reading   255 haven] ⟨heaven⟩ D   256 Though] ⟨But⟩ M   260 Stern
⟨His⟩ M   261 While] ⟨And⟩ M

A mortal sovereign holds her dangerous throne,
And thou may'st find a new Calypso there.   265
Sweet Florence! could another ever share
This wayward, loveless heart, it would be thine:
But check'd by every tie, I may not dare
To cast a worthless offering at thy shrine,
Nor ask so dear a breast to feel one pang for mine.   270

31.

Thus Harold deem'd, as on that lady's eye
He look'd, and met its beam without a thought,
Save Admiration glancing harmless by:
Love kept aloof, albeit not far remote,
Who knew his votary often lost and caught,   275
But knew him as his worshipper no more,
And ne'er again the boy his bosom sought:
Since now he vainly urg'd him to adore,
Well deem'd the little God his ancient sway was o'er.

32.

Fair Florence found, in sooth with some amaze,   280
One who, 'twas said, still sigh'd to all he saw,
Withstand, unmov'd, the lustre of her gaze,
Which others hail'd with real, or mimic awe,
Their hope, their doom, their punishment, their law;
All that gay Beauty from her bondsmen claims: 285
And much she marvell'd that a youth so raw
Nor felt, nor feign'd at least, the oft-told flames,
Which, though sometimes they frown, yet rarely anger
    dames.

33.

Little knew she that seeming marble-heart,
Now mask'd in silence or withheld by pride,   290
Was not unskilful in the spoiler's art,
And spread its snares licentious far and wide;
Nor from the base pursuit had turn'd aside,

268 every tie] ⟨timely thought⟩ *M*   271 deem'd] spoke *M; cor. in D*   288 rarely]
never *M, D*

As long as aught was worthy to pursue:
But Harold on such arts no more relied;   295
And had he doated on those eyes so blue,
Yet never would he join the lover's whining crew.

34.

Not much he kens, I ween, of woman's breast,
Who thinks that wanton thing is won by sighs;
What careth she for hearts when once possess'd?   300
Do proper homage to thine idol's eyes;
But not too humbly, or she will despise
Thee and thy suit, though told in moving tropes:
Disguise ev'n tenderness, if thou art wise;
Brisk Confidence still best with woman copes;   305
Pique her and soothe in turn, soon Passion crowns thy hopes.

35.

'Tis an old lesson; Time approves it true,
And those who know it best, deplore it most;
When all is won that all desire to woo,
The paltry prize is hardly worth the cost: 310
Youth wasted, minds degraded, honour lost,
These are thy fruits, successful Passion! these!
If, kindly cruel, early Hope is crost,
Still to the last it rankles, a disease,
Not to be cur'd when Love itself forgets to please.   315

36.

Away! nor let me loiter in my song,
For we have many a mountain-path to tread,
And many a varied shore to sail along,
By pensive Sadness, not by Fiction, led—
Climes, fair withal as ever mortal head   320
Imagin'd in its little schemes of thought;
Or e'er in new Utopias were ared,
To teach man what he might be, or he ought;
If that corrupted thing could ever such be taught.

296 so] ⟨of⟩ M   298 kens] ⟨knows⟩ M   305 Confidence] Impudence M; cor. in
D   311 minds degraded,] ⟨wretches born, and⟩ M   320 fair] strange M, D
321 Imagin'd . . . schemes] ⟨Suspected . . . pride⟩ M

37.

Dear Nature is the kindest mother still,   325
Though alway changing, in her aspect mild;
From her bare bosom let me take my fill,
Her never-wean'd, though not her favour'd child.
Oh! she is fairest in her features wild,
Where nothing polish'd dares pollute her path: 330
To me by day or night she ever smil'd,
Though I have mark'd her when none other hath,
And sought her more and more, and lov'd her best in wrath.

38.

Land of Albania! where Iskander rose,
Theme of the young, and beacon of the wise,   335
And he his name-sake, whose oft-baffled foes
Shrunk from his deeds of chivalrous emprize:
Land of Albania! let me bend mine eyes
On thee, thou rugged nurse of savage men!
The cross descends, thy minarets arise,   340
And the pale crescent sparkles in the glen,
Through many a cypress grove within each city's ken.

39.

Childe Harold sail'd, and pass'd the barren spot,
Where sad Penelope o'erlook'd the wave;
And onward view'd the mount, not yet forgot,   345
The lover's refuge, and the Lesbian's grave.
Dark Sappho! could not verse immortal save
That breast imbued with such immortal fire?
Could she not live who life eternal gave?
If life eternal may await the lyre,   350
That only Heaven to which Earth's children may aspire.

40.

'Twas on a Grecian autumn's gentle eve
Childe Harold hail'd Leucadia's cape afar;
A spot he long'd to see, nor cared to leave:
Oft did he mark the scenes of vanish'd war,   355

328 ⟨Her not unconscious though her weakly / rudest child⟩ *M*   332 mark'd] seen
M, D   347 immortal] exhaustless *M*   349 Could she] ⟨Could'st thou⟩ *M*
354 ⟨And here his ? must grieve⟩ *M*   355 did he mark] ⟨had he marked⟩ *M*

Actium, Lepanto, fatal Trafalgar;
Mark them unmov'd, for he would not delight
(Born beneath some remote inglorious star)
In themes of bloody fray, or gallant fight,
But loath'd the bravo's trade, and laugh'd at martial
    wight.   360

41.

But when he saw the evening star above
Leucadia's far-projecting rock of woe,
And hail'd the last resort of fruitless love,
He felt, or deem'd he felt, no common glow:
And as the stately vessel glided slow   365
Beneath the shadow of that ancient mount,
He watch'd the billows' melancholy flow,
And, sunk albeit in thought as he was wont,
More placid seem'd his eye, and smooth his pallid front.

42.

Morn dawns; and with it stern Albania's hills,   370
Dark Suli's rocks, and Pindus' inland peak,
Rob'd half in mist, bedew'd with snowy rills,
Array'd in many a dun and purple streak,
Arise; and, as the clouds along them break,
Disclose the dwelling of the mountaineer: 375
Here roams the wolf, the eagle whets his beak,
Birds, beasts of prey, and wilder men appear,
And gathering storms around convulse the closing year.

43.

Now Harold felt himself at length alone,
And bade to Christian tongues a long adieu;   380
Now he adventur'd on a shore unknown,
Which all admire, but many dread to view:
His breast was arm'd 'gainst fate, his wants were few;

357 Mark . . . would] ⟨Saw . . . did⟩ M   359 In . . .] ⟨Albeit he knew not fear⟩ M
bloody . . . gallant] ⟨gallant . . . bootless⟩ M   360 But . . . trade] ⟨And looked askance
on Mars / And scorned the boaster's tale⟩ M   367 watch'd the billows'] ⟨heard the
water's⟩ M   368-9 And roused him more from thought than he was wont | While
Pleasure almost ⟨smiled along⟩ seemed to smooth his pallid front M, D   377 Birds,
beasts of] Beasts, birds of M; cor. in D

Peril he sought not, but ne'er shrank to meet,
The scene was savage, but the scene was new;   385
This made the ceaseless toil of travel sweet,
Beat back keen winter's blast, and welcom'd summer's heat.

44.

Here the red cross, for still the cross is here,
Though sadly scoff'd at by the circumcis'd,
Forgets that pride to pamper'd Priesthood dear;   390
Churchman and votary alike despis'd.
Foul Superstition! howsoe'er disguis'd,
Idol, saint, virgin, prophet, crescent, cross,
For whatsoever symbol thou art priz'd,
Thou sacerdotal gain, but general loss!   395
Who from true worship's gold can separate thy dross?

45.

Ambracia's gulph behold, where once was lost
A world for woman, lovely, harmless thing!
In yonder rippling bay, their naval host
Did many a Roman chief and Asian king   400
To doubtful conflict, certain slaughter bring:
Look where the second Caesar's trophies rose!
Now, like the hands that rear'd them, withering:
Imperial Anarchs, doubling human woes!
GOD! was thy globe ordain'd for such to win and lose?   405

46.

From the dark barriers of that rugged clime,
Ev'n to the centre of Illyria's vales,
Childe Harold pass'd o'er many a mount sublime,
Through lands scarce notic'd in historic tales;
Yet in fam'd Attica such lovely dales   410
Are rarely seen; nor can fair Tempe boast
A charm they know not; lov'd Parnassus fails,
Though classic ground and consecrated most,
To match some spots that lurk within this lowering coast.

398 harmless] harmful *M alternate reading*   400 king] Thing *M*   402 the
second] ⟨victorious⟩ *M*   403 rear'd] ⟨caused⟩ *M*   404 Anarchs] ⟨wretches⟩ *M*
405 ordain'd] ⟨ere made⟩ *M*   409 scarce notic'd] ⟨unnoticed⟩ *M*

47.

He pass'd bleak Pindus, Acherusia's lake,   415
And left the primal city of the land,
And onwards did his further journey take
To greet Albania's chief, whose dread command
Is lawless law; for with a bloody hand
He sways a nation, turbulent and bold: 420
Yet here and there some daring mountain-band
Disdain his power, and from their rocky hold
Hurl their defiance far, nor yield, unless to gold.

48.

Monastic Zitza! from thy shady brow,
Thou small, but favour'd spot of holy ground!   425
Where'er we gaze, around, above, below,
What rainbow tints, what magic charms are found!
Rock, river, forest, mountain, all abound,
And bluest skies that harmonize the whole:
Beneath, the distant torrent's rushing sound   430
Tells where the volum'd cataract doth roll
Between those hanging rocks, that shock yet please the soul.

49.

Amidst the grove that crowns yon tufted hill,
Which, were it not for many a mountain nigh
Rising in lofty ranks, and loftier still,   435
Might well itself be deem'd of dignity,
The convent's white walls glisten fair on high:
Here dwells the caloyer, nor rude is he,
Nor niggard of his cheer; the passer by
Is welcome still; nor heedless will he flee   440
From hence, if he delight kind Nature's sheen to see.

50.

Here in the sultriest season let him rest,
Fresh is the green beneath those aged trees;
Here winds of gentlest wing will fan his breast,
From heaven itself he may inhale the breeze: 445

416 primal] ⟨chiefest⟩ M   417 further] ⟨willing⟩ M   423 unless] except
M, D   437 fair] ⟨far⟩ D   444 of gentlest wing] if winds there be M; cor. in D

The plain is far beneath—oh! let him seize
Pure pleasure while he can; the scorching ray
Here pierceth not, impregnate with disease:
Then let his length the loitering pilgrim lay,
And gaze, untir'd, the morn, the noon, the eve away.   450

51.

Dusky and huge, enlarging on the sight,
Nature's volcanic amphitheatre,
Chimaera's alps extend from left to right:
Beneath, a living valley seems to stir;
Flocks play, trees wave, streams flow, the mountain-fir
Nodding above: behold black Acheron!   456
Once consecrated to the sepulchre.
Pluto! if this be hell I look upon,
Close sham'd Elysium's gates, my shade shall seek for none!

52.

Ne city's towers pollute the lovely view;   460
Unseen is Yanina, though not remote,
Veil'd by the screen of hills: here men are few,
Scanty the hamlet, rare the lonely cot;
But, peering down each precipice, the goat
Browseth; and, pensive o'er his scattered flock,   465
The little shepherd in his white capote
Doth lean his boyish form along the rock,
Or in his cave awaits the tempest's short-liv'd shock.

53.

Oh! where, Dodona! is thine aged grove,
Prophetic fount, and oracle divine?   470
What valley echo'd the response of Jove?
What trace remaineth of the thunderer's shrine?
All, all forgotten—and shall man repine

446 The plain] ⟨Low Earth⟩ M   451, 453 M transposed then corrected
452 Nature's volcanic] ⟨A rolling caverned⟩ M   459 Close ... gates] Keep Heaven
for better souls M; cor. in D   Close] ⟨Shut⟩ D   464–5 ⟨But frequent is the lamb,
the kid, the goat— | And watching pensive with his browsing flock⟩ M   468 ⟨Counting
the hours beneath yon skies unerring shock⟩ M   469 Oh ... thine aged] ⟨But ... thy
sacred⟩ MC   470 Prophetic fount] Thy holy founts MC; cor. in M   471 What]
⟨Whose⟩ MC   472 What trace ⟨remains of Greece⟩ remaineth MC   473 ⟨His
name now⟩ MC

That his frail bonds to fleeting life are broke?
Cease, fool! the fate of gods may well be thine: 475
Wouldst thou survive the marble or the oak?
When nations, tongues, and worlds must sink beneath the
    stroke!

54.

Epirus' bounds recede, and mountains fail;
Tir'd of up-gazing still, the wearied eye
Reposes gladly on as smooth a vale   480
As ever Spring yclad in grassy dye:
Ev'n on a plain no humble beauties lie,
Where some bold river breaks the long expanse,
And woods along the banks are waving high,
Whose shadows in the glassy waters dance,   485
Or with the moon-beam sleep in midnight's solemn trance.

55.

The Sun had sunk behind vast Tomerit,
And Laos wide and fierce came roaring by;
The shades of wonted night were gathering yet,
When, down the steep banks winding warily,   490
Childe Harold saw, like meteors in the sky,
The glittering minarets of Tepalen,
Whose walls o'erlook the stream; and drawing nigh,
He heard the busy hum of warrior-men
Swelling the breeze that sigh'd along the lengthening
    glen.   495

56.

He pass'd the sacred Haram's silent tower,
And underneath the wide o'erarching gate
Survey'd the dwelling of this chief of power,
Where all around proclaim'd his high estate.
Amidst no common pomp the despot sate,   500
While busy preparation shook the court,
Slaves, eunuchs, soldiers, guests, and santons wait;
Within, a palace, and without, a fort:
Here men of every clime appear to make resort.

474 When his frail hands to ⟨mouldering earth⟩ / ⟨fluttering⟩ / fleeting life are broke *MC*
482 no humble] ⟨some humbler⟩ *M*   497 wide] ⟨high⟩ *M*   502 santons]
⟨vassals⟩ *M*   504 appear] appeared *M*

57.

Richly caparison'd, a ready row   505
Of armed horse, and many a warlike store
Circled the wide extending court below:
Above, strange groups adorn'd the corridore;
And oft-times through the Area's echoing door
Some high-capp'd Tartar spurr'd his steed away: 510
The Turk, the Greek, the Albanian, and the Moor,
Here mingled in their many-hued array,
While the deep war-drum's sound announc'd the close of day.

58.

The wild Albanian kirtled to his knee,
With shawl-girt head and ornamented gun,   515
And gold-embroider'd garments, fair to see;
The crimson-scarfed men of Macedon;
The Delhi with his cap of terror on,
And crooked glaive; the lively, supple Greek;
And swarthy Nubia's mutilated son;   520
The bearded Turk that rarely deigns to speak,
Master of all around, too potent to be meek,

59.

Are mix'd conspicuous: some recline in groups,
Scanning the motley scene that varies round;
There some grave Moslem to devotion stoops,   525
And some that smoke, and some that play, are found;
Here the Albanian proudly treads the ground;
Half whispering there the Greek is heard to prate;
Hark! from the mosque the nightly solemn sound,
The Muezzin's call doth shake the minaret,   530
'There is no god but God!—to prayer—lo! God is great.'

60.

Just at this season Ramazani's fast
Through the long day its penance did maintain:
But when the lingering twilight hour was past,
Revel and feast assum'd the rule again: 535

508 Above] ⟨Where⟩ D   513 war-drum's] Tocsin's M; cor. in D   523–31 All
verb forms in the stanza were originally in the past tense in M

Now all was bustle, and the menial train
Prepar'd and spread the plenteous board within;
The vacant gallery now seem'd made in vain,
But from the chambers came the mingling din,
As page and slave anon were passing out and in.   540

61.

Here woman's voice is never heard: apart,
And scarce permitted, guarded, veil'd, to move,
She yields to one her person and her heart,
Tam'd to her cage, nor feels a wish to rove:
For, not unhappy in her master's love,   545
And joyful in a mother's gentlest cares,
Blest cares! all other feelings far above!
Herself more sweetly rears the babe she bears,
Who never quits the breast, no meaner passion shares.

62.

In marble-pav'd pavilion, where a spring   550
Of living water from the centre rose,
Whose bubbling did a genial freshness fling,
And soft voluptuous couches breath'd repose,
ALI reclin'd, a man of war and woes;
Yet in his lineaments ye cannot trace,   555
While Gentleness her milder radiance throws
Along that aged venerable face,
The deeds that lurk beneath, and stain him with disgrace.

63.

It is not that yon hoary lengthening beard
Ill suits the passions which belong to youth;   560
Love conquers age—so Hafiz hath averr'd,
So sings the Teian, and he sings in sooth—

542 guarded . . . move] ⟨even for health⟩ to rove *M*   542, 544 move . . . rove] rove . . .
move *M, D, edns. 1–6*
545–9   For boyish minions of unhallowed love
               The shameless torch of wild desire is lit,
               Caressed, preferred even to woman's self above,
               Whose forms for Nature's gentler errors fit
               All frailties mote excuse save that which they commit. *M; cor. in D*
555 cannot] ⟨could⟩ not *M*   560 Delights to mingle with the lip of youth *M; cor. in D*

But crimes that scorn the tender voice of Ruth,
Beseeming all men ill, but most the man
In years, have marked him with a tyger's tooth;   565
Blood follows blood, and, through their mortal span,
In bloodier acts conclude those who with blood began.

64.

'Mid many things most new to ear and eye
The pilgrim rested here his weary feet,
And gaz'd around on Moslem luxury,   570
Till quickly wearied with that spacious seat
Of Wealth and Wantonness, the choice retreat
Of sated Grandeur from the city's noise:
And were it humbler it in sooth were sweet;
But Peace abhorreth artificial joys,   575
And Pleasure, leagued with Pomp, the zest of both destroys.

65.

Fierce are Albania's children, yet they lack
Not virtues, were those virtues more mature.
Where is the foe that ever saw their back?
Who can so well the toil of war endure?   580
Their native fastnesses not more secure
Than they in doubtful time of troublous need:
Their wrath how deadly! but their friendship sure,
When Gratitude or Valour bids them bleed,
Unshaken rushing on where'er their chief may lead.   585

66.

Childe Harold saw them in their chieftain's tower
Thronging to war in splendour and success;
And after view'd them, when, within their power,
Himself awhile the victim of distress;

563 But 'tis those ne'er forgotten acts of truth *M, D, edns. 1–6*   565 have marked]
that mark *M, D, edns. 1–6*   566–7 ⟨Has markèd even he, and where they can |
Those who in blood begin in blood conclude their span⟩ *M*
568–72   Childe Harold with that chief held colloquy
                               Yet what they spake it boots not to repeat;
                               Converse may little charm strange ear or eye;
                               Albeit he rested in that spacious seat
                               Of Moslem luxury the choice retreat *M; cor. in D*
var. 4 Albeit . . . spacious] ⟨Four days / Some time . . . worthy⟩ *M*   576 zest] ⟨taste⟩ *M*
580 toil] toils *M*   583 how] ⟨is⟩ *M*   deadly] ⟨dreadful⟩ *D*

That saddening hour when bad men hotlier press: 590
But these did shelter him beneath their roof,
When less barbarians would have cheered him less,
And fellow-countrymen have stood aloof—
In aught that tries the heart how few withstand the proof!

67.

It chanc'd that adverse winds once drove his bark   595
Full on the coast of Suli's shaggy shore,
When all around was desolate and dark;
To land was perilous, to sojourn more;
Yet for awhile the mariners forbore,
Dubious to trust where treachery might lurk: 600
At length they ventur'd forth, though doubting sore
That those who loathe alike the Frank and Turk
Might once again renew their ancient butcher-work.

68.

Vain fear! the Suliotes stretch'd the welcome hand,
Led them o'er rocks and past the dangerous swamp,   605
Kinder than polish'd slaves though not so bland,
And pil'd the hearth, and wrung their garments damp,
And fill'd the bowl, and trimm'd the cheerful lamp,
And spread their fare; though homely, all they had:
Such conduct bears Philanthropy's rare stamp—   610
To rest the weary and to soothe the sad,
Doth lesson happier men, and shames at least the bad.

69.

It came to pass, that when he did address
Himself to quit at length this mountain-land,
Combin'd marauders half-way barr'd egress,   615
And wasted far and near with glaive and brand;
And therefore did he take a trusty band
To traverse Acarnania's forest wide,
In war well season'd, and with labours tann'd,
Till he did greet white Achelous' tide,   620
And from his further bank Aetolia's wolds espied.

591 beneath] ⟨within⟩ M   610 rare] ⟨fair⟩ M   611 rest] ⟨soothe⟩ M

70.

Where lone Utraikey forms its circling cove,
And weary waves retire to gleam at rest,
How brown the foliage of the green hill's grove,
Nodding at midnight o'er the calm bay's breast,   625
As winds come lightly whispering from the west,
Kissing, not ruffling, the blue deep's serene:—
Here Harold was receiv'd a welcome guest;
Nor did he pass unmov'd the gentle scene,
For many a joy could he from Night's soft presence glean. 630

71.

On the smooth shore the night-fires brightly blaz'd,
The feast was done, the red wine circling fast,
And he that unawares had there ygaz'd
With gaping wonderment had star'd aghast;
For ere night's midmost, stillest hour was past   635
The native revels of the troop began;
Each Palikar his sabre from him cast,
And bounding hand in hand, man link'd to man,
Yelling their uncouth dirge, long daunc'd the kirtled clan.

72.

Childe Harold at a little distance stood   640
And view'd, but not displeas'd, the revelrie,
Nor hated harmless mirth, however rude:
In sooth, it was no vulgar sight to see
Their barbarous, yet their not indecent, glee,
And, as the flames along their faces gleam'd,   645
Their gestures nimble, dark eyes flashing free,
The long wild locks that to their girdles stream'd,
While thus in concert they this lay half sang, half scream'd:

I.

Tambourgi! Tambourgi! thy 'larum afar
Gives hope to the valiant, and promise of war;   650
All the sons of the mountains arise at the note,
Chimariot, Illyrian, and dark Suliote!

645 along] ⟨upon⟩ M   647 to] ⟨down⟩ M   649 'larum] tocsin Υ, M; cor.
in D   651 All the] The Υ, M   652 Illyrian] ⟨Albanian⟩ Υ

2.

Oh! who is more brave than a dark Suliote,
In his snowy camese and his shaggy capote?
To the wolf and the vulture he leaves his wild flock,   655
And descends to the plain like the stream from the rock.

3.

Shall the sons of Chimari, who never forgive
The fault of a friend, bid an enemy live?
Let those guns so unerring such vengeance forego?
What mark is so fair as the breast of a foe?   660

4.

Macedonia sends forth her invincible race;
For a time they abandon the cave and the chase:
But those scarfs of blood-red shall be redder, before
The sabre is sheath'd and the battle is o'er.

5.

Then the pirates of Parga that dwell by the waves,   665
And teach the pale Franks what it is to be slaves,
Shall leave on the beach the long galley and oar,
And track to his covert the captive on shore.

6.

I ask not the pleasures that riches supply,
My sabre shall win what the feeble must buy;   670
Shall win the young bride with her long flowing hair,
And many a maid from her mother shall tear.

7.

I love the fair face of the maid in her youth,
Her caresses shall lull me, her music shall sooth;
Let her bring from the chamber her many-ton'd lyre, 675
And sing us a song on the fall of her sire.

655 vulture] robber *Y*   657 Chimari, who] Chimaera that *Y*; *cor. in M*
663 of . . . before] ⟨now so white shall be crimson before⟩ *Y*   671 bride . . . hair]
minions with long flowing hair *Y*, *M*, *D*   673–6, 677–80 *the stanzas are transposed
in Y*   673 fair face] ⟨soft lips⟩ *Y*   in her] and the *Y*, *M*; *cor. in D*   674 Their
caresses shall lull us, their voices shall soothe *Y*, *M*; *cor. in D*   675 her . . . the
chamber] them . . . their chambers *Y*, *M*; *cor. in D*   676 her sire] their Sires *Y*, *M*;
cor. in D

8.

Remember the moment when Previsa fell,
The shrieks of the conquer'd, the conquerors' yell;
The roofs that we fir'd, and the plunder we shar'd,
The wealthy we slaughter'd, the lovely we spar'd.   680

9.

I talk not of mercy, I talk not of fear;
He neither must know who would serve the Vizier:
Since the days of our prophet the Crescent ne'er saw
A chief ever glorious like Ali Pashaw.

10.

Dark Muchtar his son to the Danube is sped,   685
Let the yellow-hair'd Giaours view his horse-tail with
   dread;
When his Delhis come dashing in blood o'er the banks,
How few shall escape from the Muscovite ranks!

11.

Selictar! unsheath then our chief's scimitār:
Tambourgi! thy 'larum gives promise of war.   690
Ye mountains, that see us descend to the shore,
Shall view us as victors, or view us no more!

73.

Fair Greece! sad relic of departed worth!
Immortal, though no more! though fallen, great!
Who now shall lead thy scatter'd children forth,   695
And long accustom'd bondage uncreate?
Not such thy sons who whilome did await,
The hopeless warriors of a willing doom,
In bleak Thermopylae's sepulchral strait—
Oh! who that gallant spirit shall resume,   700
Leap from Eurotas' banks, and call thee from the tomb?

686 yellow-hair'd] yellow *Y*   687–8 ⟨See his Delhis are dashing in blood through
their ranks | And the Muscovites flee but in vain from the Banks⟩ *Y*   How . . . escape]
⟨Not many will see⟩ *Y*   690 'larum] tocsin *Y*, *M*; *cor. in* D   693 relic] mother *Y*
⟨widow⟩ *M*   694 ⟨Immortal ruin of a mortal state⟩ Immortal monument of mortal
fate *Y*   695 lead] call *Y*   697 Not . . .] ⟨Each⟩ *Y*   698 The . . .]
⟨The shock of battle without / The warriors of battle without⟩ *Y*   hopeless] ⟨willing⟩ *Y*
helpless *Y*, *M*   701 Leap . . .] ⟨Wake the⟩ *Y*   call . . . tomb] ⟨lead / call⟩ wake ye
from your tomb *Y*

74.

Spirit of freedom! when on Phyle's brow
Thou sat'st with Thrasybulus and his train,
Couldst thou forebode the dismal hour which now
Dims the green beauties of thine Attic plain?   705
Not thirty tyrants now enforce the chain,
But every carle can lord it o'er thy land;
Nor rise thy sons, but idly rail in vain,
Trembling beneath the scourge of Turkish hand,
From birth till death enslav'd; in word, in deed unmann'd. 710

75.

In all save form alone, how chang'd! and who
That marks the fire still sparkling in each eye,
Who but would deem their bosoms burn'd anew
With thy unquenched beam, lost Liberty!
And many dream withal the hour is nigh   715
That gives them back their fathers' heritage:
For foreign arms and aid they fondly sigh,
Nor solely dare encounter hostile rage,
Or tear their name defil'd from Slavery's mournful page.

76.

Hereditary bondsmen! know ye not   720
Who would be free themselves must strike the blow?
By their right arms the conquest must be wrought?
Will Gaul or Muscovite redress ye? no!
True, they may lay your proud despoilers low,
But not for you will Freedom's altars flame.   725
Shades of the Helots! triumph o'er your foe!
Greece! change thy lords, thy state is still the same;
Thy glorious day is o'er, but not thine years of shame.

77.

The city won for Allah from the Giaour,
The Giaour from Othman's race again may wrest;   730
And the Serai's impenetrable tower
Receive the fiery Frank, her former guest;

710 ⟨A fawning feeble race, untaught, enslaved, unmanned⟩ M   714 lost] fair M;
c r. in D   717 For . . . and]⟨To . . . for⟩ M   729 for Allah] by Mahmet MA

On Wahab's rebel brood who dared divest
The prophet's tomb of all its pious spoil,
May wind their path of blood along the West;   735
But ne'er will freedom seek this fated soil,
But slave succeed to slave through years of endless toil.

78.

Yet mark their mirth—ere lenten days begin,
That penance which their holy rites prepare
To shrive from man his weight of mortal sin,   740
By daily abstinence and nightly prayer;
But ere his sackcloth garb Repentance wear,
Some days of joyaunce are decreed to all,
To take of pleasaunce each his secret share,
In motley robe to dance at masking ball,   745
And join the mimic train of merry Carnival.

79.

And whose more rife with merriment than thine,
Oh Stamboul! once the empress of their reign?
Though turbans now pollute Sophia's shrine,
And Greece her very altars eyes in vain: 750
(Alas! her woes will still pervade my strain!)
Gay were her minstrels once, for free her throng,
All felt the common joy they now must feign,
Nor oft I've seen such sight, nor heard such song,
As woo'd the eye, and thrill'd the Bosphorus along.   755

80.

Loud was the lightsome tumult of the shore,
Oft Music chang'd, but never ceas'd her tone,
And timely echo'd back the measur'd oar,
And rippling waters made a pleasant moan:

733 rebel] ⟨impious⟩ *MA*   735 wind . . . blood] ⟨pour with blood the path⟩ *MA*
736 ne'er] ⟨not far⟩ *MA*   738 days] ⟨time⟩ *MA*   739 That . . . their] The . . .
the *MA*   748 reign] ⟨Main⟩ *H*   749 Though] ⟨strangers enter there / now⟩
Sophia's shrine *MA*   751 ⟨Who would not deem her free to see their / thy train⟩
MA   752 her . . . her] thy . . . thy *MA*   754 heard] ⟨viewed⟩ *MA*   756 was]
is *MA*   of] on *1831, 1832, C, More*   757 tone] ⟨note⟩ *H*   759 pleasant]
pleasing *MA, H*

The Queen of tides on high consenting shone,   760
And when a transient breeze swept o'er the wave,
'Twas, as if darting from her heavenly throne,
A brighter glance her form reflected gave,
Till sparkling billows seem'd to light the banks they lave.

81.

Glanc'd many a light caique along the foam,   765
Danc'd on the shore the daughters of the land,
Ne thought had man or maid of rest or home,
While many a languid eye and thrilling hand
Exchang'd the look few bosoms may withstand,
Or gently prest, return'd the pressure still: 770
Oh Love! young Love! bound in thy rosy band,
Let sage or cynic prattle as he will,
These hours, and only these, redeem Life's years of ill!

82.

But, midst the throng in merry masquerade,
Lurk there no hearts that throb with secret pain,   775
Even through the closest searment half betrayed?
To such the gentle murmurs of the main
Seem to re-echo all they mourn in vain;
To such the gladness of the gamesome crowd
Is source of wayward thought and stern disdain: 780
How do they loathe the laughter idly loud,
And long to change the robe of revel for the shroud!

83.

This must he feel, the true-born son of Greece,
If Greece one true-born patriot still can boast:
Not such as prate of war, but skulk in peace,   785
The bondman's peace, who sighs for all he lost,
Yet with smooth smile his tyrant can accost,
And wield the slavish sickle, not the sword:
Ah! Greece! they love thee least who owe thee most;
Their birth, their blood, and that sublime record   790
Of hero sires, who shame thy now degenerate horde!

764 banks] ⟨shore⟩ *MA*, *H*   771 band] ⟨chain⟩ *MA*   773 These hours are
cheaply bought by ⟨years of future⟩ future years of ill *MA*; These hours are cheaply bought
by years of after ill *H*

84.

When riseth Lacedemon's hardihood,
When Thebes Epaminondas rears again,
When Athens' children are with hearts endued,
When Grecian mothers shall give birth to men,   795
Then may'st thou be restored; but not till then.
A thousand years scarce serve to form a state;
An hour may lay it in the dust: and when
Can man its shatter'd splendour renovate,
Recal its virtues back, and vanquish Time and Fate?   800

85.

And yet how lovely in thine age of woe,
Land of lost gods and godlike men! art thou!
Thy vales of ever-green, thy hills of snow
Proclaim thee Nature's varied favourite now:
Thy fanes, thy temples to thy surface bow,   805
Commingling slowly with heroic earth,
Broke by the share of every rustic plough:
So perish monuments of mortal birth,
So perish all in turn, save well-recorded Worth;

86.

Save where some solitary column mourns   810
Above its prostrate brethren of the cave;
Save where Tritonia's airy shrine adorns
Colonna's cliff, and gleams along the wave;
Save o'er some warrior's half-forgotten grave,
Where the grey stones and unmolested grass   815
Ages, but not oblivion, feebly brave,
While strangers only not regardless pass,
Lingering like me, perchance, to gaze, and sigh 'Alas!'

87.

Yet are thy skies as blue, thy crags as wild;
Sweet are thy groves, and verdant are thy fields,   820
Thine olive ripe as when Minerva smil'd,
And still his honied wealth Hymettus yields;

794 hearts] arts D, edns. 1–8   803 hills crags D

There the blithe bee his fragrant fortress builds,
The freeborn wanderer of thy mountain-air;
Apollo still thy long, long summer gilds,   825
Still in his beam Mendeli's marbles glare;
Art, Glory, Freedom fail, but Nature still is fair.

88.

Where'er we tread 'tis haunted, holy ground;
No earth of thine is lost in vulgar mould,
But one vast realm of wonder spreads around,   830
And all the Muse's tales seem truly told,
Till the sense aches with gazing to behold
The scenes our earliest dreams have dwelt upon:
Each hill and dale, each deepening glen and wold
Defies the power which crush'd thy temples gone: 835
Age shakes Athena's tower, but spares gray Marathon.

89.

The sun, the soil, but not the slave, the same;
Unchanged in all except its foreign lord—
Preserves alike its bounds and boundless fame
The Battle-field, where Persia's victim horde   840
First bowed beneath the brunt of Hellas' sword,
As on the morn to distant Glory dear,
When Marathon became a magic word;
Which utter'd, to the hearer's eye appear
The camp, the host, the fight, the conqueror's career,   845

90.

The flying Mede, his shaftless broken bow;
The fiery Greek, his red pursuing spear;
Mountains above, Earth's, Ocean's plain below;
Death in the front, Destruction in the rear!

826 Mendeli's] ⟨Pentele's⟩ D   827 fail] fails edns. 1–6   838 lord] ⟨lords⟩ L
839 bounds and] ⟨form / friend—its⟩ L   840 horde] ⟨hordes⟩ L   841 Hellas'
sword] ⟨Attic swords⟩ L   842 As] ⟨When⟩ L   843 Marathon] ⟨Freedom⟩ L
844 hearer's] listener's L   845 The camp, the host] ⟨The plain, the host⟩ The host,
the plain L   the conqueror's career] ⟨the triumph and the tear / the Greek's pursuing spear⟩
L   846 ⟨The tears of Asia / Hellas for her ? ⟩ | ⟨The shattered Mede with / who flies
with broken bow⟩ L   847 his] ⟨with⟩ L   848 Earth's . . . plain] ⟨the plain—the
sea⟩ L   849 front] van L

Such was the scene—what now remaineth here?   850
What sacred trophy marks the hallow'd ground,
Recording Freedom's smile and Asia's tear?
The rifled urn, the violated mound,
The dust thy courser's hoof, rude stranger! spurns around.

91.

Yet to the remnants of thy splendour past   855
Shall pilgrims, pensive, but unwearied, throng;
Long shall the voyager, with th' Ionian blast,
Hail the bright clime of battle and of song;
Long shall thine annals and immortal tongue
Fill with thy fame the youth of many a shore;   860
Boast of the aged! lesson of the young!
Which sages venerate and bards adore,
As Pallas and the Muse unveil their awful lore.

92.

The parted bosom clings to wonted home,
If aught that's kindred cheer the welcome hearth;   865
He that is lonely hither let him roam,
And gaze complacent on congenial earth.
Greece is no lightsome land of social mirth;
But he whom Sadness sootheth may abide,
And scarce regret the region of his birth,   870
When wandering slow by Delphi's sacred side,
Or gazing o'er the plains where Greek and Persian died.

93.

Let such approach this consecrated land,
And pass in peace along the magic waste:
But spare its relics—let no busy hand   875
Deface the scenes, already how defac'd!
Not for such purpose were these altars plac'd:
Revere the remnants nations once rever'd:

851 What . . .] ⟨No marble⟩ L   852 ⟨To tell what Asia trembled but to
hear⟩ L   855 Yet] Long M, D, edns. 1–6   857 with th' Ionian] ⟨from the
convulsed⟩ M   860 many a shore] ⟨happier shores⟩ M   862 venerate and bards]
⟨reverence and the bards⟩ M   863 unveil . . . lore] ⟨display . . . store⟩ M   866 He
that is] ⟨But he that's⟩ M   874 pass] ⟨walk⟩ G   875 busy] wanton G
876 defac'd] effaced G

So may our country's name be undisgrac'd,
So may'st thou prosper where thy youth was rear'd,   880
By every honest joy of love and life endear'd!

94.

For thee, who thus in too protracted song
Hast sooth'd thine idlesse with inglorious lays,
Soon shall thy voice be lost amid the throng
Of louder minstrels in these later days: 885
To such resign the strife for fading bays—
Ill may such contest now the spirit move
Which heeds nor keen reproach nor partial praise;
Since cold each kinder heart that might approve,
And none are left to please when none are left to love. 890

95.

Thou too art gone, thou lov'd and lovely one!
Whom youth and youth's affection bound to me;
Who did for me what none beside have done,
Nor shrank from one albeit unworthy thee.
What is my being? thou hast ceas'd to be!   895
Nor staid to welcome here thy wanderer home,
Who mourns o'er hours which we no more shall see—
Would they had never been, or were to come!
Would he had ne'er return'd to find fresh cause to roam!

96.

Oh! ever loving, lovely, and belov'd!   900
How selfish Sorrow ponders on the past,
And clings to thoughts now better far remov'd!
But Time shall tear thy shadow from me last.
All thou could'st have of mine, stern Death! thou hast;
The parent, friend, and now the more than friend: 905
Ne'er yet for one thine arrows flew so fast,
And grief with grief continuing still to blend,
Hath snatch'd the little joy that life had yet to lend.

---

882 in] ⟨with⟩ G   883 thine . . . inglorious] ⟨? in wildest⟩ G   886 such] these G
888 keen] stern G, D   889 Since ⟨hushed⟩ each ⟨gentler⟩ heart that mote approve G
891 Thou too art] ⟨But thou art⟩ MB   894 albeit unworthy] ⟨unworthy such as⟩ MB
899 he] I D   903 ⟨Till Time the Comforter shall come at last⟩ MB

97.

Then must I plunge again into the crowd,
And follow all that Peace disdains to seek?   910
Where Revel calls, and Laughter, vainly loud,
False to the heart, distorts the hollow cheek,
To leave the flagging spirit doubly weak;
Still o'er the features, which perforce they cheer,
To feign the pleasure or conceal the pique,   915
Smiles form the channel of a future tear,
Or raise the writhing lip with ill-dissembled sneer.

98.

What is the worst of woes that wait on age?
What stamps the wrinkle deeper on the brow?
To view each lov'd one blotted from life's page,   920
And be alone on earth, as I am now.
Before the Chastener humbly let me bow:
O'er hearts divided and o'er hopes destroy'd,
Roll on, vain days! full reckless may ye flow,
Since Time hath reft whate'er my soul enjoy'd,   925
And with the ills of Eld mine earlier years alloy'd.

Childe Harold's Pilgrimage

CANTO THE THIRD

Afin que cette application vous forçât à penser à autre chose.
Il n'y a en vérité de remède que celui-là et le temps. *Lettre du
Roi de Prusse à D'Alembert, Sept. 7, 1776.*

I.

Is thy face like thy mother's, my fair child!
Ada! sole daughter of my house and heart?

909 must I] let me *MB*   910 all that] ⟨Pleasures⟩ *MB*   911 vainly] ⟨feigned /
light and⟩ *MB*   912 hollow] ⟨joyless⟩ *MB*   915 To . . . pleasure] ⟨Gloss oer the
grievance⟩ *MB*   pleasure] pleasaunce *MB*   pique,] pique *all early edns., C, OSA*
916 channel] ⟨furrow⟩ *MB*   917 Or . . . sneer] ⟨And . . . leer⟩ *MB*   922–3 bow:
. . . destroy'd,] bow, . . . destroy'd *all edns.*   924–5 Though Time not yet hath tinged
my locks with snow | Yet hath he reft whateer my soul enjoyed *MB, D alternate reading*

Copy text : *CHP III* (third issue), collated with *MSS. M, BM, S, MC, B, SB, H, Smith
1831, 1832, C, More*
     epigraph   *not in M, BM, S*
     2 sole] ⟨sweet⟩ *B*

When last I saw thy young blue eyes they smiled,
And then we parted,—not as now we part,
But with a hope.—

              Awaking with a start,   5
The waters heave around me; and on high
The winds lift up their voices: I depart,
Whither I know not; but the hour's gone by,
When Albion's lessening shores could grieve or glad mine eye.

2.

Once more upon the waters! yet once more!   10
And the waves bound beneath me as a steed
That knows his rider. Welcome, to their roar!
Swift be their guidance, wheresoe'er it lead!
Though the strain'd mast should quiver as a reed,
And the rent canvas fluttering strew the gale,   15
Still must I on; for I am as a weed,
Flung from the rock, on Ocean's foam, to sail
Where'er the surge may sweep, or tempest's breath prevail.

3.

In my youth's summer I did sing of One,
The wandering outlaw of his own dark mind;   20
Again I seize the theme then but begun,
And bear it with me, as the rushing wind
Bears the cloud onwards: in that Tale I find
The furrows of long thought, and dried-up tears,
Which, ebbing, leave a sterile track behind,   25
O'er which all heavily the journeying years
Plod the last sands of life,—where not a flower appears.

4.

Since my young days of passion—joy, or pain,
Perchance my heart and harp have lost a string,

6 heave] ⟨are⟩ *B*   8 hour's] day's *B, BM; cor. in MC*   9 When ⟨leaving⟩ Albion's fading shores ⟨could *?* could vent a sigh⟩ could grieve my gazing eye *B, BM*; lessening . . . or glad mine eye *S, MC*   12 That] Who *B, S, BM*   13 Swift be] ⟨Welcome⟩ *BM*   14 strain'd] ⟨strained⟩ bowed *S*   should . . . as] ⟨should⟩ may . . . like *B*   15 fluttering strew] shatter in *B*; tattering strew *S*   16 must] will *B* ⟨would⟩ *BM*   17 rock] ⟨cliff⟩ *B*   18 ⟨Where the *?* tide that recks not⟩ *B*   surge may sweep] tide may float *B, cor. in S, MC*   or tempest's] the tempest's *all edns.*   21 ⟨And now I seize again that theme begun⟩ *B*   25 track] waste *B, cor. in BM*   26 heavily] ⟨sickly / heavy plod⟩ *B*   27 Plod] ⟨To⟩ Plough *B* 28 my . . . or] ⟨those . . . and⟩ *M*   29 harp have] harp ⟨alike⟩ have *M*

And both may jar: it may be, that in vain   30
I would essay as I have sung to sing.
Yet, though a dreary strain, to this I cling;
So that it wean me from the weary dream
Of selfish grief or gladness—so it fling
Forgetfulness around me—it shall seem   35
To me, though to none else, a not ungrateful theme.

5.

He, who grown aged in this world of woe,
In deeds, not years, piercing the depths of life,
So that no wonder waits him; nor below
Can love, or sorrow, fame, ambition, strife,   40
Cut to his heart again with the keen knife
Of silent, sharp endurance: he can tell
Why thought seeks refuge in lone caves, yet rife
With airy images, and shapes which dwell
Still unimpair'd, though old, in the soul's haunted cell.   45

6.

'Tis to create, and in creating live
A being more intense, that we endow
With form our fancy, gaining as we give
The life we image, even as I do now.
What am I? Nothing; but not so art thou,   50
Soul of my thought! with whom I traverse earth,
Invisible but gazing, as I glow
Mix'd with thy spirit, blended with thy birth,
And feeling still with thee in my crush'd feeling's dearth.

31 as I have sung] of ⟨him⟩ all I sang *M*   32 dreary strain] ⟨twice-told⟩ mournful tale *M*
⟨the tale⟩ *BM*   34 fling] ⟨will⟩ fling *M*   37 grown aged in] ⟨hath long withstood⟩
M   38 ⟨In acts not years—and pierced the caves of life⟩ By acts not years hath pierced
the depths of life *M, cor. in BM*   deeds] ⟨deeds⟩ acts *S*   40 fame, ambition] ⟨Agony
—Fame⟩ *M*   42 silent, sharp endurance] ⟨secret silent feeling⟩ *M*   43 thought
. . . yet] ⟨Truth seeks refuge in such haunts though⟩ *M*   44 which] that *M, cor. in BM*
45 old] worn *M*   46 create] ⟨seek⟩ *M*   47 A . . . that] A ⟨better⟩
brighter being ⟨and a⟩ that *M*   48 fancy, gaining] fancies—⟨and in⟩ gaining *M*
49 The life we] ⟨A life to⟩ *M*   52 ⟨Heedless of hopeless love / Thoughtful of / Un-
bending⟩ *M*   but gazing] ⟨but seeing⟩ though gazing *M*   54 crush'd ˙own *M, cor.
in BM*

7.

Yet must I think less wildly:—I *have* thought   55
Too long and darkly, till my brain became,
In its own eddy boiling and o'erwrought,
A whirling gulf of phantasy and flame:
And thus, untaught in youth my heart to tame,
My springs of life were poison'd. 'Tis too late!   60
Yet am I chang'd; though still enough the same
In strength to bear what time can not abate,
And feed on bitter fruits without accusing Fate.

8.

Something too much of this:—but now 'tis past,
And the spell closes with its silent seal.   65
Long absent HAROLD re-appears at last;
He of the breast which fain no more would feel,
Wrung with the wounds which kill not, but ne'er heal;
Yet Time, who changes all, had altered him
In soul and aspect as in age: years steal   70
Fire from the mind as vigour from the limb;
And life's enchanted cup but sparkles near the brim.

9.

His had been quaff'd too quickly, and he found
The dregs were wormwood; but he fill'd again,
And from a purer fount, on holier ground,   75
And deem'd its spring perpetual; but in vain!

55 ⟨I must not think and I must not⟩ *M*   wildly] deeply *M, cor. in BM*   56 darkly]
⟨deeply⟩ *M*   57 eddy boiling] ⟨maze entangled⟩ *M*   58 A whirling gulf] A
⟨dizzy world / whirling pool⟩ *M*   59 ⟨And being thus my heart⟩
And thus without a guide my heart to tame *M, cor. in BM*   60 ⟨My wishes and
wisdom / My visions have been deadly but to me⟩ *M*   were] are *M, cor. in BM*
61 Yet . . . though] ⟨Now I am changed yet⟩ *M*   though] but *M*   am] ⟨was⟩ *BM*
62 ⟨To bear unbent the very ills Time⟩ *M*   In . . . bear] To bear unbent ⟨my⟩ *M* ⟨To bear
unbent / live beneath / Fitly to bear⟩ *BM*   63 ⟨And to sustain them as I strike these
chords anew⟩ *M*   And feed] ⟨Now live⟩ *M*   65 closes] ⟨binds⟩ *M* ⟨closes ? / reas-
sumes⟩ *BM*   66 re-appears at last] ⟨thou art not / is returned⟩ at last *M*
67 the breast] the ⟨cold chill⟩ breast *M*   which . . . would] that ⟨never / strove not⟩ strove no
more to *M, cor. in BM*   68 Wrung] Scarred *M, cor. in BM*   which] that *S, cor. in
M*   70 age: years] age:—⟨and souls⟩ years *M*   71 Fire . . . as vigour from] ⟨The
Vigour from the Spirit as⟩ from *M*   72 life's] ⟨the Life's most⟩ *M*   74 were]
of *M, cor. in BM*   75 fount, on] ⟨source and⟩ *M*   76 its] ⟨it⟩ the *M*

Still round him clung invisibly a chain
Which gall'd for ever, fettering though unseen,
And heavy though it clank'd not; worn with pain,
Which pined although it spoke not, and grew keen,   80
Entering with every step, he took, through many a scene.

10.

Secure in guarded coldness, he had mix'd
Again in fancied safety with his kind,
And deem'd his spirit now so firmly fix'd
And sheath'd with an invulnerable mind,   85
That, if no joy, no sorrow lurk'd behind;
And he, as one, might midst the many stand
Unheeded, searching through the crowd to find
Fit speculation! such as in strange land
He found in wonder-works of God and Nature's hand.   90

11.

But who can view the ripened rose, nor seek
To wear it? who can curiously behold
The smoothness and the sheen of beauty's cheek,
Nor feel the heart can never all grow old?
Who can contemplate Fame through clouds unfold   95
The star which rises o'er her steep, nor climb?
Harold, once more within the vortex, roll'd
On with the giddy circle, chasing Time,
Yet with a nobler aim than in his youth's fond prime.

77 ⟨Still oer him hung invisibly the chain⟩ *M*   78 Which . . . fettering] That ⟨bound⟩
galled forever ⟨fast⟩ fettering *M*   79 worn with pain] and ⟨felt keen⟩ with pain *M*
⟨linked by pain⟩ *BM*   worn] and *M*   80 and grew keen] ⟨twas I ween / and felt
keen⟩ *M*   grew] ⟨sunk⟩ *BM*   81 Entering . . . many a] ⟨Falling . . . every⟩ *M*
through] ⟨with⟩ *BM*   82 in guarded] in ⟨his⟩ curbing *M*   84 his . . . firmly] ⟨the
spirit in itself so⟩ *M*   86 no] ⟨with⟩ *M*   88 searching through] ⟨and unheeding
of / heedless / gazing⟩ *M*   89 such . . . land] ⟨as upon / in some strange land / in
stranger's land⟩ *M*   90 He found in] ⟨He found the⟩ Shines through the *M, cor. in BM*
91 But . . . rose] Who can behold the flower ⟨long time⟩ at noon *M*   92 To
pluck it—⟨from⟩ who can ⟨calmly / long⟩ steadfastly behold *M*   94–5 ⟨Nor feel how
Wisdom ceases to be cold | And that the heart can never quel⟩ *M*   94 Nor] ⟨And⟩ *S*
95 through clouds] ⟨on far steeps⟩ *M*   96 The] ⟨A⟩ *M*   97 Harold]
⟨Even⟩ Harold *M*   98 chasing] ⟨scattering⟩ *M*   99 nobler aim . . . youth's fond
prime] ⟨steadier step . . . earlier time⟩ *M*   fond] gay *M, BM, S, cor. in MC*

12.

But soon he knew himself the most unfit   100
Of men to herd with Man; with whom he held
Little in common; untaught to submit
His thoughts to others, though his soul was quell'd
In youth by his own thoughts; still uncompell'd,
He would not yield dominion of his mind   105
To spirits against whom his own rebell'd;
Proud though in desolation; which could find
A life within itself, to breathe without mankind.

13.

Where rose the mountains, there to him were friends;
Where roll'd the ocean, thereon was his home;   110
Where a blue sky, and glowing clime, extends,
He had the passion and the power to roam;
The desert, forest, cavern, breaker's foam,
Were unto him companionship; they spake
A mutual language, clearer than the tome   115
Of his land's tongue, which he would oft forsake
For Nature's pages glass'd by sunbeams on the lake.

14.

Like the Chaldean, he could watch the stars,
Till he had peopled them with beings bright
As their own beams; and earth, and earth-born jars,   120
And human frailties, were forgotten quite:
Could he have kept his spirit to that flight
He had been happy; but this clay will sink
Its spark immortal, envying it the light
To which it mounts, as if to break the link   125
That keeps us from yon heaven which woos us to its brink.

---

100 But . . . knew] ⟨Fool! to not to know⟩ M   105 He] He ⟨held⟩ M   106 spirits] ⟨fables⟩ M   107 though] ⟨even⟩ BM   109–10 Where there were mountains— there for him were friends | Where there was Ocean—there he was at home M, cor. in BM   113 desert] ⟨desert's sand⟩ M   115 A . . .] ⟨To him a language of a⟩ M clearer] ⟨drawn⟩ M   116 land's tongue] land's ⟨native⟩ tongue M   117 ⟨To read in brighter pages glassed in the shining lake⟩ M ⟨To read a fairer⟩ BM 118 he . . . stars] he ⟨adored the stars⟩ could gaze on stars M   119 Till . . .] ⟨Not in the ?⟩ M   121 human] ⟨mortal⟩ M   122 to] ⟨on⟩ M   124 spark immortal] ⟨heavenly immortality⟩ M immortal] ⟨celestial⟩ M light] ⟨sight⟩ M   125 as if] ⟨breaking⟩ as if M   126 Which keeps us from that heaven on which we love to think M, cor. in BM

15.

But in Man's dwellings he became a thing
Restless and worn, and stern and wearisome,
Droop'd as a wild-born falcon with clipt wing,
To whom the boundless air alone were home: 130
Then came his fit again, which to o'ercome,
As eagerly the barr'd-up bird will beat
His breast and beak against his wiry dome
Till the blood tinge his plumage, so the heat
Of his impeded soul would through his bosom eat.   135

16.

Self-exiled Harold wanders forth again,
With nought of hope left, but with less of gloom;
The very knowledge that he lived in vain,
That all was over on this side the tomb,
Had made Despair a smilingness assume,   140
Which, though 'twere wild,—as on the plundered wreck
When mariners would madly meet their doom
With draughts intemperate on the sinking deck,—
Did yet inspire a cheer, which he forbore to check.

17.

Stop!—for thy tread is on an Empire's dust!   145
An Earthquake's spoil is sepulchred below!
Is the spot mark'd with no colossal bust?
Nor column trophied for triumphal show?
None; but the moral's truth tells simpler so,
As the ground was before, thus let it be;—   150
How that red rain hath made the harvest grow!
And is this all the world has gained by thee,
Thou first and last of fields! king-making Victory?

127 Man's . . . he] ⟨the . . . Harold⟩ *M*   he became] ⟨Harold was⟩ *BM*   128 worn.
⟨wearisome⟩   stern] cold *M* ⟨evil / fierce⟩ *BM*   131 his] ⟨the⟩ *M*   132 As . .]
barr'd-up] As ⟨gainst the cage the prisoned⟩ *M*   133 His . . .] ⟨His bosom on the bars
⟨—till⟩ *M*   breast and beak] ⟨bound up bosom⟩ *M*   136 Self-exiled] ⟨And lonely⟩ *M*
140 smilingness] ⟨cheerfulness⟩ *M*   141 Which ⟨although / if twere false as on the
sinking deck⟩ *M*   143 on . . . deck] ⟨plundering while they wreck⟩ *M*   146 spoil]
⟨work⟩ *M* ⟨soil⟩ *MC*   149 moral's . . . so] ⟨ground / truth⟩ moral truth ⟨shines better⟩
so *M*   150 thus . . . be] and still must be *M, cor. in BM*   151 rain] ⟨blood⟩ *MC*
152 is this . . . has] this is . . . hath *M, cor. in BM*

18.

And Harold stands upon this place of skulls,
The grave of France, the deadly Waterloo!   155
How in an hour the power which gave annuls
Its gifts, transferring fame as fleeting too!
In 'pride of place' here last the eagle flew,
Then tore with bloody talon the rent plain,
Pierced by the shaft of banded nations through;   160
Ambition's life and labours all were vain;
He wears the shattered links of the world's broken chain.

19.

Fit retribution! Gaul may champ the bit
And foam in fetters;—but is Earth more free?
Did nations combat to make *One* submit;   165
Or league to teach all kings true sovereignty?
What! shall reviving Thraldom again be
The patched-up idol of enlightened days?
Shall we, who struck the Lion down, shall we
Pay the Wolf homage? proffering lowly gaze   170
And servile knees to thrones? No; *prove* before ye praise!

20.

If not, o'er one fallen despot boast no more!
In vain fair cheeks were furrowed with hot tears
For Europe's flowers long rooted up before
The trampler of her vineyards; in vain years   175
Of death, depopulation, bondage, fears,
Have all been borne, and broken by the accord
Of roused-up millions: all that most endears

---

155 deadly] fatal *M*   158 Here ⟨its⟩ his last flight the haughty Eagle flew *M, cor.
to S in BM*;   Here his last 'Pride of Place' the eagle flew *S, cor. in MC*   159 ⟨Then
bit with bloody beak / talons the rent soil⟩ *M*   160 banded] ⟨battling⟩ *M*
161 Ambition's] ⟨How honour⟩ *M*   162 And Gaul must wear the links of her own
broken chain *M, cor. in BM*   163 Gaul may] let her *M*   165 Did nations]
⟨Was all man's⟩ *M*   *One*] One ⟨more⟩ *S*   166 all kings true] ⟨their kings—so⟩ *M*
⟨all men true⟩ *S*   168 The . . .] ⟨The boast to brighter⟩ *M*   of . . . days] of /
in . . . ⟨men / earth⟩ *M*   169 struck] ⟨felled⟩ smote *M*   170 Pay the
wolf worship—⟨and yield up to birth⟩ proffer of / him blind praise *M cancelled*
171 And . . .] ⟨And have ye to the moans / And have ye blind and⟩ *M*   to thrones] ⟨to things
those wretch⟩ ⟨before we reach the power⟩ *M*   172 despot] tyrant *M*   173 In
vain fair] ⟨Those lovely⟩ *M*   were] are *S*   174 long rooted] ⟨of Manhood⟩ *M*
176 ⟨Of nation's massacred / smitten—slaughters death and chains⟩ *M*   177 accord]
⟨strength / might⟩ *M*   178 millions] nations   most] ⟨eer⟩ *M*

Glory, is when the myrtle wreathes a sword
Such as Harmodius drew on Athens' tyrant lord.   180

21.

There was a sound of revelry by night,
And Belgium's capital had gathered then
Her Beauty and her Chivalry, and bright
The lamps shone o'er fair women and brave men;
A thousand hearts beat happily; and when   185
Music arose with its voluptuous swell,
Soft eyes look'd love to eyes which spake again,
And all went merry as a marriage-bell;
But hush! hark! a deep sound strikes like a rising knell!

22.

Did ye not hear it?—No; 'twas but the wind,   190
Or the car rattling o'er the stony street;
On with the dance! let joy be unconfined;
No sleep till morn, when Youth and Pleasure meet
To chase the glowing Hours with flying feet—
But, hark!—that heavy sound breaks in once more,   195
As if the clouds its echo would repeat;
And nearer, clearer, deadlier than before!
Arm! Arm! and out—it is—the cannon's opening roar!

23.

Within a windowed niche of that high hall
Sate Brunswick's fated chieftain; he did hear   200
That sound the first amidst the festival,
And caught its tone with Death's prophetic ear;
And when they smiled because he deem'd it near,

179 ⟨Its / The greatest memory of the fiercest fight⟩ *M*   a] the *S, cor. in M*   the . . . a]
⟨such . . . the⟩ *BM*   180 drew] ⟨wore / turned⟩ *M*   181 There . . .] ⟨Now he is⟩ *M*
184 ⟨Lamps shone on lovely dames and gallant men⟩ *M*   women] ladies *M, cor. in BM*
185 ⟨And / Soft eyes looked love to eyes which answered when⟩ *M*   186 Music arose]
⟨The music soar / arose⟩ *M*   191 o'er] ⟨through⟩ *M*   194 glowing] glaring *S*
195 that] ⟨you⟩ that *M*   196 would] did *M*   197 With a slow deep and
⟨deadly⟩ dread-inspiring roar *M cancelled*   nearer] ⟨deeper⟩ *M*   198 Arm! . . .] ⟨Oh
tis the⟩ *M*   and out] it is *all edns.*   cannon's opening] opening cannon's *M*
199 hall] wall *S*   200 Sate . . .] ⟨And quick with⟩ *M*   201 That . . .] ⟨His
coming death⟩ *M*   202 And] And ⟨he⟩ *M*
203–7   And the hoped Vengeance for a ⟨Father's line⟩ sire so dear
               And him who died at Jena when so well
               His filial heart had mourned through many a year

His heart more truly knew that peal too well
Which stretch'd his father on a bloody bier,   205
And roused the vengeance blood alone could quell:
He rush'd into the field, and, foremost fighting, fell.

24.

Ah! then and there was hurrying to and fro,
And gathering tears, and tremblings of distress,
And cheeks all pale, which but an hour ago   210
Blush'd at the praise of their own loveliness;
And there were sudden partings, such as press
The life from out young hearts, and choking sighs
Which ne'er might be repeated; who could guess
If ever more should meet those mutual eyes,   215
Since upon nights so sweet such awful morn could rise?

25.

And there was mounting in hot haste: the steed,
The mustering squadron, and the clattering car,
Went pouring forward in impetuous speed,
And swiftly forming in the ranks of war;   220
And the deep thunder peal on peal afar;
And near, the beat of the alarming drum
Roused up the soldier ere the morning star;
While throng'd the citizens with terror dumb,
Or whispering, with white lips—'The foe! They come! they
    come!'   225

⟨Bound him to gallant⟩ Roused him to valiant fury nought could
    quell *M cancelled*
And when they smiled ⟨at him who deemed it near⟩
⟨What others⟩ His heart replying knew that sound too well
⟨For it had rested / hurled upon⟩ a bloody bier
And ⟨exiled him with / sent the son with⟩ roused ⟨that⟩ vengeance
    ⟨many a life must⟩ ⟨lives⟩ blood alone could quell
⟨But rushing⟩ to the field ⟨he⟩ foremost fought and fell *M*
204 more truly] ⟨replying / more surely⟩ *BM*   209 And . . .] ⟨And mounting tears in
eyes so⟩ *M*   tremblings] tremors *M*   210 ⟨And cheeks grew pale which late did
blush and glow⟩ *M*   211 Blush'd . . . praise] ⟨With a sweet conscience⟩ *M*   at]
⟨before⟩ *M*   212 such as press] which did press *M, cor. in BM*   213 Like death
upon young hearts—and ⟨mutual⟩ choaking sighs *M, cor. in BM*   214 might] ⟨would⟩
M   216 Oh that on nights so soft—⟨so sad / dread a⟩ such heavy morn should rise
M   nights] night *1831, 1832, C, More*   218 mustering] ⟨rolling⟩ *M*   219 Went]
⟨The / And⟩ Are *M*   in] with *all edns.*   221 ⟨And the deep din is rolling
still from far⟩ And the deep thunder rolling still afar *M, cor. in BM*   222 beat] ⟨beat-
ing⟩ *M*   223 Roused up the soldier] ⟨Which roused the warrior⟩ Rousing the soldier
M, cor. in BM   224 While . . . citizens] And ⟨fear⟩ making ⟨the⟩ citizens *M*
225 white] pale *M*   'The . . . come!'] ⟨'the Desolation's come'⟩ *M*

26.

And wild and high the 'Cameron's gathering' rose!
The war-note of Lochiel, which Albyn's hills
Have heard, and heard, too, have her Saxon foes:—
How in the noon of night that pibroch thrills,
Savage and shrill! But with the breath which fills   230
Their mountain-pipe, so fill the mountaineers
With the fierce native daring which instils
The stirring memory of a thousand years,
And Evan's, Donald's fame rings in each clansman's ears!

27.

And Ardennes waves above them her green leaves,   235
Dewy with nature's tear-drops, as they pass,
Grieving, if aught inanimate e'er grieves,
Over the unreturning brave,—alas!
Ere evening to be trodden like the grass
Which now beneath them, but above shall grow   240
In its next verdure, when this fiery mass
Of living valour, rolling on the foe
And burning with high hope, shall moulder cold and low.

28.

Last noon beheld them full of lusty life,
Last eve in Beauty's circle proudly gay,   245
The midnight brought the signal-sound of strife,
The morn the marshalling in arms,—the day
Battle's magnificently-stern array!
The thunder-clouds close o'er it, which when rent
The earth is covered thick with other clay,   250
Which her own clay shall cover, heaped and pent,
Rider and horse,—friend, foe,—in one red burial blent!

228 and . . . have] and so have heard S, BM, cor. in C ⟨a willing ?⟩ M   229 noon]
⟨dead⟩ M   231 Their] ⟨That / This⟩ BM   235 Ardennes] Soignies M, BM, S, cor.
in MC   waves] ⟨shed / waved⟩ M   237 aught] ⟨things⟩ M   e'er grieves] may grieve S
238 Over] ⟨Above⟩ BM   239 Ere . . .] ⟨Thus speeding on to be trod down⟩ M
240 but] ⟨then⟩ M   245 eve . . . proudly] ⟨Evening amidst Beauty's circle⟩ M
246 brought] ⟨passed⟩ M   249 which] ⟨and⟩ M   251 shall] ⟨must⟩ M

29.

Their praise is hymn'd by loftier harps than mine;
Yet one I would select from that proud throng,
Partly because they blend me with his line,   255
And partly that I did his sire some wrong,
And partly that bright names will hallow song;
And his was of the bravest, and when shower'd
The death-bolts deadliest the thinn'd files along,
Even where the thickest of war's tempest lower'd,   260
They reach'd no nobler breast than thine, young, gallant
    Howard!

30.

There have been tears and breaking hearts for thee,
And mine were nothing, had I such to give;
But when I stood beneath the fresh green tree,
Which living waves where thou didst cease to live,   265
And saw around me the wide field revive
With fruits and fertile promise, and the Spring
Come forth her work of gladness to contrive,
With all her reckless birds upon the wing,
I turn'd from all she brought to those she could not bring. 270

31.

I turn'd to thee, to thousands, of whom each
And one as all a ghastly gap did make
In his own kind and kindred, whom to teach
Forgetfulness were mercy for their sake;
The Archangel's trump, not Glory's, must awake   275
Those whom they thirst for; though the sound of Fame
May for a moment soothe, it cannot slake

253 Their . . . loftier] ⟨To praise the great be other / To hymn their praises be other⟩ *M*
by loftier] on mightier *M*   255 blend me with] ⟨trace me in⟩ *M*   257 And
partly] ⟨And mostly⟩ But chiefly *M*   bright] ⟨brave⟩ *M*   258 his] ⟨theirs⟩ *M*
260 of war's] of ⟨the⟩ war's *M*   261 breast] ⟨heart⟩ *M*   262 breaking] broken
M   264 fresh green] ⟨tall / sheltering / beauteous⟩ *M*   265 living] ⟨with its⟩ *M*
266 wide field] ⟨spring⟩ *M*   267 ⟨With all its reckless birds upon the wing /
Doing its work of gladness—and the spring⟩ *M*   268 Come forth her] ⟨Doing⟩ its *M*
269 her] its *M*   270 turn'd from] ⟨hated⟩ *M*   to] ⟨for⟩ *M*   she . . . she]
it . . . it *M*   272 all a] all ⟨did in his⟩ a *M*   273 own kind] own ⟨kindred kind's⟩
kind *M*   275 The . . .] ⟨For Glory's trumpet is not⟩ *M*   276 though . . . of] ⟨and
their very⟩ *M*   277 May . . .] ⟨Which / In the same hour / moment will soothe
the⟩ *M*

The fever of vain longing, and the name
So honoured but assumes a stronger, bitterer claim.

32.

They mourn, but smile at length; and, smiling, mourn: 280
The tree will wither long before it fall;
The hull drives on, though mast and sail be torn;
The roof-tree sinks, but moulders on the hall
In massy hoariness; the ruined wall
Stands when its wind-worn battlements are gone; 285
The bars survive the captive they enthral;
The day drags through though storms keep out the sun;
And thus the heart will break, yet brokenly live on:

33.

Even as a broken mirror, which the glass
In every fragment multiplies; and makes 290
A thousand images of one that was,
The same, and still the more, the more it breaks;
And thus the heart will do which not forsakes,
Living in shattered guise, and still, and cold,
And bloodless, with its sleepless sorrow aches, 295
Yet withers on till all without is old,
Shewing no visible sign, for such things are untold.

34.

There is a very life in our despair,
Vitality of poison,— a quick root
Which feeds these deadly branches; for it were 300
As nothing did we die; but Life will suit

278 vain] ⟨deep⟩ M   282 ⟨And dead within behold the Spring return⟩ M
mast and sail] sail and mast M   283 the] ⟨its⟩ M   284 In . . .] ⟨And the ruined
long outlive / survive⟩ ⟨In strong fragments⟩ M   285 Stands when] ⟨Will stand
though / But halfway stands when⟩ M   286 ⟨As man doth oer what he can neer
recall⟩ ⟨Despair will live in fire / And Desolation lives the most of all⟩ M   The bars] The
⟨large⟩ bars M   287 ⟨And Day has⟩ It still is day though clouds keep out the sun M,
cor. in BM   The . . . through] ⟨Tis still the day⟩ BM   288 break . . . on] break and
⟨break⟩ the cold breast live on M   291 A . . . of one that] ⟨The . . . for one that⟩ of one
which M   292 and still the more] ⟨a thousand such⟩ M   295 with] ⟨as⟩ M
297 visible] ⟨outward⟩ M   298 our] ⟨our⟩ such M   299 ⟨Like activeness
of poison—a deep root⟩ M   Vitality] ⟨An⟩ activity M   300 these] the S
301 did we die] ⟨could we die / did they kill⟩ M

Itself to Sorrow's most detested fruit,
Like to the apples on the Dead Sea's shore,
All ashes to the taste: Did man compute
Existence by enjoyment, and count o'er   305
Such hours 'gainst years of life,—say, would he name three-
    score?

35.

The Psalmist numbered out the years of man:
They are enough; and if thy tale be *true*,
Thou, who didst grudge him even that fleeting span,
More than enough, thou fatal Waterloo!   310
Millions of tongues record thee, and anew
Their children's lips shall echo them, and say—
'Here, where the sword united nations drew,
Our countrymen were warring on that day!'
And this is much, and all which will not pass away.   315

36.

There sunk the greatest, nor the worst of men,
Whose spirit antithetically mixt
One moment of the mightiest, and again
On little objects with like firmness fixt,
Extreme in all things! hadst thou been betwixt,   320
Thy throne had still been thine, or never been;
For daring made thy rise as fall: thou seek'st
Even now to re-assume the imperial mien,
And shake again the world, the Thunderer of the scene!

---

302 Sorrow's most detested] ⟨sorrow and this the wretched⟩ *M*   303 shore] ⟨brink /
bank⟩ *M*   304 All . . .] ⟨Ashes all ashes to the taste / Food and with ashes ashes
for⟩ *M*   305 Existence] ⟨His⟩ Existence *M*   306 Such hours] ⟨His joys⟩ *M*
307 ⟨And ten—the Psalmist's numbered years to man?⟩ *M*   308 ⟨It may be⟩ But
not his ⟨sorrows⟩ pleasure such might be a task *M cancelled*   309 fleeting] petty *M*
⟨paltry⟩ *BM*   310 thou] Oh *M*   311 Millions] ⟨A / Ten thousand⟩ *M*
312 lips shall echo] voice shall ⟨speak of⟩ *M, cor. in BM*   313 With a smooth / such
vain feeling *M cancelled*   sword . . . drew] ⟨chief / mightiest men / choice of earth their
falchions drew⟩ *M*   nations] Europe *M*   314 I had a kinsman warring on that day *M*
315 which] that *S*   316 There] ⟨Then⟩ *M*   319 On little thoughts ⟨as⟩ with
equal firmness fixed *M*   320 hadst thou been] ⟨could⟩ hadst thou ⟨between⟩ been *M*
322 For thou hadst risen as fallen—and now thou seek'st *M*   323 A moment to
react ⟨on that⟩ upon the scene *M cancelled*   Even now] An hour *M*   324 And shake
again the world] ⟨Which then thou wouldst shake again⟩ And shake the world again *M*;
And ⟨fain wouldst⟩ shake *BM*

37.

Conqueror and captive of the earth art thou!   325
She trembles at thee still, and thy wild name
Was ne'er more bruited in men's minds than now
That thou art nothing, save the jest of Fame,
Who wooed thee once, thy vassal, and became
The flatterer of thy fierceness, till thou wert   330
A god unto thyself; nor less the same
To the astounded kingdoms all inert,
Who deem'd thee for a time whate'er thou didst assert.

38.

Oh, more or less than man—in high or low,
Battling with nations, flying from the field;   335
Now making monarchs' necks thy footstool, now
More than thy meanest soldier taught to yield;
An empire thou couldst crush, command, rebuild,
But govern not thy pettiest passion, nor,
However deeply in men's spirits skill'd,   340
Look through thine own, nor curb the lust of war,
Nor learn that tempted Fate will leave the loftiest star.

39.

Yet well thy soul hath brook'd the turning tide
With that untaught innate philosophy,
Which, be it wisdom, coldness, or deep pride,   345
Is gall and wormwood to an enemy.
When the whole host of hatred stood hard by,
To watch and mock thee shrinking, thou hast smiled
With a sedate and all-enduring eye;—

326 She trembles] ⟨We tremble⟩   and . . . name] and ⟨still thy⟩ thy dark name *M*
wild] ⟨strange⟩ *BM*   327 ne'er . . . minds] ⟨never felt⟩ neer more rife within
men's mouths *M*   bruited in] ⟨rife within / deeply⟩ *BM*   329 ⟨Who tost thee too
and fro till⟩ Who wooed thee as thy vassal and became *M*   once] ⟨as⟩ *BM*
330 ⟨Thy worst of foes thy⟩ ⟨Thy Flatterer until / in / till thyself making⟩ *M*
332 astounded kingdoms all] astonished nations all *M*; astounded ⟨nations who⟩ *BM*
333 whate'er thou] ⟨all that thou⟩ *M*   334 Oh . . . man] ⟨And then not less than man /
But thou not more than man⟩ *M*   338 command] ⟨or couldst⟩ *M*   340 in men's
spirits] ⟨in the minds of others⟩ *M*   341 Look through] ⟨Now to⟩ *M*   nor] and
S   342 Nor . . . tempted Fate] ⟨Which⟩ Nor learn that ⟨Fate at last / too⟩ M
343 brook'd] ⟨taen⟩ *M*   345 coldness] weakness *M, cor. in BM*   346 ⟨Works
like to woe / Will ever disappoint an enemy⟩ *M*   348 To watch thee shrinking—⟨still
thou⟩ calmly hadst thou smiled *M, cor. in BM*   349 With a ⟨sad⟩ sedate ⟨though not
unfeeling⟩ eye *M*

When Fortune fled her spoil'd and favourite child,   350
He stood unbowed beneath the ills upon him piled.

40.

Sager than in thy fortunes; for in them
Ambition steel'd thee on too far to show
That just habitual scorn which could contemn
Men and their thoughts; 'twas wise to feel, not so   355
To wear it ever on thy lip and brow,
And spurn the instruments thou wert to use
Till they were turn'd unto thine overthrow:
'Tis but a worthless world to win or lose;
So hath it proved to thee, and all such lot who choose.   360

41.

If, like a tower upon a headlong rock,
Thou hadst been made to stand or fall alone,
Such scorn of man had help'd to brave the shock;
But men's thoughts were the steps which paved thy throne,
Their admiration thy best weapon shone;   365
The part of Philip's son was thine, not then
(Unless aside thy purple had been thrown)
Like stern Diogenes to mock at men;
For sceptred cynics earth were far too wide a den.

42.

But quiet to quick bosoms is a hell,   370
And *there* hath been thy bane; there is a fire
And motion of the soul which will not dwell
In its own narrow being, but aspire
Beyond the fitting medium of desire;

350 When . . . and] ⟨And thus when Fortune left her⟩ M   351 He . . .] ⟨Still hath
he stood / Still stood he yet⟩ M   ills] griefs M   352 Sager] Greater M ⟨greater⟩ BM
353 ⟨Ambition maddened thee and made thee tired⟩ M   steel'd] lured M, cor. in BM
354 just] ⟨just⟩ true M   355 thoughts . . . wise] thoughts : ⟨a madness few⟩ twas
⟨just⟩ M   356 ever . . . brow] ⟨often thus insolently⟩ ever on thy brow and lip M
lip] lips S, cor. in MC   360 So . . .] ⟨But such were not thy thoughts / But empire
was thy / As twice it⟩ M   361 headlong] ⟨barren⟩ M   363 man . . . brave]
earth . . . stand M   364 were] are S, cor. in MC   365 Their] ⟨And⟩ their M
369 were] is M   371 hath . . . fire] has . . . ⟨stir⟩ M   372 will not] ⟨cannot⟩ M
373 narrow being] ⟨contemplation⟩ M   374 fitting] ⟨lawful⟩ M

And, but once kindled, quenchless evermore,   375
Preys upon high adventure, nor can tire
Of aught but rest; a fever at the core,
Fatal to him who bears, to all who ever bore.

43.

This makes the madmen who have made men mad
By their contagion; Conquerors and Kings,   380
Founders of sects and systems, to whom add
Sophists, Bards, Statesmen, all unquiet things
Which stir too strongly the soul's secret springs,
And are themselves the fools to those they fool;
Envied, yet how unenviable! what stings   385
Are theirs! One breast laid open were a school
Which would unteach mankind the lust to shine or rule:

44.

Their breath is agitation, and their life
A storm whereon they ride, to sink at last,
And yet so nurs'd and bigotted to strife,   390
That should their days, surviving perils past,
Melt to calm twilight, they feel overcast
With sorrow and supineness, and so die;
Even as a flame unfed, which runs to waste
With its own flickering, or a sword laid by   395
Which eats into itself, and rusts ingloriously.

45.

.   He who ascends to mountain-tops, shall find
The loftiest peaks most wrapt in clouds and snow;
He who surpasses or subdues mankind,
Must look down on the hate of those below.   400

---

375 quenchless] ⟨never⟩ quenchless M   376 ⟨It assails⟩ Curses itself and all around
M *cancelled*   Feeds ⟨ever in⟩ on itself and all things—nor can tire M, *cor. in BM*
378 Fatal . . . bears] ⟨Which curseth him who / And curse to him who⟩ M   379 These
are the ⟨vilains⟩ madmen who do make men mad M, *cor. in BM*   381 to whom add]
⟨such as add / gay or sad⟩ M   382 Sophists . . .] ⟨This / And take away from⟩ ⟨Chiefs,
sages⟩ M   383 ⟨Which stir the blood to boiling / too lively in its spring⟩ M   strongly]
deeply M ⟨warmly⟩ BM   384 And are] And ⟨which⟩ are M   385 ⟨Yet⟩ envied M
386 breast] heart S   387 shine] lead M   388 breath] ⟨life⟩ M   389 A]
⟨The⟩ M   390 to] in S   392 calm . . . feel] ⟨soft⟩ . . . are M   twilight] tranquillity
S   feel] ⟨are⟩ BM   394 Even as] ⟨Like to⟩ M   397 ascends to] ⟨will stand
on⟩ M   to mountain-tops] the loftiest peaks S   400 those] all M

Though high *above* the sun of glory glow,
And far *beneath* the earth and ocean spread,
Round him are icy rocks, and loudly blow
Contending tempests on his naked head,
And thus reward the toils which to those summits led.   405

46.

Away with these! true Wisdom's world will be
Within its own creation, or in thine,
Maternal Nature! for who teems like thee,
Thus on the banks of thy majestic Rhine?
There Harold gazes on a work divine,   410
A blending of all beauties; streams and dells,
Fruit, foliage, crag, wood, cornfield, mountain, vine,
And chiefless castles breathing stern farewells
From gray but leafy walls, where Ruin greenly dwells.

47.

And there they stand, as stands a lofty mind,   415
Worn, but unstooping to the baser crowd,
All tenantless, save to the crannying wind,
Or holding dark communion with the cloud.
There was a day when they were young and proud,
Banners on high, and battles pass'd below;   420
But they who fought are in a bloody shroud,
And those which waved are shredless dust ere now,
And the bleak battlements shall bear no future blow.

48.

Beneath these battlements, within those walls,
Power dwelt amidst her passions; in proud state   425
Each robber chief upheld his armed halls,
Doing his evil will, nor less elate

402 ocean] ⟨waters⟩ M   403 icy rocks] ⟨rocks of ice⟩ M   404 naked] single
M, *cor. in* BM   405 thus] these M, *cor. in* BM   406 true Wisdom's] the wise
man's M   407 its] his M   or] and S   408 Maternal . . . who] ⟨Repeopled⟩
Nature ⟨yet⟩ what M   410 gazes on a] views thy M   413 And ⟨ruined / craggy /
knightless⟩ Castles ⟨full of⟩ stern farewells M   414 but leafy . . . greenly] and ghastly
. . . proudly M, *cor. in* BM   415 lofty] ⟨single⟩ M   416 ⟨Alone a thousand
smiling things that crowd⟩ ⟨Oer the⟩ Worn but ⟨unmixed⟩ unstooping to the grovelling
crowd M   baser crowd] ⟨things below⟩ BM   417 All] ⟨These⟩ M   418 Or]
⟨And⟩ M   422 dust ere] tatters M   424 Beneath] Below M   these . . . those]
these . . . these M; those . . . those S   425 Power . . . her] ⟨Hath dwelt a world of⟩ M
in] ⟨and⟩ in S   427 evil will, nor] ⟨will of evil and⟩ M

Than mightier heroes of a longer date.
What want these outlaws conquerors should have
But History's purchased page to call them great?   430
A wider space, an ornamented grave?
Their hopes were not less warm, their souls were full as brave.

49.

In their baronial feuds and single fields,
What deeds of prowess unrecorded died!
And Love, which lent a blazon to their shields,   435
With emblems well devised by amorous pride,
Through all the mail of iron hearts would glide;
But still their flame was fierceness, and drew on
Keen contest and destruction near allied,
And many a tower for some fair mischief won,   440
Saw the discoloured Rhine beneath its ruin run.

50.

But Thou, exulting and abounding river!
Making thy waves a blessing as they flow
Through banks whose beauty would endure for ever
Could man but leave thy bright creation so,   445
Nor its fair promise from the surface mow
With the sharp scythe of conflict,—then to see
Thy valley of sweet waters, were to know
Earth paved like Heaven; and to seem such to me
Even now what wants thy stream?—that it should Lethe be.

51.

A thousand battles have assail'd thy banks,   451
But these and half their fame have pass'd away,
And Slaughter heap'd on high his weltering ranks;
Their very graves are gone, and what are they?

428 heroes] conquerors *M*   429 outlaws conquerors] ⟨ruffians / robbers⟩ outlaws that a king *M*   430 But . . . call] But ⟨verse to⟩ History's vain page to ⟨make⟩ *M*
432 souls . . . brave] hearts were ⟨not⟩ far more brave *M*   433 feuds . . . fields]
⟨strifes and petty feuds⟩ *M*   436 emblems well] ⟨gay device⟩ emblemed signs *M*
437 ⟨Even⟩ through *M*   439 Keen] ⟨In their hurried⟩ Deep *M*   441 beneath
its ruin] ⟨below / within⟩ beneath it redly *M*   445 Could] ⟨If⟩ Would *M*
446-7 Nor mar it frequent with an impious show | Of arms and ⟨hostile⟩ angry conflict—
then to see *M, cor. in BM*   449 Earth . . . seem] Earth's dreams of Heaven and ⟨seem-
ing⟩ *M, cor. in BM*   450 Even now what] But one thing *M*   453 on high]
⟨them here⟩ *M*   his] its *S*   454 ⟨But⟩ their *M*

Thy tide wash'd down the blood of yesterday,   455
And all was stainless, and on thy clear stream
Glass'd with its dancing light the sunny ray;
But o'er the blackened memory's blighting dream
Thy waves would vainly roll, all sweeping as they seem.

52.

Thus Harold inly said, and pass'd along,   460
Yet not insensibly to all which here
Awoke the jocund birds to early song
In glens which might have made even exile dear:
Though on his brow were graven lines austere,
And tranquil sternness which had ta'en the place   465
Of feelings fiercer far but less severe,
Joy was not always absent from his face,
But o'er it in such scenes would steal with transient trace.

53.

Nor was all love shut from him, though his days
Of passion had consumed themselves to dust.   470
It is in vain that we would coldly gaze
On such as smile upon us; the heart must
Leap kindly back to kindness, though disgust
Hath wean'd it from all worldlings: thus he felt,
For there was soft remembrance, and sweet trust   475
In one fond breast, to which his own would melt,
And in its tenderer hour on that his bosom dwelt.

54.

And he had learn'd to love,—I know not why,
For this in such as him seems strange of mood,—

455 wash'd] ⟨swept⟩ M   457 Glass'd . . . dancing] ⟨Danced⟩ with ⟨a / his⟩ its
wonted M   dancing] glancing BM *alternate reading*   458 But oer the ⟨scarred⟩ mind's
⟨lightest / least / dark⟩ marred thoughts—though but a dream M   But oer the ⟨minds /
blackness of the / Reflection's dream⟩ BM   459 Thy . . .] ⟨Thou canst not sweep
away⟩ M   461 insensibly . . . which] ⟨insensibly⟩ insensible to ⟨what⟩ all that M
insensibly] insensible C   463 In glens] ⟨And⟩ in valleys M   might have made] ⟨made
such spots⟩ M   464 on . . . graven] in his ⟨spirit⟩ were ⟨written⟩ M   466 fierier]
fiercer S   but] though M   468 But . . . steal . . . trace] ⟨But⟩ And . . . ⟨pass⟩ . . .
⟨pace⟩ M   469 his] ⟨the⟩ M   472 the] ⟨and⟩ the M   473 Leap . . . to]
Repose itself on M, *cor. in* BM   474 all] ⟨the⟩ M   475 ⟨And⟩ there ⟨were the⟩
soft ⟨remembrances⟩ M   476 In . . . to] ⟨From . . . at⟩ M   477 tenderer]
⟨distant / softer⟩ M   hour] ⟨mood⟩ hours M   479 seems . . . mood] ⟨seemed passing
strange⟩ M

The helpless looks of blooming infancy,   480
Even in its earliest nurture; what subdued,
To change like this, a mind so far imbued
With scorn of man, it little boots to know;
But thus it was; and though in solitude
Small power the nipp'd affections have to grow,   485
In him this glowed when all beside had ceased to glow.

55.

And there was one soft breast, as hath been said,
Which unto his was bound by stronger ties
Than the church links withal; and, though unwed,
That love was pure, and, far above disguise,   490
Had stood the test of mortal enmities
Still undivided, and cemented more
By peril, dreaded most in female eyes;
But this was firm, and from a foreign shore
Well to that heart might his these absent greetings pour! 495

I.

The castled crag of Drachenfels
Frowns o'er the wide and winding Rhine,
Whose breast of waters broadly swells
Between the banks which bear the vine,
And hills all rich with blossomed trees,   500
And fields which promise corn and wine,
And scattered cities crowning these,
Whose far white walls along them shine,
Have strewed a scene, which I should see
With double joy wert *thou* with me!   505

480 looks] ⟨face⟩ M   481 what subdued] what ⟨a / this change⟩ M   482 To . . .]
⟨In him was nothing / Him to this change⟩ M   mind] soul M   like . . . mind] a mind
like this S   far] ⟨much⟩ BM   483 scorn] ⟨cold⟩ scorn M   484 thus . . . in]
⟨so it was—and even in⟩ M   485 ⟨The nipped affections have no power to grow⟩ M
power the] power ⟨such youth⟩ the M   486 glowed . . . glow] ⟨more increased when
others ceased to grow⟩ M   glowed] grew M   487 And] But M   488 his] him S
489 links] ⟨makes⟩ M   490 *That* love was] Yet was it M, *cor. in* BM   492 and]
and ⟨to⟩ M   494 was . . . foreign] ⟨had stood and to his native⟩ M   495 Well
. . .] ⟨Thus to that far⟩ M   Thus to that heart did his its ⟨absent feelings⟩ thoughts in
absence pour M, *cor. in* BM   498 broadly] ⟨proudly⟩ S   499 Between] ⟨Beneath⟩
ML   501 which] that M, BM, S

2.

And peasant girls, with deep blue eyes,
And hands which offer early flowers,
Walk smiling o'er this paradise;
Above, the frequent feudal towers
Through green leaves lift their walls of grey,   510
And many a rock which steeply lours,
And noble arch in proud decay,
Look o'er this vale of vintage-bowers;
But one thing want these banks of Rhine,—
Thy gentle hand to clasp in mine!   515

3.

I send the lilies given to me;
Though long before thy hand they touch,
I know that they must withered be,
But yet reject them not as such;
For I have cherish'd them as dear,   520
Because they yet may meet thine eye,
And guide thy soul to mine even here,
When thou behold'st them drooping nigh,
And knowst them gathered by the Rhine,
And offered from my heart to thine!   525

4.

The river nobly foams and flows,
The charm of this enchanted ground,
And all its thousand turns disclose
Some fresher beauty varying round;
The haughtiest breast its wish might bound   530
Through life to dwell delighted here;
Nor could on earth a spot be found
To nature and to me so dear,
Could thy dear eyes in following mine
Still sweeten more these banks of Rhine!   535

509 Above] On high *ML*   512 And noble] And ⟨many⟩ noble *ML*
513 Look] Looks *M*   516 lilies given] flowers they gave *ML*, *cor. in M*
521 yet] still *ML*   522 And ⟨thy / turn thy tender memory / spirit⟩ here *ML*
523 them drooping] these strangers *ML*   525 from] by *S*   534 in
following] now follow *ML*   535 Still] And *ML*

56.

By Coblentz, on a rise of gentle ground,
There is a small and simple pyramid,
Crowning the summit of the verdant mound;
Beneath its base are heroes' ashes hid,
Our enemy's,—but let not that forbid   540
Honour to Marceau! o'er whose early tomb
Tears, big tears, gush'd from the rough soldier's lid,
Lamenting and yet envying such a doom,
Falling for France, whose rights he battled to resume.

57.

Brief, brave, and glorious was his young career,—   545
His mourners were two hosts, his friends and foes;
And fitly may the stranger lingering here
Pray for his gallant spirit's bright repose;
For he was Freedom's champion, one of those,
The few in number, who had not o'erstept   550
The charter to chastise which she bestows
On such as wield her weapons; he had kept
The whiteness of his soul, and thus men o'er him wept.

58.

Here Ehrenbreitstein, with her shattered wall
Black with the miner's blast, upon her height   555
Yet shows of what she was, when shell and ball
Rebounding idly on her strength did light;
A tower of victory! from whence the flight
Of baffled foes was watch'd along the plain:
But Peace destroy'd what War could never blight,   560
And laid those proud roofs bare to Summer's rain—
On which the iron shower for years had pour'd in vain.

537 is] stands *M*   538 verdant] grassy *M, cor. in BM*   539 base] stone *M*
540 Our] ⟨An⟩ *BM*   541 Honour to] A sigh for *M, cor. in BM*   542 gush'd]
rushed *M, BM, S, C*   543 such a] such *S*   544 battled] ⟨perished⟩ *M*   550 had]
have *M*   553 thus men o'er] ⟨men above⟩ *M*   554 Here . . . shattered wall]
And . . . shivered ⟨strength⟩ *M*   557 ⟨An idle seige⟩ All vain and idly on her strength
⟨would⟩ did light *M, cor. in BM*   561 laid . . . bare to Summer's rain] ⟨made . . . open⟩
to hail and rain *M, cor. in BM*   562 for] of *S*

59.

Adieu to thee, fair Rhine! How long delighted
The stranger fain would linger on his way!
Thine is a scene alike where souls united   565
Or lonely Contemplation thus might stray;
And could the ceaseless vultures cease to prey
On self-condemning bosoms, it were here,
Where Nature, nor too sombre nor too gay,
Wild but not rude, awful yet not austere,   570
Is to the mellow Earth as Autumn to the year.

60.

Adieu to thee again! a vain adieu!
There can be no farewell to scene like thine;
The mind is coloured by thy every hue;
And if reluctantly the eyes resign   575
Their cherish'd gaze upon thee, lovely Rhine!
'Tis with the thankful glance of parting praise;
More mighty spots may rise—more glaring shine,
But none unite in one attaching maze
The brilliant, fair, and soft,—the glories of old days,   580

61.

The negligently grand, the fruitful bloom
Of coming ripeness, the white city's sheen,
The rolling stream, the precipice's gloom,
The forest's growth, and Gothic walls between,
The wild rocks shaped as they had turrets been   585
In mockery of man's art; and these withal
A race of faces happy as the scene,

563 How long delighted] ⟨the passing stranger⟩ M   How] ⟨too⟩ M ⟨though⟩ BM
564 ⟨Too long would linger on his destined way⟩ M   565 where] for M, cor. in BM
566 On lonely ⟨Meditation⟩ Contemplation calm to stray M   might] ⟨to⟩ BM
567 And . . . ceaseless] ⟨Gorging on thee the⟩ M   ceaseless] sleepless M, BM, S
568 ⟨For on self-assassins bosoms for a time⟩ M   570 Rustic not rude—sublime ⟨but⟩
yet not austere M, cor. in BM   571 as . . . to] ⟨the . . . on⟩ M   572 a vain
adieu] ⟨but vain the mind⟩ M   574 by] with M, cor. in BM   575 the eyes]
⟨it must⟩ M   these eyes S   578 More mighty scenes may rise—⟨and growth may
shine⟩ more ⟨gaudy⟩ glaring shine M   579 attaching] enchanted M ⟨enchanting⟩ BM
580 The fertile—fair—⟨the grand with glories of past days⟩ M, cor. in BM   582 the
white] ⟨with the far⟩ M   584 Gothic] ⟨castled⟩ M   585 The] ⟨The⟩ And S
had turrets] too towers M   586 these] ⟨these⟩ there S   587 faces . . . scene]
⟨happy faces rarely seen⟩ M

Whose fertile bounties here extend to all,
Still springing o'er thy banks, though Empires near them fall.

62.

But these recede. Above me are the Alps,   590
The palaces of Nature, whose vast walls
Have pinnacled in clouds their snowy scalps,
And throned Eternity in icy halls
Of cold sublimity, where forms and falls
The avalanche—the thunderbolt of snow!   595
All which expands the spirit, yet appals,
Gather around these summits, as to show
How Earth may pierce to Heaven, yet leave vain man below.

63.

But ere these matchless heights I dare to scan,
There is a spot should not be pass'd in vain,—   600
Morat! the proud, the patriot field! where man
May gaze on ghastly trophies of the slain,
Nor blush for those who conquered on that plain;
Here Burgundy bequeath'd his tombless host,
A bony heap, through ages to remain,   605
Themselves their monument;—the Stygian coast
Unsepulchred they roam'd, and shriek'd each wandering
    ghost.

64.

While Waterloo with Cannae's carnage vies,
Morat and Marathon twin names shall stand;

588 Whose . . .] ⟨In other Mens / Scenes⟩ M   Whose] ⟨Nature's⟩ M   extend] ⟨seemed / showed⟩ M   fertile] ⟨teeming⟩ BM   589 Still . . . though] And ⟨soon⟩ rise upon thy banks while M, cor. in BM   590 recede] ⟨are fled⟩ M   594 ⟨Below⟩ Around in crystal grandeur—⟨yonder⟩ to where falls M; Of cold ⟨and awful splendour-lo! where⟩ falls BM   595 The . . . of] The Avalanche ⟨with⟩ the thunder-clouds of M   596 which] that all edns.   yet] ⟨or⟩ M   597 Gather around] ⟨Then gather on⟩ M   as to show] ⟨and there grow⟩ M   598 How . . . pierce] ⟨Where earth ascends⟩ M   yet leave] and leaves M   600 a spot] a ⟨field I now⟩ spot M   601 Morat! ⟨the patriot's field where still may man⟩ M   602 ⟨Gazes on the trophies of the slain⟩ May gaze upon the trophies oer the slain M   603 that] the S   605 A] ⟨The / In⟩ M   boney] lonely S   606 the . . . coast] ⟨as barbarians boast / they are near the coast⟩ ⟨by⟩ the Stygian coast M   607 Unsepulchred . . . shriek'd] ⟨Of / But better such should be / No shade of these can reach⟩ Unsepulchred may roam—and shriek M   608 While] ⟨But / Let⟩ M   609 twin . . . stand] ⟨shall be twin names⟩ M

They were true Glory's stainless victories,   610
Won by the unambitious heart and hand
Of a proud, brotherly, and civic band,
All unbought champions in no princely cause
Of vice-entail'd Corruption; they no land
Doom'd to bewail the blasphemy of laws   615
Making kings' rights divine, by some Draconic clause.

65.

By a lone wall a lonelier column rears
A gray and grief-worn aspect of old days,
'Tis the last remnant of the wreck of years,
And looks as with the wild-bewildered gaze   620
Of one to stone converted by amaze,
Yet still with consciousness; and there it stands
Making a marvel that it not decays,
When the coeval pride of human hands,
Levell'd Aventicum, hath strewed her subject lands.   625

66.

And there—oh! sweet and sacred be the name!—
Julia—the daughter, the devoted—gave
Her youth to Heaven; her heart, beneath a claim
Nearest to Heaven's, broke o'er a father's grave.
Justice is sworn 'gainst tears, and hers would crave   630
The life she lived in; but the judge was just,
And then she died on him she could not save.
Their tomb was simple, and without a bust,
And held within their urn one mind, one heart, one dust.

610 They . . .] ⟨For they are / Oer the⟩   Glory's] Glory's ⟨battles⟩ M, BM   611 the
. . . and] the ⟨manly heart and freeman's⟩ M   612 Of a proud] Fought by the M
613 All] Of M   614 Of . . . Corruption] Of ⟨despotic Vice and Idiotry⟩ M   they no
land] their proud land M   615 Doom'd . . .] ⟨Which curses ? to / kingly rights divine⟩
Groaned not beneath ⟨hereditary⟩ the blasphemy of laws M   617 By] ⟨In⟩ M
618 grief-worn] grieflike M   619 'Tis] ⟨Like to⟩ M   remnant] relic M
620 And . . .] ⟨And ? once might⟩ M   the] a M   621 Of . . . by] ⟨As⟩ . . . in M
623 The spirit of Winter's ⟨vain⟩ morn and darkness rays M cancelled   Making] ⟨Marvel-
ling⟩ Making M   624 When . . .] ⟨But yet here was ever the⟩ When here / even upon
⟨that⟩ the hill which still commands M, BM   625 ⟨Aventicum oerlooked and ruled
these valiant lands⟩ M   hath . . . subject] ⟨lay crushed / fallen⟩ hath strewed her valiant M
628 beneath] ⟨unto⟩ M   633 ⟨And they lie simply⟩—decked with no vain
bust M   634 their . . . mind ⟨one⟩ its urn—one ⟨word⟩ M ,cor. in BM

67.

But these are deeds which should not pass away,   635
And names that must not wither, though the earth
Forgets her empires with a just decay,
The enslavers and the enslaved, their death and birth;
The high, the mountain-majesty of worth
Should be, and shall, survivor of its woe,   640
And from its immortality look forth
In the sun's face, like yonder Alpine snow,
Imperishably pure beyond all things below.

68.

Lake Leman woos me with its crystal face,
The mirror where the stars and mountains view   645
The stillness of their aspect in each trace
Its clear depth yields of their far height and hue:
There is too much of man here, to look through
With a fit mind the might which I behold;
But soon in me shall Loneliness renew   650
Thoughts hid, but not less cherish'd than of old,
Ere mingling with the herd had penn'd me in their fold.

69.

To fly from, need not be to hate, mankind;
All are not fit with them to stir and toil,
Nor is it discontent to keep the mind   655
Deep in its fountain, lest it overboil
In the hot throng, where we become the spoil
Of our infection, till too late and long
We may deplore and struggle with the coil,
In wretched interchange of wrong for wrong   660
'Midst a contentious world, striving where none are strong.

644 Lake] But *M, cor. in BM*   646 aspect] aspects *M*   647 Its . . . yields] The
clear depths yield *M*   652 had . . . me] had ⟨coupled me to⟩ ⟨fixed⟩ me *M*
654 fit with] ⟨fitted for⟩ *M*   655 Nor is it] ⟨It is not⟩ *M*   656 Deep . . . fountain]
In its own deepness *M*   658 our] its *M*   660 In] ⟨Returning⟩ In ⟨the⟩ *M*
661 'Midst . . .] ⟨One of a striving / In a most struggle⟩ One of a worthless ⟨crowd who⟩
world to strive where none are strong *M, cor. in BM*

70.

There, in a moment, we may plunge our years
In fatal penitence, and in the blight
Of our own soul, turn all our blood to tears,
And colour things to come with hues of Night;   665
The race of life becomes a hopeless flight
To those that walk in darkness: on the sea,
The boldest steer but where their ports invite,
But there are wanderers o'er Eternity
Whose bark drives on and on, and anchored ne'er shall be. 670

71.

Is it not better, then, to be alone,
And love Earth only for its earthly sake?
By the blue rushing of the arrowy Rhone,
Or the pure bosom of its nursing lake,
Which feeds it as a mother who doth make   675
A fair but froward infant her own care,
Kissing its cries away as these awake;—
Is it not better thus our lives to wear,
Than join the crushing crowd, doom'd to inflict or bear?

72.

I live not in myself, but I become   680
Portion of that around me; and to me,
High mountains are a feeling, but the hum
Of human cities torture: I can see
Nothing to loathe in nature, save to be
A link reluctant in a fleshly chain,   685
Class'd among creatures, when the soul can flee,

662 plunge our years] ⟨fix / stamp our fates⟩ M   663 and . . . blight] ⟨grown early gray / and all with a cast / in turn⟩ M   664 Of . . . soul] ⟨Of a false die⟩ M   665 And colour things] ⟨And make the past⟩ And colour all things M   666 ⟨And then there will not be no⟩ And then their life becomes a hopeless flight M   race] ⟨rest⟩ BM   667 on] oer M, cor. in BM   668 their ports] ⟨thy shores⟩ M the ports M, S   669 o'er] through M   670 drives] ⟨still⟩ drives M   673 By] ⟨Through⟩ M   674 pure] ⟨smooth⟩ sweet M, cor. in BM   675 it as] it ⟨with⟩ as M   677 To its young cries and kisses all awake M, cor. in BM   678 Is] ⟨Were⟩ M   679 join . . . crowd] ⟨be amongst the doomed / make / yield or join in⟩ M   680 live] ⟨breathe⟩ M   682 High] ⟨These⟩ M   683 human] peopled M   684 save] but M   685 ⟨Thus a link reluctant in a chain⟩ M   fleshly] ⟨living⟩ M   686 ⟨Oh I could breathe all in comingledly⟩ Class'd among] Classing with M, cor. in BM

And with the sky, the peak, the heaving plain
Of ocean, or the stars, mingle, and not in vain.

73.

And thus I am absorb'd, and this is life:
I look upon the peopled desart past,   690
As on a place of agony and strife,
Where, for some sin, to Sorrow I was cast,
To act and suffer, but remount at last
With a fresh pinion; which I feel to spring,
Though young, yet waxing vigorous, as the blast   695
Which it would cope with, on delighted wing,
Spurning the clay-cold bonds which round our being cling.

74.

And when, at length, the mind shall be all free
From what it hates in this degraded form,
Reft of its carnal life, save what shall be   700
Existent happier in the fly and worm,—
When elements to elements conform,
And dust is as it should be, shall I not
Feel all I see, less dazzling, but more warm?
The bodiless thought? the Spirit of each spot?   705
Of which, even now, I share at times the immortal lot?

75.

Are not the mountains, waves, and skies, a part
Of me and of my soul, as I of them?
Is not the love of these deep in my heart
With a pure passion? should I not contemn   710

687 And . . . peak] And with the air—the ⟨cliff / mount⟩ M   692 ⟨Where I am for
some guilt to baffling being⟩ M   693 act] ⟨battle⟩ sink M ⟨sting / crawl⟩ BM
694 which . . . to] and I feel it M, cor. in BM   695 yet . . . as] and feeble—⟨unequal⟩
not equal to M cancelled   waxing] growing M   696 Which . . . on] ⟨Still with a
growing and⟩ M   would] shall M   697 Spurning . . . round our being] ⟨Leaving⟩ . . .
partly round me M   our being] ⟨man's spirit⟩ BM   698 the . . . all] ⟨my Spirit
shall be⟩ M   699 what] ⟨all⟩ M   700 its] ⟨all⟩ M, BM   702 When . . .]
⟨I know what / Then Nature will be mine⟩ M   704 ⟨Feel the same soon / Be all as
I am partly now still warm⟩ M   705 the . . . spot] ⟨found in every spot⟩   of] in M
706 Of which] ⟨Where⟩ M   707 mountains . . . a] ⟨waters and this earth a /
mountain, waves and skies a⟩ universe a breathing M   708 as] ⟨and⟩ M   710 With
a pure] ⟨Purer than⟩ M

All objects, if compared with these? and stem
A tide of suffering, rather than forego
Such feelings for the hard and worldly phlegm
Of those whose eyes are only turn'd below,
Gazing upon the ground, with thoughts which dare not glow?

76.

But this is not my theme; and I return
To that which is immediate, and require
Those who find contemplation in the urn,
To look on One, whose dust was once all fire,
A native of the land where I respire   720
The clear air for a while—a passing guest,
Where he became a being,—whose desire
Was to be glorious; 'twas a foolish quest,
The which to gain and keep, he sacrificed all rest.

77.

Here the self-torturing sophist, wild Rousseau,   725
The apostle of affliction, he who threw
Enchantment over passion, and from woe
Wrung overwhelming eloquence, first drew
The breath which made him wretched; yet he knew
How to make madness beautiful, and cast   730
O'er erring deeds and thoughts, a heavenly hue
Of words, like sunbeams, dazzling as they past
The eyes, which o'er them shed tears feelingly and fast.

78.

His love was passion's essence—as a tree
On fire by lightning; with ethereal flame   735
Kindled he was, and blasted; for to be
Thus, and enamoured, were in him the same.

712 rather than forego] ⟨to behold once grow⟩ M   713 ⟨The birthplace of my spirit /
My spirit's birthplace⟩ And change those feelings for the unworldly phlegm M   Such]
⟨These⟩ BM   715 And gaze upon the ground with sordid thoughts and slow M
716 my . . . I] the time—I must M   717 require] ⟨as now⟩ M   721 passing]
⟨quiet⟩ M   725 self-torturing] ⟨self-loving⟩ M   729 yet] ⟨well⟩ M   731 ⟨Oer
deeds and thoughts of Error the bright hue⟩ M   732 Of] ⟨With⟩ M   733 ⟨Over
eyes which wept before them sent tears flowing swift and fast⟩ M   which . . . and] that
oer them shed deep tears which flamed too M   735 by . . . ethereal] ⟨with lightening
—with celestial⟩ M   736 for] ⟨and⟩ M   737 ⟨Like him enamoured were to die
the same⟩ M

But his was not the love of living dame,
Nor of the dead who rise upon our dreams,
But of ideal beauty, which became   740
In him existence, and o'erflowing teems
Along his burning page, distempered though it seems.

79.

This breathed itself to life in Júlie, *this*
Invested her with all that's wild and sweet;
This hallowed, too, the memorable kiss   745
Which every morn his fevered lip would greet,
From hers, who but with friendship his would meet;
But to that gentle touch, through brain and breast
Flash'd the thrill'd spirit's love-devouring heat;
In that absorbing sigh perchance more blest,   750
Than vulgar minds may be with all they seek possest.

80.

His life was one long war with self-sought foes,
Or friends by him self-banish'd; for his mind
Had grown Suspicion's sanctuary, and chose
For its own cruel sacrifice, the kind,   755
'Gainst whom he raged with fury strange and blind.
But he was phrenzied,—wherefore, who may know?
Since cause might be which skill could never find;
But he was phrenzied by disease or woe,
To that worst pitch of all, which wears a reasoning show. 760

81.

For then he was inspired, and from him came,
As from the Pythian's mystic cave of yore,
Those oracles which set the world in flame,
Nor ceased to burn till kingdoms were no more:

738 But . . .] ⟨But his was not so fair⟩ *M*   739 rise upon] ⟨dwell / haunt us in⟩ *M*
742 Along . . .] ⟨In all his thoughts preyed⟩ *M*   Along his] ⟨On every⟩ *M*   744 all
that's wild] ⟨radiance fair⟩ *M*   748 But . . .] ⟨But this was worth⟩ *M*   749 ⟨Gushed
the wild / fresh spirit's self-consuming heat⟩ *M*   750 In . . . perchance] ⟨Even in that
vain clinging sigh / And in a single wretch's sigh⟩ *M*   751 with] ⟨who⟩ *M*   752 His
. . . war] ⟨But his life was one struggle⟩ *M*   753 self-banish'd] ⟨far-banished⟩ *M*
755 sacrifice, the kind] ⟨workings the most kind⟩ *M*   756 'Gainst . . . fury] ⟨And
these he raged with phrenzy⟩ *M*   757 who may] ⟨none can⟩ *M*   758 Since
. . . which . . . find] ⟨Though⟩ . . . ⟨which some could truly find⟩ and leaves no trace behind
M   762 Pythian's mystic] ⟨Pythian in her⟩ *M*

Did he not this for France? which lay before   765
Bowed to the inborn tyranny of years?
Broken and trembling, to the yoke she bore,
Till by the voice of him and his compeers,
Roused up to too much wrath which follows o'ergrown fears?

82.

They made themselves a fearful monument!   770
The wreck of old opinions—things which grew
Breathed from the birth of time: the veil they rent,
And what behind it lay, all earth shall view.
But good with ill they also overthrew,
Leaving but ruins, wherewith to rebuild   775
Upon the same foundation, and renew
Dungeons and thrones, which the same hour re-fill'd,
As heretofore, because ambition was self-will'd.

83.

But this will not endure, nor be endured!
Mankind have felt their strength, and made it felt.   780
They might have used it better, but, allured
By their new vigour, sternly have they dealt
On one another; pity ceased to melt
With her once natural charities. But they,
Who in oppression's darkness caved had dwelt,   785
They were not eagles, nourish'd with the day;
What marvel then, at times, if they mistook their prey?

84.

What deep wounds ever closed without a scar?
The heart's bleed longest, and but heal to wear
That which disfigures it; and they who war   790
With their own hopes, and have been vanquish'd, bear

767 ⟨Yet in his mood ? she who bore⟩ M   768 Till . . . him] ⟨The yoke so long that
he⟩ M   769 up] ⟨him⟩ M   770 They . . . themselves] ⟨He . . . himself⟩ M
771 The . . . things] ⟨A⟩ . . . thoughts M   772 Breathed from the . . . they] Born with
the . . . ⟨was⟩ M   773 And what ⟨behind⟩ within it lay even let me view M   all
earth] ⟨we long⟩ BM   774 with . . . also] alas ! with ill they M   775 ⟨And
left us but wide ruins to rebuild⟩ M   777 Dungeons . . .] ⟨On the same site⟩ M
784 But] ⟨and⟩ M   785 caved] ⟨long⟩ deep M   786 with the day] ⟨in the ray⟩
M   788 What] ⟨The / No⟩ M

Silence, but not submission: in his lair
Fix'd Passion holds his breath, until the hour
Which shall atone for years; none need despair:
It came, it cometh, and will come,—the power   795
To punish or forgive—in *one* we shall be slower.

85.

Clear, placid Leman! thy contrasted lake,
With the wild world I dwelt in, is a thing
Which warns me, with its stillness, to forsake
Earth's troubled waters for a purer spring.   800
This quiet sail is as a noiseless wing
To waft me from distraction; once I loved
Torn ocean's roar, but thy soft murmuring
Sounds sweet as if a sister's voice reproved,
That I with stern delights should e'er have been so moved. 805

86.

It is the hush of night, and all between
Thy margin and the mountains, dusk, yet clear,
Mellowed and mingling, yet distinctly seen,
Save darken'd Jura, whose capt heights appear
Precipitously steep; and drawing near,   810
There breathes a living fragrance from the shore,
Of flowers yet fresh with childhood; on the ear
Drops the light drip of the suspended oar,
Or chirps the grasshopper one good-night carol more;

87.

He is an evening reveller, who makes   815
His life an infancy, and sings his fill;
At intervals, some bird from out the brakes,
Starts into voice a moment, then is still.

792 his] ⟨its⟩ M   793 Fix'd . . .] ⟨Crushed and the Passions shut⟩ M   Passion . . .
breath] ⟨Passion's breath holds⟩ M   795 and] and ⟨it⟩ M   796 *one*] ⟨both⟩ M
798 wild] wide *1st edn., all issues*   801 quiet . . . as] ⟨sail which bears me seems⟩ M
802 distraction] Contention M ⟨convulsion⟩ BM   803 soft] ⟨sweet⟩ M   807 yet]
⟨yet⟩ and M   809 darken'd] ⟨the far dark⟩ M   813 Drops] ⟨Sinks⟩ M
814 chirps] ⟨sings⟩ M   815 He is ⟨in / for⟩ an endless evening reveller M *cancelled*
816 infancy, and] infancy ⟨gay / green thoughts⟩ and M   817 ⟨Him merry with
light talking with his mate⟩ M   intervals] ⟨times⟩ M   818 Starts into voice] ⟨Breaks
into song⟩ M

There seems a floating whisper on the hill,
But that is fancy, for the starlight dews   820
All silently their tears of love instil,
Weeping themselves away, till they infuse
Deep into Nature's breast the spirit of her hues.

88.

Ye stars! which are the poetry of heaven!
If in your bright leaves we would read the fate   825
Of men and empires,—'tis to be forgiven,
That in our aspirations to be great,
Our destinies o'erleap their mortal state,
And claim a kindred with you; for ye are
A beauty and a mystery, and create   830
In us such love and reverence from afar,
That fortune, fame, power, life, have named themselves a star.

89.

All heaven and earth are still—though not in sleep,
But breathless, as we grow when feeling most;
And silent, as we stand in thoughts too deep:—   835
All heaven and earth are still: From the high host
Of stars, to the lull'd lake and mountain-coast,
All is concentered in a life intense,
Where not a beam, nor air, nor leaf is lost,
But hath a part of being, and a sense   840
Of that which is of all Creator and defence.

90.

Then stirs the feeling infinite, so felt
In solitude, where we are *least* alone;
A truth, which through our being then doth melt
And purifies from self: it is a tone,   845

821 All...] ⟨Are of / so silent on the thoughts⟩ M   tears ... instil] ⟨loving tears dis⟩ M   822 ⟨In / That upon / Deep into Nature's bosom—and infuse⟩ M   823 the ... hues] the existence which they lose M, cor. in BM   830 ⟨A mystery and a beauty⟩ BM   832 That when Ambition bows, tis only to a star Smith, cor. in BM   only to a] ⟨only to his⟩ BM   833 though] ⟨but⟩ M   834 But...] ⟨But in such full existence⟩ M   835 too] ⟨quite⟩ M   837 to] ⟨and⟩ to M   838 a] ⟨the⟩ M   840 hath a] has its M   841 Of...] ⟨Which is? fallen heaven when / Of that which governs all⟩ M   842 It is a voiceless feeling—⟨only⟩ chiefly felt M, cor. in BM   843 In ... where] ⟨Alone—where truly / Alone—in sooth where⟩ M   844 our being] ⟨the soul⟩ M   845 And...] ⟨And is purified⟩ M

The soul and source of music, which makes known
Eternal harmony, and sheds a charm,
Like to the fabled Cytherea's zone,
Binding all things with beauty;—'twould disarm
The spectre Death, had he substantial power to harm.   850

91.

Not vainly did the early Persian make
His altar the high places and the peak
Of earth-o'ergazing mountains, and thus take
A fit and unwall'd temple, there to seek
The Spirit, in whose honour shrines are weak,   855
Uprear'd of human hands. Come, and compare
Columns and idol-dwellings, Goth or Greek,
With Nature's realms of worship, earth and air,
Nor fix on fond abodes to circumscribe thy prayer!

92.

The sky is changed!—and such a change! Oh night,   860
And storm, and darkness, ye are wondrous strong,
Yet lovely in your strength, as is the light
Of a dark eye in woman! Far along,
From peak to peak, the rattling crags among
Leaps the live thunder! Not from one lone cloud,   865
But every mountain now hath found a tongue,
And Jura answers, through her misty shroud,
Back to the joyous Alps, who call to her aloud!

93.

And this is in the night:—Most glorious night!
Thou wert not sent for slumber! let me be   870

846 Of a most inward music—which ⟨once⟩ makes known *M, cor. in BM*   850 had
... power] ⟨if he had real power⟩ *M*   851 Not ... early] ⟨And⟩ ... outrapt *M*
852 altar ... peak] ⟨altars ... peaks⟩ *M*   853 earth-o'ergazing] earth-oerhanging *S*
854 A fit] ⟨The wide⟩ *M*   there] ⟨that⟩ *M*   unwall'd] unrivalled *S, cor. in MC*
856 Come] ⟨go⟩ *M*   857 or] and *M*   858 With] With ⟨these / the⟩ *M*
859 Nor fix ... thy] ⟨Nor to the same / Nor to fix⟩ ... your *M*   860 The sky] ⟨But
this⟩ *BM*   and] ⟨it⟩ and *M*   861 ye are wondrous] ⟨Precipices⟩ *M* wondrous]
⟨wonderful⟩ *M*   862 Yet] ⟨And⟩ *M*   864 rattling crags] ⟨sounding rocks⟩ *M*
866 now ... a] ⟨hath its Tempest⟩ *M*   867 through her] ⟨from its⟩ *M*   868 joyous
... who] ⟨roaring ... that⟩ *M*   869–70 Most ... wert] Oh ... art *M*

A sharer in thy fierce and far delight,—
A portion of the tempest and of thee!
How the lit lake shines, a phosphoric sea,
And the big rain comes dancing to the earth!
And now again 'tis black,—and now, the glee   875
Of the loud hills shakes with its mountain-mirth,
As if they did rejoice o'er a young earthquake's birth.

94.

Now, where the swift Rhone cleaves his way between
·Heights which appear as lovers who have parted
In hate, whose mining depths so intervene,   880
That they can meet no more, though broken-hearted;
Though in their souls, which thus each other thwarted,
Love was the very root of the fond rage
Which blighted their life's bloom, and then departed:—
Itself expired, but leaving them an age   885
Of years all winters,—war within themselves to wage.

95.

Now, where the quick Rhone thus hath cleft his way,
The mightiest of the storms hath ta'en his stand:
For here, not one, but many, make their play,
And fling their thunder-bolts from hand to hand,   890
Flashing and cast around: of all the band,
The brightest through these parted hills hath fork'd
His lightnings,—as if he did understand,
That in such gaps as desolation work'd,
There the hot shaft should blast whatever therein lurk'd. 895

872 ⟨And⟩ a portion of the Storm—a part of thee *M*   873 How . . . a . . . sea]
⟨Now⟩ . . . as a fiery sea *M, cor. in BM*   875 and] ⟨to the⟩ and *M*   877 o'er
a young] ⟨upon an⟩ *M* ⟨As they had found an heir and feasted ⟩oer his birth⟩ *M*
879 Heights] ⟨Crags⟩ *M*   as] like *M*   879–80 ⟨Hills that look like brethren—with
twin heights / Of a like aspect⟩ *M*   880 In . . . mining] ⟨And⟩ In hate ⟨which tells
where⟩ *M*   884 Which] Which ⟨shared that / strove in⟩ *M*   bloom] ⟨fruits⟩ *M*
886 years all winters] ⟨long / separation dreary⟩ *M*   887 hath cleft] ⟨doth cleave⟩ *M*
888 mightiest . . . ta'en] ⟨strongest . . . made⟩ *M*   891 cast around] ⟨passing on / flung
along⟩ *M*   892 through . . . fork'd] ⟨oer . . . sped⟩ *M*   893 His ⟨sheeted⟩ lightnings *M*   895 blast] blast ⟨the⟩ *M*

96.

Sky, mountains, river, winds, lake, lightnings! ye!
With night, and clouds, and thunder, and a soul
To make these felt and feeling, well may be
Things that have made me watchful; the far roll
Of your departing voices, is the knoll   900
Of what in me is sleepless,—if I rest.
But where of ye, oh tempests! is the goal?
Are ye like those within the human breast?
Or do ye find, at length, like eagles, some high nest?

97.

Could I embody and unbosom now   905
That which is most within me,—could I wreak
My thoughts upon expression, and thus throw
Soul, heart, mind, passions, feelings, strong or weak,
All that I would have sought, and all I seek,
Bear, know, feel, and yet breathe—into *one* word,   910
And that one word were Lightning, I would speak;
But as it is, I live and die unheard,
With a most voiceless thought, sheathing it as a sword.

98.

The morn is up again, the dewy morn,
With breath all incense, and with cheek all bloom,   915
Laughing the clouds away with playful scorn,
And living as if earth contain'd no tomb,—
And glowing into day: we may resume
The march of our existence: and thus I,
Still on thy shores, fair Leman! may find room   920
And food for meditation, nor pass by
Much, that may give us pause, if pondered fittingly.

896 Sky, mountains . . . lake] Sky—⟨thou art⟩ mountains . . . lake ⟨and⟩ *M*   898 To
make] That makes *M*   901 if I rest] ⟨I shall rest⟩ *M*   905 embody] ⟨unbody⟩
MC   906 most] ⟨great⟩ *M*   908 mind] mind ⟨and all passions / feelings⟩ *M*
910 Bear . . .] ⟨Or even ? / ? all that I shall⟩ *M*   913 ⟨A / And / But / In most
voiceless hope—sheathed as a bloodless sword / In voiceless thought—my heart the sheath⟩
M   916 with] ⟨in⟩ *M*   917 living as if] ⟨joys fair as if⟩ *M*   918 we]
⟨alike⟩ we *M*

99.

Clarens! sweet Clarens, birth-place of deep Love!
Thine air is the young breath of passionate thought;
Thy trees take root in Love; the snows above   925
The very Glaciers have his colours caught,
And sun-set into rose-hues sees them wrought
By rays which sleep there lovingly: the rocks,
The permanent crags, tell here of Love, who sought
In them a refuge from the worldly shocks,   930
Which stir and sting the soul with hope that woos, then
    mocks.

100.

Clarens! by heavenly feet thy paths are trod,—
Undying Love's, who here ascends a throne
To which the steps are mountains; where the god
Is a pervading life and light,—so shown   935
Not on those summits solely, nor alone
In the still cave and forest: o'er the flower
His eye is sparkling, and his breath hath blown,
His soft and summer breath, whose tender power
Passes the strength of storms in their most desolate hour. 940

101.

All things are here of *him;* from the black pines,
Which are his shade on high, and the loud roar
Of torrents, where he listeneth, to the vines
Which slope his green path downward to the shore,
Where the bowed waters meet him, and adore,   945

924 Thine air is] ⟨Thine is⟩ Thy air is *M*   925 Thy ... in] ⟨Love is⟩ Thy trees
⟨have grown from⟩ *M*   926 Glaciers] ⟨snows⟩ *M*   928 By ... there] By ⟨his⟩
rays which ⟨sleep⟩ twine there *M*   929 crags ... who sought] ⟨rocks ... the vine⟩
⟨which⟩ sought *M*   who] which *BM*   930 In them] ⟨Grow⟩ *M*   931 Which]
Which ⟨shake⟩ *M*   that] which *BM*   932 Clarens—sweet Clarens—thou art Love's
abode *M, cor. in BM*   933 Love's ... ascends] Love ... hath made *M, cor. in BM*
934 To ... are] ⟨And girded it with⟩ *M*   the] thy *M*   935 ⟨In a pervading spirit
which is shown⟩ *M*   Is ... light] In ... ⟨hope⟩ *M*   936 ⟨From the steep summit to
the rushing Rhone⟩ *M*   on] in *M*   938 eye is sparkling] ⟨heart is glistening /
springing⟩ *M*   939 tender] ⟨searching⟩ *M*   940 Passes ... their] ⟨Surpasses
the strong storm's in its⟩ *M*   942 Which ...] Which ⟨he retires⟩ *M*   943 listeneth]
⟨muses⟩ *M*   945 bowed waters] ⟨calm Lake doth⟩ *M*

Kissing his feet with murmurs; and the wood,
The covert of old trees, with trunks all hoar,
But light leaves, young as joy, stands where it stood,
Offering to him, and his, a populous solitude,

102.

A populous solitude of bees and birds,   950
And fairy-form'd and many-coloured things,
Who worship him with notes more sweet than words,
And innocently open their glad wings,
Fearless and full of life: the gush of springs,
And fall of lofty fountains, and the bend   955
Of stirring branches, and the bud which brings
The swiftest thought of beauty, here extend,
Mingling, and made by Love, unto one mighty end.

103.

He who hath loved not, here would learn that lore,
And make his heart a spirit; he who knows   960
That tender mystery, will love the more,
For this is Love's recess, where vain men's woes,
And the world's waste, have driven him far from those,
For 'tis his nature to advance or die;
He stands not still, but or decays, or grows   965
Into a boundless blessing, which may vie
With the immortal lights, in its eternity!

104.

'Twas not for fiction chose Rousseau this spot,
Peopling it with affections; but he found

946 ⟨Rippling to his footsteps⟩ BM   947 The . . .] The ⟨wood of a⟩ M   948 ⟨The
branches young as Heaven stand where they stood⟩ M   light] ⟨quiet⟩ M   951 ⟨And
beautiful and variegated things⟩ M   952 notes more sweet] sweeter voice M, cor. in
BM ⟨sweeter voice / tones⟩ MC   953 And . . .] ⟨In innocent⟩ M   954 gush]
sound M, cor, in BM   955 fall] ⟨falling⟩ falls M   956 bud . . . brings] ⟨leaf . . .
flings⟩ M   957 swiftest] ⟨quickest⟩ M   958 and made] and ⟨making j⟩ made M
959 learn] ⟨catch⟩ M   lore] love 1st edn., all issues, cor. in H, SB   960 And . . .]
⟨He who loves / And he / Making⟩ M   knows] ⟨hath⟩ M   961 That . . .] ⟨Loved
and still / And still doth love—would learn to love the more / What that mystery⟩ Tha t
mystery would learn to love the more M   tender . . . will] ⟨gentle . . . would⟩ BM
962 ⟨For this is his chief altar where the woes / For this is his very altar / Here is his⟩ M
963 And . . . far from those] ⟨Of m⟩ From . . . to repose M, cor. in BM   964 For]
And M   advance] ⟨advance / proceed⟩ BM   966 may] shall M, cor. in BM
968 ⟨It is not that Rousseau hath made—but found / made this spot⟩ M   'Twas . . .]
⟨And tis not that⟩ M   for] ⟨in⟩ M

It was the scene which passion must allot   970
To the mind's purified beings; 'twas the ground
Where early Love his Psyche's zone unbound,
And hallowed it with loveliness: 'tis lone,
And wonderful, and deep, and hath a sound,
And sense, and sight of sweetness; here the Rhone   975
Hath spread himself a couch, the Alps have rear'd a throne.

105.

Lausanne! and Ferney! ye have been the abodes
Of names which unto you bequeath'd a name;
Mortals, who sought and found, by dangerous roads,
A path to perpetuity of fame: 980
They were gigantic minds, and their steep aim,
Was, Titan-like, on daring doubts to pile
Thoughts which should call down thunder, and the flame
Of Heaven, again assail'd, if Heaven the while
On man and man's research could deign do more than smile.

106.

The one was fire and fickleness, a child,
Most mutable in wishes, but in mind,
A wit as various,—gay, grave, sage, or wild,—
Historian, board, philosopher, combined;
He multiplied himself among mankind,   990
The Proteus of their talents: But his own
Breathed most in ridicule,—which, as the wind,
Blew where it listed, laying all things prone,—
Now to o'erthrow a fool, and now to shake a throne.

971 To . . . purified] To her ⟨own brighter⟩ more purified M   the mind's] ⟨her more⟩ BM
973 loveliness: 'tis] ⟨Beauty—it is⟩ M   974 deep] ⟨sweet⟩ M   975 And . . .]
⟨A sweetness⟩ M   here the] ⟨the swift⟩ M   976 spread] ⟨made⟩ M   978 names]
⟨men⟩ M   979 Mortals . . . dangerous] ⟨Men . . . ranging⟩ M   981 They]
These M   983 should] ⟨should⟩ might M   984 again] once more M, cor. in BM
986 a] ⟨the⟩ M   was] ⟨all⟩ BM   987 ⟨Of wishes the most mutable: in mind⟩ M
988–92   A Scorner as ranging: gay ⟨or⟩ grave ⟨or⟩ sage—or wild
                Coping with all and leaving all behind
                Within himself existed all mankind
                And laughing at their faults betrayed ⟨revealed⟩ his own
                His own was ridicule—which as the wind M
988 wit as various] ⟨Power as varying⟩ BM   989 ⟨Coping with all and leaving all
behind⟩ BM   990 ⟨Within himself existed all⟩ Mankind BM   991 ⟨And laughing
at their faults betrayed⟩ his own BM   of their] of S   992 Breathed most in] ⟨His
arm was⟩ BM   993 laying . . . prone] ⟨with a force and / and could shake a throne⟩
M   994 Now . . .] ⟨To overthrow a fool or just shake⟩ M

107.

The other, deep and slow, exhausting thought,   995
And hiving wisdom with each studious year,
In meditation dwelt, with learning wrought,
And shaped his weapon with an edge severe,
Sapping a solemn creed with solemn sneer;
The lord of irony,—that master-spell,   1000
Which stung his foes to wrath, which grew from fear,
And doom'd him to the zealot's ready Hell,
Which answers to all doubts so eloquently well.

108.

Yet, peace be with their ashes,—for by them,
If merited, the penalty is paid;   1005
It is not ours to judge,—far less condemn;
The hour must come when such things shall be made
Known unto all,—or hope and dread allay'd
By slumber, on one pillow,—in the dust,
Which, thus much we are sure, must lie decay'd;   1010
And when it shall revive, as is our trust,
'Twill be to be forgiven, or suffer what is just.

109.

But let me quit man's works, again to read
His Maker's, spread around me, and suspend
This page, which from my reveries I feed,   1015
Until it seems prolonging without end.
The clouds above me to the white Alps tend,
And I must pierce them, and survey whate'er
May be permitted, as my steps I bend
To their most great and growing region, where   1020
The earth to her embrace compels the powers of air.

995 exhausting thought] concentering ⟨years⟩ thought M, cor. in BM   996 And
hiving] ⟨Of meditation⟩ And gathering M, cor. in BM   997 with] ⟨in⟩ M ⟨or⟩ BM
998 shaped] ⟨dipped⟩ M   999 Sapping . . .] ⟨Fond of⟩ M   1000 The lord . . . that]
The ⟨unconquered⟩ Lord . . . ⟨so⟩ that M   that] whose BM   1001 Which stung his
⟨raging⟩ swarming foes with rage and fear M   to . . . from] ⟨with mingling wrath and⟩ BM
1003 Which] ⟨That⟩ M   1004 But peace to both their ashes—⟨if to⟩ them M
1007 The hour must . . . shall] The time must . . . will M   1008 and dread allay'd]
⟨forever laid⟩ and fear allayed M   1009 By slumber . . . in the dust] ⟨With fear⟩ In
sleep . . . ⟨Let us dream⟩ M   1010 ⟨The fire within will not be all decayed⟩ M   lie]
be M   1014 around] before M   1015 from my reveries] ⟨in / with my lowly
thoughts⟩ M   1017 clouds above] clouds ⟨be⟩ above M   1020 their . . . growing]
that most ⟨mighty⟩ M, cor. in BM

110.

Italia! too, Italia! looking on thee,
Full flashes on the soul the light of ages,
Since the fierce Carthaginian almost won thee,
To the last halo of the chiefs and sages,   1025
Who glorify thy consecrated pages;
Thou wert the throne and grave of empires; still,
The fount at which the panting mind assuages
Her thirst of knowledge, quaffing there her fill,
Flows from the eternal source of Rome's imperial hill. 1030

111.

Thus far I have proceeded in a theme
Renewed with no kind auspices:—to feel
We are not what we have been, and to deem
We are not what we should be,—and to steel
The heart against itself; and to conceal,   1035
With a proud caution, love, or hate, or aught,—
Passion or feeling, purpose, grief or zeal,—
Which is the tyrant spirit of our thought,
Is a stern task of soul:—No matter,—it is taught.

112.

And for these words, thus woven into song,   1040
It may be that they are a harmless wile,—
The colouring of the scenes which fleet along,
Which I would seize, in passing, to beguile
My breast, or that of others, for a while.
Fame is the thirst of youth,—but I am not   1045
So young as to regard men's frown or smile,
As loss or guerdon of a glorious lot;
I stood and stand alone,—remembered or forgot.

1022 too] Oh *M*   1024 fierce] proud *M*   1025 To . . . of the] ⟨Down⟩ to . . .
of ⟨thy⟩ *M*   1026 glorify] ⟨brighten and⟩ *M*   1028 mind] ⟨Soul⟩ *M*
1032 kind] ⟨bright⟩ *M*   1036 proud] ⟨stern⟩ *BM*   1037 Passion . . .] ⟨That
works⟩ *M*   grief] wish *M, cor. in BM*   1039 stern task] hard ⟨strife⟩ *M*
1040 thus . . . song] I weave into a song *M, cor. in BM*   1041 ⟨I know that they
are nothing / They are but as a self-deceiving wile⟩ *M*   1042 The shadows of the
things which pass along *M, cor. in BM*   fleet] float *S*   1043 Which I] ⟨And⟩ I *M*
1044 My . . .] ⟨My thought and⟩ *M*   or] ⟨and⟩ *BM*   1045 thirst of youth,—but]
⟨dream of Boyhood⟩—and *M*   1046 men's] the *M*; man's *S*   1047 Of crowds
as making an immortal lot *M, cor. in BM* ⟨of crowds conferring . . .⟩ *BM*

113.

I have not loved the world, nor the world me;
I have not flattered its rank breath, nor bow'd   1050
To its idolatries a patient knee,—
Nor coin'd my cheek to smiles,—nor cried aloud
In worship of an echo; in the crowd
They could not deem me one of such; I stood
Among them, but not of them; in a shroud   1055
Of thoughts which were not their thoughts, and still could,
Had I not filed my mind, which thus itself subdued.

114.

I have not loved the world, nor the world me,—
But let us part fair foes; I do believe,
Though I have found them not, that there may be   1060
Words which are things,—hopes which will not deceive,
And virtues which are merciful, nor weave
Snares for the failing: I would also deem
O'er others' griefs that some sincerely grieve;
That two, or one, are almost what they seem,—   1065
That goodness is no name, and happiness no dream.

115.

My daughter! with thy name this song begun—
My daughter! with thy name thus much shall end—
I see thee not,—I hear thee not,—but none
Can be so wrapt in thee; thou art the friend   1070
To whom the shadows of far years extend:
Albeit my brow thou never should'st behold,
My voice shall with thy future visions blend,
And reach into thy heart,—when mine is cold,—
A token and a tone, even from thy father's mould.   1075

1050 have not flattered] ⟨did not flatter⟩ M   1051 patient] ⟨lowly⟩ M
1052 cheek] heart M ⟨life⟩ BM   1053 In . . .] ⟨In hollow echo / Worshippers /
That business was no wrong / That strength could no wrong⟩ M   in] ⟨even⟩ in M
1054 such] ⟨them⟩ M, BM   1056 which] that M   1057 Had . . .] ⟨Were I⟩ M
1061 which . . . which] that . . . that M   will] ⟨do⟩ BM   1062 which] that M
1064 Oer misery unmixedly some grieve M, S, cor. in BM   1067 this] my B
1075 A . . . a] ⟨Singing with thy⟩ B

116.

To aid thy mind's development,—to watch
Thy dawn of little joys,—to sit and see
Almost thy very growth,—to view thee catch
Knowledge of objects,—wonders yet to thee!
To hold thee lightly on a gentle knee,   1080
And print on thy soft cheek a parent's kiss,—
This, it should seem, was not reserv'd for me;
Yet this was in my nature:—as it is,
I know not what is there, yet something like to this.

117.

Yet, though dull Hate as duty should be taught,   1085
I know that thou wilt love me; though my name
Should be shut from thee, as a spell still fraught
With desolation,—and a broken claim:
Though the grave closed between us,—'twere the same,
I know that thou wilt love me; though to drain   1090
My blood from out thy being, were an aim,
And an attainment,—all would be in vain,—
Still thou would'st love me, still that more than life retain.

118.

The child of love,—though born in bitterness,
And nurtured in convulsion,—of thy sire   1095
These were the elements,—and thine no less.
As yet such are around thee,—but thy fire
Shall be more tempered, and thy hope far higher.
Sweet be thy cradled slumbers! O'er the sea,
And from the mountains where I now respire,   1100
Fain would I waft such blessing upon thee,
As, with a sigh, I deem thou might'st have been to me!

1076 aid] view *B* ⟨watch⟩ *BM*   1078 Almost ... growth,—] ⟨Thy very growth,
almost⟩ *B*   to view thee] ⟨to sit and⟩ *S*   1081 on ... cheek] thy soft cheek with *B*
on] ⟨upon⟩ *BM*   1082 This ... seem] ⟨All this it seems⟩ *B*   1083 as it is]
⟨and from ?⟩ *B*   1084 something] ⟨little⟩ *B*   1085 as] like *B*   1087 shut]
⟨kept⟩ *B*   1089 'twere] still *B*   1090 wilt] ⟨wouldst⟩ *B*   1091 *My*] ⟨Thy⟩ *B*
1092 all] it *B*   1095 nurtured] nourished *B*, cor. in *BM* convulsion,—of *BM, MC,
More*; convulsion. Of *1st edn., all issues, 1818–56*; convulsion! Of *C*   1096 were] ⟨are⟩
B   1097 are] ⟨were⟩ *B*   1098 Shall] Will *B*   1099–1100 sea ... where I now
respire] ⟨waves ... I would waft a dream⟩ *B*   1101 such] ⟨a⟩ *B*   1102 with
... deem] from my soul I dream *B*, cor. in *BM*

Childe Harold's Pilgrimage

CANTO THE FOURTH

Visto ho Toscana, Lombardia, Romagna,
Quel Monte che divide, e quel che serra
Italia, e un mare e l'altro, che la bagna.
ARIOSTO, *Satira* [IV. 58–60].

Venice, January 2, 1818.

TO

JOHN HOBHOUSE, ESQ. A.M., F.R.S.

&c. &c. &c.

MY DEAR HOBHOUSE,

AFTER an interval of eight years between the composition of the
first and last cantos of Childe Harold, the conclusion of the poem is
about to be submitted to the public. In parting with so old a friend
it is not extraordinary that I should recur to one still older and
5 better,—to one who has beheld the birth and death of the other,
and to whom I am far more indebted for the social advantages of an
enlightened friendship, than—though not ungrateful—I can, or
could be, to Childe Harold, for any public favour reflected through
the poem on the poet,—to one, whom I have known long, and
10 accompanied far, whom I have found wakeful over my sickness and
kind in my sorrow, glad in my prosperity and firm in my adversity,
true in counsel and trusty in peril—to a friend often tried and
never found wanting;—to yourself.

In so doing, I recur from fiction to truth, and in dedicating to you
15 in its complete, or at least concluded state, a poetical work which

Copy text : *CHP IV* (first edn., second issue for Dedication, text, and notes up to, but not
including, the note for st. 52, line 2; first edn., first issue for the remaining notes); collated
with *MSS. B, H, BA, E, N,* and *Proofs A, B, C* ; the copy of *CHP IV* with B's corrections
and annotations (*Text M*); all issues of *CHP IV*

epigraph   *not in B*
Dedication
    2–3 is . . . be] is *B*   5 has beheld] beheld *B*   6 advantages] ⟨gratification⟩ *B*
7–8 can . . . be] can be *B*   9 poet—⟨none but I accompanied⟩ to one *B*   10 wakeful over] ⟨watchful in⟩ *B*   15 in its . . . state] in its ⟨uncompleted⟩ state *B*

is the longest, the most thoughtful and comprehensive of my compositions, I wish to do honour to myself by the record of many years intimacy with a man of learning, of talent, of steadiness, and of honour. It is not for minds like ours to give or to receive flattery; yet the praises of sincerity have ever been permitted to the voice of friendship; and it is not for you, nor even for others, but to relieve a heart which has not elsewhere, or lately, been so much accustomed to the encounter of good-will as to withstand the shock firmly, that I thus attempt to commemorate your good qualities, or rather the advantages which I have derived from their exertion. Even the recurrence of the date of this letter, the anniversary of the most unfortunate day of my past existence, but which cannot poison my future while I retain the resource of your friendship, and of my own faculties, will henceforth have a more agreeable recollection for both, inasmuch as it will remind us of this my attempt to thank you for an indefatigable regard, such as few men have experienced, and no one could experience without thinking better of his species and of himself.

It has been our fortune to traverse together, at various periods, the countries of chivalry, history, and fable—Spain, Greece, Asia Minor, and Italy; and what Athens and Constantinople were to us a few years ago, Venice and Rome have been more recently. The poem also, or the pilgrim, or both, have accompanied me from first to last; and perhaps it may be a pardonable vanity which induces me to reflect with complacency on a composition which in some degree connects me with the spot where it was produced, and the objects it would fain describe; and however unworthy it may be deemed of those magical and memorable abodes, however short it may fall of our distant conceptions and immediate impressions, yet as a mark of respect for what is venerable, and of feeling for what is glorious, it has been to me a source of pleasure in the production, and I part with it with a kind of regret, which I hardly suspected that events could have left me for imaginary objects.

16 and comprehensive] ⟨and perhaps the best⟩ B   17 to myself by] to myself ⟨and justice to both in recording / I have lived long enough and seen enough and felt enough ? are useless but not⟩ by B   20 yet the praises] and the servility of the Age has shown itself best in our Country rather in deeds than words—but the praises B   21 relieve] ⟨ease⟩ B   22 elsewhere, or] very B   24 commemorate] record B, cor. in H   25–33 Even . . . of himself] not in B   36 what] that which B   37 years ago ⟨we have recently⟩ Venice B   recently. ⟨My poem and my pilgrim⟩ The B   39 may be ⟨one of those⟩ a B   41 connects me in some degree with the spots where B   42 would fain] would B   43 magical] ⟨mighty⟩ B   46 me ⟨its own⟩ a source B

With regard to the conduct of the last canto, there will be found
50 less of the pilgrim than in any of the preceding, and that little
slightly, if at all, separated from the author speaking in his own
person. The fact is, that I had become weary of drawing a line which
every one seemed determined not to perceive: like the Chinese in
Goldsmith's 'Citizen of the World', whom nobody would believe to
55 be a Chinese, it was in vain that I asserted, and imagined, that I had
drawn, a distinction between the author and the pilgrim; and the
very anxiety to preserve this difference, and disappointment at
finding it unavailing, so far crushed my efforts in the composition,
that I determined to abandon it altogether—and have done so. The
60 opinions which have been, or may be, formed on that subject, are
now a matter of indifference; the work is to depend on itself, and
not on the writer; and the author, who has no resources in his own
mind beyond the reputation, transient or permanent, which is to
arise from his literary efforts, deserves the fate of authors.

65   In the course of the following Canto it was my intention, either
in the text or in the notes, to have touched upon the present state
of Italian literature, and perhaps of manners. But the text, within
the limits I proposed, I soon found hardly sufficient for the labyrinth
of external objects and the consequent reflections; and for the whole
70 of the notes, excepting a few of the shortest, I am indebted to
yourself, and these were necessarily limited to the elucidation of
the text.

   It is also a delicate, and no very grateful task, to dissert upon the

55–6 and . . . a] and as I imagined drew a *B*   57 and] and some *B*   64–5 authors.
In the] authors.—But let me not be ungrateful—from literary men in general, at least
those worthy of the name I have experienced nothing but ⟨liberality⟩ the most liberal conduct & kind & honourable dealing—and this was from those who had ⟨at one period by
the⟩ they reacted through the many & various opportunities given to them—the premature
attacks of an undistinguishing moment of blind anger and boyish vivacity—could neither
have been blamed—nor answered.—If I allude to this it is because ⟨the⟩ I think such circumstances honourable to the literary men who practised such forebearance—and 'if we have
writ our annals true' it is also a fact new ⟨to⟩ in our literary history which has hitherto been
too much checquered with 'quarrels' and 'calamities'. Whatever say the sophists of the
literary commonwealth—however we may have dwindled from the standards or our fathers
in genius—in ⟨the purity⟩ invention—in strength—and depth of conception and composition
—we are at least thus sapient in the courtesies of life & exempt from the envy & irritability
of even the Augustan Age of English Letters and should there be any one who at an
early & less thinking period should have deviated into ⟨unprovoked⟩ undeserved satire he
has probably not ceased to feel far greater regret than could be experienced by the objects
of such attacks—now forgotten—that he has been forgiven—a humiliating recollection
only to a base mind—because it arises from an unwillingness to be found in the wrong and
alas ! what are & what ever have been those self-optimists whose 'whatever is—is right' ? In the
B   69–71 for the greatest part of the notes I am ⟨chiefly⟩ indebted to Yourself ⟨and I am
much mistaken if the ?⟩ and these were *B*   73 It is also perhaps ⟨too delicate⟩ a delicate *B*
73–4 to . . . dissimilar] to touch upon the literature and manners of a foreign people *B*

literature and manners of a nation so dissimilar; and requires an
attention and impartiality which would induce us,—though per-   75
haps no inattentive observers, nor ignorant of the language or
customs of the people amongst whom we have recently abode,—
to distrust, or at least defer our judgment, and more narrowly
examine our information. The state of literary party runs as high
or higher than even on the question of Romantic or Classical as   80
they call it, so that for a stranger to steer impartially between
them is next to impossible. It may be enough then, at least for my
purpose, to quote from their own beautiful language—'Mi pare che
in un paese tutto poetico, che vanta la lingua la più nobile ed
insieme la più dolce, tutte tutte le vie diverse si possono tentare,   85
e che sinche la patria di Alfieri e di Monti non ha perduto l'antico
valore, in tutte essa dovrebbe essere la prima.' Italy has great names
still—Canova, Monti, Ugo Foscolo, Pindemonti, Visconti, Morelli,
Cicognara, Albrizzi, Mezzophanti, Mai, Mustoxidi, Aglietti, and
Vacca, will secure to the present generation an honourable place in   90
most of the departments of Art, Science, and Belles Lettres; and in
some the very highest—Europe—the World—has but one Canova.

It has been somewhere said by Alfieri, that 'La pianta uomo
nasce più robusta in Italia che in qualunque altra terra—e che gli
stessi atroci delitti che vi si commettono ne sono una prova.'   95
Without subscribing to the latter part of his proposition, a dangerous doctrine, the truth of which may be disputed on better grounds,
namely, that the Italians are in no respect more ferocious than their
neighbours, that man must be wilfully blind, or ignorantly heedless,
who is not struck with the extraordinary capacity of this people,   100
or, if such a word be admissible, their *capabilities*, the facility of their
acquisitions, the rapidity of their conceptions, the fire of their
genius, their sense of beauty, and amidst all the disadvantages
of repeated revolutions, the desolation of battles and the despair
of ages, their still unquenched 'longing after immortality',—the   105
immortality of independence. And when we ourselves, in riding

76–9 nor . . . information] nor ⟨so far⟩ altogether ignorant of the language and customs
of the nation with whom we have abode—could induce us to doubt of qualifications and
distrust our judgments and information. *B*   79–81 literary . . . that] literary, as well
as political party, appears to run, or to *have* run, so high, that *B, H, all proofs, all edns.;
present text represents B's correction in Text M*   82–3 then . . . quote] then ⟨perhaps⟩
for my purpose at least—⟨to name the names of Monti, Visconti, Foscolo, Pindemonti,
Morelli, Cicognara⟩ to quote *B*   96–7 a dangerous doctrine] which would be a dangerous
doctrine *B*   104 the . . . battles] ⟨the despair of ages and⟩ the desolation of ⟨wars⟩ battles
B   106–8 in . . . chorus] heard ⟨the rude⟩ in riding round the walls of Rome ⟨the rude
ditty⟩ the simple lament of the labourers ⟨singing⟩ chorus *B*

round the walls of Rome, heard the simple lament of the labourers'
chorus, 'Roma! Roma! Roma! Roma non è più come era prima',
it was difficult not to contrast this melancholy dirge with the
110 bacchanal roar of the songs of exultation still yelled from the London taverns, over the carnage of Mont St. Jean, and the betrayal of
Genoa, of Italy, of France, and of the world, by men whose conduct
you yourself have exposed in a work worthy of the better days of
our history. For me,

115
          'Non movero mai corda
        Ove la turba di sue ciance assorda.'

    What Italy has gained by the late transfer of nations, it were
useless for Englishmen to enquire, till it becomes ascertained that
England has acquired something more than a permanent army and
120 a suspended Habeas Corpus: it is enough for them to look at home.
For what they have done abroad, and especially in the South,
'Verily they *will have* their reward', and at no very distant period.
    Wishing you, my dear Hobhouse, a safe and agreeable return to
that country whose real welfare can be dearer to none than to
125 yourself, I dedicate to you this poem in its completed state; and
repeat once more how truly I am ever

                      Your obliged
                And affectionate friend,
                        BYRON.

I.

    I stood in Venice, on the Bridge of Sighs;
    A palace and a prison on each hand:
    I saw from out the wave her structures rise
    As from the stroke of the enchanter's wand:
    A thousand years their cloudy wings expand   5
    Around me, and a dying Glory smiles
    O'er the far times, when many a subject land
    Look'd to the winged Lion's marble piles,
Where Venice sate in state, thron'd on her hundred isles!

108 era] fosse *Proof D*   ⟨fosse⟩ *Proof B*   109 this melancholy] the simple and
melancholy *B*   110 of . . . from] of deliverance & triumph still yelled in *B*
111 betrayal] betrayers *B*   117 has] may have *B*   124 real welfare] ⟨well
being⟩ welfare *B*
Text
    4 of the] of some *Gifford's correction in Proof B*; of the / an *E*   6 Around] Above
E   9 hundred] seventy *B*; seventy / hundred *H alternate readings*

2.

She looks a sea Cybele, fresh from ocean,   10
Rising with her tiara of proud towers
At airy distance, with majestic motion,
A ruler of the waters and their powers:
And such she was;—her daughters had their dowers
From spoils of nations, and the exhaustless East   15
Pour'd in her lap all gems in sparkling showers.
In purple was she robed, and of her feast
Monarchs partook, and deem'd their dignity increas'd.

3.

In Venice Tasso's echoes are no more,
And silent rows the songless gondolier;
Her palaces are crumbling to the shore,   20
And music meets not always now the ear:
Those days are gone—but Beauty still is here.
States fall, arts fade—but Nature doth not die,
Nor yet forget how Venice once was dear,   25
The pleasant place of all festivity,
The revel of the earth, the masque of Italy!

4.

But unto us she hath a spell beyond
Her name in story, and her long array
Of mighty shadows, whose dim forms despond   30
Above the dogeless city's vanish'd sway;
Ours is a trophy which will not decay
With the Rialto; Shylock and the Moor,
And Pierre, can not be swept or worn away—
The keystones of the arch! though all were o'er,   35
For us repeopled were the solitary shore.

---

11 with] ⟨from⟩ BA   12 airy] a far BA, H, Proofs A, C, cor. in Proof B
14 such] so BA ; so / such H alternate readings   15 From spoils of many nations—
and the East BA, cor. in H   17 In . . . of]⟨And⟩ In . . . at BA, cor. in H   18 partook]
sate down BA, cor. in H   22 ceaseless music meets not ⟨always⟩ now the ear B, H
alternate reading   26 pleasant place] pleasure-place B   28 unto] upon H alternate
reading   spell beyond]⟨magic more⟩ B   29 Her . . . and]⟨Than her past Glory,
than⟩ /⟨Her vanishing Glory and⟩ B   30 ⟨Of trophies, triumphs, and of pleasures⟩ B
31 ⟨Of / Oer⟩ Above B   34 And Pierre ⟨uphold⟩ can not B   36 For us ⟨were⟩
repeopled B

5.

The beings of the mind are not of clay;
Essentially immortal, they create
And multiply in us a brighter ray
And more beloved existence: that which Fate   40
Prohibits to dull life, in this our state
Of mortal bondage, by these spirits supplied
First exiles, then replaces what we hate;
Watering the heart whose early flowers have died,
And with a fresher growth replenishing the void.   45

6.

Such is the refuge of our youth and age,
The first from Hope, the last from Vacancy;
And this worn feeling peoples many a page,
And, may be, that which grows beneath mine eye:
Yet there are things whose strong reality   50
Outshines our fairy-land; in shape and hues
More beautiful than our fantastic sky,
And the strange constellations which the Muse
O'er her wild universe is skilful to diffuse:

7.

I saw or dreamed of such,—but let them go—   55
They came like truth, and disappeared like dreams;
And whatsoe'er they were—are now but so:
I could replace them if I would, still teems
My mind with many a form which aptly seems
Such as I sought for, and at moments found;   60
Let these too go—for waking Reason deems
Such over-weening phantasies unsound,
And other voices speak, and other sights surround.

---

38 create] ⟨produce⟩ B   39 ⟨In us⟩ And . . . brighter ray / day B   41 ⟨Denies
to the dull trick of life⟩ B   our] ⟨the⟩ B   42 mortal] ⟨our⟩ B   43 ⟨Replaces
what⟩ First B   44 ⟨Peopling the heart⟩ Watering . . . early ⟨plants⟩ have B
47 from] ⟨when⟩ B   48 worn] wan C, OSA   49 grows] grows / springs ⟨ spreads
B alternate readings   51 ⟨The brain o⟩ermasters & hath shapes and hues⟩ B   Outshines our fairy-land] ⟨Surpass⟩ our fairies—things B, cor. in H   54 ⟨Paints on her⟩ B
56 and] ⟨but⟩ B   58 still] for B, H, cor. in Proof B   59 mind] ⟨thought⟩ B
61 Let these too] ⟨But let them⟩ B

8.

I've taught me other tongues—and in strange eyes
Have made me not a stranger; to the mind   65
Which is itself, no changes bring surprise;
Nor is it harsh to make, nor hard to find
A country with—ay, or without mankind;
Yet was I born where men are proud to be,
Not without cause; and should I leave behind   70
The inviolate island of the sage and free,
And seek me out a home by a remoter sea,

9.

Perhaps I loved it well: and should I lay
My ashes in a soil which is not mine,
My spirit shall resume it—if we may   75
Unbodied choose a sanctuary. I twine
My hopes of being remembered in my line
With my land's language: if too fond and far
These aspirations in their scope incline,—
If my fame should be, as my fortunes are,   80
Of hasty growth and blight, and dull Oblivion bar

10.

My name from out the temple where the dead
Are honoured by the nations—let it be—
And light the laurels on a loftier head!
And be the Spartan's epitaph on me—   85
'Sparta hath many a worthier son than he.'
Meantime I seek no sympathies, nor need;
The thorns which I have reaped are of the tree
I planted,—they have torn me,—and I bleed:
I should have known what fruit would spring from such
    a seed.   90

64 taught . . . tongues] ⟨learned another tongue⟩ *B*   66 changes bring] ⟨? things⟩ changes can *B*, *cor. in H*   67 ⟨And tis not hard nor harsh to make or find⟩ *B* 69 ⟨Where the bright sun is⟩ *B*   70 should] ⟨if⟩ though *B*   72 And ⟨make myself⟩ a home ⟨beneath a softer⟩ sea *B*   73 Perhaps . . . should] ⟨Yet have . . . when⟩ *B* 74 My] Mine *B, H, cor. in Proof B*   76–7 I . . . line] ⟨to pine Albeit is not my nature and I twine⟩ *B*   77 ⟨My hope of Memory⟩ *B*   78 ⟨Around⟩ With . . . language —⟨it may⟩ if too *B*   79 These] ⟨My⟩ *B*   80 If ⟨Fortune⟩ my fame *B* 84 loftier] ⟨worthier⟩ *B*   85 ⟨And be⟩ And ⟨place⟩ be *B*   89 I . . . torn] ⟨Which I had planted—they tore⟩ *B*   90 ⟨And⟩ I *B*

11.

The spouseless Adriatic mourns her lord;
And, annual marriage now no more renewed,
The Bucentaur lies rotting unrestored,
Neglected garment of her widowhood!
St. Mark yet sees his lion where he stood   95
Stand, but in mockery of his withered power,
Over the proud Place where an Emperor sued,
And monarchs gazed and envied in the hour
When Venice was a queen with an unequalled dower.

12.

The Suabian sued, and now the Austrian reigns—   100
An Emperor tramples where an Emperor knelt;
Kingdoms are shrunk to provinces, and chains
Clank over sceptred cities; nations melt
From power's high pinnacle, when they have felt
The sunshine for a while, and downward go   105
Like lauwine loosen'd from the mountain's belt;
Oh for one hour of blind old Dandolo!
Th' octogenarian chief, Byzantium's conquering foe.

13.

Before St. Mark still glow his steeds of brass,
Their gilded collars glittering in the sun;   110
But is not Doria's menace come to pass?
Are they *not bridled?*—Venice, lost and won,
Her thirteen hundred years of freedom done,
Sinks, like a sea-weed, into whence she rose!
Better be whelm'd beneath the waves, and shun,   115
Even in destruction's depth, her foreign foes,
From whom submission wrings an infamous repose.

91 spouseless . . . lord] ⟨widowed . . . Doge⟩ B   94 ⟨The withered / need of⟩ Neglected B
97 Over . . . Place] ⟨Even on the pillar⟩ H   100 and] ⟨where⟩ BA   102 Kingdoms
. . to] And kingdoms shrink to BA   106 ⟨Like the huge Avalanche⟩ Like Lauwines
BA   108 Byzantium's . . . foe] ⟨who quelled the imperial / Eastern foe⟩ / Empire's
all conquering foe BA   109 still glow] ⟨appear⟩ yet glow BA, cor. in H   114 into]
unto C   116 depth] breast BA

14.

In youth she was all glory,—a new Tyre,—
Her very by-word sprung from victory,
The 'Planter of the Lion', which through fire   120
And blood she bore o'er subject earth and sea;
Though making many slaves, herself still free,
And Europe's bulwark 'gainst the Ottomite;
Witness Troy's rival, Candia! Vouch it, ye
Immortal waves that saw Lepanto's fight!   125
For ye are names no time nor tyranny can blight.

15.

Statues of glass—all shiver'd—the long file
Of her dead Doges are declin'd to dust;
But where they dwelt, the vast and sumptuous pile
Bespeaks the pageant of their splendid trust;   130
Their sceptre broken, and their sword in rust,
Have yielded to the stranger: empty halls,
Thin streets, and foreign aspects, such as must
Too oft remind her who and what enthrals,
Have flung a desolate cloud o'er Venice' lovely walls.   135

16.

When Athens' armies fell at Syracuse,
And fetter'd thousands bore the yoke of war,
Redemption rose up in the Attic Muse,
Her voice their only ransom from afar:
See! as they chant the tragic hymn, the car   140
Of the o'ermaster'd victor stops, the reins
Fall from his hands—his idle scimitar
Starts from its belt—he rends his captive's chains,
And bids him thank the bard for freedom and his strains.

---

124 Vouch it] ⟨Witness⟩ BA   127 shiver'd] ⟨broken⟩ B   129 But] ⟨And⟩ B
130 splendid] ⟨prisoned⟩ H   131 ⟨But⟩ Their B   132 to the ⟨sway of strangers⟩
stranger B   135 flung] ⟨left / fixed⟩ B   137 ⟨And dead or captive / captive
thousands owned / felt the doom of Fate⟩ BA   139 And ⟨sang her chained⟩ / won
her hopeless children from afar BA, cor. in H   140 ⟨Even as they sang the strain⟩
BA   hymn] ⟨strain⟩ BA   141 o'ermastered] ⟨insulting⟩ BA   143 ⟨Stops⟩
Starts . . . his ⟨pursuer's⟩ chains BA   144 And sends him ⟨ransomeless⟩ / home to
bless the poet for his strains BA, cor. in H

17.

Thus, Venice, if no stronger claim were thine,   145
Were all thy proud historic deeds forgot,
Thy choral memory of the Bard divine,
Thy love of Tasso, should have cut the knot
Which ties thee to thy tyrants; and thy lot
Is shameful to the nations,—most of all,   150
Albion! to thee: the Ocean queen should not
Abandon Ocean's children; in the fall
Of Venice think of thine, despite thy watery wall.

18.

I lov'd her from my boyhood—she to me
Was as a fairy city of the heart,   155
Rising like water-columns from the sea,
Of joy the sojourn, and of wealth the mart;
And Otway, Radcliffe, Schiller, Shakspeare's art,
Had stamp'd her image in me, and even so,
Although I found her thus, we did not part,   160
Perchance even dearer in her day of woe,
Than when she was a boast, a marvel, and a show.

19.

I can repeople with the past—and of
The present there is still for eye and thought,
And meditation chasten'd down, enough;   165
And more, it may be, than I hoped or sought;
And of the happiest moments which were wrought
Within the web of my existence, some
From thee, fair Venice! have their colours caught:
There are some feelings Time can not benumb,   170
Nor Torture shake, or mine would now be cold and dumb.

145 stronger] other *BA*   146 ⟨Thy choral Memory⟩ *BA*   148 of . . . cut] of
Tasso's Muse should cut *BA*   ⟨The knot ? Gordian⟩ *BA*   149 ties . . . tyrants] ties
thee to a tyrant *BA*; ⟨tied⟩ thee to thy tyrants *H*   150 most of all] ⟨and / but the
most⟩ *BA*   151 the] ⟨for⟩ the *BA*   152 Abandon] Forget the *BA*   153 despite
. . . wall] for come it will and shall *BA*, *cor. in H*   158 And . . . Schiller] And
Otway's—Schiller's—Radcliffe's *B* Radcliffe] Ratcliff *CHP IV* (*issues 1–4*)   159 in]
⟨on⟩ *B*   160 Although I . . . did] Though I have . . . will *B, cor. in H*   165 chasten'd
down] ⟨more matured⟩ *B*   167 of . . . moments] ⟨thus my happiest days⟩ *B*
169 From] ⟨To⟩ *B*   170–1 ⟨The past at least is mine—whateer may come | But when
the heart is full the lips must needs be dumb.⟩ *B*   171 mine . . . be] else mine now
were *B*

20.

But from their nature will the tannen grow
Loftiest on loftiest and least shelter'd rocks,
Rooted in barrenness, where nought below
Of soil supports them 'gainst the Alpine shocks   175
Of eddying storms; yet springs the trunk, and mocks
The howling tempest, till its height and frame
Are worthy of the mountains from whose blocks
Of bleak, grey, granite, into life it came,
And grew a giant tree;—the mind may grow the same.   180

21.

Existence may be borne, and the deep root
Of life and sufferance make its firm abode
In bare and desolated bosoms: mute
The camel labours with the heaviest load,
And the wolf dies in silence,—not bestow'd   185
In vain should such example be; if they,
Things of ignoble or of savage mood,
Endure and shrink not, we of nobler clay
May temper it to bear,—it is but for a day.

22.

All suffering doth destroy, or is destroy'd,   190
Even by the sufferer; and, in each event
Ends:—Some, with hope replenish'd and rebuoy'd,
Return to whence they came—with like intent,
And weave their web again; some, bow'd and bent,
Wax gray and ghastly, withering ere their time,   195
And perish with the reed on which they leant;
Some seek devotion, toil, war, good or crime,
According as their souls were form'd to sink or climb:

172 ⟨But there are minds which as the Tannen grow⟩ B   But from ⟨its aims⟩ their BA
175 'gainst] ⟨in⟩ B   176 ⟨Of storms and whirlwinds—yet it grows / springs⟩ and
mocks B   177 howling . . . till] ⟨passing . . . and⟩ B   178 from] ⟨on⟩ B
179 bleak, grey] ⟨shrubless⟩ B   180 the . . . grow] ⟨So our Minds may be⟩ B
181 Existence] ⟨And to be / flourish⟩ / ⟨Destruction⟩ B   183 bare . . . bosoms] ⟨rocks
and unsupporting places⟩ B   187 savage] ⟨cruel⟩ B   190 ⟨For Suffering either⟩ B
191 ⟨By that which⟩ B   192 with ⟨amplest⟩ hopes B   193 like] ⟨the same⟩ B
196 And perish ⟨piece and⟩ with B   197 seek] ⟨in⟩ B   198 ⟨Seek / Betake them
as their mind⟩ / ⟨Even as their⟩ soul was formed . . . climb B

23.

But ever and anon of griefs subdued
There comes a token like a scorpion's sting,   200
Scarce seen, but with fresh bitterness imbued;
And slight withal may be the things which bring
Back on the heart the weight which it would fling
Aside for ever: it may be a sound—
A tone of music,—summer's eve—or spring,   205
A flower—the wind—the ocean—which shall wound,
Striking the electric chain wherewith we are darkly bound;

24.

And how and why we know not, nor can trace
Home to its cloud this lightning of the mind,
But feel the shock renew'd, nor can efface   210
The blight and blackening which it leaves behind,
Which out of things familiar, undesign'd,
When least we deem of such, calls up to view
The spectres whom no exorcism can bind,
The cold—the changed—perchance the dead—anew,   215
The mourn'd, the loved, the lost—too many!—yet how few!

25.

But my soul wanders; I demand it back
To meditate amongst decay, and stand
A ruin amidst ruins; there to track
Fall'n states and buried greatness, o'er a land   220
Which *was* the mightiest in its old command,
And *is* the loveliest, and must ever be
The master-mould of Nature's heavenly hand,
Wherein were cast the heroic and the free,
The beautiful, the brave—the lords of earth and sea,   225

199 griefs subdued] ⟨things that were⟩ B   201 with fresh bitterness] ⟨bitter—and with woe⟩ B   204 Aside . . . sound] ⟨Away . . . tone⟩ B   205 A ⟨tone⟩ of Music;—⟨twilight even in Spring / Eventide in spring⟩ B   206 ⟨The / A calm sea shore⟩ A flower—⟨the Ocean⟩ the wind—the Ocean—⟨touch alone⟩ which ⟨thus⟩ shall wound B   207 wherewith] wherein B   209 Back to its cloud this lightning ⟨which hath flashed⟩ B   213 to view] ⟨again⟩ B   215 changed . . . anew] ⟨false . . . in vain⟩ B   216 loved] ⟨hated / betrothed⟩ B   217 I demand] ⟨and I will have⟩ B   218 amongst] among B   220 greatness] ⟨Empires⟩ B   224 heroic] ⟨conquering⟩ H

26.

The commonwealth of kings, the men of Rome!
And even since, and now, fair Italy!
Thou art the garden of the world, the home
Of all Art yields, and Nature can decree;
Even in thy desart, what is like to thee?   230
Thy very weeds are beautiful, thy waste
More rich than other climes' fertility;
Thy wreck a glory, and thy ruin graced
With an immaculate charm which can not be defaced.

27.

The Moon is up, and yet it is not night—   235
Sunset divides the sky with her—a sea
Of glory streams along the Alpine height
Of blue Friuli's mountains; Heaven is free
From clouds, but of all colours seems to be
Melted to one vast Iris of the West,   240
Where the Day joins the past Eternity;
While, on the other hand, meek Dian's crest
Floats through the azure air—an island of the blest!

28.

A single star is at her side, and reigns
With her o'er half the lovely heaven; but still   245
Yon sunny sea heaves brightly, and remains
Roll'd o'er the peak of the far Rhaetian hill,
As Day and Night contending were, until
Nature reclaim'd her order:—gently flows
The deep-dyed Brenta, where their hues instil   250
The odorous purple of a new-born rose,
Which streams upon her stream, and glass'd within it glows,

---

228 the home] and home *B, H, cor. in Proof B*   236 a] ⟨the⟩ *BA*   241 joins
the] ⟨mingles⟩ *BA*   242 crest] ⟨breast⟩ *BA*   246 Yon . . . heaves] ⟨That . . .
rolls⟩ *BA*   247 peak . . . hill] ⟨rock of the far distant⟩ hill *BA*   249 Nature
⟨proclaimed the victory, — ?⟩ reclaim'd *BA*   250 ⟨The Brenta at / like a mirror⟩ /
⟨The gentle Brenta where the / their reflected hues instil⟩ / The ⟨blended⟩ Brenta . . . instil
BA   251 purple] ⟨colour⟩ *BA*   252 Which ⟨as the⟩ streams upon her
stream—⟨and in its mirror glows⟩ *BA*   upon] ⟨along⟩ *H*

29.

Fill'd with the face of heaven, which, from afar,
Comes down upon the waters; all its hues,
From the rich sunset to the rising star,   255
Their magical variety diffuse:
And now they change; a paler shadow strews
Its mantle o'er the mountains; parting day
Dies like the dolphin, whom each pang imbues
With a new colour as it gasps away,   260
The last still loveliest, till—'tis gone—and all is gray.

30.

There is a tomb in Arqua;—rear'd in air,
Pillar'd in their sarcophagus, repose
The bones of Laura's lover: here repair
Many familiar with his well-sung woes,   265
The pilgrims of his genius. He arose
To raise a language, and his land reclaim
From the dull yoke of her barbaric foes:
Watering the tree which bears his lady's name
With his melodious tears, he gave himself to fame.   270

31.

They keep his dust in Arqua, where he died;
The mountain-village where his latter days
Went down the vale of years; and 'tis their pride—
An honest pride—and let it be their praise,
To offer to the passing stranger's gaze   275
His mansion and his sepulchre; both plain
And venerably simple, such as raise
A feeling more accordant with his strain
Than if a pyramid form'd his monumental fane.

255 sunset] ⟨twilight⟩ BA   261 ⟨And loveliest still⟩ BA   262 There is a tomb] ⟨I sit me down⟩ B   263 ⟨In its sarcophagus⟩ B   265 Many ⟨the⟩ familiar B   familiar with] ⟨the pilgrims of⟩ H   267 To . . . land] ⟨To raise his trampled Nation and⟩ B   268 ⟨With his melodious tears⟩ / ⟨Her tongue from desolation / language from the Goth⟩ B   276 sepulchre] monument B, cor. in H   278 ⟨A softer / kinder feeling of⟩ B   279 monumental] sepulchral B, cor. in H

32.

And the soft quiet hamlet where he dwelt   280
Is one of that complexion which seems made
For those who their mortality have felt,
And sought a refuge from their hopes decay'd
In the deep umbrage of a green hill's shade,
Which shows a distant prospect far away   285
Of busy cities, now in vain display'd,
For they can lure no further; and the ray
Of a bright sun can make sufficient holiday,

33.

Developing the mountains, leaves, and flowers,
And shining in the brawling brook, where-by,   290
Clear as its current, glide the sauntering hours
With a calm languor, which, though to the eye
Idlesse it seem, hath its morality.
If from society we learn to live,
'Tis solitude should teach us how to die;   295
It hath no flatterers; vanity can give
No hollow aid; alone—man with his God must strive:

34.

Or, it may be, with demons, who impair
The strength of better thoughts, and seek their prey
In melancholy bosoms, such as were ·   300
Of moody texture from their earliest day,
And loved to dwell in darkness and dismay,
Deeming themselves predestin'd to a doom
Which is not of the pangs that pass away;
Making the sun like blood, the earth a tomb,   305
The tomb a hell, and hell itself a murkier gloom.

35.

Ferrara! in thy wide and grass-grown streets,
Whose symmetry was not for solitude,

280 hamlet] ⟨village⟩ B   287 lure] ⟨tempt⟩ H   288 sun ⟨suffices⟩ can make B
291 ⟨The dreaming⟩ B   294 ⟨Society's the school which taught⟩ to live B   295 ⟨In⟩
Solitude ⟨we best may learn to die⟩ B   297 No ⟨aid⟩ hollow aid,—⟨the Soul must
unsupport⟩ alone ⟨the Soul with God must strive⟩ B   299 seek] ⟨make⟩ B   300 In]
⟨Of⟩ B   304 ⟨Which dies not nor can ever pass away⟩ B   306 hell . . . murkier
⟨life one universal⟩ B; hell a more infernal H *alternate reading*

There seems as 'twere a curse upon the seats
Of former sovereigns, and the antique brood   310
Of Este, which for many an age made good
Its strength within thy walls, and was of yore
Patron or tyrant, as the changing mood
Of petty power impell'd, of those who wore
The wreath which Dante's brow alone had worn before. 315

36.

And Tasso is their glory and their shame.
Hark to his strain! and then survey his cell!
And see how dearly earn'd Torquato's fame,
And where Alfonso bade his poet dwell:
The miserable despot could not quell   320
The insulted mind he sought to quench, and blend
With the surrounding maniacs, in the hell
Where he had plung'd it. Glory without end
Scatter'd the clouds away—and on that name attend

37.

The tears and praises of all time; while thine   325
Would rot in its oblivion—in the sink
Of worthless dust, which from thy boasted line
Is shaken into nothing; but the link
Thou formest in his fortunes bids us think
Of thy poor malice, naming thee with scorn—   330
Alfonso! how thy ducal pageants shrink
From thee! if in another station born,
Scarce fit to be the slave of him thou mad'st to mourn:

38.

Thou! form'd to eat, and be despis'd, and die,
Even as the beasts that perish, save that thou   335
Hadst a more splendid trough and wider sty:
He! with a glory round his furrow'd brow,

310 antique brood] ⟨guilty blood⟩ *B*   312 strength] ⟨praise⟩ *B*   313 or] ⟨and⟩ *B*
314 impell'd . . . wore] ⟨directed . . . bore⟩ *B*   317 Hark . . . strain] ⟨Go—hear his
lyre⟩ *B*   318 Torquato's] ⟨his useless⟩ *B*   324 that] ⟨his⟩ *B*   326 sink]
⟨crowd⟩ *B*   328 but] ⟨save⟩ *B*   329 ⟨That name⟩ *B*   331 how] ⟨see⟩ *B*
332 ⟨And thou for no one useful purpose born⟩ *B*   333 Scarce . . . slave] ⟨Had scarcely /
Wert made⟩ to be the groom *B*   334 be despis'd] ⟨propagate⟩ *B*   337 ⟨And⟩
He *B*

Which emanated then, and dazzles now
In face of all his foes, the Cruscan quire;
And Boileau, whose rash envy could allow   340
No strain which shamed his country's creaking lyre,
That whetstone of the teeth—monotony in wire!

39.

Peace to Torquato's injur'd shade! 'twas his
In life and death to be the mark where Wrong
Aim'd with her poison'd arrows; but to miss.   345
Oh, victor unsurpass'd in modern song!
Each year brings forth its millions; but how long
The tide of generations shall roll on,
And not the whole combin'd and countless throng
Compose a mind like thine? though all in one   350
Condens'd their scatter'd rays, they would not form a sun.

40.

Great as thou art, yet paralleled by those,
Thy countrymen, before thee born to shine,
The Bards of Hell and Chivalry: first rose
The Tuscan father's comedy divine;   355
Then, not unequal to the Florentine,
The southern Scott, the minstrel who call'd forth
A new creation with his magic line,
And, like the Ariosto of the North,
Sang ladye-love and war, romance and knightly worth.   360

41.

The lightning rent from Ariosto's bust
The iron crown of laurel's mimic'd leaves;
Nor was the ominous element unjust,
For the true laurel-wreath which Glory weaves

339 quire] ⟨crew / host⟩ B   340 And ⟨baffled Gaul whose rancour⟩ could
allow B   341 ⟨No name which shamed his natio / country's paltry few⟩ B   which]
⟨that⟩ B, H   342 ⟨Who torture into / Who ape the / scrape the measured lyre of
their own tuneless⟩ B   That . . . of] ⟨Which grates upon⟩ B   343 ⟨Torquato!⟩ B
346 victor . . . in] ⟨ever / never equalled Chief / Lord of⟩ B   348 on] ⟨down /
oer⟩ B   349 ⟨Without a mind like thine⟩ B   350 ⟨Could mount into a mind
like thine⟩ B   Compose] ⟨Could make⟩ B   351 a] the B; a / the H alternate readings

Is of the tree no bolt of thunder cleaves,   365
And the false semblance but disgraced his brow;
Yet still, if fondly Superstition grieves,
Know, that the lightning sanctifies below
Whate'er it strikes;—yon head is doubly sacred now.

42.

Italia! oh Italia! thou who hast   370
The fatal gift of beauty, which became
A funeral dower of present woes and past,
On thy sweet brow is sorrow plough'd by shame,
And annals graved in characters of flame.
Oh God! that thou wert in thy nakedness   375
Less lovely or more powerful, and could'st claim
Thy right, and awe the robbers back, who press
To shed thy blood, and drink the tears of thy distress;

43.

Then might'st thou more appal; or, less desired,
Be homely and be peaceful, undeplored   380
For thy destructive charms; then, still untired,
Would not be seen the armed torrents pour'd
Down the deep Alps; nor would the hostile horde
Of many-nation'd spoilers from the Po
Quaff blood and water; nor the stranger's sword   385
Be thy sad weapon of defence, and so,
Victor or vanquish'd, thou the slave of friend or foe.

44.

Wandering in youth, I traced the path of him,
The Roman friend of Rome's least-mortal mind,
The friend of Tully: as my bark did skim   390
The bright blue waters with a fanning wind,

---

373 And on thy ⟨sweet⟩ brow ⟨with brands of⟩ in characters of flame *B, cancelled*
374 ⟨To write the words of sorrow and of shame⟩ *B*   And . . . graved] ⟨Are annals cut⟩ *B*
376 powerful, and could'st] ⟨strong and thus / thereby⟩ *B*   377 right] rights *B*
378 ⟨To the divided spoil⟩ *B* ⟨To riot in thy tears⟩ / To ⟨drink⟩ shed *B*   380 undeplored]
⟨unbetrayed⟩ *B*   381 For thy destructive] ⟨To death by thy vain⟩ *B*   384 from
the Po] ⟨of the foe⟩ *B*   385 ⟨With blood and water quench their thirst⟩ *B*   386 sad]
⟨sole⟩ *B*   387 thou] ⟨still⟩ *B*   388 ⟨In my youth I pursued the voyage of him⟩ *B*
Wandering in youth] ⟨In my wandering youth⟩ *B*   389 least-] ⟨most⟩ *B*   391 bright]
⟨active⟩ *B*

Came Megara before me, and behind
Aegina lay, Piraeus on the right,
And Corinth on the left; I lay reclined
Along the prow, and saw all these unite   395
In ruin, even as he had seen the desolate sight;

45.

For Time hath not rebuilt them, but uprear'd
Barbaric dwellings on their shattered site,
Which only make more mourn'd and more endear'd
The few last rays of their far-scattered light,   400
And the crush'd relics of their vanish'd might.
The Roman saw these tombs in his own age,
These sepulchres of cities, which excite
Sad wonder, and his yet surviving page
The moral lesson bears, drawn from such pilgrimage.   405

46.

That page is now before me, and on mine
His country's ruin added to the mass
Of perish'd states he mourn'd in their decline,
And I in desolation: all that *was*
Of then destruction *is*; and now, alas!   410
Rome—Rome imperial, bows her to the storm,
In the same dust and blackness, and we pass
The skeleton of her Titanic form,
Wrecks of another world, whose ashes still are warm.

47.

Yet, Italy! through every other land   415
Thy wrongs should ring, and shall, from side to side;
Mother of Arts! as once of arms; thy hand
Was then our guardian, and is still our guide;

397 ⟨Ages ha⟩ For . . . but ⟨hath reared⟩ B   399 Which ⟨but the more recall how⟩
only ⟨under more⟩ make B   400 last rays] ⟨frail relics⟩ B   401 ⟨The crumbling⟩
relics of their ⟨favoured⟩ might B   402 tombs] ⟨things / spots⟩ B   403 sepulchres]
⟨carcases⟩ B   405 such] ⟨this / his⟩ B   406 on] ⟨to⟩ B   407 ⟨I add his
Country's ruin to the mass⟩ B   408 perish'd . . . mourn'd] ⟨broken . . . saw⟩ B
409 And I in ⟨death⟩ desolation B   411 bows . . . storm] ⟨lays her giant length /
form⟩ / ⟨lays her with the worm⟩ B   412 blackness] ⟨ashes⟩ B   413 ⟨The
skeleton of her titanic strength / oer which the lazy worm⟩ B   414 ⟨Preys where
once⟩ / ⟨Which overlooked / overspread the earth⟩ / ⟨Far scatt / Shivered and spread⟩ B
415 Yet] Oh BA

Parent of our Religion! whom the wide
Nations have knelt to for the keys of heaven!   420
Europe, repentant of her parricide,
    Shall yet redeem thee, and, all backward driven,
Roll the barbarian tide, and sue to be forgiven.

48.

But Arno wins us to the fair white walls,
Where the Etrurian Athens claims and keeps   425
A softer feeling for her fairy halls.
    Girt by her theatre of hills, she reaps
Her corn, and wine, and oil, and Plenty leaps
To laughing life, with her redundant horn.
    Along the banks where smiling Arno sweeps   430
Was modern Luxury of Commerce born,
And buried Learning rose, redeem'd to a new morn.

49.

There, too, the Goddess loves in stone, and fills
The air around with beauty; we inhale
The ambrosial aspect, which, beheld, instils   435
    Part of its immortality; the veil
Of heaven is half undrawn; within the pale
We stand, and in that form and face behold
    What Mind can make, when Nature's self would fail;
And to the fond idolaters of old   440
Envy the innate flash which such a soul could mould:

50.

We gaze and turn away, and know not where,
Dazzled and drunk with beauty, till the heart
Reels with its fulness; there—for ever there—
    Chain'd to the chariot of triumphal Art,   445

---

424 wins us to] ⟨winds gliding through⟩ *B*   425 Where] ⟨Of⟩ *B*   426 for
her ⟨youth⟩ fairy *B*   428 and Plenty] ⟨where⟩ plenty *B*   431 ⟨And modern⟩ /
⟨Where luxury who would / might willingly be born⟩ *B*   432 ⟨And buried learning
broke forth to a fresher morn⟩ *B*   433 There, too] ⟨And there⟩ *B*   loves in] breathes
in ⟩ loves from / in *B*; loves from / in *H alternate readings*   434 we inhale] ⟨all / and
we draw⟩ *B*   435 ⟨As from a fountain which / of the immortal hills⟩ *B*   439 would]
⟨could⟩ *B*   440 to] ⟨in⟩ *B*   441 flash . . . soul] ⟨sense . . . form⟩ *B*   442 ⟨From
her was dr⟩ *B*   turn] ⟨pass⟩ *B*   443 For we are drunk with beauty—and the heart
B, cor. in H   444 there . . . there] ⟨the enchanted air⟩ *B*

We stand as captives, and would not depart.
Away!—there need no words, nor terms precise,
The paltry jargon of the marble mart,
Where Pedantry gulls Folly—we have eyes:
Blood—pulse—and breast, confirm the Dardan Shepherd's
   prize.   450

51.

Appear'dst thou not to Paris in this guise?
Or to more deeply blest Anchises? or,
In all thy perfect goddess-ship, when lies
Before thee thy own vanquish'd Lord of War?
And gazing in thy face as toward a star,   455
Laid on thy lap, his eyes to thee upturn,
Feeding on thy sweet cheek! while thy lips are
With lava kisses melting while they burn,
Showered on his eyelids, brow, and mouth, as from an urn!

52.

Glowing, and circumfused in speechless love,   460
Their full divinity inadequate
That feeling to express, or to improve,
The gods become as mortals, and man's fate
Has moments like their brightest; but the weight
Of earth recoils upon us;—let it go!   465
We can recal such visions, and create,
From what has been, or might be, things which grow
Into thy statue's form, and look like gods below.

53.

I leave to learned fingers, and wise hands,
The artist and his ape, to teach and tell   470

447 words, nor terms] ⟨terms nor words⟩ B   450 breast, confirm] ⟨bosom bestow⟩ B
Dardan] Idan B alternate reading   451 ⟨Didst thou not ? to him appear, or to that /
him⟩ BA Appear'dst thou not] Seemedst thou not ⟨thus⟩ BA; Seemedst thou not /
Appear'dst thou not / Didst thou not seem H alternate readings   452 ⟨Still happier
Pastor⟩ BA   454 ⟨Beside thee thy ?⟩ BA   455 ⟨Oh ? upon thy lips⟩ BA
456 his . . . upturn] ⟨with upward glance his eyes⟩ BA   457 ⟨Feed on thy sweet
sweet cheek & thee in turn⟩ BA   458 ⟨With kisses which as lava melt and burn⟩ BA
459 ⟨Showerest upon his brow & eyes & mouth as from⟩ BA   460 circumfused] ⟨all
diffused⟩ BA   461 Their full] ⟨Even their⟩ BA   463 man's] our BA   465 Of
earth ⟨& heaven⟩ recoils BA   go] ⟨pass⟩ BA   466 ⟨We can remember such an
hour⟩ BA   visions] ⟨moments⟩ BA   467 ⟨From such an hour that might have been
or was⟩ / ⟨Such bubbles / Thoughts like the statue's form / From something or from nothing
things which glow⟩ BA

How well his connoisseurship understands
The graceful bend, and the voluptuous swell:
Let these describe the undescribable:
I would not their vile breath should crisp the stream
Wherein that image shall for ever dwell;   475
The unruffled mirror of the loveliest dream
That ever left the sky on the deep soul to beam.

54.

In Santa Croce's holy precincts lie
Ashes which make it holier, dust which is
Even in itself an immortality,   480
Though there were nothing save the past, and this,
The particle of those sublimities
Which have relaps'd to chaos:—here repose
Angelo's, Alfieri's bones, and his,
The starry Galileo, with his woes;   485
Here Machiavelli's earth, return'd to whence it rose.

55.

These are four minds, which, like the elements,
Might furnish forth creation:—Italy!
Time, which hath wrong'd thee with ten thousand rents
Of thine imperial garment, shall deny,   490
And hath denied, to every other sky,
Spirits which soar from ruin:—thy decay
Is still impregnate with divinity,
Which gilds it with revivifying ray;
Such as the great of yore, Canova is to-day.   495

56.

But where repose the all Etruscan three—
Dante, and Petrarch, and, scarce less than they,

471 his] his ⟨innate⟩ B   474 their . . . breath] ⟨that a word⟩ B   479 it . . . which is] them . . . ⟨is here⟩ BA   481 ⟨Angelo—Alfieri / There Galileo / Though nothing save the past and this⟩ Even were there nothing save the past and this BA 482 The particle] The ⟨elements of Mind⟩ particles BA   486 Here] ⟨And⟩ H 487 These] ⟨Here⟩ H   488 forth creation] ⟨out⟩ a universe BA; forth ⟨a universe⟩ H   490 Of . . . garment] ⟨And ruins of thy beauty⟩ / Of . . . garments BA 492 ⟨The⟩ Spirits which ⟨spring⟩ / soar like thine;—⟨in⟩ from thy decay BA, cor. in H 493 Still springs some ⟨work⟩ / son of thy divinity BA, cor. in H   494 ⟨Which gilds thy ruins with reviving ray⟩ BA   Which] ⟨And⟩ H   495 And what there was of yore—Canova is today. BA, cor. in H   496 the all] the ⟨thrice⟩ BA

The Bard of Prose, creative spirit! he
Of the Hundred Tales of love—where did they lay
Their bones, distinguish'd from our common clay   500
In death as life? Are they resolv'd to dust,
And have their country's marbles nought to say?
Could not her quarries furnish forth one bust?
Did they not to her breast their filial earth entrust?

57.

Ungrateful Florence! Dante sleeps afar,   505
Like Scipio, buried by the upbraiding shore;
Thy factions, in their worse than civil war,
Proscribed the bard whose name for evermore
Their children's children would in vain adore
With the remorse of ages; and the crown   510
Which Petrarch's laureate brow supremely wore,
Upon a far and foreign soil had grown,
His life, his fame, his grave, though rifled—not thine own.

58.

Boccaccio to his parent earth bequeathed
His dust,—and lies it not her Great among,   515
With many a sweet and solemn requiem breath'd
O'er him who form'd the Tuscan's siren tongue?
That music in itself, whose sounds are song,
The poetry of speech? No;—even his tomb
Uptorn, must bear the hyaena bigot's wrong,   520
No more amidst the meaner dead find room,
Nor claim a passing sigh, because it told for *whom*!

498 ⟨Their great Contemporary⟩ spirit—he *BA*   499 Of . . . love] ⟨Of Love's
hundred tales⟩ *BA*   506 upbraiding] ⟨sounding⟩ / sea-beat *BA*   507 in their]
⟨with⟩ thy *BA*   510 crown] ⟨Fame⟩ *BA*   511 ⟨Of Petrarch grew⟩ *BA*   laureate
brow supremely] ⟨brow in other ?⟩ *BA*   513 life] ⟨birth⟩ *BA*   514 earth] ⟨soil⟩ *BA*
515–22   The dust derived from thence—doth it not lie
                      With many a sweet and solemn requiem breathed
                      Oer him who formed the tongue of Italy
                      That music in itself whose harmony
                      Asks for no tune to make it song;—No—torn
                      From earth—and scattered while the silent sky
                      Hushed its indignant winds—with quiet scorn
                      The Hyaena bigots thus forbade a World to mourne. *BA, cor. in H*
518 sounds are song] ⟨song / note to aid its sound⟩ tune is song *BA*   519–20 even . . .
wrong] ⟨twas uptorn / Insulted while gazing on that coward's wrong⟩ *H*   522 ⟨Of notes
like this / Human hyaenas⟩ *BA*

59.

And Santa Croce wants their mighty dust;
Yet for this want more noted, as of yore
The Caesar's pageant, shorn of Brutus' bust,   525
Did but of Rome's best Son remind her more:
Happier Ravenna! on thy hoary shore,
Fortress of falling empire! honoured sleeps
The immortal exile;—Arqua, too, her store
Of tuneful relics proudly claims and keeps,   530
While Florence vainly begs her banish'd dead and weeps.

60.

What is her pyramid of precious stones?
Of porphyry, jasper, agate, and all hues
Of gem and marble, to encrust the bones
Of merchant-dukes? the momentary dews   535
Which, sparkling to the twilight stars, infuse
Freshness in the green turf that wraps the dead,
Whose names are mausoleums of the Muse,
Are gently prest with far more reverent tread
Than ever paced the slab which paves the princely head. 540

61.

There be more things to greet the heart and eyes
In Arno's dome of Art's most princely shrine,
Where Sculpture with her rainbow sister vies;
There be more marvels yet—but not for mine;
For I have been accustomed to entwine   545
My thoughts with Nature rather in the fields,
Than Art in galleries: though a work divine
Calls for my spirit's homage, yet it yields
Less than it feels, because the weapon which it wields

524 ⟨The elder born / ⁇ eldest—brightest⟩ BA   525 pageant] ⟨triumph⟩ BA
528 Fortress of falling] ⟨Shelter of exiled⟩ BA   529 Arqua, too] ⟨happy⟩ Arqua
⟨still⟩ BA   531 ⟨While blushing Florence woos the dead in / While Florence from
afar endures her loss & weeps⟩ BA   vainly begs] begs in vain BA   532 her] ⟨thy⟩ BA
536 Which sparkle in the twilight and infuse BA, cor. in H   537 that] ⟨which⟩ H
540 paves the] paves a BA   541–2 ⟨Oh that community which is the curse | Of travel
—where on either hand⟩ B   542 Arno's dome of] these abodes of B   543 rainbow]
⟨rosy⟩ B   548 for . . . yet] ⟨up my voice for homage and⟩ B   549 weapon which]
⟨weapon which⟩ / instrument B

62.

Is of another temper, and I roam   550
By Thrasimene's lake, in the defiles
Fatal to Roman rashness, more at home;
For there the Carthaginian's warlike wiles
Come back before me, as his skill beguiles
The host between the mountains and the shore,   555
Where Courage falls in her despairing files,
And torrents, swoln to rivers with their gore,
Reek through the sultry plain, with legions scatter'd o'er,

63.

Like to a forest fell'd by mountain winds;
And such the storm of battle on this day,   560
And such the phrenzy, whose convulsion blinds
To all save carnage, that, beneath the fray,
An earthquake reel'd unheededly away!
None felt stern Nature rocking at his feet,
And yawning forth a grave for those who lay   565
Upon their bucklers for a winding sheet;
Such is the absorbing hate when warring nations meet!

64.

The Earth to them was as a rolling bark
Which bore them to Eternity; they saw
The Ocean round, but had no time to mark   570
The motions of their vessel; Nature's law,
In them suspended, reck'd not of the awe
Which reigns when mountains tremble, and the birds
Plunge in the clouds for refuge and withdraw
From their down-toppling nests; and bellowing herds 575
Stumble o'er heaving plains, and man's dread hath no words.

550 temper . . . roam] order . . . ⟨stand⟩ B, H, cor. in Proof B   554 as his skill] as ⟨he will⟩ his skill B   556 falls in her despairing] ⟨perished in unyielding⟩ B   558 through] in H, cor. in Proof B   legions] ⟨carnage⟩ B   562 beneath] ⟨amidst / above⟩ B 564 ⟨And⟩ none B   565 ⟨To die as yawning⟩ B   567 ⟨The Quick⟩ B   when . . . nations] ⟨of nations when they⟩ B   574 Fly to the clouds for refuge and withdraw B, H, cor. in Proofs A, B   575 From their unsteady nests the ⟨scared / roaring⟩ herds B, cor. in H

65.

Far other scene is Thrasimene now;
Her lake a sheet of silver, and her plain
Rent by no ravage save the gentle plough;
Her aged trees rise thick as once the slain   580
Lay where their roots are; but a brook hath ta'en—
A little rill of scanty stream and bed—
A name of blood from that day's sanguine rain;
And Sanguinetto tells ye where the dead
Made the earth wet, and turn'd the unwilling waters red. 585

66.

But thou, Clitumnus! in thy sweetest wave
Of the most living crystal that was e'er
The haunt of river nymph, to gaze and lave
Her limbs where nothing hid them, thou dost rear
Thy grassy banks whereon the milk-white steer   590
Grazes; the purest god of gentle waters!
And most serene of aspect, and most clear;
Surely that stream was unprofaned by slaughters—
A mirror and a bath for Beauty's youngest daughters!

67.

And on thy happy shore a temple still,   595
Of small and delicate proportion, keeps,
Upon a mild declivity of hill,
Its memory of thee; beneath it sweeps
Thy current's calmness; oft from out it leaps
The finny darter with the glittering scales,   600
Who dwells and revels in thy glassy deeps;
While, chance, some scatter'd water-lily sails
Down where the shallower wave still tells its bubbling tales.

576 Stumble o'er heaving plains] Stumble oer heaving ⟨fields⟩ B ⟨Roam oer the heaving
plains⟩ H   577 is] ⟨was⟩ B   580 Her] ⟨The⟩ H   rise] ⟨lay⟩ B   581 are;
but] are ⟨twined⟩ B   583 sanguine] crimson B   585 Made ⟨fat⟩ the earth
⟨with⟩ wet B   586 sweetest] ⟨sweet clear⟩ B   588 river] ⟨water⟩ B   589 dost
rear] ⟨didst neer⟩ B   590 whereon] ⟨where graze⟩ B   591 gentle] ⟨quiet⟩ B
596 keeps] ⟨beams⟩ B   597 mild] ⟨mild⟩ / green B   602–3 ⟨There is a course
where lover's evening tales | Should murmur to thy stream⟩ B   603 where . . . still]
⟨with the sparkling wave which⟩ B

68.

Pass not unblest the Genius of the place!
If through the air a zephyr more serene   605
Win to the brow, 'tis his; and if ye trace
Along his margin a more eloquent green,
If on the heart the freshness of the scene
Sprinkle its coolness, and from the dry dust
Of weary life a moment lave it clean   610
With Nature's baptism,—'tis to him ye must
Pay orisons for this suspension of disgust.

69.

The roar of waters!—from the headlong height
Velino cleaves the wave-worn precipice;
The fall of waters! rapid as the light   615
The flashing mass foams shaking the abyss;
The hell of waters! where they howl and hiss,
And boil in endless torture; while the sweat
Of their great agony, wrung out from this
Their Phlegethon, curls round the rocks of jet   620
That gird the gulf around, in pitiless horror set,

70.

And mounts in spray the skies, and thence again
Returns in an unceasing shower, which round,
With its unemptied cloud of gentle rain,
Is an eternal April to the ground,   625
Making it all one emerald:—how profound
The gulf! and how the giant element
From rock to rock leaps with delirious bound,
Crushing the cliffs, which, downward worn and rent
With his fierce footsteps, yield in chasms a fearful vent   630

---

610 lave] ⟨make⟩ B   614 Velino ⟨cleaves the mountains like / with his voice / the
sound⟩ B   616 flashing . . . shaking] ⟨foaming mass whirls⟩ into B; flashing mass
foams into H, cor. in Proof B   617 where they howl] ⟨whence they roar⟩ B   618 in
endless . . . while] ⟨as torn in . . . and⟩ B   620 curls round] ⟨ascends the⟩ B
621 the gulf] ⟨their gulphs⟩ B   623 an unceasing] ⟨a perpetual⟩ B   624 ⟨The
eternal April of a⟩ B   unempted cloud] ⟨still hurried⟩ B   626 all one] as an B;
H alternate reading   627 gulf] ⟨depth⟩ B   628 Leaps on from rock to rock—⟨and
mound to mound⟩ with mighty bound B   630 footsteps ⟨lie in rugged⟩ yield B

71.

To the broad column which rolls on, and shows
More like the fountain of an infant sea
Torn from the womb of mountains by the throes
Of a new world, than only thus to be
Parent of rivers, which flow gushingly,   635
With many windings, through the vale:—Look back!
Lo! where it comes like an eternity,
As if to sweep down all things in its track,
Charming the eye with dread,—a matchless cataract,

72.

Horribly beautiful! but on the verge,   640
From side to side, beneath the glittering morn,
An Iris sits, amidst the infernal surge,
Like Hope upon a death-bed, and, unworn
Its steady dyes, while all around is torn
By the distracted waters, bears serene   645
Its brilliant hues with all their beams unshorn:
Resembling, 'mid the torture of the scene,
Love watching Madness with unalterable mien.

73.

Once more upon the woody Apennine,
The infant Alps, which—had I not before   650
Gazed on their mightier parents, where the pine
Sits on more shaggy summits, and where roar
The thundering lauwine—might be worshipp'd more;
But I have seen the soaring Jungfrau rear
Her never-trodden snow, and seen the hoar   655
Glaciers of bleak Mont-Blanc both far and near,
And in Chimari heard the thunder-hills of fear,

631 rolls . . . shows] ⟨goes roaring on⟩ B   633 womb] heart / womb B   635 flow]
⟨go⟩ B   637 Lo! where] ⟨Behind⟩ B   638 sweep down] ⟨cover⟩ B   639 ⟨The
eye will reel with⟩ B   Charming . . . dread] ⟨A beautiful dismay⟩ B   641 side to]
⟨either⟩ B   645 bears serene] ⟨with a⟩ bears ⟨aloft⟩ B   646 brilliant] ⟨many⟩ B
647 ⟨Preserving an ascendancy⟩ B   ⟨Looking amidst the terrors of⟩ the scene B
648 Love watching ⟨over⟩ Madness with ⟨unaltered⟩ mien B   650 before] ⟨so long⟩ B
652 ⟨Dares not ascend the summit / Clothes a more rocky summit⟩ B   654 soaring
Jungfrau] virgin ⟨mountain⟩ B; virgin Jungfrau H   656 ⟨Baldness of the white moun-
tain⟩ B   bleak] ⟨far⟩ B   657 ⟨And stood / midst Chimari stood the thunder hills
of fear⟩ B

74.

Th' Acroceraunian mountains of old name
And on Parnassus seen the eagles fly
Like spirits of the spot, as 'twere for fame,   660
For still they soared unutterably high:
I've look'd on Ida with a Trojan's eye;
Athos, Olympus, Aetna, Atlas, made
These hills seem things of lesser dignity,
All, save the lone Soracte's height, displayed   665
Not *now* in snow, which asks the lyric Roman's aid

75.

For our remembrance, and from out the plain
Heaves like a long-swept wave about to break,
And on the curl hangs pausing: not in vain
May he, who will, his recollections rake   670
And quote in classic raptures, and awake
The hills with Latian echoes; I abhorr'd
Too much, to conquer for the poet's sake,
The drill'd dull lesson, forced down word by word
In my repugnant youth, with pleasure to record   675

76.

Aught that recals the daily drug which turn'd
My sickening memory; and, though Time hath taught
My mind to meditate what then it learn'd,
Yet such the fix'd inveteracy wrought
By the impatience of my early thought,   680
That, with the freshness wearing out before
My mind could relish what it might have sought,
If free to choose, I cannot now restore
Its health; but what it then detested, still abhor.

659 seen] ⟨saw⟩ B   660 spot] place B   662 I've] ⟨And⟩ B   663 ⟨And Atlas
and Olympus—and to me / beheld⟩ B Athos—Olympus—⟨Atlas—all which have⟩ / Afric's
Atlas made B   664 ⟨These hills are not the first of / in majesty⟩ B   665 ⟨None⟩
All B   666 Not *now*] ⟨But not⟩ B   668 Heaves like a ⟨wave upon the⟩ long B
671 And ⟨shall⟩ quote B   673 conquer] ⟨ponder⟩ B   674 dull lesson] ⟨command⟩ B
676 which turn'd] ⟨that gorged⟩ B   678 meditate] ⟨taste the⟩ / meditate / analyse B
679 the . . . inveteracy] ⟨my⟩ / the inveterate impression B   681 wearing out] being
gone B, H, cor. in Proof B   684 it then detested] ⟨I⟩ then abhorred—must B

77.

Then farewell, Horace; whom I hated so,   685
Not for thy faults, but mine; it is a curse
To understand, not feel thy lyric flow,
To comprehend, but never love thy verse,
Although no deeper Moralist rehearse
Our little life, nor Bard prescribe his art,   690
Nor livelier Satirist the conscience pierce,
    Awakening without wounding the touch'd heart,
Yet fare thee well—upon Soracte's ridge we part.

78.

Oh Rome! my country! city of the soul!
The orphans of the heart must turn to thee,   695
Lone mother of dead empires! and controul
In their shut breasts their petty misery.
What are our woes and sufferance? Come and see
The cypress, hear the owl, and plod your way
O'er steps of broken thrones and temples, Ye!   700
    Whose agonies are evils of a day—
A world is at our feet as fragile as our clay.

79.

The Niobe of nations! there she stands,
Childless and crownless, in her voiceless woe;
An empty urn within her withered hands,   705
Whose holy dust was scatter'd long ago;
The Scipios' tomb contains no ashes now;
The very sepulchres lie tenantless
Of their heroic dwellers: dost thou flow,
    Old Tiber! through a marble wilderness?   710
Rise, with thy yellow waves, and mantle her distress!

685 so] ⟨thus⟩ B   686 a] ⟨my⟩ B   689 deeper] ⟨nobler⟩ B   692 without]
but not B   693 fare thee well] ⟨farewell then⟩ B   696 ⟨Whence Glory Power
Mighty Majesty⟩ / ⟨What are the petty woes we would condole⟩ B   697 ⟨With one
another⟩ B   699 hear the] ⟨and look the⟩ B   702 our . . . our] ⟨thy . . . thy⟩ B
704 voiceless woe] ⟨human age⟩ / tearless ⟨trance⟩ B; ⟨tearless / withered⟩ woe H
706 Whose] ⟨dust as her⟩ holy B   708 lie tenantless] ⟨give up the dead⟩ B
711 ⟨Watering⟩ B

80.

The Goth, the Christian, Time, War, Flood, and Fire,
Have dealt upon the seven-hill'd city's pride;
She saw her glories star by star expire,
And up the steep barbarian monarchs ride,   715
Where the car climb'd the capitol; far and wide
Temple and tower went down, nor left a site:—
Chaos of ruins! who shall trace the void,
O'er the dim fragments cast a lunar light,
And say, 'here was, or is', where all is doubly night?   720

81.

The double night of ages, and of her,
Night's daughter, Ignorance, hath wrapt and wrap
All round us; we but feel our way to err:
The ocean hath his chart, the stars their map,
And Knowledge spreads them on her ample lap;   725
But Rome is as the desart, where we steer
Stumbling o'er recollections; now we clap
Our hands, and cry 'Eureka!' it is clear—
When but some false mirage of ruin rises near.

82.

Alas! the lofty city! and alas!   730
The trebly hundred triumphs! and the day
When Brutus made the dagger's edge surpass
The conqueror's sword in bearing fame away!
Alas, for Tully's voice, and Virgil's lay,
And Livy's pictur'd page!—but these shall be   735
Her resurrection; all beside—decay.
Alas, for Earth, for never shall we see
That brightness in her eye she bore when Rome was free!

714 star by star] one by one *BA*   716 climb'd] rolled *BA*   717 nor left
⟨behind⟩ *BA*   718 ⟨Vestige of ruin / Their / A vestige white and⟩ *BA*   trace] ⟨fill⟩
BA   719-20 ⟨The / And / Redecorate the fragments; fill the place | Of levelled fanes
—or say⟩ *BA*   720 is doubly] ⟨around is⟩ *BA*   721 ages] Ruin *BA, cor. in H*
722 hath . . . wrapt] Alas! has wrapt *BA*   723 we . . . way] ⟨and we wander but⟩ *BA*
724 ⟨Alas! the sacred city⟩ *BA*   725 ⟨The Earth⟩ *BA*   726 as] ⟨but⟩ *BA*
728 clear] ⟨here⟩ *BA*   730 lofty] ⟨glorious⟩ *BA*   732 made the ⟨dagger holy⟩
dagger's *BA*   733 conqueror's] ⟨warrior's⟩ *BA*   734 Virgil's lay] ⟨Trajan's
sway⟩ / Titus' sway *BA*   735 pictur'd] ⟨sounding⟩ *H*   ⟨The Consular⟩ And Virgil's
verse—the first and last ⟨may / shall⟩ must be *BA*   737 we] ⟨she⟩ *BA*   738 ⟨A
second Rome⟩ *BA*   That] ⟨Such⟩ *H*

83.

Oh thou, whose chariot roll'd on Fortune's wheel,
Triumphant Sylla! Thou, who didst subdue   740
Thy country's foes ere thou would pause to feel
The wrath of thy own wrongs, or reap the due
Of hoarded vengeance till thine eagles flew
O'er prostrate Asia;—thou, who with thy frown
Annihilated senates—Roman, too,   745
With all thy vices, for thou didst lay down
With an atoning smile a more than earthly crown—

84.

The dictatorial wreath,—couldst thou divine
To what would one day dwindle that which made
Thee more than mortal? and that so supine   750
By aught than Romans Rome should thus be laid?
She who was named Eternal, and array'd
Her warriors but to conquer—she who veil'd
Earth with her haughty shadow, and display'd,
Until the o'er-canopied horizon fail'd,   755
Her rushing wings—Oh! she who was Almighty hail'd!

85.

Sylla was first of victors; but our own
The sagest of usurpers, Cromwell; he
Too swept off senates while he hewed the throne
Down to a block—immortal rebel! See   760
What crimes it costs to be a moment free
And famous through all ages! but beneath
His fate the moral lurks of destiny;

741 wouldst *1831*, *1832*, *C*, *More* would *all MSS.*, *proofs, and CHP IV–1829*
742 reap] pour *B*   746 lay] ⟨throw⟩ *B*   748 wreath] ⟨Laurel⟩ *B*   750 so
supine] ⟨how supine⟩ *B*   751 ⟨Into such dust deserted Rome would fade⟩ / ⟨In self-
woven sackcloth Rome shouldst be laid⟩ *B*   753 veil'd] ⟨hid⟩ *B*   754 ⟨The Earth
beneath / within her shadow & displayed⟩ *B*   755 ⟨Her wings as with the horizon
& was hailed / Her wings until oerspread horizons failed⟩ *B*   756 ⟨The rushing
of her wings & was Almighty hailed⟩ *B*   757 ⟨First ?⟩ Sylla supreme of ⟨mortals /
villains⟩ / victors save our own *BA*   758 sagest] ablest *BA*   759 Too . . .
senates] Who ⟨by⟩ swept ⟨down⟩ / off Senates *BA*   760 ⟨Into a block of leaving⟩ *BA*
block] ⟨scaffold⟩ *BA*   rebel] Villain *BA*, *cor. in H*   762 ⟨And glorious through
immortal ages⟩ *BA*   but beneath] ⟨while our faith⟩ *BA*   763 ⟨May through this
mortal ? to destiny⟩ *BA*

His day of double victory and death
Beheld him win two realms, and, happier, yield his breath. 765

86.

The third of the same moon whose former course
Had all but crown'd him, on the selfsame day
Deposed him gently from his throne of force,
And laid him with the earth's preceding clay.
And show'd not Fortune thus how fame and sway,   770
And all we deem delightful, and consume
Our souls to compass through each arduous way,
Are in her eyes less happy than the tomb?
Were they but so in man's, how different were his doom!

87.

And thou, dread statue! yet existent in   775
The austerest form of naked majesty,
Thou who beheldest, 'mid the assassins' din,
At thy bath'd base the bloody Caesar lie,
Folding his robe in dying dignity,
An offering to thine altar from the queen   780
Of gods and men, great Nemesis! did he die,
And thou, too, perish, Pompey? have ye been
Victors of countless kings, or puppets of a scene?

88.

And thou, the thunder-stricken nurse of Rome!
She-wolf! whose brazen-imaged dugs impart   785
The milk of conquest yet within the dome
Where, as a monument of antique art,
Thou standest:—Mother of the mighty heart,
Which the great founder suck'd from thy wild teat,
Scorch'd by the Roman Jove's etherial dart,   790
And thy limbs black with lightning—dost thou yet
Guard thine immortal cubs, nor thy fond charge forget?

764 ⟨Which shows in him the happiness of death⟩ BA   765 ⟨Worcester—Dunbar
—⟩ BA   two realms] ⟨the world⟩ BA   766 former] ⟨forward⟩ BA   768 ⟨Gently⟩
Deposed BA   770 fame] ⟨power⟩ BA   772 compass . . . arduous] ⟨gain / seek⟩
compass ⟨every wicked⟩ BA   774 Were . . . so] ⟨Would⟩ Were ⟨it⟩ but so BA   man's
. . . his] ⟨our's . . . our⟩ BA   776 ⟨Austerest majesty⟩ B   777 'mid] 'midst B
785 dugs] ⟨teats / breasts⟩ B   787 as] ⟨thou / in⟩ B   789 Which ⟨great from⟩ the
great . . . ⟨breast⟩ / teat B   791 dost thou yet] ⟨thou dost rest / yet⟩ B   792 ⟨Thy
foster-children⟩ B

89.

Thou dost;—but all thy foster-babes are dead—
The men of iron; and the world hath rear'd
Cities from out their sepulchres: men bled   795
In imitation of the things they fear'd,
And fought and conquer'd, and the same course steer'd,
At apish distance; but as yet none have,
Nor could, the same supremacy have near'd,
Save one vain man, who is not in the grave,   800
But, vanquish'd by himself, to his own slaves a slave—

90.

The fool of false dominion—and a kind
Of bastard Caesar, following him of old
With steps unequal: for the Roman's mind
Was modell'd in a less terrestrial mould,   805
With passions fiercer, yet a judgment cold,
And an immortal instinct which redeem'd
The frailties of a heart so soft, yet bold,
Alcides with the distaff now he seem'd
At Cleopatra's feet,—and now himself he beam'd,   810

91.

And came—and saw—and conquer'd! But the man
Who would have tamed his eagles down to flee,
Like a train'd falcon, in the Gallic van,
Which he, in sooth, long led to victory,
With a deaf heart which never seem'd to be   815
A listener to itself, was strangely fram'd;
With but one weakest weakness—vanity,
Coquettish in ambition—still he aim'd—
At what? can he avouch—or answer what he claim'd?

---

793 dead] ⟨gone⟩ B, H   794 rear'd] ⟨built⟩ B .   795 men] ⟨and⟩ B   797 the]
⟨their⟩ B   798 but ⟨none now⟩ as yet B   799 could] ⟨shall⟩ B   812 Who
⟨borrowed his⟩ would B   813 train'd] taught B, cor. in H   814 he ⟨long⟩ in B
815 deaf heart which] ⟨cold⟩ heart that B   816 ⟨Of such a⟩ B   817 ⟨To / Of
pettier / selfish passions which raged angrily⟩ B   819 At] And C; At what—can he
⟨reply—his lusting is unnamed⟩ B

92.

And would be all or nothing—nor could wait   820
For the sure grave to level him; few years
Had fix'd him with the Caesars in his fate,
On whom we tread: For *this* the conqueror rears
The arch of triumph! and for this the tears
And blood of earth flow on as they have flowed,   825
An universal deluge, which appears
Without an ark for wretched man's abode,
And ebbs but to reflow!—Renew thy rainbow, God!

93.

What from this barren being do we reap?
Our senses narrow, and our reason frail,   830
Life short, and truth a gem which loves the deep,
And all things weigh'd in custom's falsest scale;
Opinion an omnipotence,—whose veil
Mantles the earth with darkness, until right
And wrong are accidents, and men grow pale   835
Lest their own judgments should become too bright,
And their free thoughts be crimes, and earth have too much
    light.

94.

And thus they plod in sluggish misery,
Rotting from sire to son, and age to age,
Proud of their trampled nature, and so die,   840
Bequeathing their hereditary rage
To the new race of inborn slaves, who wage
War for their chains, and rather than be free,
Bleed gladiator-like, and still engage
Within the same arena where they see   845
Their fellows fall before, like leaves of the same tree.

822 fix'd] ⟨placed⟩ *B*   827 wretched man's] ⟨man's wretched⟩ *B*   828 And
only ebbs to flow—⟨War is / How long/ How oft how long Oh God!⟩/ ⟨Send out⟩ thy
rainbow God! *B*   ebbs . . . reflow] ⟨only ebbs to flow⟩ *H*   829 ⟨What are we—and
what shall we know⟩ *BA*   830 ⟨With⟩ senses narrow ⟨and with⟩ reason ⟨weak⟩ *BA*
834 Mantles] ⟨Darkens⟩ *BA*   835 And wrong ⟨& Vice & Virtue⟩ are *BA*   837 be]
⟨grow⟩ *BA*   838 And thus ⟨in some dull⟩ they ⟨sleep in some dull certainty⟩ *BA*
840 ⟨For such existence is as much to die⟩ / ⟨And bequeathing / Truth stygmatized / And
proud of their petty prejudice—and die⟩ *BA*   nature, and so] natures—till they *BA*
844 ⟨Butcher⟩ *BA*

95.

I speak not of men's creeds—they rest between
Man and his Maker—but of things allowed,
Averr'd, and known,—and daily, hourly seen—
The yoke that is upon us doubly bowed,　　　　850
And the intent of tyranny avowed,
The edict of Earth's rulers, who are grown
The apes of him who humbled once the proud,
And shook them from their slumbers on the throne;
Too glorious, were this all his mighty arm had done.　855

96.

Can tyrants but by tyrants conquered be,
And Freedom find no champion and no child
Such as Columbia saw arise when she
Sprung forth a Pallas, armed and undefiled?
Or must such minds be nourished in the wild,　　　860
Deep in the unpruned forest, 'midst the roar
Of cataracts, where nursing Nature smiled
On infant Washington? Has Earth no more
Such seeds within her breast, or Europe no such shore?

97.

But France got drunk with blood to vomit crime,　865
And fatal have her Saturnalia been
To Freedom's cause, in every age and clime;
Because the deadly days which we have seen,
And vile Ambition, that built up between
Man and his hopes an adamantine wall,　　　　870
And the base pageant last upon the scene,

847 they] ⟨those⟩ BA　　　848 Man . . . Maker] ⟨God & His works⟩ BA
849 Averr'd] ⟨And seen⟩ BA　　853 once the] ⟨them when⟩ BA　　855 ⟨And how the
World ? & do what he hath done!⟩ BA　　glorious] ⟨happy⟩ BA　　859 Sprung ⟨from
? Nation—young & undefiled⟩ BA　　860 in] ⟨by⟩ BA　　861 Deep in the ⟨lone
Savannah where⟩ the roar BA　　　862 Of cataracts ⟨the quiet earth beguiled⟩ BA
863 ⟨Of the young ?⟩ BA　　　865 ⟨Too long hath Earth been drunk with blood and
crime⟩ BA　　　866 ⟨And Freedom's span⟩ Her span of Freedom hath but fatal been
BA　　　867 To that of every coming age and clime BA　　　869 that . . .
between] which ⟨opposing / vainly / across⟩ built up between BA　　　871 pageant
⟨which⟩ last BA

Are grown the pretext for the eternal thrall
Which nips life's tree, and dooms man's worst—his second
    fall.

98.

Yet, Freedom! yet thy banner, torn, but flying,
Streams like the thunder-storm *against* the wind;   875
Thy trumpet voice, though broken now and dying,
The loudest still the tempest leaves behind;
Thy tree hath lost its blossoms, and the rind,
Chopp'd by the axe, looks rough and little worth,
But the sap lasts,—and still the seed we find   880
Sown deep, even in the bosom of the North;
So shall a better spring less bitter fruit bring forth.

99.

There is a stern round tower of other days,
Firm as a fortress, with its fence of stone,
Such as an army's baffled strength delays,   885
Standing with half its battlements alone,
And with two thousand years of ivy grown,
The garland of eternity, where wave
The green leaves over all by time o'erthrown;—
What was this tower of strength? within its cave   890
What treasure lay so lock'd, so hid?—A woman's grave.

100.

But who was she, the lady of the dead,
Tombed in a palace? Was she chaste and fair?
Worthy a king's—or more—a Roman's bed?
What race of chiefs and heroes did she bear?   895
What daughter of her beauties was the heir?
How lived—how loved—how died she? Was she not
So honoured—and conspicuously there,
    Where meaner relics must not dare to rot,
Placed to commemorate a more than mortal lot?   900

872 Are grown the] ⟨Will now be the⟩ *BA*   873 Which ⟨sapped / cut down⟩ /
fells life's tree and dooms ⟨man to a⟩ second fall *BA*   nips] fells *H, cor. in Proof B*
880 seed] seeds *N, H, cor. in Proof B*   886 Standing with half] ⟨And⟩ standing with
its / with all⟩ *B*   887 grown] ⟨strown⟩ *B*   888 The garland] ⟨That blossom⟩
B   891 ⟨So massily begirt—what lay⟩ *B*   lock'd] ⟨girt⟩ *B*   894 ⟨A⟩ Worthy *B*
896 ⟨And⟩ what *B*

101.

Was she as those who love their lords, or they
Who love the lords of others? such have been,
Even in the olden time Rome's annals say.
Was she a matron of Cornelia's mien,
Or the light air of Egypt's graceful queen,　　　　905
Profuse of joy—or 'gainst it did she war,
Inveterate in virtue? Did she lean
To the soft side of the heart, or wisely bar
Love from amongst her griefs?—for such the affections are.

102.

Perchance she died in youth: it may be, bowed　　　910
With woes far heavier than the ponderous tomb
That weighed upon her gentle dust, a cloud
Might gather o'er her beauty, and a gloom
In her dark eye, prophetic of the doom
Heaven gives its favourites—early death; yet shed　　　915
A sunset charm around her, and illume
With hectic light, the Hesperus of the dead,
Of her consuming cheek the autumnal leaf-like red.

103.

Perchance she died in age—surviving all,
Charms, kindred, children—with the silver grey　　　920
On her long tresses, which might yet recal,
It may be, still a something of the day
When they were braided, and her proud array
And lovely form were envied, praised, and eyed
By Rome—But whither would Conjecture stray?　　　925
Thus much alone we know—Metella died,
The wealthiest Roman's wife; Behold his love or pride!

901 as] ⟨of / like⟩ B　　　902 have been] ⟨there were⟩ / had been B; had been H, cor. in Proof B　　　903 olden time Rome's] old time Roman B, H, cor. in Proof B
906 Profuse of ⟨beauty and of love / passion or⟩ / ⟨love⟩ joy B　　　908 To ⟨frailty⟩ of the heart or ⟨greatly mar⟩ / ⟨nobly⟩ bar B　　　909 ⟨Implacably in duty / sublime⟩ / ⟨Gainst Love⟩ / Love from ⟨her duties still a conqueress in the war⟩ B　　　910 ⟨Died she in youth or⟩ B　　　911 woes] ⟨grief⟩ B　　　912 dust] ⟨ashes⟩ B　　　915 ⟨Which is the happiest⟩—early B　　　916 charm ⟨along her cheek⟩ around B　　　917 With hectic ⟨light / beaming the crimson / autumnal leaflike red⟩ B　　　918 ⟨Of the bright cheek that / which glows—and in that blush is dead / the Hesperus of the dead⟩ B
921 ⟨Of years upon her tresses which recall⟩ B　　　924 were] ⟨was⟩ B　　　926 Thus] This B　　　927 ⟨The wife of Rome's⟩ B

104.

I know not why—but standing thus by thee
It seems as if I had thine inmate known,
Thou tomb! and other days come back on me   930
With recollected music, though the tone
Is changed and solemn, like the cloudy groan
Of dying thunder on the distant wind;
Yet could I seat me by this ivied stone
Till I had bodied forth the heated mind   935
Forms from the floating wreck which Ruin leaves behind;

105.

And from the planks, far shattered o'er the rocks,
Built me a little bark of hope, once more
To battle with the ocean and the shocks
Of the loud breakers, and the ceaseless roar   940
Which rushes on the solitary shore
Where all lies foundered that was ever dear:
But could I gather from the wave-worn store
Enough for my rude boat, where should I steer?
There woos no home, nor hope, nor life, save what is here. 945

106.

Then let the winds howl on! their harmony
Shall henceforth be my music, and the night
The sound shall temper with the owlet's cry,
As I now hear them, in the fading light
Dim o'er the bird of darkness' native site,   950
Answering each other on the Palatine,
With their large eyes, all glistening grey and bright,
And sailing pinions.—Upon such a shrine
What are our petty griefs?—let me not number mine.

107.

Cypress and ivy, weed and wallflower grown   955
Matted and mass'd together, hillocks heap'd

930 Thou] ⟨Oh⟩ B   931 recollected] ⟨an internal⟩ B   932 cloudy] ⟨last low⟩ B
933 wind] ⟨gale / storm⟩ B   934 ⟨And⟩ yet I could ⟨sit me⟩ / seat me B   935 ⟨Till
all I called forth even from the mind / with heated mind⟩ B   942 lies] ⟨was⟩ B
945 There woos . . . life] I have . . . ⟨heart⟩ B   947 ⟨wherefore⟩ and the night B
949 them . . . fading] ⟨it . . . moon of⟩ B   950 Dim o'er . . . native] ⟨Rise from . . . for-
ward⟩ B   954 let . . . number] ⟨I shrink to think of⟩ B   955 weed and wallflower]
⟨arch and column⟩ B   956 heap'd] ⟨piled / reared⟩ B

On what were chambers, arch crush'd, column strown
In fragments, chok'd up vaults, and frescos steep'd
In subterranean damps, where the owl peep'd,
Deeming it midnight:—Temples, baths, or halls?   960
Pronounce who can; for all that Learning reap'd
From her research hath been, that these are walls—
Behold the Imperial Mount! 'tis thus the mighty falls.

108.

There is the moral of all human tales;
'Tis but the same rehearsal of the past,   965
First Freedom, and then Glory—when that fails,
Wealth, vice, corruption,—barbarism at last.
And History, with all her volumes vast,
Hath but *one* page,—'tis better written here,
Where gorgeous Tyranny had thus amass'd   970
All treasures, all delights, that eye or ear,
Heart, soul could seek, tongue ask—Away with words! draw
          near,

109.

Admire, exult—despise—laugh, weep,—for here
There is such matter for all feeling:—Man!
Thou pendulum betwixt a smile and tear,   975
Ages and realms are crowded in this span,
This mountain, whose obliterated plan
The pyramid of empires pinnacled,
Of Glory's gewgaws shining in the van
Till the sun's rays with added flame were fill'd!   980
Where are its golden roofs? where those who dared to build?

957 On . . . crush'd] In . . . ⟨and⟩ B   959 where . . . peep'd] ⟨wherein have creeped⟩ B
960 ⟨The reptile which / Scorpion and blindworm oer the⟩ B   966 ⟨Glory to such
a position and⟩ when it fails B   that] ⟨it⟩ H   967 corruption] ⟨decay—and⟩ B
970 thus] ⟨most⟩ B   973 ⟨Oh ho ho ho / Approach—behold⟩ / ⟨Admire laugh weep
whateer for here there is⟩ / ⟨Admire—contemn—laugh weep whateer for here⟩ BA
974 ⟨Oh ho ho ho thou creature of a man⟩ BA   all feeling :—Man !] ⟨thy feelings—what⟩
BA   975 ⟨Is man—and what is⟩ / Thou ⟨sad⟩ pendulum BA   976 ⟨Behold
thine ages⟩ / Ages ⟨and Empires / conquests—glass⟩ BA   977 ⟨Behold thou—of
palaces where⟩ BA   978 ⟨Had Power⟩ BA   979 And ⟨stood⟩ shone of Glory's
gewgaws in the van BA, cor. in H   980 ⟨Making⟩ And the Sun's rays with
flames more dazzling filled BA   981 ⟨From roofs of gold / golden roofs⟩ BA   roofs—
⟨gone / and still all⟩ where BA   its] ⟨thy⟩ H

110.

Tully was not so eloquent as thou,
Thou nameless column with the buried base!
What are the laurels of the Caesar's brow?
Crown me with ivy from his dwelling-place.   985
Whose arch or pillar meets me in the face,
Titus or Trajan's? No—'tis that of Time:
Triumph, arch, pillar, all he doth displace
Scoffing; and apostolic statues climb
To crush the imperial urn, whose ashes slept sublime,   990

111.

Buried in air, the deep blue sky of Rome,
And looking to the stars: they had contain'd
A spirit which with these would find a home,
The last of those who o'er the whole earth reign'd,
The Roman globe, for after none sustain'd,   995
But yielded back his conquests:—he was more
Than a mere Alexander, and, unstain'd
With household blood and wine, serenely wore
His sovereign virtues—still we Trajan's name adore.

112.

Where is the rock of Triumph, the high place   1000
Where Rome embraced her heroes? where the steep
Tarpeian? fittest goal of Treason's race,
The promontory whence the Traitor's Leap
Cured all ambition. Did the conquerors heap
Their spoils here? Yes; and in yon field below,   1005
A thousand years of silenced factions sleep—
The Forum, where the immortal accents glow,
And still the eloquent air breathes—burns with Cicero!

986 or pillar] ⟨of triumph⟩ B   988 ⟨Triumph and arch and all he doth erase⟩ /
Triumph . . . doth deface B   989 Scoffing—and ⟨bids the sun⟩ apostolic B
990 crush . . . slept] fling . . . lay B, H; spill / break . . . slept cor. in Proof B   992 stars
⟨for⟩ they B   996 his] ⟨their⟩ B   997 Alexander, and] ⟨soldier all⟩ B   999 we]
⟨men⟩ B   1001 embraced] ⟨received⟩ BA   1003 promontory] ⟨State Leucadia⟩
BA   1007–8 There first did Tully's burning accents glow? | Yes—eloquently
still—the echoes tell me so. BA, H   1007 The Forum, where ⟨still⟩ the immortal
accents glow Proof B

113.

The field of freedom, faction, fame, and blood:
Here a proud people's passions were exhaled,   1010
From the first hour of empire in the bud
To that when further worlds to conquer fail'd;
But long before had Freedom's face been veil'd,
And Anarchy assumed her attributes;
Till every lawless soldier who assail'd   1015
Trod on the trembling senate's slavish mutes,
Or raised the venal voice of baser prostitutes.

114.

Then turn we to her latest tribune's name,
From her ten thousand tyrants turn to thee,
Redeemer of dark centuries of shame—   1020
The friend of Petrarch—hope of Italy—
Rienzi! last of Romans! While the tree
Of Freedom's withered trunk puts forth a leaf,
Even for thy tomb a garland let it be—
The forum's champion, and the people's chief—   1025
Her new-born Numa thou—with reign, alas! too brief.

115.

Egeria! sweet creation of some heart
Which found no mortal resting-place so fair
As thine ideal breast; whate'er thou art
Or wert,—a young Aurora of the air,   1030
The nympholepsy of some fond despair;
Or, it might be, a beauty of the earth,
Who found a more than common votary there
Too much adoring; whatsoe'er thy birth,
Thou wert a beautiful thought, and softly bodied forth.   1035

1010 were exhaled] ⟨rose & rolled⟩ *BA*   1013 face] brow *BA*   1015 lawless
soldier] ⟨petty tyrant / miscreant⟩ *BA*   1016 Appalled ⟨the Senate's hirelings and
mutes⟩ / the trembling Senate's slavish mutes *BA*   1017 baser] ⟨worse⟩ *BA*
1018 ⟨Then to her latest Tribune turn—a name⟩ *BA*   1027 heart] ⟨mind⟩ *B*
1029 breast] ⟨bosom⟩ *B*   1030 young] ⟨summer⟩ *B*   1031 ⟨Or it might⟩ *B*
The nympholepsy] The ⟨brilliant⟩ / lovely madness *B, cor. in H*   1033 a] some *H,*
cor. in Proof B   1034 ⟨Who⟩ too *B*

116.

The mosses of thy fountain still are sprinkled
With thine Elysian water-drops; the face
Of thy cave-guarded spring, with years unwrinkled,
Reflects the meek-eyed genius of the place,
Whose green, wild margin now no more erase   1040
Art's works; nor must the delicate waters sleep,
Prisoned in marble, bubbling from the base
Of the cleft statue, with a gentle leap
The rill runs o'er, and round, fern, flowers, and ivy, creep,

117.

Fantastically tangled; the green hills   1045
Are clothed with early blossoms, through the grass
The quick-eyed lizard rustles, and the bills
Of summer-birds sing welcome as ye pass;
Flowers fresh in hue, and many in their class,
Implore the pausing step, and with their dyes   1050
Dance in the soft breeze in a fairy mass;
The sweetness of the violet's deep blue eyes,
Kiss'd by the breath of heaven, seems coloured by its skies.

118.

Here didst thou dwell, in this enchanted cover,
Egeria! thy all heavenly bosom beating   1055
For the far footsteps of thy mortal lover;
The purple Midnight veil'd that mystic meeting
With her most starry canopy, and seating
Thyself by thine adorer, what befel?
This cave was surely shaped out for the greeting   1060
Of an enamour'd Goddess, and the cell
Haunted by holy Love—the earliest oracle!

1036 still are] ⟨ever⟩ B   1037 thine] ⟨the⟩ its B   1038 with years un-
wrinkled] ⟨which never wrinkled⟩ B   1039 meek-eyed] ⟨gentle⟩ B   1040 margin
now] region ⟨which⟩ B   1041 ⟨The⟩ Art's labours—nor ⟨in prisoned waters flow⟩ /
the delicate waters sleep B   1042 Prisoned] Dungeoned H, cor. in Proof B
1043 cleft . . . with a] ⟨rent . . . the rill's⟩ B   1044 rill runs] ⟨rills run⟩ B
1049 fresh] ⟨sweet⟩ B   1050 the . . . step] your . . . steps B   1051 ⟨But further
the⟩ Dance in the ⟨breeze like fairies⟩ soft B   1053 Kiss'd by . . . its] ⟨Tinges . . .
her⟩ B   1055 heavenly] ⟨celestial⟩ B   1056 For] ⟨With⟩ B   1057 ⟨And the
blue purple midnight flung her mantle oer⟩ B   1060 shaped . . . the] ⟨formed for
other⟩ B

119.

And didst thou not, thy breast to his replying,
Blend a celestial with a human heart;
And Love, which dies as it was born, in sighing,   1065
Share with immortal transports? could thine art
Make them indeed immortal, and impart
The purity of heaven to earthly joys,
Expel the venom and not blunt the dart—
The dull satiety which all destroys—   1070
And root from out the soul the deadly weed which cloys?

120.

Alas! our young affections run to waste,
Or water but the desart; whence arise
But weeds of dark luxuriance, tares of haste,
Rank at the core, though tempting to the eyes,   1075
Flowers whose wild odours breathe but agonies,
And trees whose gums are poison; such the plants
Which spring beneath her steps as Passion flies
O'er the world's wilderness, and vainly pants
For some celestial fruit forbidden to our wants.   1080

121.

Oh Love! no habitant of earth thou art—
An unseen seraph, we believe in thee,
A faith whose martyrs are the broken heart,
But never yet hath seen, nor e'er shall see
The naked eye, thy form, as it should be;   1085
The mind hath made thee, as it peopled heaven,
Even with its own desiring phantasy,
And to a thought such shape and image given,
As haunts the unquench'd soul—parch'd—wearied—wrung
    —and riven.

1064 ⟨Feel the quick throbbing / tumult of a⟩ human heart *B*   1065 ⟨And the sweet
sorrow of that pangless sighing / of its mutual dying⟩ / ⟨And the sweet death which Love
resembles dying / which exults in dying⟩ / ⟨And the sweet sorrow of its deathless dying⟩ *B*
dies] ⟨end⟩ *B*   1066 transports] ⟨kisses⟩ *B*   1069 Expel the venom] ⟨Extract
the venom⟩ / Efface the poison *B, cor. in H*   1070 The dull] ⟨And the sad⟩ *B*
1071 soul] heart *B, cor. in H*   1072 Alas] ⟨And all⟩ *H*   1074 tares of haste] ⟨all
debased⟩ *H*   1078 her] ⟨the⟩ *H*   1081 ⟨Oh Love! thou art no habitant of Earth⟩
H   1083 ⟨And can point out thy time and place of birth⟩ *H*

122.

Of its own beauty is the mind diseased,   1090
And fevers into false creation:—where,
Where are the forms the sculptor's soul hath seized?
In him alone. Can Nature shew so fair?
Where are the charms and virtues which we dare
Conceive in boyhood and pursue as men,   1095
The unreach'd Paradise of our despair,
Which o'er-informs the pencil and the pen,
And overpowers the page where it would bloom again?

123.

Who loves, raves—'tis youth's frenzy—but the cure
Is bitterer still; as charm by charm unwinds   1100
Which robed our idols, and we see too sure
Nor worth nor beauty dwells from out the mind's
Ideal shape of such; yet still it binds
The fatal spell, and still it draws us on,
Reaping the whirlwind from the oft-sown winds;   1105
The stubborn heart, its alchemy begun,
Seems ever near the prize,—wealthiest when most undone.

124.

We wither from our youth, we gasp away—
Sick—sick; unfound the boon—unslaked the thirst,
Though to the last, in verge of our decay,   1110
Some phantom lures, such as we sought at first—
But all too late,—so are we doubly curst.
Love, fame, ambition, avarice—'tis the same,
Each idle—and all ill—and none the worst—
For all are meteors with a different name,   1115
And Death the sable smoke where vanishes the flame.

1099 frenzy . . . cure] madness—⟨we were not⟩ BA, cor. in H   1100 ⟨Formed
for such Utopia⟩ BA   1102 ⟨There is no worth or beauty save the⟩ Mind! BA
1103 Ideal] The Mind's own BA, cor. in H   1105 whirlwind ⟨we have sown in⟩ from
BA   1106 ⟨For stubborn still the heart when most undone⟩ | ⟨Alchemically | The
stubborn heart like Alchemists⟩ The stubborn heart ⟨deems | when | by its own⟩ Alchemy
⟨is neer won⟩ BA   1107 Seems ever near] ⟨Still closest⟩ Seems closest to BA, cor. in H
1108 gasp] ⟨pant⟩ H   1112 so are we] so we are H, cor. in Proof B   1114 Each]
⟨All⟩ H   1115 meteors . . . different] ⟨visions . . . separate⟩ H

125.

Few—none—find what they love or could have loved,
Though accident, blind contact, and the strong
Necessity of loving, have removed
Antipathies—but to recur, ere long,   1120
Envenomed with irrevocable wrong;
And Circumstance, that unspiritual god
And miscreator, makes and helps along
Our coming evils with a crutch-like rod,
Whose touch turns Hope to dust,—the dust we all have   1225
    trod.

126.

Our life is a false nature—'tis not in
The harmony of things,—this hard decree,
This uneradicable taint of sin,
This boundless upas, this all-blasting tree,
Whose root is earth, whose leaves and branches be   1130
The skies which rain their plagues on men like dew—
Disease, death, bondage—all the woes we see—
And worse, the woes we see not—which throb through
The immedicable soul, with heart-aches ever new.

127.

Yet let us ponder boldly—'tis a base   1135
Abandonment of reason to resign
Our right of thought—our last and only place
Of refuge; this, at least, shall still be mine:
Though from our birth the faculty divine
Is chain'd and tortured—cabin'd, cribb'd, confined,   1140
And bred in darkness, lest the truth should shine
Too brightly on the unprepared mind,
The beam pours in, for time and skill will couch the blind.

128.

Arches on arches! as it were that Rome,
Collecting the chief trophies of her line,   1145

1118 Though] ⟨But⟩ H   1127 hard] bad BA   1133 throb] ⟨go / pulse⟩ BA
1134 heart-aches] ⟨throbs⟩ / pangs BA   1145 the chief trophies] ⟨her great records /
annals⟩ B

Would build up all her triumphs in one dome,
Her Coliseum stands; the moonbeams shine
As 'twere its natural torches, for divine
Should be the light which streams here, to illume
This long-explored but still exhaustless mine   1150
Of contemplation; and the azure gloom
Of an Italian night, where the deep skies assume

129.

Hues which have words, and speak to ye of heaven,
Floats o'er this vast and wondrous monument,
And shadows forth its glory. There is given   1155
Unto the things of earth, which time hath bent,
A spirit's feeling, and where he hath leant
His hand, but broke his scythe, there is a power
And magic in the ruined battlement,
For which the palace of the present hour   1160
Must yield its pomp, and wait till ages are its dower.

130.

Oh Time! the beautifier of the dead,
Adorner of the ruin, comforter
And only healer when the heart hath bled—
Time! the corrector where our judgments err,   1165
The test of truth, love,—sole philosopher,
For all beside are sophists, from thy thrift,
Which never loses though it doth defer—
Time, the avenger! unto thee I lift
My hands, and eyes, and heart, and crave of thee a gift: 1170

131.

Amidst this wreck, where thou hast made a shrine
And temple more divinely desolate,

1146 build up all] ⟨gather all⟩ B   1147 stands] ⟨rises⟩ B   1149 Should . . . light]
⟨Like her own light⟩ B   to illume] ⟨not by day⟩ / ⟨and⟩ illume B   1151 contemplation]
⟨meditation⟩ B   1152 an] ⟨Rome's⟩ B   1154 Floats oer this ⟨wondrous monument
of earth⟩ B   1155 ⟨To shadow⟩ forth B   1156 ⟨To⟩ Unto the things ⟨which⟩ of
earth ⟨which / where years have spent⟩ B   1157 ⟨The / Their / A spiritual repose⟩ B
1159 And magic in] ⟨Whose throne is on⟩ / ⟨Which / More⟩ And magic ⟨of⟩ B   1160 For
which] ⟨Than in⟩ / ⟨To⟩ which B   1164 And only] ⟨Of grief, sole⟩ B   1165 corrector
where] ⟨Avenger when⟩ B   1166 sole] ⟨wisdom⟩ B   1167 ⟨Of⟩ For . . . sophists,
⟨unto thee⟩ from B   1168 Which . . . it doth] ⟨Who . . . thou dost⟩ B   1170 crave]
beg B   1171 Amidst] ⟨these ruins⟩ where thou ⟨art most great⟩ B   1172 ⟨And
giving beauty⟩ And ⟨sanctuary thou / all⟩ divinely B

Among thy mightier offerings here are mine,
Ruins of years—though few, yet full of fate:—
If thou hast ever seen me too elate, 1175
Hear me not; but if calmly I have borne
Good, and reserved my pride against the hate
Which shall not whelm me, let me not have worn
This iron in my soul in vain—shall *they* not mourn?

132.

And thou, who never yet of human wrong 1180
Left'st the unbalanced scale, great Nemesis!
Here, where the ancient paid thee homage long—
Thou, who didst call the Furies from the abyss,
And round Orestes bade them howl and hiss
For that unnatural retribution—just, 1185
Had it but been from hands less near—in this
Thy former realm, I call thee from the dust!
Dost thou not hear my heart?—Awake! thou shalt, and must.

133.

It is not that I may not have incurr'd
For my ancestral faults or mine the wound 1190
I bleed withal, and, had it been conferr'd
With a just weapon, it had flowed unbound;
But now my blood shall not sink in the ground;
To thee I do devote it—*thou* shalt take
The vengeance, which shall yet be sought and found, 1195
Which if *I* have not taken for the sake—
But let that pass—I sleep, but thou shalt yet awake.

1173 ⟨Amidst more worthy⟩ offerings *B*   1174 ⟨My youth's past—years all few⟩ /
⟨Years few but full⟩ *B*   1176 but . . . borne] ⟨but if that I have sustained⟩ / but if
⟨humbly I sustained⟩ *B*   1180 human] ⟨mortal⟩ *B*   1181 Left'st] *Text M,
Proof B* Lost *CHP IV (all issues), 1819–29;* Left *B, H, Proof C, 1831, 1832, C, More,
OSA*   1182 ancient] ⟨Roman⟩ *B*   1184 them howl and] ⟨the black snake⟩ *B*
1186 Although it were from other hands; in this *B, cor. in H*   1188 ⟨And holy &
seeking⟩ *B*   1190 Or for my father's ⟨or my⟩ faults ⟨and⟩ mine ⟨a⟩ wound *B*
1192 By ⟨injured⟩ a just *B*   1193 not sink] ⟨sink not⟩ *B*   1194 ⟨To thee it is
devot⟩ *B*   *thou* shalt take] ⟨most alone⟩ *B*   1195 yet . . . and] ⟨heavily be⟩ *B*
1196 ⟨If that I antedate in⟩ *B*   1197 shalt] ⟨art⟩ / wilt *B*

134.

And if my voice break forth, 'tis not that now
I shrink from what is suffered: let him speak
Who hath beheld decline upon my brow,　　　　　　1200
Or seen my mind's convulsion leave it weak;
But in this page a record will I seek.
Not in the air shall these my words disperse,
Though I be ashes; a far hour shall wreak
The deep prophetic fulness of this verse,　　　　　　1205
And pile on human heads the mountain of my curse!

135.

That curse shall be Forgiveness.—Have I not—
Hear me, my mother Earth! behold it, Heaven!—
Have I not had to wrestle with my lot?
Have I not suffered things to be forgiven?　　　　　　1210
Have I not had my brain seared, my heart riven,
Hopes sapp'd, name blighted, Life's life lied away?
And only not to desperation driven,
Because not altogether of such clay
As rots into the souls of those whom I survey.　　　　　　1215

1198 'tis . . . now] ⟨it is not that⟩ B   1200 ⟨What⟩ Who ⟨hath beheld me quiver /
humbler in⟩ hath B   1201 Or ⟨found my mind convulsed⟩ / ⟨my internal spirit changed
or weak⟩ seen . . . leave it ⟨blenched or⟩ weak B   1202 a . . . will] ⟨the . . . which⟩ B
1203 ⟨Shall stand and when that hour shall come and come / of that remorse / from out
the deep⟩ / ⟨Shall come though I be ashes and shall pile / heap / come and wreak⟩ / ⟨It will⟩ /
⟨Then not in vain I registered my curse⟩ / ⟨In fire the Measure / The fiery prophecy / The
fullness of my / The fullness of my prophecy or curse⟩ B
1204 ⟨Tis written that an hour of deep remorse⟩ / ⟨Shall come though I be ashes and shall
wreak⟩ B   far] ⟨deep / slow⟩ B   1205 ⟨The fullness / Thee⟩ B   this] ⟨my⟩ B
1215a–i *stanza in BA, H not printed*

> If to forgive be 'heaping coals of fire'
> As God hath spoken—on the heads of foes
> Mine should be a Volcano—and rise higher
> Than o'er the Titans crushed Olympus rose
> Than Athos soars, or blazing Aetna glows:
> True—they who stung were creeping things—but what
> Than serpent's teeth infects with deadlier throes.
> The Lion may be goaded by the gnat—
> Who sucks the slumberer's blood—the Eagle? no, the Bat. H

1215e Athos soars] ⟨Pelion towers⟩ BA   1215f they] those BA   creeping] petty
BA, cor. in H   1215g ⟨More fatal than the sting of reptile's bite / Amphisbaena's
bite / folding serpent's bite⟩ BA   teeth . . . deadlier] stings produce more deadly BA, cor.
in H   1215h ⟨The Lion's bite is noble⟩ BA   goaded] ⟨punished⟩ BA tortured BA,
cor. in H   1215i suck's the ⟨sleeping⟩ slumberer's BA

136.

From mighty wrongs to petty perfidy
Have I not seen what human things could do?
From the loud roar of foaming calumny
To the small whisper of the as paltry few,
And subtler venom of the reptile crew,   1220
The Janus glance of whose significant eye,
Learning to lie with silence, would *seem* true,
And without utterance, save the shrug or sigh,
Deal round to happy fools its speechless obloquy.

137.

But I have lived, and have not lived in vain: 1225
My mind may lose its force, my blood its fire,
And my frame perish even in conquering pain,
But there is that within me which shall tire
Torture and Time, and breathe when I expire;
Something unearthly, which they deem not of,   1230
Like the remembered tone of a mute lyre,
Shall on their softened spirits sink, and move
In hearts all rocky now the late remorse of love.

138.

The seal is set.—Now welcome, thou dread power
Nameless, yet thus omnipotent, which here   1235
Walk'st in the shadow of the midnight hour
With a deep awe, yet all distinct from fear;
Thy haunts are ever where the dead walls rear
Their ivy mantles, and the solemn scene
Derives from thee a sense so deep and clear   1240
That we become a part of what has been,
And grow unto the spot, all-seeing but unseen.

1219 as paltry] ⟨genial⟩ *BA* ⟨as⟩ paltry *H, cor. in Proof B*   1234 ⟨Now welcome
silence; welcome too | thou dread Power⟩ *B*   1235 thus . . . here] ⟨here . . . now⟩ *B*
1236 ⟨In⟩ Walkst *B*   1238 haunts] ⟨traces⟩ *B*   1239 solemn scene] solemn
⟨arch⟩ *B*; ⟨busy⟩ scene *H*   1240 sense . . . clear] ⟨memory . . . dear⟩ *B*

139.

And here the buzz of eager nations ran,
In murmured pity, or loud-roared applause,
As man was slaughtered by his fellow man.   1245
And wherefore slaughtered? wherefore, but because
Such were the bloody Circus' genial laws,
And the imperial pleasure.—Wherefore not?
What matters where we fall to fill the maws
Of worms—on battle-plains or listed spot?   1250
Both are but theatres where the chief actors rot.

140.

I see before me the Gladiator lie:
He leans upon his hand—his manly brow
Consents to death, but conquers agony,
And his drooped head sinks gradually low—   1255
And through his side the last drops, ebbing slow
From the red gash, fall heavy, one by one,
Like the first of a thunder-shower; and now
The arena swims around him—he is gone,
Ere ceased the inhuman shout which hail'd the wretch who
    won.   1260

141.

He heard it, but he heeded not—his eyes
Were with his heart, and that was far away;
He reck'd not of the life he lost nor prize,
But where his rude hut by the Danube lay
There were his young barbarians all at play,   1265
There was their Dacian mother—he, their sire,
Butcher'd to make a Roman holiday—
All this rush'd with his blood—Shall he expire
And unavenged?—Arise! ye Goths, and glut your ire!

1243 ⟨What shall we call thee? Dread thou art or / Love or⟩ B ⟨Here shone⟩ B
1245 As man was ⟨vanquish⟩ slaughtered B   1246 And wherefore so? in very sooth
because B, H, cor. in Proof B   1249 where we] ⟨if we⟩ B   1250 in . . . spot] ⟨in
battle / open battle's⟩ on battle plains ⟨and the spot⟩ B   1252 ⟨Here⟩ I B   1253 He
leans . . . manly] ⟨Leaning . . . mute⟩ B   1254 Consents . . . conquers] ⟨Yielding . . .
conquering⟩ B   1255 sinks] ⟨sunk⟩ B   1256 And through] ⟨While from⟩ B
1257 red . . . heavy] wide . . . ⟨faintly⟩ / bigly B, cor. in H   1258 ⟨Like the last of a
shower⟩ B   first] last B   1259 arena] ⟨earth / theatre⟩ B   1264 where] ⟨of⟩ B
1266 Dacian . . . he] ⟨Thracian . . . and⟩ B   1267 Butcher'd] ⟨Slaughtered⟩ B
1269 Arise . . . your] ⟨no—soon the Goths shall glut their⟩ B

142.

But here, where Murder breathed her bloody stream;   1270
And here, where buzzing nations choked the ways,
And roar'd or murmur'd like a mountain stream
Dashing or winding as its torrent strays;
Here, where the Roman million's blame or praise
Was death or life, the playthings of a crowd,   1275
My voice sounds much—and fall the stars' faint rays
On the arena void—seats crush'd—walls bow'd—
And galleries, where my steps seem echoes strangely loud.

143.

A ruin—yet what ruin! from its mass
Walls, palaces, half-cities, have been reared;   1280
Yet oft the enormous skeleton ye pass
And marvel where the spoil could have appeared.
Hath it indeed been plundered, or but cleared?
Alas! developed, opens the decay,
When the colossal fabric's form is neared: 1285
It will not bear the brightness of the day,
Which streams too much on all years, man, have reft away.

144.

But when the rising moon begins to climb
Its topmost arch, and gently pauses there;
When the stars twinkle through the loops of time,   1290
And the low night-breeze waves along the air
The garland-forest, which the grey walls wear,
Like laurels on the bald first Caesar's head;
When the light shines serene but doth not glare,

1270 But here ⟨blood exhaled⟩ where B   1271 And] ⟨But⟩ B   1272 ⟨The⟩ And
roared ⟨and⟩ / or B   1273 ⟨Winding or⟩ B   strays] lays B, H, cor. in Proof B
1275 ⟨Was a death warrant and⟩ B   or] and B, cor. in H   1276 sounds . . . fall the]
⟨is . . . the high⟩ B   1277 ⟨Shrink / Fallen on its pile / vanished seats benches—and⟩ B
crush'd] ⟨rent⟩ B   1279 A] ⟨The⟩ B   1280 reared] ⟨built⟩ B   1281 enormous]
⟨colossal⟩ B   1282 ⟨So rent and plundered⟩ / ⟨Ere this⟩ B   1284 Alas! ⟨the
ruin / desolation no⟩ developed ⟨the⟩ opens B   1285 fabric's] ⟨limbs⟩ B   1287 ⟨The
Temple of the Night⟩ B   years . . . have] ⟨Time . . . hath⟩ B   1288 ⟨But in the night
the / when the fire⟩ B   1289 gently pauses] ⟨⸮ people⟩ B   1291 And the low]
⟨When its light⟩ B   1292 ⟨Its Ivy forest / The forest which along it⟩ B   the grey
walls] ⟨its walls doth⟩ B   1294 serene] ⟨distinct⟩ B

Then in this magic circle raise the dead: 1295
Heroes have trod this spot—'tis on their dust ye tread.

145.

'While stands the Coliseum, Rome shall stand;
When falls the Coliseum, Rome shall fall;
And when Rome falls—the World.' From our own land
Thus spake the pilgrims o'er this mighty wall   1300
In Saxon times, which we are wont to call
Ancient; and these three mortal things are still
On their foundations, and unaltered all;
Rome and her Ruin past Redemption's skill,
The World, the same wide den—of thieves, or what ye will.

146.

Simple, erect, severe, austere, sublime—   1306
Shrine of all saints and temple of all gods,
From Jove to Jesus—spared and blest by time;
Looking tranquillity, while falls or nods
Arch, empire, each thing round thee, and man plods   1310
His way through thorns to ashes—glorious dome!
Shalt thou not last? Time's scythe and tyrants' rods
Shiver upon thee—sanctuary and home
Of art and piety—Pantheon!—pride of Rome!

147.

Relic of nobler days, and noblest arts!   1315
Despoiled yet perfect, with thy circle spreads
A holiness appealing to all hearts—
To art a model; and to him who treads
Rome for the sake of ages, Glory sheds

1295 Then ⟨walk and in this⟩ circle *B*   1296 ⟨They will obey the call⟩ *B*   ⟨The
Hero race who trod the imperial earth / dust ye tread⟩ *B*   spot] ⟨dust⟩ *B*   1301 ⟨In
the old Saxon days which we would call⟩ *B*   are] were *B*   1302 and ⟨all⟩
these . . . are ⟨yet⟩ *B*   1303 and unaltered] ⟨but how altered⟩ *B*   1305 The
World ⟨the den of thieves⟩ / ⟨the same mixed scene of⟩ thieves *B*   1306 Simple—
⟨severe—austere—erect—⟩ sublime *B*   1307 Shrine] ⟨Church⟩ *B*   1308 Jesus—
⟨with⟩ spared *B*   1310 ⟨The⟩ Arch *B*   1314 ⟨Of Art and Nature⟩ / ⟨Art's
model—World's shrine⟩ / ⟨Art's natural⟩ *B*   Pantheon . . . of] ⟨the pride of proudest⟩
B   1315 ⟨Pantheon⟩ of *B*   1316 Despoiled . . . spreads] ⟨Spoiled . . . is / rolls⟩ *B*
1317 appealing] ⟨pertaining⟩ *H*   1318 and to] ⟨unto⟩ *B*   1319 ages,] ⟨ancient⟩ *B*

Her light through thy sole aperture; to those   1320
Who worship, here are altars for their beads;
And they who feel for genius may repose
Their eyes on honoured forms, whose busts around them
    close.

148.

There is a dungeon, in whose dim drear light
What do I gaze on? Nothing: Look again!   1325
Two forms are slowly shadowed on my sight—
Two insulated phantoms of the brain:
It is not so; I see them full and plain—
An old man, and a female young and fair,
Fresh as a nursing mother, in whose vein   1330
The blood is nectar:—but what doth she there,
With her unmantled neck, and bosom white and bare?

149.

Full swells the deep pure fountain of young life,
Where *on* the heart and *from* the heart we took
Our first and sweetest nurture, when the wife,   1335
Blest into mother, in the innocent look,
Or even the piping cry of lips that brook
No pain and small suspense, a joy perceives
Man knows not, when from out its cradled nook
She sees her little bud put forth its leaves—   1340
What may the fruit be yet?—I know not—Cain was Eve's.

150.

But here youth offers to old age the food,
The milk of his own gift:—it is her sire
To whom she renders back the debt of blood
Born with her birth. No; he shall not expire   1345

While in those warm and lovely veins the fire
Of health and holy feeling can provide
Great Nature's Nile, whose deep stream rises higher
Than Egypt's river:—from that gentle side
Drink, drink and live, old man! Heaven's realm holds no
  such tide.   1350

151.

The starry fable of the milky way
Has not thy story's purity; it is
A constellation of a sweeter ray,
And sacred Nature triumphs more in this
Reverse of her decree, than in the abyss   1355
Where sparkle distant worlds:—Oh, holiest nurse!
No drop of that clear stream its way shall miss
To thy sire's heart, replenishing its source
With life, as our freed souls rejoin the universe.

152.

Turn to the Mole which Hadrian rear'd on high,   1360
Imperial mimic of old Egypt's piles,
Colossal copyist of deformity,
Whose travelled phantasy from the far Nile's
Enormous model, doom'd the artist's toils
To build for giants, and for his vain earth   1365
His shrunken ashes raise this dome: How smiles
The gazer's eye with philosophic mirth,
To view the huge design which sprung from such a birth!

153.

But lo! the dome—the vast and wondrous dome,
To which Diana's marvel was a cell—   1370
Christ's mighty shrine above his martyr's tomb!
I have beheld the Ephesian's miracle—

1349 from] ⟨where⟩ B   1350 ⟨Imbibe⟩ Drink B   1351 ⟨And⟩ the starry B
1353 ⟨The triumph of Affection⟩ B   1355 ⟨Her⟩ Reverse of her ⟨own⟩ decree B
1357 clear stream] ⟨pure font⟩ B   1358 ⟨To its original fountain but repierce⟩ / ⟨To
its first spring but thy sire's heart⟩ / ⟨Thy sire's heart with⟩ B   1360 which . . .
high] ⟨the now / once aspiring mass⟩ / ⟨the mass which once arose / which held the dead⟩ B
1361 ⟨Where the Imp⟩ B   1362 ⟨Advance⟩ B   1364 doom'd] ⟨turned⟩ B
1365 build . . . vain earth] ⟨labour . . . vain dust / vile⟩ earth B   1367 The ⟨calm⟩ / now
spectator with ⟨no guilty⟩ / a sanctioned mirth B   1368 huge] vast B, H, cor. in
Proof B   1369 ⟨I stand beneath the dome! the wondrous dome⟩ B Look to the ⟨holier⟩
dome! the vast B   1370 marvel] ⟨temple⟩ B   1371 ⟨To⟩ Lo! Christ's great
shrine above ⟨the Apostle's⟩ tomb B

Its columns strew the wilderness, and dwell
The hyaena and the jackall in their shade;
I have beheld Sophia's bright roofs swell   1375
Their glittering mass i' the sun, and have survey'd
Its sanctuary the while the usurping Moslem pray'd;

154.

But thou, of temples old, or altars new,
Standest alone—with nothing like to thee—
Worthiest of God, the holy and the true.   1380
Since Zion's desolation, when that He
Forsook his former city, what could be,
Of earthly structures, in his honour piled,
Of a sublimer aspect? Majesty,
Power, Glory, Strength, and Beauty, all are aisled   1385
In this eternal ark of worship undefiled.

155.

Enter: its grandeur overwhelms thee not;
And why? it is not lessened; but thy mind,
Expanded by the genius of the spot,
Has grown colossal, and can only find   1390
A fit abode wherein appear enshrined
Thy hopes of immortality; and thou
Shalt one day, if found worthy, so defined,
See thy God face to face, as thou dost now
His Holy of Holies, nor be blasted by his brow.   1395

156.

Thou movest—but increasing with the advance,
Like climbing some great Alp, which still doth rise,
Deceived by its gigantic elegance;
Vastness which grows—but grows to harmonize—
All musical in its immensities;   1400

1373 dwell] ⟨tell⟩ B   1375 I have ⟨looked⟩ B   bright] round B, cor. in H
1376 Their glittering ⟨breastplates⟩ in the sun B   1377 Its ⟨saint⟩ sanctuary ⟨which⟩
the B   1383 piled] ⟨reared⟩ B   1385 Glory—⟨Beauty⟩—Strength B
1386 ⟨Within⟩ In ⟨his⟩ B   1387 grandeur] ⟨greatness⟩ B   1388 ⟨Because⟩
And B   1391 ⟨A fitting place of⟩ B appear⟨ed⟩ Proof B   1394 as] ⟨even⟩ as B
1395 Holy of Holies] ⟨Earthly Palace⟩ B   1396 movest—but increasing] ⟨pausest—
but still / yet opening⟩ B   1397 still doth rise] ⟨rises still⟩ B   1399–1401 ⟨And
fair proportions which beguile the eyes | And marble / Paintings and marble of so many dyes |
And glorious high altar where forever burns⟩ B

Rich marbles— richer painting—shrines where flame
The lamps of gold—and haughty dome which vies
In air with Earth's chief structures, though their frame
Sits on the firm-set ground—and this the clouds must claim.

157.

Thou seest not all; but piecemeal thou must break,   1405
To separate contemplation, the great whole;
And as the ocean many bays will make,
That ask the eye—so here condense thy soul
To more immediate objects, and control
Thy thoughts until thy mind hath got by heart   1410
Its eloquent proportions, and unroll
In mighty graduations, part by part,
The glory which at once upon thee did not dart,

158.

Not by its fault—but thine: Our outward sense
Is but of gradual grasp—and as it is   1415
That what we have of feeling most intense
Outstrips our faint expression; even so this
Outshining and o'erwhelming edifice
Fools our fond gaze, and greatest of the great
Defies at first our Nature's littleness,   1420
Till, growing with its growth, we thus dilate
Our spirits to the size of that they contemplate.

159.

Then pause, and be enlightened; there is more
In such a survey than the sating gaze
Of wonder pleased, or awe which would adore   1425
The worship of the place, or the mere praise
Of art and its great masters, who could raise

1402 haughty] ⟨mighty⟩ B   1403 though] ⟨as⟩ B   1404 ground] ⟨earth⟩ B
1405 piecemeal thou] ⟨part by part⟩ B   1408 ask] ⟨claim⟩ B   1409 immediate]
⟨universal⟩ B   1410 thoughts ⟨lest⟩ until B   1411 ⟨The Giant's limbs—
& by degrees unroll⟩ / ⟨Its giant eloquence—& thus unroll⟩ / ⟨Its eloquent immensity⟩ B
1412 graduations] ⟨portions albeit⟩ B   1414 outward] ⟨narrow⟩ B   1415 Is . . .
grasp] ⟨Cannot keep pace with Mind⟩ B   as] ⟨thus⟩ B   1417 faint expression]
⟨language⟩ B   so] ⟨as⟩ B   1421 dilate] ⟨create⟩ B   1422 that] ⟨what⟩ B
1423 pause . . . more] ⟨gaze . . . that⟩ B   1424 In such ⟨employment more⟩ than
the ⟨mere gaze⟩ B   1425 wonder . . . awe] ⟨pleasing wonder—or that⟩ B

What former time, nor skill, nor thought could plan;
The fountain of sublimity displays
Its depth, and thence may draw the mind of man   1430
Its golden sands, and learn what great conceptions can.

160.

Or, turning to the Vatican, go see
Laocoon's torture dignifying pain—
A father's love and mortal's agony
With an immortal's patience blending:—Vain   1435
The struggle; vain, against the coiling strain
And gripe, and deepening of the dragon's grasp,
The old man's clench; the long envenomed chain
Rivets the living links,—the enormous asp
Enforces pang on pang, and stifles gasp on gasp.   1440

161.

Or view the Lord of the unerring bow,
The God of life, and poesy, and light—
The Sun in human limbs arrayed, and brow
All radiant from his triumph in the fight;
The shaft hath just been shot—the arrow bright   1445
With an immortal's vengeance; in his eye
And nostril beautiful disdain, and might,
And majesty, flash their full lightnings by,
Developing in that one glance the Deity.

162.

But in his delicate form—a dream of Love,   1450
Shaped by some solitary nymph, whose breast
Long'd for a deathless lover from above,
And madden'd in that vision—are exprest

1428 What Earth nor time—⟨could Thought / could parallel⟩ / nor former Thought could ⟨frame⟩ / plan *B, cor. in H*   1429 fountain] ⟨deep fount⟩ *B*   1430 ⟨But with a nobler sense⟩ *B*   Its depth ⟨before your eye / and ye return not as ye came / and he who would explain it can / developed in the mind of man⟩ *B*   may draw] ⟨the observant⟩ *B* 1431 ⟨Here / May gather⟩ / ⟨In that which genius did⟩ *B*   learn] ⟨view⟩ *B*   1432 go see] ⟨behold⟩ *B*   1433 ⟨Laocoon giving dignity⟩ *B*   1434 ⟨And blending in his love and agony⟩ *B*   1437 And ⟨dart of⟩ gripe . . . dragon's ⟨bite⟩ *B*   1438 clench; ⟨the writhing boys⟩ the long *B*   1439 ⟨Shackles its living rings; around⟩ the enormous Asp *B*   1440 stifles] ⟨presses⟩ *B*   1441 view] ⟨on⟩ *B*   1442 life . . . light] ⟨light . . . life⟩ *B*   1444 his . . . fight] ⟨the . . . strife⟩ *B*   1445 bright] ⟨rife⟩ *B* 1448 their full] ⟨in their⟩ *B*   1449 ⟨And in⟩ *B*   1450 a] ⟨the⟩ *B*   1451 breast] ⟨heart⟩ *B*   1453 vision] ⟨fancy⟩ *B*

All that ideal beauty ever bless'd
The mind with in its most unearthly mood,   1455
When each conception was a heavenly guest—
A ray of immortality—and stood,
Starlike, around, until they gathered to a god!

163.

And if it be Prometheus stole from Heaven
The fire which we endure, it was repaid   1460
By him to whom the energy was given
Which this poetic marble hath array'd
With an eternal glory—which, if made
By human hands, is not of human thought;
And Time himself hath hallowed it, nor laid   1465
One ringlet in the dust—nor hath it caught
A tinge of years, but breathes the flame with which 'twas
    wrought.

164.

But where is he, the Pilgrim of my song,
The being who upheld it through the past?
Methinks he cometh late and tarries long.   1470
He is no more—these breathings are his last;
His wanderings done, his visions ebbing fast,
And he himself as nothing:—if he was
Aught but a phantasy, and could be class'd
With forms which live and suffer—let that pass—   1475
His shadow fades away into Destruction's mass,

165.

Which gathers shadow, substance, life, and all
That we inherit in its mortal shroud,
And spreads the dim and universal pall
Through which all things grow phantoms; and the cloud
Between us sinks and all which ever glowed,   1481

1455 with in . . . unearthly] ⟨withall . . . fevered⟩ B   1457 ⟨And⟩ a ray B
1458 ⟨Before its / the eye unveiled to image forth a god⟩ B   1461 By ⟨whom⟩ him
to whom ⟨this⟩ energy B   1462 this . . . hath] ⟨the . . . so⟩ B   1467 flame . . .
wrought] ⟨youth Apollo sought⟩ / ⟨fire⟩ with . . . wrought B   1474 ⟨More⟩ Aught
than B, H, cor. in Proof B   1476 His shadow . . . Destruction's] ⟨The / His phantom
. . . the general⟩ B   1478 That] ⟨Which⟩ B   1480 grow] ⟨are⟩ B   1481 ⟨Sinks
Between B

Till Glory's self is twilight, and displays
A melancholy halo scarce allowed
To hover on the verge of darkness; rays
Sadder than saddest night, for they distract the gaze,   1485

166.

And send us prying into the abyss,
To gather what we shall be when the frame
Shall be resolv'd to something less than this
Its wretched essence; and to dream of fame,
And wipe the dust from off the idle name   1490
We never more shall hear,—but never more,
Oh, happier thought! can we be made the same:
It is enough in sooth that *once* we bore
These fardels of the heart—the heart whose sweat was gore.

167.

Hark! forth from the abyss a voice proceeds,   1495
A long low distant murmur of dread sound,
Such as arises when a nation bleeds
With some deep and immedicable wound;
Through storm and darkness yawns the rending ground,
The gulf is thick with phantoms, but the chief   1500
Seems royal still, though with her head discrown'd,
And pale, but lovely, with maternal grief
She clasps a babe, to whom her breast yields no relief.

168.

Scion of chiefs and monarchs, where art thou?
Fond hope of many nations, art thou dead?   1505
Could not the grave forget thee, and lay low
Some less majestic, less beloved head?
In the sad midnight, while thy heart still bled,
The mother of a moment, o'er thy boy,
Death hush'd that pang for ever: with thee fled   1510
The present happiness and promised joy
Which fill'd the imperial isles so full it seem'd to cloy.

1482 is] ⟨grows⟩ *B*   1491 but] ⟨and⟩ *B*   1498 deep and] ⟨confirmed⟩ *BA*
1499 ⟨A shadow stands before me⟩ *BA*   storm] ⟨mist⟩ *BA*   1501 Seems] ⟨Is⟩
BA   1504 chiefs and] ⟨many⟩ *BA*   1505 ⟨And⟩ Fond *BA*   1507 Some]
A *BA*   1508 the] ⟨that⟩ *H*

169.

Peasants bring forth in safety.—Can it be,
Oh thou that wert so happy, so adored!
Those who weep not for kings shall weep for thee,   1515
And Freedom's heart, grown heavy, cease to hoard
Her many griefs for ONE; for she had pour'd
Her orisons for thee, and o'er thy head
Beheld her Iris.—Thou, too, lonely lord,
And desolate consort—vainly wert thou wed!   1520
The husband of a year! the father of the dead!

170.

Of sackcloth was thy wedding garment made;
Thy bridal's fruit is ashes: in the dust
The fair-haired Daughter of the Isles is laid,
The love of millions! How we did entrust   1525
Futurity to her! and, though it must
Darken above our bones, yet fondly deem'd
Our children should obey her child, and bless'd
Her and her hoped-for seed, whose promise seem'd
Like stars to shepherds' eyes:—'twas but a meteor beam'd.

171.

Woe unto us, not her; for she sleeps well: 1531
The fickle reek of popular breath, the tongue
Of hollow counsel, the false oracle,
Which from the birth of monarchy hath rung
Its knell in princely ears, till the o'erstung   1535
Nations have arm'd in madness, the strange fate
Which tumbles mightiest sovereigns, and hath flung

1514 so adored] and adored *BA*   1516 And] ⟨Even⟩ *BA*
1518–21   Her prayer for thee and in thy coming power
                    Beheld her Iris.—Thou too lonely Lord
                    And desolate consort ⟨bitt⟩ deadly is thy dower
                    The husband of a year—the father of an hour. *BA, cor. in H*
1520 deadly *BA*; fatal *H*   1523 Thy bridal *BA*   1524 Isles] ⟨West⟩ *BA*
1525 How we did] ⟨They who did⟩ *BA*   1526 though] ⟨while⟩ *BA*   1527 our]
⟨their⟩ *BA*   1528 Our] ⟨Their⟩ *BA*   1529 seed . . . promise] ⟨offering . . . coming⟩
BA   1532 reek . . . tongue] ⟨breath of popular worth, the false⟩ *BA*   tongue] ⟨voice⟩
BA   1534 ⟨Which teaches princely Spirits to rejoice⟩ *BA*   1536 arm'd . . . fate
⟨? to arms—all the wars⟩ *BA*   1537 tumbles mightiest] ⟨reaches crowned⟩ *BA*

Against their blind omnipotence a weight
Within the opposing scale, which crushes soon or late,—

172.

These might have been her destiny; but no,   1540
Our hearts deny it: and so young, so fair,
Good without effort, great without a foe;
But now a bride and mother—and now *there!*
How many ties did that stern moment tear!
From thy Sire's to his humblest subject's breast   1545
Is linked the electric chain of that despair,
Whose shock was as an earthquake's, and opprest
The land which loved thee so that none could love thee best.

173.

Lo, Nemi! navelled in the woody hills
So far, that the uprooting wind which tears   1550
The oak from his foundation, and which spills
The ocean o'er its boundary, and bears
Its foam against the skies, reluctant spares
The oval mirror of thy glassy lake;
And, calm as cherish'd hate, its surface wears   1555
A deep cold settled aspect nought can shake,
All coiled into itself and round, as sleeps the snake.

174.

And near Albano's scarce divided waves
Shine from a sister valley;—and afar
The Tiber winds, and the broad ocean laves   1560
The Latian coast where sprung the Epic war,
'Arms and the Man', whose re-ascending star
Rose o'er an empire;—but beneath thy right
Tully reposed from Rome;—and where yon bar

1538 Against] ⟨Through all⟩ *BA*   1539 Which sinks the opposing scale—and crushes
them in ⟨its⟩ hate. *BA, cor. in H*   1542 ⟨But now a / Admired abroad—Great with-
out⟩ / ⟨And ? for none save flatterers—without foe⟩ *BA*   1544 ⟨In that abyss / Then⟩
BA   stern] dread *BA*   1545 his . . . breast] ⟨thy . . . heart⟩ *BA*   1546 the ⟨chain⟩
electric *BA*   1547 opprest] ⟨apart⟩ *BA*   1548 thee . . . none] ⟨her . . . no one⟩
BA   1551 which] that *BA*   1552 its] ⟨his⟩ *BA*   1553 against] ⟨into⟩ *BA*
1555 And . . . cherish'd . . . its] ⟨But . . . mortal⟩ / speechless . . . ⟨thy *BA*   cherish'd]
⟨speechless / songless⟩ *H*   1557 All] ⟨And⟩ *BA*   1559 from] ⟨through⟩ *BA*
1563 but] ⟨but⟩ / there *BA*

Of girdling mountains intercepts the sight   1565
The Sabine farm was till'd, the weary bard's delight.

175.

But I forget.—My pilgrim's shrine is won,
And he and I must part,—so let it be,—
His task and mine alike are nearly done;
Yet once more let us look upon the sea;   1570
The midland ocean breaks on him and me,
And from the Alban Mount we now behold
Our friend of youth, that ocean, which when we
Beheld it last by Calpe's rock unfold
Those waves, we followed on till the dark Euxine roll'd 1575

176.

Upon the blue Symplegades: long years—
Long, though not very many, since have done
Their work on both; some suffering and some tears
Have left us nearly where we had begun:
Yet not in vain our mortal race hath run,   1580
We have had our reward—and it is here;
That we can yet feel gladden'd by the sun,
And reap from earth, sea, joy almost as dear
As if there were no man to trouble what is clear.

177.

Oh! that the Desert were my dwelling place,   1585
With one fair Spirit for my minister,
That I might all forget the human race,
And, hating no one, love but only her!
Ye Elements!—in whose ennobling stir
I feel myself exalted—Can ye not   1590
Accord me such a being? Do I err
In deeming such inhabit many a spot?
Though with them to converse can rarely be our lot.

1565 intercepts] circle on *BA*   1566 weary] wearied *BA*   1567 shrine]
⟨goal⟩ *B*   1572 Mount we] ⟨Mountain⟩ *B*   1575 Those] Its *B, cor. in H*   dark]
⟨black⟩ *B*   1577 since have] ⟨have since⟩ *B*   1578 on both] ⟨upon us⟩ *B*   some
suffering] much suffering *B*   1583 sea . . . as] ⟨and sea a joy as⟩ *B*   1592 inhabit
exist in *BA, cor. in H*

178.

There is a pleasure in the pathless woods,
There is a rapture on the lonely shore,   1595
There is society, where none intrudes,
By the deep Sea, and music in its roar:
I love not Man the less, but Nature more,
From these our interviews, in which I steal
From all I may be, or have been before,   1600
To mingle with the Universe, and feel
What I can ne'er express, yet can not all conceal.

179.

Roll on, thou deep and dark blue ocean—roll!
Ten thousand fleets sweep over thee in vain;
Man marks the earth with ruin—his control   1605
Stops with the shore;—upon the watery plain
The wrecks are all thy deed, nor doth remain
A shadow of man's ravage, save his own,
When, for a moment, like a drop of rain,
He sinks into thy depths with bubbling groan,   1610
Without a grave, unknell'd, uncoffin'd, and unknown.

180.

His steps are not upon thy paths,—thy fields
Are not a spoil for him,—thou dost arise
And shake him from thee; the vile strength he wields
For earth's destruction thou dost all despise,   1615
Spurning him from thy bosom to the skies,
And send'st him, shivering in thy playful spray
And howling, to his Gods, where haply lies
His petty hope in some near port or bay,
And dashest him again to earth:—there let him lay.   1620

1599 in which] wherein *BA, cor. in H*   1604 sweep] ⟨pass⟩ *B*   1606 Stops]
⟨Ceases⟩ *B*   1607 thy deed] ⟨thine own⟩ *B*   1609 When ⟨sinking⟩ for *B*
1611 unknell'd] unearthed *B, H, cor. in Proof B*   uncoffin'd] ⟨unmourned⟩ *B*   1612 thy
fields] ⟨his⟩ fields *B*   1614 shake] ⟨tear⟩ *B*   1615 For] To *B*   all] ⟨so⟩ *B*
1618 Gods] saints *H alternate reading* ⟨saints⟩ *Proof B*   1620 again to earth] to earth
again *B, H, cor. in Proof B*

181.

The armaments which thunderstrike the walls
Of rock-built cities, bidding nations quake,
And monarchs tremble in their capitals,
The oak leviathans, whose huge ribs make
Their clay creator the vain title take   1625
Of lord of thee, and arbiter of war;
These are thy toys, and, as the snowy flake,
They melt into thy yeast of waves, which mar
Alike the Armada's pride, or spoils of Trafalgar.

182.

Thy shores are empires, changed in all save thee—   1630
Assyria, Greece, Rome, Carthage, what are they?
Thy waters washed them power while they were free,
And many a tyrant since; their shores obey
The stranger, slave, or savage; their decay
Has dried up realms to desarts:—not so thou,   1635
Unchangeable save to thy wild waves' play—
Time writes no wrinkle on thine azure brow—
Such as creation's dawn beheld, thou rollest now.

183.

Thou glorious mirror, where the Almighty's form
Glasses itself in tempests; in all time,   1640
Calm or convuls'd—in breeze, or gale, or storm,
Icing the pole, or in the torrid clime
Dark-heaving;—boundless, endless, and sublime—
The image of Eternity—the throne
Of the Invisible; even from out thy slime   1645

1621 thunderstrike] ⟨thunder down⟩ *BA*   1622 bidding] ⟨making⟩ *BA*
1623 tremble] ⟨humble⟩ *BA*   1624 ⟨Those broken / oaken citadels which made and
make⟩ *BA*   1625 ⟨Man in his vanity the title take⟩ *BA* Their vain creator Man the
title take *BA, cor. in H*   1627 ⟨What worthy to ? like the flake⟩ / These are thy toys
⟨and thus melt like the snow⟩ *BA*   1628 ⟨Of snow they melt into thy foam⟩ *BA*
yeast of] ⟨yeasty⟩ *BA*   1629 ⟨The proudest ? away—the⟩ spoils of Trafalgar. *BA*
1631 Assyria . . . Rome] Greece—Rome—Assyria *BA*   1632 washed them power *BA*,
H, all proofs, Text M, 1831, 1832, C, More; wasted them *Gifford cor. in Proof B, CHP IV,
edns. 1819–1829*   1633 ⟨when⟩ their *BA*   1636 to . . . waves'] in thy tempests' *BA* ⟨while
thy tempests⟩ *H*   1637 on] ⟨in⟩ *BA*   1638 ⟨Creation's morn / dawn beheld
thee⟩ *BA*   1639 form] ⟨force⟩ *B*   1640 Glasses] Reflects *B*   1642 Icing the] ⟨In /
At the iced⟩ *B*   1643 Dark-heaving] ⟨Varied but / Foaming still⟩ *B*   1644 the
throne] ⟨and space⟩ *B*   1645 ⟨For who hath fixed thy limits⟩ *B*   from out] from *B*

The monsters of the deep are made; each zone
Obeys thee; thou goest forth, dread, fathomless, alone.

184.

And I have loved thee, Ocean! and my joy
Of youthful sports was on thy breast to be
Borne, like thy bubbles, onward: from a boy   1650
I wantoned with thy breakers—they to me
Were a delight; and if the freshening sea
Made them a terror—'twas a pleasing fear,
For I was as it were a child of thee,
And trusted to thy billows far and near,   1655
And laid my hand upon thy mane—as I do here.

185.

My task is done—my song hath ceased—my theme
Has died into an echo; it is fit
The spell should break of this protracted dream.
The torch shall be extinguish'd which hath lit   1660
My midnight lamp—and what is writ, is writ,—
Would it were worthier! but I am not now
That which I have been—and my visions flit
Less palpably before me—and the glow
Which in my spirit dwelt, is fluttering, faint, and low.   1665

186.

Farewell! a word that must be, and hath been—
A sound which makes us linger;—yet—farewell!
Ye! who have traced the Pilgrim to the scene
Which is his last, if in your memories dwell
A thought which once was his, if on ye swell   1670
A single recollection, not in vain
He wore his sandal-shoon, and scallop-shell;
Farewell! with *him* alone may rest the pain,
If such there were—with *you*, the moral of his strain!

1646 are made] ⟨go forth⟩ B   1647 dread—⟨path⟩ fathomless B   1648 And I
⟨do⟩ have B   1655 billows] waters B   1658 ⟨Is dying in the echo—it is time⟩ B
1659 The . . . break] ⟨To break the spell⟩ B   1660-1 ⟨And what will be the fate
of this my rhyme | May not be of my augury⟩ B   1660 ⟨And now the⟩ B   hath] ⟨was⟩ B
1661 ⟨Even in the sun⟩ B   1666 that] which B, H, cor. in H   1667 Fatal—and
yet it shakes me not—farewell B   1668 the Pilgrim] my Pilgrim B, H, cor. in Proof B
1670 A ⟨shred of⟩ thought B   1672 sandal-shoon, and] ⟨Sandals and the⟩ B
1674 were] ⟨was⟩ B

NOTES

6. The little village of Castri stands partly on the site of Delphi. Along the path of the mountain, from Chrysso, are the remains of sepulchres hewn in and from the rock: 'One,' said the guide, 'of a king who broke his neck hunting.' His Majesty had certainly chosen the fittest spot for such an achievement.

A little above Castri is a cave, supposed the Pythian, of immense depth; the upper part of it is paved, and now a cow-house.

On the other side of Castri stands a Greek monastery; some way above which is the cleft in the rock, with a range of caverns difficult of ascent, and apparently leading to the interior of the mountain; probably to the Corycian Cavern mentioned by Pausanias. From this part descend the fountain and the 'Dews of Castalie'. [B]

255. The Convent of 'Our Lady of Punishment', *Nossa Señora de Pena*, on the summit of the rock. Below, at some distance, is the Cork Convent, where St. Honorius dug his den, over which is his epitaph. From the hills, the sea adds to the beauty of the view. [B]

Since the publication of this Poem, I have been informed of the mis-apprehension of the term *Nossa Señora de Pena*. It was owing to the want of the *tilde*, or mark over the *ñ*, which alters the signification of the word: with it, *Peña* signifies a rock; without it, *Pena* has the sense I adopted. I do not think it necessary to alter the passage, as though the common acceptation affixed to it is 'our Lady of the Rock', I may well assume the other sense from the severities practised there. [B, 2nd edn.]

269. It is a well-known fact, that in the year 1809 the assassinations in the streets of Lisbon and its vicinity were not confined by the Portuguese to their countrymen; but that Englishmen were daily butchered: and so far from redress being obtained, we were requested not to interfere if we perceived any compatriot defending himself against his allies. I was once stopped

---

6. of the mountain] by the mountainside *NL*   hewn . . . rock] and some entire hewn in the rock *NL*   hunting] hunting on the Hill *NL*   the upper . . . now] the upper part now *NL;* the upper part is floored and now *D*   a Greek] a *NL*   with a range . . . Pausanias] with apparently a ⟨succession⟩ range of caverns leading to the interior of the mountain probably to the cavern mentioned by Pausanias *NL*
255. Below] Beneath *M, D*   over] and over *M*
269. redress . . . we were] the survivors obtaining redress, they were *D*   if . . . allies] if they perceived their compatriot defending himself against his amiable allies *D*

in the way to the theatre at eight o'clock in the evening, when the streets were not more empty than they generally are at that hour, opposite to an open shop, and in a carriage with a friend; had we not fortunately been armed, I have not the least doubt that we should have adorned a tale instead of telling one. The crime of assassination is not confined to Portugal: in Sicily and Malta we are knocked on the head at a handsome average nightly, and not a Sicilian or Maltese is ever punished! [B]

288. The Convention of Cintra was signed in the palace of the Marchese Marialva. The late exploits of Lord Wellington have effaced the follies of Cintra. He has, indeed, done wonders: he has perhaps changed the character of a nation, reconciled rival superstitions, and baffled an enemy who never retreated before his predecessors. [B]

333. The extent of Mafra is prodigious; it contains a palace, convent, and most superb church. The six organs are the most beautiful I ever beheld in point of decoration; we did not hear them, but were told that their tones were correspondent to their splendour. Mafra is termed the Escurial of Portugal. [B]

389–90. Count Julian's daughter, the Helen of Spain. Pelagius preserved his independence in the fastnesses of the Asturias, and the descendents of his followers, after some centuries, completed their struggle by the conquest of Granada. [B]

508. 'Vivā el Rey Fernando!'—Long live King Ferdinand! is the chorus of most of the Spanish patriotic songs: they are chiefly in dispraise of the old king Charles, the Queen, and the Prince of Peace. I have heard many of them; some of the airs are beautiful. Godoy, the *Principe de la Paz*, was born at Badajoz, on the frontiers of Portugal, and was originally in the ranks of the Spanish Guards, till his person attracted the queen's eyes, and raised him to the dukedom of Alcudia, &c. &c. It is to this man that the Spaniards universally impute the ruin of their country. [B]

539. All who have seen a battery will recollect the pyramidal form in which shot and shells are piled. The Sierra Morena was fortified in every defile through which I passed on my way to Seville. [B]

269. friend . . . had] friend by three of our allies and had *D*   one] it *D*
333. correspondent] ⟨equal⟩ *D*
389–90. When Cava's father Count Julian called in the Moors to avenge her rape on Roderick the King of the Goths, a few of the natives with Pelagius at their head retired into the Asturias and preserved their independence. *M, cor. in D*
508. Long live] Live *M*   chiefly] mostly *M*   many of them] many *M*
539. Every one who has seen a battery will recollect the shape of the heaps in which the shot or shells are piled nearby for action, to be that of a small pyramid. *M, D*   defile] ⟨pass⟩ *M* through which I passed] where I ⟨have seen it⟩ passed *M*   where I have passed *D*

584. Such were the exploits of the Maid of Saragoza. When the author was at Seville she walked daily in the Prado, decorated with medals and orders, by command of the Junta. [B]

706. This was written at Thebes, and consequently in the best situation for asking and answering such a question; not as the birthplace of Pindar, but as the capital of Boeotia, where the first riddle was propounded and solved. [B]

927. The Honourable J.★ W.★★ of the Guards, who died of a fever at Coimbra. I had known him ten years, the better half of his life, and the happiest part of mine.

In the short space of one month I have lost *her* who gave me being, and most of those who had made that being tolerable. To me the lines of Young are no fiction:

> 'Insatiate archer! could not one suffice?
> Thy shaft flew thrice, and thrice my peace was slain,
> And thrice ere thrice yon moon had fill'd her horn.'

I should have ventured a verse to the memory of the late Charles Skinner Matthews, Fellow of Downing College, Cambridge, were he not too much above all praise of mine. His powers of mind, shown in the attainment of greater honours, against the ablest candidates, than those of any graduate on record at Cambridge, have sufficiently established his fame on the spot where it was acquired, while his softer qualities live in the recollection of friends who loved him too well to envy his superiority. [B]

CANTO II

6. We can all feel, or imagine, the regret with which the ruins of cities, once the capitals of empires, are beheld; the reflections suggested by such objects are too trite to require recapitulation. But never did the littleness of man, and the vanity of his very best virtues, of patriotism to exalt, and of valour to defend his country, appear more conspicuous in the record of what Athens was, and the certainty of what she now is. This theatre of contention between mighty factions, of the struggles of orators, the exaltation and deposition of tyrants, the triumph and punishment of generals, is now become a scene of petty intrigue and perpetual disturbance, between the bickering agents of certain British nobility and gentry. 'The wild foxes, the owls and serpents in the ruins of Babylon', were surely less degrading than such inhabitants.

---

584. Saragoza . . . decorated] Saragossa of whom I doubt not England has long ere now heard a full account particularly as Sir John Carr of ? celebrity was at Seville at the same time. ⟨I was there⟩ and mentioned that he had paid a visit to this new Joan of Arc. *M*
When I was at Seville she was walking the Prado daily ornamented *M, D*
706. answering] solving *D*

The Turks have the plea of conquest for their tyranny, and the Greeks have only suffered the fortune of war, incidental to the bravest; but how are the mighty fallen, when two painters contest the privilege of plundering the Parthenon, and triumph in turn, according to the tenor of each succeeding firman! Sylla could but punish, Philip subdue, and Xerxes burn Athens; but it remained for the paltry Antiquarian, and his despicable agents, to render her contemptible as himself and his pursuits.

The Parthenon, before its destruction in part by fire during the Venetian siege, had been a temple, a church, and a mosque. In each point of view it is an object of regard; it changed its worshippers; but still it was a place of worship thrice sacred to devotion: its violation is a triple sacrilege. But

> 'Man, vain man,
> Drest in a little brief authority,
> Plays such fantastic tricks before high heaven
> As make the angels weep.' [B]

38. It was not always the custom of the Greeks to burn their dead; the greater Ajax in particular was interred entire. Almost all the chiefs became gods after their decease, and he was indeed neglected, who had not annual games near his tomb, or festivals in honour of his memory by his countrymen, as Achilles, Brasidas, &c. and at last even Antinous, whose death was as heroic as his life was infamous. [B]

101. At this moment (January 3, 1809 [i.e. 1810]), besides what has been already deposited in London, an Hydroit vessel is in the Piraeus to receive every portable relic. Thus, as I heard a young Greek observe in common with many of his countrymen—for, lost as they are, they yet feel on this occasion— thus may Lord Elgin boast of having ruined Athens. An Italian painter of the first eminence, named Lusieri, is the agent of devastation; and, like the Greek *finder* of Verres in Sicily, who followed the same profession, he has proved the able instrument of plunder. Between this artist and the French Consul Fauvel, who wishes to rescue the remains for his own government, there is now a violent dispute concerning a car employed in their conveyance, the wheel of which—I wish they were both broken upon it—has been locked up by the Consul, and Lusieri has laid his complaint before the Waywode. Lord Elgin has been extremely happy in his choice of Signor Lusieri. During

38. became] ⟨had become⟩ *M*   near] ⟨over⟩ near *M*
101. deposited] stolen and deposited *M*   London] ⟨Picadilly⟩ *M*   thus may Lord] thus may my Lord *M*   painter . . . named] painter named *M*   who wishes] who however merely wishes *M*   both broken] broke *M*   and Lusieri has laid] while Lusieri laid *M*   the Waywode. Lord Elgin] the Waywode. ⟨But⟩ worse than all are the ravages committed in the Parthenon, but I have no patience to detail these barbarities. *M*

a residence of ten years in Athens, he never had the curiosity to proceed as far as Sunium, till he accompanied us in our second excursion. However, his works, as far as they go, are most beautiful; but they are almost all unfinished. While he and his patrons confine themselves to tasting medals, appreciating cameos, sketching columns, and cheapening gems, their little absurdities are as harmless as insect or fox-hunting, maiden-speechifying, barouche-driving, or any such pastime: but when they carry away three or four shiploads of the most valuable and massy relics that time and barbarism have left to the most injured and most celebrated of cities; when they destroy, in a vain attempt to tear down, those works which have been the admiration of ages, I know no motive which can excuse, no name which can designate, the perpetrators of this dastardly devastation. It was not the least of the crimes laid to the charge of Verres, that he had plundered Sicily, in the manner since imitated at Athens. The most unblushing impudence could hardly go farther than to affix the name of its plunderer to the walls of the Acropolis; while the wanton and useless defacement of the whole range of the basso-relievos, in one compartment of the temple, will never permit that name to be pronounced by an observer without execration.

On this occasion I speak impartially: I am not a collector or admirer of collections, consequently no rival; but I have some early prepossession in favour of Greece, and do not think the honour of England advanced by plunder, whether of India or Attica.

Another noble Lord has done better, because he has done less: but some others, more or less noble, yet 'all honourable men', have done *best*, because, after a deal of excavation and execration, bribery to the Waywode, mining and countermining, they have done nothing at all. We had such ink-shed, and wine-shed, which almost ended in bloodshed! Lord E's 'prig',—see Jonathan Wylde for the definition of 'priggism',—quarrelled with another, *Gropius* by name (a very good name too for his business) and muttered something about satisfaction, in a verbal answer to a note of the poor Prussian: this was stated at table to Gropius, who laughed, but could eat no dinner afterwards. The rivals were not reconciled when I left Greece. I have reason to remember their squabble, for they wanted to make me their arbitrator. [B]

107–8. I cannot resist availing myself of the permission of my friend Dr. Clarke, whose name requires no comment with the public, but whose sanction will add tenfold weight to my testimony, to insert the following extract from a very obliging letter of his to me, as a note to the above lines:—

'When the last of the Metopes was taken from the Parthenon, and, in

---

101. absurdities] ⟨foibles⟩ *D*   execration. On this] execration.
                    Aspice quos Scoto Pallas concedit honores
                    Stat nomen subter, facta superque vide!
On this *D*   Another] Lord————'s collector *edns. 1–2, D*   prepossession] ⟨prejudice⟩ *D*
whether] ⟨either⟩ *D*

moving of it, great part of the superstructure with one of the triglyphs was thrown down by the workmen whom Lord Elgin employed, the Disdar, who beheld the mischief done to the building, took his pipe from his mouth, dropped a tear, and, in a supplicating tone of voice, said to Lusieri; Τέλος!— I was present.'

The Disdar alluded to was the father of the present Disdar. [B, 2nd edn.]

118–19. According to Zosimus, Minerva and Achilles frightened Alaric from the Acropolis; but others relate that the Gothic King was nearly as mischievous as the Scottish peer. [B]

338. Albania comprises part of Macedonia, Illyria, Chaonia, and Epirus. Iskander is the Turkish word for Alexander; and the celebrated Scanderbeg (Lord Alexander) is alluded to in the third and fourth lines of the thirty-eighth stanza. I do not know whether I am correct in making Scanderbeg the countryman of Alexander, who was born at Pella in Macedon, but Mr. Gibbon terms him so, and adds Pyrrhus to the list, in speaking of his exploits.

Of Albania Gibbon remarks, that a country 'within sight of Italy is less known than the interior of America'. Circumstances, of little consequence to mention, led Mr. Hobhouse and myself into that country before we visited any other part of the Ottoman dominions; and with the exception of Major Leake, then officially resident at Joannina, no other Englishmen have ever advanced beyond the capital into the interior, as that gentleman very lately assured me. Ali Pacha was at that time (October, 1809) carrying on war against Ibrahim Pacha, whom he had driven to Berat, a strong fortress which he was then besieging: on our arrival at Joannina we were invited to Tepaleni, his Highness's birth-place, and favourite Serai, only one day's distance from Berat; at this juncture the Vizier had made it his head quarters.

After some stay in the capital, we accordingly followed; but though furnished with every accommodation and escorted by one of the Vizier's secretaries, we were nine days (on account of the rains) in accomplishing a journey which, on our return, barely occupied four.

On our route we passed two cities, Argyrocastro and Libochabo, apparently little inferior to Yanina in size; and no pencil or pen can ever do justice to the scenery in the vicinity of Zitza and Delvinachi, the frontier village of Epirus and Albania proper.

On Albania and its inhabitants I am unwilling to descant, because this will be done so much better by my fellow-traveller, in a work which may probably precede this in publication, that I as little wish to follow as I would to anticipate him. But some few observations are necessary to the text.

The Arnaouts, or Albanese, struck me forcibly by their resemblance to the Highlanders of Scotland, in dress, figure, and manner of living. Their very

118–19. others relate] other historians relate with more truth *M*
338. advanced] ⟨went⟩ *D*   days . . . in] days in *D*   four] ⟨three⟩ *D*   descant] ⟨say much⟩ *D*

mountains seemed Caledonian with a kinder climate. The kilt, though white; the spare, active form; their dialect, Celtic in its sound; and their hardy habits, all carried me back to Morven. No nation are so detested and dreaded by their neighbours as the Albanese: the Greeks hardly regard them as Christians, or the Turks as Moslems; and in fact they are a mixture of both, and sometimes neither. Their habits are predatory: all are armed; and the red-shawled Arnaouts, the Montenegrins, Chimariots, and Gegdes are treacherous; the others differ somewhat in garb, and essentially in character. As far as my own experience goes, I can speak favourably. I was attended by two, an Infidel and a Mussulman, to Constantinople and every other part of Turkey which came within my observation; and more faithful in peril, or indefatigable in service, are rarely to be found. The Infidel was named Basilius, the Moslem, Dervish Tahiri; the former a man of middle age, and the latter about my own. Basili was strictly charged by Ali Pacha in person to attend us; and Dervish was one of fifty who accompanied us through the forests of Acarnania to the banks of Achelous, and onward to Messalunghi in Aetolia. There I took him into my own service, and never had occasion to repent it till the moment of my departure.

When in 1810, after the departure of my friend Mr. H[obhouse] for England, I was seized with a severe fever in the Morea, these men saved my life by frightening away my Physician, whose throat they threatened to cut if I was not cured within a given time. To this consolatory assurance of posthumous retribution, and a resolute refusal of Dr. Romanelli's prescriptions, I attributed my recovery. I had left my last remaining English servant at Athens; my dragoman was as ill as myself, and my poor Arnaouts nursed me with an attention which would have done honour to civilization.

They had a variety of adventures; for the Moslem, Dervish, being a remarkably handsome man, was always squabbling with the husbands of Athens; insomuch that four of the principal Turks paid me a visit of remonstrance at the Convent, on the subject of his having taken a woman from the bath—whom he had lawfully bought however—a thing quite contrary to etiquette.

Basili also was extremely gallant amongst his own persuasion, and had the greatest veneration for the church, mixed with the highest contempt of churchmen, whom he cuffed upon occasion in a most heterodox manner. Yet he never passed a church without crossing himself; and I remember the risk he ran in entering St. Sophia, in Stambol, because it had once been a place of his worship. On remonstrating with him on his inconsistent proceedings, he invariably answered, 'our church is holy, our priests are thieves'; and then he crossed himself as usual, and boxed the ears of the first 'papas'

338. Infidel ... Mussulman] ⟨Christian ... Turk⟩ D   To this ... recovery] I laughed so much ⟨that⟩ as to induce a violent perspiration, to which——and a resolute refusal of Dr. Romanelli's prescriptions, I attribute my present Individuality. D   last remaining] only D which ... civilization] too kind for civilization D

who refused to assist in any required operation, as was always found to be necessary where the priest had any influence with the Cogia Bashi of his village. Indeed a more abandoned race of miscreants cannot exist than the lower orders of the Greek clergy.

When preparations were made for my return, my Albanians were summoned to receive their pay. Basili took his with an awkward show of regret at my intended departure, and marched away to his quarters with his bag of piastres. I sent for Dervish, but for some time he was not to be found; at last he entered, just as Signor Logotheti, father to the ci-devant Anglo-consul of Athens, and some other of my Greek acquaintances paid me a visit. Dervish took the money, but on a sudden dashed it to the ground; and clasping his hands, which he raised to his forehead, rushed out of the room weeping bitterly. From that moment to the hour of my embarkation he continued his lamentations, and all our efforts to console him only produced this answer, 'Μά φεινει', 'He leaves me'. Signor Logotheti, who never wept before for any thing less than the loss of a para, melted; the padre of the convent, my attendants, my visitors—and I verily believe that even 'Sterne's foolish fat scullion' would have left her 'fish-kettle', to sympathize with the unaffected and unexpected sorrow of this barbarian.

For my own part, when I remembered that, a short time before my departure from England, a noble and most intimate associate had excused himself from taking leave of me because he had to attend a relation 'to a milliner's', I felt no less surprised than humiliated by the present occurrence and the past recollection.

That Dervish would leave me with some regret was to be expected: when master and man have been scrambling over the mountains of a dozen provinces together, they are unwilling to separate; but his present feelings, contrasted with his native ferocity, improved my opinion of the human heart. I believe this almost feudal fidelity is frequent amongst them. One day, on our journey over Parnassus, an Englishman in my service gave him a push in some dispute about the baggage, which he unluckily mistook for a blow; he spoke not, but sat down leaning his head upon his hands. Foreseeing the consequences, we endeavoured to explain away the affront, which produced the following answer:—'I *have been* a robber, I *am* a soldier; no captain ever struck me; *you* are my master, I have eaten your bread, but by *that* bread! (a usual oath) had it been otherwise, I would have stabbed the dog your servant, and gone to the mountains.' So the affair ended, but from that day forward he never thoroughly forgave the thoughtless fellow who insulted him.

Dervish excelled in the dance of his country, conjectured to be a remnant of the ancient Pyrrhic: be that as it may, it is manly, and requires wonderful agility. It is very distinct from the stupid Romaika, the dull roundabout of the Greeks, of which our Athenian party had so many specimens.

The Albanians in general (I do not mean the cultivators of the earth in the provinces, who have also that appellation, but the mountaineers) have a fine cast of countenance; and the most beautiful women I ever beheld, in stature and in features, we saw *levelling* the *road* broken down by the torrents between Delvinachi and Libochabo. Their manner of walking is truly theatrical; but this strut is probably the effect of the capote, or cloak, depending from one shoulder. Their long hair reminds you of the Spartans, and their courage in desultory warfare is unquestionable. Though they have some cavalry amongst the Gegdes, I never saw a good Arnaout horseman; my own preferred the English saddles, which, however, they could never keep. But on foot they are not to be subdued by fatigue. [B]

356. Actium and Trafalgar need no further mention. The battle of Lepanto [7 Oct. 1571], equally bloody and considerable but less known, was fought in the gulph of Patras; here the author of Don Quixote lost his left hand. [B]

402. Nicopolis, whose ruins are most extensive, is at some distance from Actium, where the wall of the Hippodrome survives in a few fragments. [B]

423. Five thousand Suliotes, among the rocks and in the castle of Suli, withstood 30,000 Albanians for eighteen years: the castle at last was taken by bribery. In this contest there were several acts performed not unworthy of the better days of Greece. [B]

424. The convent and village of Zitza are four hours journey from Joannina, or Yanina, the capital of the Pachalick. In the valley the river Kalamas (once the Acheron) flows, and not far from Zitza forms a fine cataract. The situation is perhaps the finest in Greece, though the approach to Delvinachi and parts of Acarnania and Aetolia may contest the palm. Delphi, Parnassus, and, in Attica, even Cape Colonna and Port Raphti, are very inferior; as also every scene in Ionia, or the Troad: I am almost inclined to add the approach to Constantinople; but from the different features of the last, a comparison can hardly be made. [B]

488. The river Laos was full at the time the author passed it; and, immediately above Tepaleen, was to the eye as wide as the Thames at Westminster; at least in the opinion of the author and his fellow traveller, Mr. Hobhouse. In the summer it must be much narrower. It certainly is the finest river in

338. specimens.] specimens last winter. *D*, *edns. 1–8*   features] countenance *D*   courage]
⟨ability⟩ *D*
356. need no] require no *M*, *D*
402. Nicopolis . . . where] The ruins of Nicopolis are still extensive but situated at some
distance from Actium, of which *M*, *D*
423. among] on *M*
424. a fine] a very fine *M*   I . . . add] perhaps even *D*

the Levant; neither Achelous, Alpheus, Acheron, Scamander nor Cayster, approached it in breadth or beauty. [B]

649. As a specimen of the Albanian or Arnaout dialect of the Illyric, I here insert two of their most popular choral songs, which are generally chaunted in dancing by men or women indiscriminately. The first words are merely a kind of chorus without meaning, like some in our own and all other languages.

I.
Bo, Bo, Bo, Bo, Bo, Bo,
Naciarura, popuso.

I.
Lo, Lo, I come, I come; be
thou silent.

2.
Naciarura na civin
Ha pe nderini ti hin.

2.
I come, I run; open the door
that I may enter.

3.
Ha pe uderi escrotini
Ti vin ti mar servetini.

3.
Open the door by halves, that
I may take my turban.

4.
Caliriote me surme
Ea ha pe pse dua tive.

4.
Caliriotes with the dark eyes,
open the gate that I may
enter.

5.
Buo, Bo, Bo, Bo, Bo,
Gi egem spirta esimiro.

5.
Lo, Lo, I hear thee, my soul.

6.
Caliriote vu le funde
Ede vete tunde tunde.

6.
An Arnaout girl, in costly
garb, walks with graceful
pride.

7.
Caliriote me surme
Ti mi put e poi mi le.

7.
Caliriot maid of the dark eyes,
give me a kiss.

8.
Se ti puta citi mora
Si mi ri ni veti udo gia.

8.
If I have kissed thee, what
hast thou gained? My soul
is consumed with fire.

9.
Va le ni il che cadale
Celo more, more celo.

9.
Dance lightly, more gently,
and gently still.

10.
Plu hari ti tirete
Plu huron cia pra seti.

10.
Make not so much dust to
destroy your embroidered
hose.

The last stanza would puzzle a commentator: the men have certainly buskins of the most beautiful texture, but the ladies (to whom the above is supposed to be addressed) have nothing under their little yellow boots and slippers but a well-turned and sometimes very white ancle. The Arnaout girls are much handsomer than the Greeks, and their dress is far more picturesque. They preserve their shape much longer also, from being always in the open air. It is to be observed, that the Arnaout is not a *written* language; the words of this song, therefore, as well as the one which follows, are spelt according to their pronunciation. They are copied by one who speaks and understands the dialect perfectly, and who is a native of Athens.

1.

Ndi sefda tinde ulavossa
Vettimi upri vi lofsa.

1.

I am wounded by thy love,
and have loved but to
scorch myself.

2.

Ah vaisisso mi privi lofse
Si mi rini mi la vosse.

2.

Thou hast consumed me!
Ah, maid! thou hast struck
me to the heart.

3.

Uti tasa roba stua
Sitti eve tulati dua.

3.

I have said I wish no dowry,
but thine eyes and eye-
lashes.

4.

Roba stinori ssidua *
Qu mi sini vetti dua.

4.

The accursed dowry I want
not, but thee only.

5.

Qurmini dua civileni
Roba ti siarmi tildi eni.

5.

Give me thy charms, and let
the portion feed the flames.

6.

Utara pisa vaisisso me
simi rin ti hapti
Eti mi bire a piste si
gui dendroi tiltati.

6.

I have loved thee, maid, with
a sincere soul, but thou hast
left me like a withered
tree.

7.

Udi vura udorini udiri
cicova cilti mora
Udorini talti hollna u
ede caimoni mora.

7.

If I have placed my hand on
thy bosom what have I
gained? my hand is with-
drawn, but retains the flame.

I believe the two last stanzas, as they are in a different measure, ought to belong to another ballad. An idea something similar to the thought in the last lines was expressed by Socrates, whose arm having come in contact with one of his 'ὑποκολπιοι', Critobulus or Cleobulus, the philosopher complained of a shooting pain as far as his shoulder for some days after, and therefore very properly resolved to teach his disciples in future without touching them. [B]

649–92. These stanzas are partly taken from different Albinese songs, as far as I was able to make them out by the exposition of the Albinese in Romaic and Italian. [B]

703–4. Phyle, which commands a beautiful view of Athens, has still considerable remains: it was seized by Thrasybulus previous to the expulsion of the Thirty. [B]

803. On many of the mountains, particularly Liakura, the snow never is entirely melted, notwithstanding the intense heat of the Summer; but I never saw it lie on the plains even in Winter. [B]

811. Of Mount Pentelicus, from whence the marble was dug that constructed the public edifices of Athens. The modern name is Mount Mendeli. An immense cave formed by the quarries still remains, and will till the end of time. [B]

843. 'Siste Viator—heroa calcas!' was the epitaph on the famous Count Merci;—what then must be our feelings when standing on the tumulus of the two hundred (Greeks) who fell on Marathon? The principal barrow has recently been opened by Fauvel; few or no relics, as vases, &c. were found by the excavator. The plain of Marathon was offered to me for sale at the sum of sixteen thousand piastres, about nine hundred pounds! Alas!— 'Expende—quot *libras* in duce summo—invenies?'—was the dust of Miltiades worth no more? it could scarcely have fetched less if sold by *weight*. [B]

649–92. The above stanzas are partly taken from different Albinese songs as far as I have been able to make them out by the exposition of the Albinese in Romaic.—With regard to the lines in 6 and 7 it must be understood that the Albanians in common with the Turks and Greeks are addicted to Pederasty though I must say in their favour what must be said for the Turks, that I believe they prefer women, however in Albania their number is small in proportion to the male population. *M*

I.

Before I say any thing about a city of which every body, traveller or not, has thought it necessary to say something, I will request Miss Owenson, when she next borrows an Athenian heroine for her four volumes, to have the goodness to marry her to somebody more of a gentleman than a 'Disdar Aga', (who by the by is not an Aga) the most impolite of petty officers, the greatest patron of larceny Athens ever saw, (except Lord E[lgin]) and the unworthy occupant of the Acropolis, on a handsome annual stipend of 150 piastres, (eight pounds sterling) out of which he has only to pay his garrison, the most ill-regulated corps in the ill-regulated Ottoman Empire. I speak it tenderly, seeing I was once the cause of the husband of 'Ida of Athens' nearly suffering the bastinado; and because the said 'Disdar' is a turbulent husband, and beats his wife, so that I exhort and beseech Miss Owenson to sue for a separate maintenance in behalf of 'Ida'. Having premised thus much, on a matter of such import to the readers of romances, I may now leave Ida, to mention her birth-place.

Setting aside the magic of the name, and all those associations which it would be pedantic and superfluous to recapitulate, the very situation of Athens would render it the favourite of all who have eyes for art or nature. The climate, to me at least, appeared a perpetual spring; during eight months I never passed a day without being as many hours on horseback: rain is extremely rare, snow never lies in the plains, and a cloudy day is an agreeable rarity. In Spain, Portugal, and every part of the east which I visited, except Ionia and Attica, I perceived no such superiority of climate to our own; and at Constantinople, where I passed May, June, and part of July, (1810) you might 'damn the climate, and complain of spleen' five days out of seven.

The air of the Morea is heavy and unwholesome, but the moment you pass the isthmus in the direction of Megara the change is strikingly perceptible. But I fear Hesiod will still be found correct in his description of a Boeotian winter.

We found at Livadia, an 'Esprit fort' in a Greek bishop, of all free-thinkers! This worthy hypocrite rallied his own religion with great intrepidity (but not before his flock) and talked of a mass as a 'Coglioneria'. It was impossible to think better of him for this; but, for a Boeotian, he was brisk with all his absurdity. This phenomenon, (with the exception indeed of Thebes, the remains of Chaeronea, the plain of Platea, Orchomenus, Livadia, and its nominal cave of Trophonius), was the only remarkable thing we saw before we passed Mount Cithaeron.

The fountain of Dirce turns a mill: at least, my companion (who resolving to be at once cleanly and classical bathed in it) pronounced it to be the fountain

I. eight] seven *D, cor. in DA*   garrison] ⟨thirty⟩ *D*   behalf] favour *D*   magic] ⟨charm⟩ *D*
is an agreeable rarity] ⟨makes its appearance⟩ *D*   This phenomenon] This *D, cor. in DA*

of Dirce, and any body who thinks it worth while may contradict him. At Castri we drank of half a dozen streamlets, some not of the purest, before we decided to our satisfaction which was the true Castalian, and even that had a villainous twang, probably from the snow, though it did not throw us into an epic fever, like poor Dr. Chandler.

From Fort Phyle, of which large remains still exist, the Plain of Athens, Pentelicus, Hymettus, the Aegean, and the Acropolis, burst upon the eye at once; in my opinion, a more glorious prospect than even Cintra or Istambol. Not the view from the Troad, with Ida, the Hellespont, and the more distant Mount Athos, can equal it, though so superior in extent.

I heard much of the beauty of Arcadia, but excepting the view from the monastery of Megaspelion, (which is inferior to Zitza in a command of country) and the descent from the mountains on the way from Tripolitza to Argos, Arcadia has little to recommend it beyond the name.

'Sternitur, et *dulces* moriens reminiscitur Argos.'

Virgil could have put this into the mouth of none but an Argive; and (with reverence be it spoken) it does not deserve the epithet. And if the Polynices of Statius, 'In mediis audit duo litora campis', did actually hear both shores in crossing the isthmus of Corinth, he had better ears than have ever been worn in such a journey since.

'Athens', says a celebrated topographer, 'is still the most polished city of Greece.' Perhaps it may of *Greece*, but not of the *Greeks;* for Joannina in Epirus is universally allowed, amongst themselves, to be superior in the wealth, refinement, learning, and dialect of its inhabitants. The Athenians are remarkable for their cunning; and the lower orders are not improperly characterized in that proverb, which classes them with 'the Jews of Salonica, and the Turks of the Negro-pont'.

Among the various foreigners resident in Athens, French, Italians, Germans, Ragusans, &c. there was never a difference of opinion in their estimate of the Greek character, though on all other topics they disputed with great acrimony.

Mr. Fauvel, the French consul, who has passed thirty years principally at Athens, and to whose talents as an artist and manners as a gentleman none who have known him can refuse their testimony, has frequently declared in my hearing, that the Greeks do not deserve to be emancipated; reasoning on the grounds of their 'national and individual depravity', while he forgot that such depravity is to be attributed to causes which can only be removed by the measure he reprobates.

Mr. Roque, a French merchant of respectability long settled in Athens, asserted with the most amusing gravity; 'Sir, they are the same *Canaille*

throw . . . like] ⟨give us a⟩ fever (as we hoped it might) like *D*   the eye] ⟨you⟩ *D*   Istambol] Islambol *edns. 1–8*   Statius] Statius who *D, edns. 1–8*   since. 'Athens] ⟨since.—Notes on Greece—Athens and the Greeks etc.⟩—'Athens *D*   and . . . improperly] ⟨but . . . improbably⟩ *D*   while such] forgetting that ⟨perhaps⟩ such *D*   most amusing] ⟨greatest⟩ *D*

that existed in *the days of Themistocles!*'—an alarming remark to the 'Laudator temporis acti'. The ancients banished Themistocles; the moderns cheat Monsieur Roque: thus great men have ever been treated!

In short, all the Franks who are fixtures, and most of the Englishmen, Germans, Danes, &c. of passage, came over by degrees to their opinion, on much the same grounds that a Turk in England would condemn the nation by wholesale, because he was wronged by his lacquey, and overcharged by his washerwomen.

Certainly it was not a little staggering when the Sieurs Fauvel and Lusieri, the two greatest demagogues of the day, who divide between them the power of Pericles and the popularity of Cleon, and puzzle the poor Waywode with perpetual differences, agreed in the utter condemnation, 'nulla virtute redemptum', of the Greeks in general, and of the Athenians in particular.

For my own humble opinion, I am loath to hazard it, knowing, as I do, that there be now in MS. no less than five tours of the first magnitude and of the most threatening aspect, all in typographical array, by persons of wit, and honour, and regular common-place books: but, if I may say this without offence, it seems to me rather hard to declare so positively and pertinaciously, as almost every body has declared, that the Greeks, because they are very bad, will never be better.

Eton and Sonnini have led us astray by their panegyrics and projects; but, on the other hand, De Pauw and Thornton have debased the Greeks beyond their demerits.

The Greeks will never be independent; they will never be sovereigns as heretofore, and God forbid they ever should! but they may be subjects without being slaves. Our colonies are not independent, but they are free and industrious, and such may Greece be hereafter.

At present, like the Catholics of Ireland and the Jews throughout the world, and such other cudgelled and heterodox people, they suffer all the moral and physical ills that can afflict humanity. Their life is a struggle against truth; they are vicious in their own defence. They are so unused to kindness, that when they occasionally meet with it they look upon it with suspicion, as a dog often beaten snaps at your fingers if you attempt to caress him. 'They are ungrateful, notoriously, abominably ungrateful!'—this is the general cry. Now, in the name of Nemesis! for what are they to be grateful? Where is the human being that ever conferred a benefit on Greek or Greeks? They are to be grateful to the Turks for their fetters, and the Franks for their broken promises and lying counsels: they are to be grateful to the artist who engraves their ruins, and to the antiquary who carries them away; to the traveller whose janissary flogs them, and to the scribbler whose journal abuses them! This is the amount of their obligations to foreigners. [B]

wronged . . . washerwoman] ⟨cheated by his valet and overcharged by his landlady⟩ *D*
colonies] colonists *edns. 10–11*   Nemesis] ⟨the whole Pantheon⟩ *D*   ruins] ⟨temples⟩ *D*

II.

Franciscan Convent, Athens, January 23, 1811.

Amongst the remnants of the barbarous policy of the earlier ages, are the traces of bondage which yet exist in different countries; whose inhabitants, however divided in religion and manners, almost all agree in oppression.

The English have at last compassionated their Negroes, and under a less bigoted government may probably one day release their Catholic brethren: but the interposition of foreigners alone can emancipate the Greeks, who, otherwise, appear to have as small a chance of redemption from the Turks, as the Jews have from mankind in general.

Of the ancient Greeks we know more than enough; at least the younger men of Europe devote much of their time to the study of the Greek writers and history, which would be more usefully spent in mastering their own. Of the moderns, we are perhaps more neglectful than they deserve; and while every man of any pretensions to learning is tiring out his youth, and often his age, in the study of the language and of the harangues of the Athenian demagogues in favour of freedom, the real or supposed descendants of these sturdy republicans are left to the actual tyranny of their masters, although a very slight effort is required to strike off their chains.

To talk, as the Greeks themselves do, of their rising again to their pristine superiority, would be ridiculous; as the rest of the world must resume its barbarism, after re-asserting the sovereignty of Greece; but there seems to be no very great obstacle, except in the apathy of the Franks, to their becoming an useful dependency, or even a free state with a proper guarantee;—under correction, however, be it spoken, for many, and well-informed men doubt the practicability even of this.

The Greeks have never lost their hope, though they are now more divided in opinion on the subject of their probable deliverers. Religion recommends the Russians; but they have twice been deceived and abandoned by that power, and the dreadful lesson they received after the Muscovite desertion in the Morea has never been forgotten. The French they dislike; although the subjugation of the rest of Europe will, probably, be attended by the deliverance of continental Greece. The islanders look to the English for succour, as they have very lately possessed themselves of the Ionian republic, Corfu excepted. But whoever shall appear with arms in their hands will be welcome; and when that day arrives, heaven have mercy on the Ottomans, they cannot expect if from the Giaours.

But instead of considering what they have been, and speculating on what they may be, let us look at them as they are.

And here it is impossible to reconcile the contrariety of opinions: some,

II. *Franciscan*] *Noctes Atticae.* Capuchin *D*   ages] ⟨nations⟩ *D*   mastering] ⟨studying⟩ *D*
strike] ⟨raise⟩ *D*   dislike] ⟨abhor⟩ *D*

particularly the merchants, decrying the Greeks in the strongest language; others, generally travellers, turning periods in their eulogy, and publishing very curious speculations grafted on their former state, which can have no more effect on their present lot, than the existence of the Incas on the future fortunes of Peru.

One very ingenious person terms them the 'natural allies' of Englishmen; another, no less ingenious, will not allow them to be the allies of any body, and denies their very descent from the ancients; a third, more ingenious than either, builds a Greek empire on a Russian foundation, and realizes (on paper) all the chimeras of Catherine II. As to the question of their descent, what can it import whether the Mainotes are the lineal Laconians or not? or the present Athenians as indigenous as the bees of Hymettus, or as the grasshoppers, to which they once likened themselves? What Englishman cares if he be of a Danish, Saxon, Norman, or Trojan blood? or who, except a Welchman, is afflicted with a desire of being descended from Caractacus?

The poor Greeks do not so much abound in the good things of this world, as to render even their claims to antiquity an object of envy; it is very cruel then, in Mr. Thornton, to disturb them in the possession of all that time has left them: viz. their pedigree, of which they are the more tenacious, as it is all they can call their own. It would be worth while to publish together, and compare, the works of Messrs. Thornton and De Pauw, Eton and Sonnini; paradox on one side, and prejudice on the other. Mr. Thornton conceives himself to have claims to public confidence from a fourteen years residence at Pera; perhaps he may on the subject of the Turks, but this can give him no more insight into the real state of Greece and her inhabitants, than as many years spent in Wapping into that of the Western Highlands.

The Greeks of Constantinople live in Fanal; and if Mr. Thornton did not oftener cross the Golden Horn than his brother merchants are accustomed to do, I should place no great reliance on his information. I actually heard one of these gentlemen boast of their little general intercourse with the city, and assert of himself with an air of triumph, that he had been but four times at Constantinople in as many years.

As to Mr. Thornton's voyages in the Black Sea with Greek vessels, they gave him the same idea of Greece as a cruize to Berwick in a Scotch smack would of Johnny Grot's house. Upon what grounds then does he arrogate the right of condemning by wholesale a body of men, of whom he can know little? It is rather a curious circumstance that Mr. Thornton, who so lavishly dispraises Pouqueville on every occasion of mentioning the Turks, has yet recourse to him as authority on the Greeks, and terms him an impartial observer. Now Dr. Pouqueville is as little entitled to that appellation, as Mr. Thornton to confer it on him.

Sonnini] Leckie D, *cor. in* D*A*   vessels] ⟨vessels to Odessa⟩ D   Johnny Grot's house] ⟨the town of Edinburgh⟩ D

The fact is, we are deplorably in want of information on the subject of the Greeks, and in particular their literature, nor is there any probability of our being better acquainted, till our intercourse becomes more intimate or their independence confirmed; the relations of passing travellers are as little to be depended on as the invectives of angry factors; but till something more can be attained, we must be content with the little to be acquired from similar sources.

However defective these may be, they are preferable to the paradoxes of men who have read superficially of the ancients, and seen nothing of the moderns, such as De Pauw; who, when he asserts that the British breed of horses is ruined by Newmarket, and that the Spartans were cowards in the field, betrays an equal knowledge of English horses and Spartan men. His 'philosophical observations' have a much better claim to the title of 'poetical'. It could not be expected that he who so liberally condemns some of the most celebrated institutions of the ancient, should have mercy on the modern Greeks; and it fortunately happens, that the absurdity of his hypothesis on their forefathers, refutes his sentence on themselves.

Let us trust then, that in spite of the prophecies of De Pauw, and the doubts of Mr. Thornton, there is a reasonable hope of the redemption of a race of men, who, whatever may be the errors of their religion and policy, have been amply punished by three centuries and a half of captivity. [B]

III.

Athens, Franciscan Convent, March 17, 1811.

'I must have some talk with this learned Theban.'

Some time after my return from Constantinople to this city I received the thirty-first number of the Edinburgh Review, as a great favour, and certainly at this distance an acceptable one, from the captain of an English frigate off Salamis. In that number, Art. 3. containing the review of a French translation of Strabo, there are introduced some remarks on the modern Greeks and their literature, with a short account of Coray, a co-translator in the French version. On those remarks I mean to ground a few observations, and the spot where I now write will I hope be sufficient excuse for introducing them in a work in some degree connected with the subject. Coray, the most celebrated of living Greeks, at least among the Franks, was born at Scio (in the Review Smyrna is stated, I have reason to think, incorrectly), and besides the translation of Beccaria and other works mentioned by the reviewer, has published a lexicon in Romaic and French, if I may trust the assurance of some Danish travellers lately arrived from Paris; but the

III. Some time . . . captain] In a note to line 550 (of the English version [i.e. *Hints*, 586–7] it is stated that I received, an acceptable present as a rare one in this country, the 31st No. of the Edinburgh Review from the Commander *MDb, MDc*   work . . . connected] work unconnected *MDb, MDc*   if I . . . Danish] which I saw in the possession of some Danish *MDb, MDc*

latest we have seen here in French and Greek is that of Gregory Zoliko-gloou. Coray has recently been involved in an unpleasant controversy with M. Gail, a Parisian commentator and editor of some translations from the Greek poets, in consequence of the Institute having awarded him the prize for his version of Hippocrates '*Περὶ ὑδάτων*', &c. to the disparagement, and consequently displeasure, of the said Gail. To his exertions literary and patriotic great praise is undoubtedly due, but a part of that praise ought not to be withheld from the two brothers Zosimado (merchants settled in Leghorn) who sent him to Paris, and maintained him, for the express purpose of eluci-dating the ancient, and adding to the modern, researches of his countrymen. Coray, however, is not considered by his countrymen equal to some who lived in the two last centuries; more particularly Dorotheus of Mitylene, whose Hellenic writings are so much esteemed by the Greeks that Miletius terms him, '*Μετὰ τὸν Θουκυδίδην καὶ Ξενοφῶντα ἄριστος Ἑλλήνων.*' (P. 224. *Ecclesiastical History*, vol. iv.)

Panagiotes Kodrikas, the translator of Fontenelle, and Kamarases, who translated Ocellus Lucanus on the Universe into French, Christodoulus, and more particularly Psalida, whom I have conversed with in Joannina, are also in high repute among their literati. The last-mentioned has published in Romaic and Latin a work on 'True Happiness', dedicated to Catherine II. But Polyzois, who is stated by the reviewer to be the only modern except Coray who has distinguished himself by a knowledge of Hellenic, if he be the Polyzois Lampanitziotes of Yanina, who has published a number of editions in Romaic, was neither more nor less than an itinerant vender of books; with the contents of which he had no concern beyond his name on the title page, placed there to secure his property in the publication; and he was, moreover, a man utterly destitute of scholastic acquirements. As the name, however, is not uncommon, some other Polyzois may have edited the Epistles of Aristaenetus.

It is to be regretted that the system of continental blockade has closed the few channels through which the Greeks received their publications, par-ticularly Venice and Trieste. Even the common grammars for children are become too dear for the lower orders. Amongst their original works the Geography of Meletius, Archbishop of Athens, and a multitude of theo-logical quartos and poetical pamphlets are to be met with: their grammars and lexicons of two, three, and four languages are numerous and excellent. Their poetry is in rhyme. The most singular piece I have lately seen is a satire in dialogue between a Russian, English, and French traveller, and the Waywode of Wallachia (or Vlackbey, as they term him), an archbishop, a merchant, and Cogia Bachi (or primate), in succession; to all of whom under the Turks the writer attributes their present degeneracy. Their songs are sometimes pretty and pathetic, but their tunes generally unpleasing to

generally unpleasing] generally ⟨speaking unpleasing⟩ unpleasant *D, cor. in DA* the ear of a Frank: the best is the famous '*Δεῦτε παῖδες τῶν Ἑλλήνων*', by the unfortunate Riga. But from a catalogue of more than sixty authors, now before me, only fifteen can be found who have touched on any theme except theology.

I am entrusted with a commission by a Greek of Athens named Marmarotouri to make arrangements, if possible, for printing in London a translation of Barthelemi's *Anacharsis* in Romaic, as he has no other opportunity, unless he dispatches the MS. to Vienna by the Black Sea and Danube.

The reviewer mentions a school established at Hecatonesi, and suppressed at the instigation of Sebastiani: he means Cidonies, or, in Turkish, Haivali; a town on the continent where that institution for a hundred students and three professors still exists. It is true that this establishment was disturbed by the Porte, under the ridiculous pretext that the Greeks were constructing a fortress instead of a college; but on investigation, and the payment of some purses to the Divan, it has been permitted to continue. The principal professor, named Veniamin (i.e. Benjamin), is stated to be a man of talent, but a free-thinker. He was born in Lesbos, studied in Italy, and is master of Hellenic, Latin, and some Frank languages; besides a smattering of the sciences.

Though it is not my intention to enter farther on this topic than may allude to the article in question, I cannot but observe that the reviewer's lamentation over the fall of the Greeks appears singular, when he closes it with these words: '*the change is to be attributed to their misfortunes rather than to any "physical degradation"*.' It may be true that the Greeks are not physically degenerated, and that Constantinople contained on the day when it changed masters as many men of six feet and upwards as in the hour of prosperity; but ancient history and modern politics instruct us that something more than physical perfection is necessary to preserve a state in vigour and independence; and the Greeks, in particular, are a melancholy example of the near connection between moral degradation and national decay.

The reviewer mentions a plan '*we believe*' by Potemkin for the purification of the Romaic, and I have endeavoured in vain to procure any tidings or traces of its existence. There was an academy in St. Petersburg for the Greeks; but it was suppressed by Paul, and has not been revived by his successor.

There is a slip of the pen, and it can only be a slip of the pen, in p. 58. No. 31. of the *Edinburgh Review*, where these words occur:—'We are told that when the capital of the East yielded to *Solyman*'—It may be presumed that this last word will, in a future edition, be altered to Mahomet II. The 'ladies of Constantinople', it seems, at that period spoke a dialect, 'which would not have disgraced the lips of an Athenian'. I do not know how that might be, but am sorry to say the ladies in general, and the Athenians in

I am entrusted . . . Danube.] *not in MDb, MDc*   in Romaic] into Romaic *D, edns. 1–6* a smattering] some knowledge *D, cor. in DA*

particular, are much altered; being far from choice either in their dialect or expressions, as the whole Attic race are barbarous to a proverb:

'Ω Aθηνα προτη χωρα
Tι γαιδαρους τρεφεις τωρα.'

In Gibbon, vol. x. p. 161, is the following sentence:—

'The vulgar dialect of the city was gross and barbarous, though the compositions of the church and palace sometimes affected to copy the purity of the Attic models.' Whatever may be asserted on the subject, it is difficult to conceive that the 'ladies of Constantinople', in the reign of the last Caesar, spoke a purer dialect than Anna Comnena wrote three centuries before: and those royal pages are not esteemed the best models of composition, although the princess 'γλωτταν ειχεν ΑΚΡΙΒΩΣ Αττικιρουσαν'. In the Fanal, and in Yanina, the best Greek is spoken: in the latter there is a flourishing school under the direction of Psalida.

There is now in Athens a pupil of Psalida's, who is making a tour of observation through Greece: he is intelligent, and better educated than a fellow-commoner of most colleges. I mention this as a proof that the spirit of inquiry is not dormant amongst the Greeks.

The Reviewer mentions Mr. Wright, the author of the beautiful poem 'Horae Ionicae', as qualified to give details of these nominal Romans and degenerate Greeks, and also of their language: but Mr. Wright, though a good poet and an able man, has made a mistake where he states the Albanian dialect of the Romaic to approximate nearest to the Hellenic; for the Albanians speak a Romaic as notoriously corrupt as the Scotch of Aberdeenshire, or the Italian of Naples. Yanina, (where, next to the Fanal, the Greek is purest) although the capital of Ali Pacha's dominions, is not in Albania but Epirus: and beyond Delvinachi in Albania Proper up to Argyrocastro and Tepaleen (beyond which I did not advance) they speak worse Greek than even the Athenians. I was attended for a year and a half by two of these singular mountaineers, whose mother tongue is Illyric, and I never heard them or their countrymen (whom I have seen, not only at home, but to the amount of twenty thousand in the army of Vely Pacha) praised for their Greek, but often laughed at for their provincial barbarisms.

I have in my possession about twenty-five letters, amongst which some

In the Fanal ... end of the volume.] *not in MDb*   In the Fanal ... the Scotch of Aberdeenshire and the Italian of Venice—I should also be happy to learn in what part of what work the Reviewer himself discovered that 'the Capitol of the East yielded to Solyman' (vide. p. 58). All his exquisite observations on the dialect spoken by the 'ladies of Constantinople of that period' go for nothing—besides we are told [MS. torn] the Greek ladies of any period, even very agreeable or accomplished, and certainly very far from having choice authors in their dialects or expressions, and as for the latter ages they produced nothing remarkable *?* Anna Comnena's *History*. The present ladies are still more degenerated, being diligently excluded from reading and writing lest their acquirements should lead to Billets Doux, so that now they are reduced to the necessity of intriguing by signs, and the most acceptable present a lover can receive is a bunch of flowers tied with a hair, a stone, or a coal, to which he must return an answer on anything but paper. *MDc*

from the Bey of Corinth, written to me by Notaras, the Cogia Bachi, and others by the dragoman of the Caimacam of the Morea (which last governs in Vely Pacha's absence) are said to be favourable specimens of their epistolary style. I also received some at Constantinople from private persons, written in a most hyperbolical style, but in the true antique character. The reader will find a fac simile of the handwriting of a good scribe, with specimens of the Romaic, in an appendix at the end of the volume.

The Reviewer proceeds, after some remarks on the tongue in its past and present state, to a paradox (page 59) on the great mischief the knowledge of his own language has done to Coray, who, it seems, is less likely to understand the ancient Greek, because he is perfect master of the modern! This observation follows a paragraph, recommending, in explicit terms, the study of the Romaic, as 'a powerful auxiliary', not only to the traveller and foreign merchant, but also to the classical scholar; in short, to every body except the only person who can be thoroughly acquainted with its uses: and by a parity of reasoning, our old language is conjectured to be probably more attainable by 'foreigners' than by ourselves! Now I am inclined to think, that a Dutch Tyro in our tongue (albeit himself of Saxon blood) would be sadly perplexed with 'Sir Tristrem,' or any other given 'Auchinlech MS.' with or without a grammar or glossary; and to most apprehensions it seems evident, that none but a native can acquire a competent, far less a complete, knowledge of our obsolete idioms. We may give the critic credit for his ingenuity, but no more believe him than we do Smollet's Lismahago, who maintains that the purest English is spoken in Edinburgh. That Coray may err is very possible; but if he does, the fault is in the man rather than in his mother tongue, which is, as it ought to be, of the greatest aid to the native student.—Here the reviewer proceeds to business on Strabo's translators, and here I close my remarks.

'Auchinlech . . . greatest aid] Auchinlech MS even though he had a hundred grammars by heart, and so far from the Reviewer's opinion being the fact, none but a native can acquire a competent knowledge of our old idioms with or without a Glossary. That Coray may be often wrong is very possible, but if he is the fault is in the man, not in the Romaic, which is and ought to be in all conscience a considerable aid *MDb, MDc*   Here the reviewer . . . time and place] The author of the article on which I offer these comments either is or is not a Traveller,—if he is not, he speaks of a language of which he can know nothing, and if he is he has travelled to very little purpose. On the Greeks or their modern tongue I shall add no observations, their dialect as far as connected with common life is not difficult of acquisition to those acquainted slightly with the ancient. If anyone wishes to make a parade of so trifling an acquisition, let him only copy half a dozen pages of a Romaic Grammar and he will pass for as great a Grecian as the 'learned Camarases' or Mr. Wright the author of the 3rd article of No. 31 of the *E. R.* —There are in England many now capable of informing us on the state of Greece and its literature, amongst them Hamilton, Walpole, Gell, and that debatable pedant Sir W. Drummond, and above all Capt. Leake, are probably the best qualified. From them I hope we shall have something very unlike the unfounded observations of 'this learned Theban'—then I take my leave with a Romaic proverb and changing one word for his edification:

Ω Εδινα προτη χωρα
Τι γαιδαρους τρεφεις τωρα

But by restoring the original he may have the satisfaction of a 'tu quoque' by way of riposte:
Ω Αθηνα προτη χωρα *MDc*

Sir W. Drummond, Mr. Hamilton, Lord Aberdeen, Dr. Clarke, Captain Leake, Mr. Gell, Mr. Walpole, and many others now in England, have all the requisites to furnish details of this fallen people. The few observations I have offered I should have left where I made them, had not the article in question, and above all the spot where I read it, induced me to advert to those pages which the advantage of my present situation enabled me to clear, or at least to make the attempt.

I have endeavoured to wave the personal feelings, which rise in despite of me in touching upon any part of the Edinburgh Review; not from a wish to conciliate the favour of its writers, or to cancel the remembrance of a syllable I have formerly published, but simply from a sense of the impropriety of mixing up private resentments with a disquisition of the present kind, and more particularly at this distance of time and place. [B]

ADDITIONAL NOTE, ON THE TURKS

The difficulties of travelling in Turkey have been much exaggerated, or rather have considerably diminished of late years. The Mussulmans have been beaten into a kind of sullen civility, very comfortable to voyagers.

It is hazardous to say much on the subject of Turks and Turkey; since it is possible to live amongst them twenty years without acquiring information, at least from themselves. As far as my own slight experience carried me I have no complaint to make; but am indebted for many civilities (I might almost say for friendship), and much hospitality, to Ali Pacha, his son Veli Pacha of the Morea, and several others of high rank in the provinces. Suleyman Aga, late Governor of Athens, and now of Thebes, was a *bon vivant*, and as social a being as ever sat cross-legged at a tray or a table. During the carnival, when our English party were masquerading, both himself and his successor were more happy to 'receive masks' than any dowager in Grosvenor-Square.

On one occasion of his supping at the convent, his friend and visitor, the Cadi of Thebes, was carried from table perfectly qualified for any club in Christendom; while the worthy Waywode himself triumphed in his fall.

In all money transactions with the Moslems, I ever found the strictest honour, the highest disinterestedness. In transacting business with them, there are none of those dirty peculations, under the name of interest, difference of exchange, commission, &c. &c. uniformly found in applying to a Greek consul to cash bills, even on the first Houses in Pera.

With regard to presents, an established custom in the East, you will rarely find yourself a loser; as one worth acceptance is generally returned by another of similar value—a horse, or a shawl.

Sir W. Drummond ... Walpole] Lord Aberdeen, Capt. Leake, Messrs. Gell, Hamilton (who I hear has published his book, Sir William Drummond *MDb* formerly published] formerly uttered *D*, *cor. in DA*

Additional Note.

information] ⟨much⟩ information *D*   more happy ... than] ⟨very glad ... as⟩ *D*

In the capital and at court the citizens and courtiers are formed in the same school with those of Christianity; but there does not exist a more honourable, friendly, and high-spirited character than the true Turkish provincial Aga, or Moslem country-gentleman. It is not meant here to designate the governors of towns, but those Agas who, by a kind of feudal tenure, possess lands and houses, of more or less extent, in Greece and Asia Minor.

The lower orders are in as tolerable discipline as the rabble in countries with greater pretensions to civilization. A Moslem, in walking the streets of our country-towns, would be more incommoded in England than a Frank in a similar situation in Turkey. Regimentals are the best travelling dress.

The best accounts of the religion, and different sects of Islamism, may be found in D'Ohsson's French; of their manners, &c. perhaps in Thornton's English. The Ottomans, with all their defects, are not a people to be despised. Equal, at least, to the Spaniards, they are superior to the Portuguese. If it be difficult to pronounce what they are, we can at least say what they are *not*: they are *not* treacherous, they are *not* cowardly, they do *not* burn heretics, they are *not* assassins, nor has an enemy advanced to *their* capital. They are faithful to their sultan till he becomes unfit to govern, and devout to their God without an inquisition. Were they driven from St. Sophia to-morrow, and the French or Russians enthroned in their stead, it would become a question, whether Europe would gain by the exchange. England would certainly be the loser.

With regard to that ignorance of which they are so generally, and sometimes justly, accused, it may be doubted, always excepting France and England, in what useful points of knowledge they are excelled by other nations. Is it in the common arts of life? In their manufactures? Is a Turkish sabre inferior to a Toledo? or is a Turk worse clothed or lodged, or fed and taught, than a Spaniard? Are their Pachas worse educated than a Grandee? or an Effendi than a Knight of St. Jago? I think not.

I remember Mahmout, the grandson of Ali Pacha, asking whether my fellow-traveller and myself were in the upper or lower House of Parliament. Now this question from a boy of ten years old proved that his education had not been neglected. It may be doubted if an English boy at that age knows the difference of the Divan from a College of Dervises; but I am very sure a Spaniard does not. How little Mahmout, surrounded, as he had been, entirely by his Turkish tutors, had learned that there was such a thing as a Parliament it were useless to conjecture, unless we suppose that his instructors did not confine his studies to the Koran.

In all the mosques there are schools established, which are very regularly attended; and the poor are taught without the church of Turkey being put

Regimentals ⟨Uniforms⟩ *D*   If ... *not*] ⟨They may be better introduced by negations⟩ *D*   question] ⟨difficult question⟩ *D* into peril. I believe the system is not yet printed, (though there is such a thing as a Turkish press, and books printed on the late military institution of the Nizam Gedidd); nor have I heard whether the Mufti and the Mollas have subscribed, or the Caimacam and the Tefterdar taken the alarm, for fear the ingenuous youth of the turban should be taught not to 'pray to God their way'. The Greeks also—a kind of Eastern Irish papists—have a college of their own at Maynooth—no, at Haivali; where the heterodox receive much the same kind of countenance from the Ottoman as the Catholic college from the English legislature. Who shall then affirm that the Turks are ignorant bigots, when they thus evince the exact proportion of Christian charity which is tolerated in the most prosperous and orthodox of all possible king-doms? But, though they allow all this, they will not suffer the Greeks to participate in their privileges: no, let them fight their battles, and pay their haratch (taxes), be drubbed in this world, and damned in the next. And shall we then emancipate our Irish Helots? Mahomet forbid! We should then be bad Mussulmans, and worse Christians; at present we unite the best of both—jesuitical faith, and something not much inferior to Turkish toleration. [B]

APPENDIX

Amongst an enslaved people, obliged to have recourse to foreign presses even for their books of religion, it is less to be wondered at that we find so few publications on general subjects than that we find any at all. The whole number of the Greeks, scattered up and down the Turkish empire and else-where, may amount, at most, to three millions; and yet, for so scanty a number, it is impossible to discover any nation with so great a proportion of books and their authors, as the Greeks of the present century. 'Ay,' but say the generous advocates of oppression, who, while they assert the ignorance of the Greeks, wish to prevent them from dispelling it, 'ay, but these are mostly, if not all, ecclesiastical tracts, and consequently good for nothing.' Well! and pray what else can they write about? It is pleasant enough to hear a Frank, particularly an Englishman, who may abuse the government of his own country; or a Frenchman, who may abuse every government ex-cept his own, and who may range at will over every philosophical, religious, scientific, sceptical, or moral subject, sneering at the Greek legends. A Greek must not write on politics, and cannot touch on science for want of instruc-tion; if he doubts, he is excommunicated and damned; therefore his country-men are not poisoned with modern philosophy: and as to morals, thanks to the Turks! there are no such things. What then is left him, if he has a turn for scribbling? Religion and holy biography: and it is natural enough that those who have so little in this life should look to the next. It is no great wonder then that in a catalogue now before me of fifty-five Greek writers,

evince] ⟨display / permit⟩ *D*   tolerated in] tolerated under the 'best of Kings' in *D*, cor. in *DA* many of whom were lately living, not above fifteen should have touched on any thing but religion. The catalogue alluded to is contained in the twenty-sixth chapter of the fourth volume of Meletius's *Ecclesiastical History*. From this I subjoin an extract of those who have written on general subjects; which will be follwed by some specimens of the Romaic.

LIST OF ROMAIC AUTHORS

Neophitus, Diakonos (the deacon) of the Morea, has published an extensive grammar, and also some political regulations, which last were left unfinished at his death.

Prokopius, of Moscopolis (a town in Epirus), has written and published a catalogue of the learned Greeks.

Seraphin, of Periclea, is the author of many works in the Turkish language, but Greek character; for the Christians of Caramania who do not speak Romaic, but read the character.

Eustathius Psalidas, of Bucharest, a physician, made the tour of England for the purpose of study (χάριν μαθήσεως): but though his name is enumerated, it is not stated that he has written any thing.

Kallinikus Torgeraus, Patriarch of Constantinople; many poems of his are extant, and also prose tracts, and a catalogue of patriarchs since the last taking of Constantinople.

Anastasius Macedon, of Naxos, member of the royal academy of Warsaw. A church biographer.

Demetrius Pamperes, a Moscopolite, has written many works, particularly 'A Commentary on Hesiod's Shield of Hercules', and two hundred tales (of what, is not specified), and has published his correspondence with the celebrated George of Trebizond, his cotemporary.

Meletius, a celebrated geographer; and author of the book from whence these notices are taken.

Dorotheus, of Mitylene, an Aristotelian philosopher: his Hellenic works are in great repute, and he is esteemed by the moderns (I quote the words of Meletius) μετὰ τὸν Θουκυδίδην καὶ Ξενοφῶντα ἄριστος ῾Ελλήνων. I add further, on the authority of a well-informed Greek, that he was so famous amongst his countrymen, that they were accustomed to say, if Thucydides and Xenophon were wanting he was capable of repairing the loss.

Marinus Count Tharboures, of Cephalonia, professor of chemistry in the academy of Padua, and member of that academy, and of those of Stockholm and Upsal. He has published, at Venice, an account of some marine animal, and a treatise on the properties of iron.

Marcus, brother to the former, famous in mechanics. He removed to St. Petersburg the immense rock on which the statue of Peter the Great was fixed in 1769. See the dissertation which he published in Paris, 1777.

George Constantine has published a four-tongued lexicon.

George Ventote; a lexicon in French, Italian, and Romaic.

There exist several other dictionaries in Latin and Romaic, French, &c. besides grammars in every modern language, except English.

Amongst the living authors the following are most elebrated:—

Athanasius Parios has written a treatise on rhetoric in Hellenic.

Christodoulos, an Acarnanian, has published, in Vienna, some physical treatises in Hellenic.

Panagiotos Kodrikas, an Athenian, the Romaic translator of Fontenelle's 'Plurality of Worlds', (a favourite work amongst the Greeks), is stated to be a teacher of the Hellenic and Arabic languages in Paris; in both of which he is an adept.

Athanasius, the Parian, author of a treatise on rhetoric.

Vicenzo Damodos, of Cephalonia, has written 'εἰς τὸ μεσοβάρβαρον', on logic and physics.

John Kamarases, a Byzantine, has translated into French Ocellus on the Universe. He is said to be an excellent Hellenist, and Latin scholar.

Gregorio Demetrius published, in Vienna, a geographical work: he has also translated several Italian authors, and printed his versions at Venice.

Of Coray and Psalida some account has been already given.

ROMAIC EXTRACTS

Ῥῶσσος, Ἄγκλος, καὶ Γάλλος κάμνοντες τὴν περιήγησιν τῆς Ἑλλάδος, καὶ βλέποντες τὴν ἀθλίαν τὴν κατάστασιν, εἰρώτησαν καταρχὰς ἕνα Γραικὸν φιλέλληνα διὰ νὰ μάθουν τὴν αἰτίαν, μετ' αὐτὸν ἕνα μητροπολίτην εἶτα ἕνα βλάχμπειν, ἔπειτα ἕνα πραγματευτὴν καὶ ἕνα προεστῶτα.

Εἰπέ μας ὦ φιλέλληνα πῶς φέρεις τὴν σκλαβίαν
καί τὴν ἀπαρίγορητον τὴν Τούρκων τυραννίαν
πῶς ταῖς ξυλαῖς καὶ ὑβρισμοὺς καὶ σηδηροδεσμίαν
παίδων, παρθένων, γυναικων ἀνήκουστον φθορείαν
Δὲν εἶσθαι ἐσεῖς ἀπόγονοι ἐκείνων τῶν Ἑλλήνων·
τῶν ἐλευθέρων καὶ σοφῶν καὶ τῶν φιλοπατρίων
καὶ πῶς ἐκεῖνοι ἀπέθνησκον γιὰ τὴν ἐλευθερίαν
καὶ τώρα ἐσεῖς ὑπούκεισθαι εἰς τέτοιαν τυραννίαν
καὶ ποῖον γένος ὡς ἐσεῖς ἐστάθη φωτισμένον
εἰς τὴν σοφίαν, δύναμην, εἰς κ' ὅλα ζακουσμένον
πῶς νῦν ἐκαταστήσατε τὴν φωτινην Ἑλλάδα
βαβα! ὡς ἕνα σκέλεθρον, ὡς σκοτεινὴν λαμπάδαν
Ὁμίλει φίλτατε Γραικέ εἰπέ μας τὴν αἰτίαν
μὴ κρύπτῃς τίποτης ἡμῶν, λύε τὴν ἀπορίαν.

'Ο ΦΙΛΕ'ΛΛΗΝΟΣ

'Ρωσσ-αγκλο-γαλλοι, 'Ελλὰς, καὶ ὄχι ἄλλοι,
ἦτον, ὡς λέτε, τόσον μεγάλη,
νῦν δὲ ἀθλία, καὶ ἀναξία
ἀφ' φοῦ ἄρχίσεν ἡ ἀμαθία.
οστ' ἠμπορούσαν νὰ τὴν ζυπνήση
τοῦτ' εἰς τὸ χεῖρον τὴν ὁδηγοῦσι
αὐτὴ στενάζει τὰ τέκνα κράζει,
στό να προκόπτουν ὅλα προστάζει
καὶ τότε ἐλπίζει ὅτι κερδίζει.
εὑρεῖν, ὅπου 'χει νῦν τὴν φλογίζει
Μά· ὅστις τολμήση να τὴν ξυπνήση
πάγει στὸν ἄδην χωρίς τινα κρίσιν.

The above is the commencement of a long dramatic satire on the Greek priesthood, princes, and gentry; it is contemptible as a composition, but perhaps curious as a specimen of their rhyme; I have the whole in MS. but this extract will be found sufficient. The Romaic in this composition is so easy as to render a version an insult to a scholar; but those who do not understand the original will excuse the following bad translation of what is in itself indifferent.

TRANSLATION

A Russian, Englishman, and Frenchman making the tour of Greece, and observing the miserable state of the country, interrogate, in turn, a Greek Patriot, to learn the cause; afterwards an Archbishop, then a Vlackbey, a Merchant, and Cogia Bachi or Primate.

> Thou friend of thy country! to strangers record
> Why bear ye the yoke of the Ottoman Lord?
> Why bear ye these fetters thus tamely display'd,
> The wrongs of the matron, the stripling, and maid?
> The descendants of Hellas's race are not ye!
> The patriot sons of the sage and the free,
> Thus sprung from the blood of the noble and brave,
> To vilely exist as the Mussulman slave!
> Not such were the fathers your annals can boast,
> Who conquered and died for the freedom you lost!
> Not such was your land in her earlier hour,
> The day-star of nations in wisdom and power!
> And still will you thus unresisting increase,
> Oh shameful dishonour! the darkness of Greece?
> Then tell us, beloved Achaean! reveal
> The cause of the woes which you cannot conceal.

The reply of the Philellenist I have not translated, as it is no better than the question of the travelling triumvirate; and the above will sufficiently show with what kind of composition the Greeks are now satisfied. I trust I have not much injured the original in the few lines given as faithfully, and as near the 'Oh, Miss Bailey! unfortunate Miss Bailey!' measure of the Romaic, as I could make them. Almost all their pieces, above a song, which aspire to the name of poetry, contain exactly the quantity of feet of

'A captain bold of Halifax who liv'd in country quarters,'

which is in fact the present heroic couplet of the Romaic.

SCENE FROM 'Ο ΚΑΦΕΝΕΣ

Translated from the Italian of Goldoni by
Speridion Vlanti.

ΣΚΗΝΗ ΚΓ'.

ΠΛΑΤΖΙΔΑ εἰς τὴν πόρταν τοῦ χανιοῦ, καὶ οἱ ἄνωθεν.

ΠΛΑ. ῏Ω Θεέ! ἀπὸ τὸ παραθύρι μοῦ ἐφάνη νὰ ἀκούσω τὴν φωνὴν τοῦ ἀνδρός μου· ἂν αὐτὸς εἶναι ἐδώ, ἔφθασα σὲ καιρὸν νὰ τὸν ξεντροπιάσω. [Εὐγαίνει ἔνας δοῦλος ἀπὸ τὸ ἐργαστήρι.] Παλικάρι, πές μου σὲ παρακαλῶ ποιὸς εἶναι ἐκεῖ εἰς ἐκείνους τοὺς ὀντάδες;

ΔΟΥΛ. Τρεῖς χρήσιμοι ἄνδρες. ῎Ενας ὁ κὺρ Εὐγένιος, ὁ ἄλλος ὁ κὺρ Μάρτιος Ναπολιτάνος, καὶ ὁ τρίτος ὁ Κὺρ Κόντε Λέανδρος Ἀρδέντης.

ΠΛΑ. (Ἀνάμεσα εἰς αὐτοὺς δὲν εἶναι ὁ Φλαμίνιος, ἂν ὅμως δὲν ἄλλαξεν ὄνομα.)

ΛΕΑ. Νὰ ζῇ ἡ καλὴ τύχη τοῦ κὺρ Εὐγενίου. [Πίνωντας.]

ΟΛΟΙ. Νὰ ζῇ, να ζῇ.

ΠΛΑ. (Αὐτὸς εἶναι ὁ ἄνδρας μου χωρὶς ἄλλο.) Καλὲ ἄνθρωπε κάμε μου τὴν χάριν νὰ μὲ συντροφεύσῃς ἀπάνω εἰς αὐτοὺς τοὺς ἀφεντάδες, ὁποῦ θέλω νὰ τοὺς παίξω μίαν. [Πρὸς τὸν δοῦλον.]

ΔΟΥ. Ὁρισμός σας· (συνηθισμένον ὀφφίκιον των δουλευτῶν) [Τὴν ἐμπάζει ἀπὸ τὸ ἐργαστήρι τοῦ παιγνιδιοῦ.]

ΡΙΔ. Καρδιὰ, καρδιὰ, κάμετε καλὴν καρδιὰν, δὲν εἶναι τίποτες. [Πρὸς τὴν Βιττόριαν.]

ΒΙΤ. Ἐγὼ αἰσθάνομαι πῶς ἀπεθαίνω. [Συνέρχεται εἰς τὸν ἑαυτόν της.]

Ἀπὸ τὰ παράθυρα τῶν ὀντάδων φαίνονται ὅλοι, ὁποῦ σηκόνωνται ἀπὸ τὸ τραπέζι συγχισμένοι, διὰ τὸν ξαφνισμὸν τοῦ Λεάνδρου βλέπωντας τὴν Πλάτζιδα, καὶ διατὶ αὐτὸς δείχνει πῶς θέλει νὰ τὴν φονεύσῃ.]

ΕΥΓ. ῎Οχι, σταθῆτε.

ΜΑΡ. Μὴν κάμνετε . . .

ΛΕΑ. Σίκω, φύγε ἀπ᾿ ἐδώ.

ΠΛΑ. Βοήθεια, βοήθεια. [Φεύγει ἀπὸ τὴν σκάλαν, ὁ Λέανδρος θέλει νὰ τὴν ἀκολουθήσῃ μὲ τὸ σπαθὶ, καὶ ὁ Εὐγ. τον βαστᾷ.]

ΤΡΑ. [Μὲ ἕνα πιάτο μὲ φαγὶ εἰς μίαν πετζέτα πηδᾷ ἀπὸ τὸ παραθύρι, καὶ φεύγει εἰς τὸν καφενέ.]

ΠΛΑ. [Εὐγαίνει ἀπὸ τὸ ἐργαστήρι του παιγνιδιου τρέχωντας, καὶ φεύγει εἰς τὸ χάνι.]

ΕΥΤ. [Μὲ ἄρματα εἰς τὸ χέρι πρὸς διαφέντευσιν τῆς Πλάτζιδας, ἐναντίον τοῦ Λεάνδρου, ὁποῦ τὴν κατατρέχει.]

ΜΑΡ. [Εὐγαίνει καὶ αὐτὸς σιγὰ σιγὰ ἀπὸ τὸ ἐργαστήρι, καὶ φεύγει λέγωντας.] Rumores fuge. [Ῥουμόρες φούγε.]

Οἱ Δοῦλοι. [Ἀπὸ τὸ ἐργαστήρι ἀπερνοῦν εἰς τὸ χάνι, καὶ κλειοὺν τὴν πόρταν.]

ΒΙΤ. [Μένει εἰς τὸν καφενέ βοηθημένη ἀπὸ τὸν Ῥιδόλφον.]

ΛΕΑ. Δόσετε τόπον· θέλω νὰ ἔμβω νὰ ἔμβω εἰς ἐκεῖνο τὸ χάνι. [Μὲ τὸ σπαθὶ εἰς τὸ χέρι ἐναντίον τοῦ Εὐγενίου.]

ΕΥΓ. Ὄχι, μὴ γένοιτο ποτέ· εἶσαι ἕνας σληρόκαρδος ἐναντίον τῆς γυναικός σου, καὶ ἐγὼ θέλει τήν διαφεντεύσω ὡς εἰς τὸ ὕστερον αἷμα.

ΛΕΑ. Σοῦ κάμνω ὅρκον πῶς θέλει τὸ μετανοιώσῃς. [Κινηγᾷ τὸν Εὐγένιον μὲ τὸ σπαθί.]

ΕΥΓ. Δὲν σὲ φοβοῦμαι. [Κατατρέχει τὸν Λέανδρον, καί τὸν βιάζει νὰ συρθῇ ὀπίσω τόσον, ὁποῦ εὑρίσκωντας ἀνοικτὸν τὸ σπῆτι τῆς χορεύτριας, ἐμβαίνει εἰς αὐτὸ, καὶ σώνεται.]

TRANSLATION

Platzida from the Door of the Hotel, and the Others.

Pla. Oh God! from the window it seemed that I heard my husband's voice. If he is here, I have arrived in time to make him ashamed. [*A Servant enters from the Shop.*] Boy, tell me, pray, who are in those chambers?

Serv. Three Gentlemen: one, Signor Eugenio; the other Signor Martio, the Neapolitan; and the third, my Lord, the Count Leander Ardenti.

Pla. Flaminio is not amongst these, unless he has changed his name.

Leander. [*Within drinking.*] Long live the good fortune of Signor Eugenio! [*The whole Company,* Long live, &c.] (Literally, Να ζῆ, νά ζῆ, May he live.)

Pla. Without doubt that is my husband. [*To the Serv.*] My good man, do me the favour to accompany me above to those Gentlemen: I have some business.

Serv. At your commands. [*Aside.*] The old office of us waiters. [*He goes out of the Gaming-House.*]

Ridolpho. [*To Victoria on another part of the stage.*] Courage, Courage, be of good cheer, it is nothing.

Victoria. I feel as if about to die. [*Leaning on him as if fainting.*]

> [*From the windows above all within are seen rising from table in confusion:* Leander *starts at the sight of* Platzida, *and appears by his gestures to threaten her life.*

Eugenio. No, stop——

Martio. Don't attempt——

Leander. Away, fly from hence!

Pla. Help! Help! [*Flies down the Stairs,* Leander *attempting to follow with his sword,* Eugenio *hinders him.*]

[Trappola *with a plate of meat leaps over the balcony from the window, and runs into the Coffee-House.*]

[Platzida *runs out of the Gaming-House, and takes shelter in the Hotel.*]

[Martio *steals softly out of the Gaming-House, and goes off exclaiming,* 'Rumores fuge'. *The Servants from the Gaming-House enter the Hotel, and shut the door.*]

[Victoria *remains in the Coffee-House assisted by* Ridolpho].

[Leander *sword in hand opposite* Eugenio *exclaims,* Give way—I will enter that hotel.]

Eugenio. No, that shall never be. You are a scoundrel to your wife, and I will defend her to the last drop of my blood.

Leander. I will give you cause to repent this. [*Menacing with his sword.*]

Eugenio. I fear you not. [*He attacks* Leander *and makes him give back so much that finding the door of the dancing girl's house open,* Leander *escapes through, and so finishes.*]

CONCLUSION

The foregoing selections from the Romaic are, of course, offered to the scholar only; and I trust that the critic will not quarrel with that part which is intended for his sole perusal, and for the faults of which I am not responsible. For the errors in the inscriptions copied from Meletius, the worthy archbishop must be himself answerable, but there is a hope that they may yet be rectified; for part of the marbles on which they are inscribed still exist, and were purchased by an English traveller in 1810. It is the opinion of one of the first scholars in this country, that if accurately given, 'they might be of great use in explaining the dialect, and consequently restoring the metres of Pindar'.

There can be little difficulty in obtaining a fac simile, but I much regret not having copied, or obtained a copy of the inscription on the spot, which, to the best of my recollection, was very legible.

himself answerable] himself responsible *all MSS., proofs, and edns.; cor. in letter to Murray, 5 Feb. 1814 (BLJ IV. 47).*

CANTO IV

1. The communication between the Ducal palace and the prisons of Venice is by a gloomy bridge, or covered gallery, high above the water, and divided by a stone wall into a passage and a cell. The state dungeons, called 'pozzi', or wells, were sunk in the thick walls of the palace; and the prisoner when taken out to die was conducted across the gallery to the other side, and being then led back into the other compartment, or cell, upon the bridge, was there strangled. The low portal through which the criminal was taken into this cell is now walled up; but the passage is still open, and is still known by the name of the Bridge of Sighs. The pozzi are under the flooring of the chamber at the foot of the bridge. They were formerly twelve, but on the first arrival of the French, the Venetians hastily blocked or broke up the deeper of these dungeons. You may still, however, descend by a trap-door, and crawl down through holes, half choked by rubbish, to the depth of two stories below the first range. If you are in want of consolation for the extinction of patrician power, perhaps you may find it there; scarcely a ray of light glimmers into the narrow gallery which leads to the cells, and the places of confinement themselves are totally dark. A small hole in the wall admitted the damp air of the passages, and served for the introduction of the prisoner's food. A wooden pallet, raised a foot from the ground, was the only furniture. The conductors tell you that a light was not allowed. The cells are about five paces in length, two and a half in width, and seven feet in height. They are directly beneath one another, and respiration is somewhat difficult in the lower holes. Only one prisoner was found when the republicans descended into these hideous recesses, and he is said to have been confined sixteen years. But the inmates of the dungeons beneath had left traces of their repentance, or of their despair, which are still visible, and may perhaps owe something to recent ingenuity. Some of the detained appear to have offended against, and others to have belonged to, the sacred body, not only from their signatures, but from the churches and belfries which they have scratched upon the walls. The reader may not object to see a specimen of the records prompted by so terrific a solitude. As nearly as they could be copied by more than one pencil, three of them are as follows:

I.

NON TI FIDAR AD ALCUNO PENSA e TACI
SE FUGIR VUOI DE SPIONI INSIDIE e LACCI
IL PENTIRTI PENTIRTI NULLA GIOVA
MA BEN DI VALOR TUO LA VERA PROVA
1607. ADI 2. GENARO. FUI RE-
TENTO P' LA BESTIEMMA P' AVER DATO
DA MANZAR A UN MORTO
IACOMO. GRITTI. SCRISSE.

2.

UN PARLAR POCHO et
NEGARE PRONTO et
UN PENSAR AL FINE PUO DARE LA VITA
A NOI ALTRI MESCHINI

1605

EGO IOHN BAPTISTA AD
ECCLESIAM CORTELLARIUS.

3.

DE CHI MI FIDO GUARDAMI DIO
DE CHI NON MI FIDO MI GUARDARO IO
$\overset{A}{V}$. LA S^{TA}. C^{H}. K^{A}. R^{NA}.

The copyist has followed, not corrected the solecisms; some of which are
however not quite so decided, since the letters were evidently scratched in
the dark. It only need be observed, that *Bestemmia* and *Mangiar* may be read
in the first inscription, which was probably written by a prisoner confined
for some act of impiety committed at a funeral: that *Cortellarius* is the name
of a parish on terra firma, near the sea: and that the last initials evidently are
put for *Viva la santa Chiesa Kattolica Romana*. [H]

10. An old writer, describing the appearance of Venice, has made use of the
above image, which would not be poetical were it not true. '*Quo fit ut qui
superne urbem contempletur, turritam telluris imaginem medio Oceano figuratam se
putet inspicere.*' Marci Antonii Sabelli *De Venetae Urbis situ* (Taurin, 1527), I.
202. [H]

19. The well known song of the gondoliers, of alternate stanzas, from Tasso's
Jerusalem, has almost died with the independence of Venice. Editions of the
poem, with the original on one column, and the Venetian variations on the
other, as sung by the boatmen, were once common, and are still to be found.
The following extract will serve to shew the difference between the Tuscan
epic and the 'Canta alla Barcariola'.

Original.

Canto l' arme pietose, e 'l capitano
  Che 'l gran Sepolcro liberò di Cristo.
Molto egli oprò col senno, e con la mano
  Molto soffri nel glorioso acquisto;
E in van l' Inferno a lui s' oppose, e in vano
  S' armò d' Asia, e di Libia il popol misto,
Che il Ciel gli diè favore, e sotto a i Santi
Segni ridusse i suoi compagni erranti.

Venetian.

L' arme pietose de cantar gho vogia,
    E de Goffredo la immortal braura
Che al fin l' ha libera co strassia, e dogia
    Del nostro buon Gesú la Sepoltura
De mezo mondo unito, e de quel Bogia
    Missier Pluton no l' ha bu mai paura:
Dio l' ha agiutá, e i compagni sparpagnai
Tutti 'l gh' i ha messi insieme i di del Dai.

Some of the elder gondoliers will, however, take up and continue a stanza of their once familiar bard.

On the 7th of last January, the author of *Childe Harold*, and another Englishman, the writer of this notice, rowed to the Lido with two singers, one of whom was a carpenter, and the other a gondolier. The former placed himself at the prow, the latter at the stern of the boat. A little after leaving the quay of the Piazzetta, they began to sing, and continued their exercise until we arrived at the island. They gave us, amongst other essays, the death of Clorinda, and the palace of Armida; and did not sing the Venetian, but the Tuscan verses. The carpenter, however, who was the cleverer of the two, and was frequently obliged to prompt his companion, told us that he could *translate* the original. He added, that he could sing almost three hundred stanzas, but had not spirits, (*morbin* was the word he used), to learn any more, or to sing what he already knew: a man must have idle time on his hands to acquire, or to repeat, and, said the poor fellow, 'look at my clothes and at me, I am starving.' This speech was more affecting than his performance, which habit alone can make attractive. The recitative was shrill, screaming, and monotonous, and the gondolier behind assisted his voice by holding his hand to one side of his mouth. The carpenter used a quiet action, which he evidently endeavoured to restrain; but was too much interested in his subject altogether to repress. From these men we learnt that singing is not confined to the gondoliers, and that, although the chant is seldom, if ever, voluntary, there are still several amongst the lower classes who are acquainted with a few stanzas.

It does not appear that it is usual for the performers to row and sing at the same time. Although the verses of the *Jerusalem* are no longer casually heard, there is yet much music upon the Venetian canals; and upon holidays, those strangers who are not near or informed enough to distinguish the words, may fancy that many of the gondolas still resound with the strains of Tasso. The writer of some remarks which appeared in the *Curiosities of Literature* must excuse his being twice quoted; for, with the exception of some phrases a little too ambitious and extravagant, he has furnished a very exact, as well as agreeable, description.

'In Venice the gondoliers know by heart long passages from Ariosto and Tasso, and often chant them with a peculiar melody. But this talent seems at present on the decline:—at least, after taking some pains, I could find no more than two persons who delivered to me in this way a passage from Tasso. I must add, that the late Mr. Berry once chanted to me a passage in Tasso in the manner, as he assured me, of the gondoliers.

'There are always two concerned, who alternately sing the strophes. We know the melody eventually by Rousseau, to whose songs it is printed; it has properly no melodious movement, and is a sort of medium between the canto fermo and the canto figurato; it approaches to the former by recitativical declamation, and to the latter by passages and course, by which one syllable is detained and embellished.

'I entered a gondola by moonlight; one singer placed himself forwards, and the other aft, and thus proceeded to St. Georgio. One began the song: when he had ended his strophe, the other took up the lay, and so continued the song alternately. Throughout the whole of it, the same notes invariably returned, but, according to the subject matter of the strophe, they laid a greater or a smaller stress, sometimes on one, and sometimes on another note, and indeed changed the enunciation of the whole strophe as the object of the poem altered.

'On the whole, however, the sounds were hoarse and screaming: they seemed, in the manner of all rude uncivilized men, to make the excellency of their singing in the force of their voice: one seemed desirous of conquering the other by the strength of his lungs; and so far from receiving delight from this scene (shut up as I was in the box of the gondola), I found myself in a very unpleasant situation.

'My companion, to whom I communicated this circumstance, being very desirous to keep up the credit of his countrymen, assured me that this singing was very delightful when heard at a distance. Accordingly we got out upon the shore, leaving one of the singers in the gondola, while the other went to the distance of some hundred paces. They now began to sing against one another, and I kept walking up and down between them both, so as always to leave him who was to begin his part. I frequently stood still and hearkened to the one and to the other.

'Here the scene was properly introduced. The strong declamatory, and, as it were, shrieking sound, met the ear from far, and called forth the attention; the quickly succeeding transitions, which necessarily required to be sung in a lower tone, seemed like plaintive strains succeeding the vociferations of emotion or of pain. The other, who listened attentively, immediately began where the former left off, answering him in milder or more vehement notes, according as the purport of the strophe required. The sleepy canals, the lofty buildings, the splendour of the moon, the deep shadows of the few gondolas, that moved like spirits hither and thither, increased the striking peculiarity of the scene; and amidst all these circumstances it was easy to confess the character of this wonderful harmony.

'It suits perfectly well with an idle solitary mariner, lying at length in his vessel at rest on one of these canals, waiting for his company, or for a fare, the tiresomeness of which situation is somewhat alleviated by the songs and poetical stories he has in memory. He often raises his voice as loud as he can, which extends itself to a vast distance over the tranquil mirror, and as all is still around, he is, as it were, in a solitude in the midst of a large and populous town. Here is no rattling of carriages, no noise of foot passengers: a silent gondola glides now and then by him, of which the splashing of the oars are scarcely to be heard.

'At a distance he hears another, perhaps utterly unknown to him. Melody and verse immediately attach the two strangers; he becomes the responsive echo to the former, and exerts himself to be heard as he had heard the other. By a tacit convention they alternate verse for verse; though the song should last the whole night through, they entertain themselves without fatigue; the hearers, who are passing between the two, take part in the amusement.

'This vocal performance sounds best at a great distance, and is then inexpressibly charming, as it only fulfils its design in the sentiment of remoteness. It is plaintive, but not dismal in its sound, and at times it is scarcely possible to refrain from tears. My companion, who otherwise was not a very delicately organized person, said quite unexpectedly: e singolare come quel canto intenerisce, e molto più quando lo cantano meglio.

'I was told that the women of Libo [sic], the long row of islands that divides the Adriatic from the Lagouns, particularly the women of the extreme districts of Malamocca and Palestrina, sing in like manner the works of Tasso to these and similar tunes.

'They have the custom, when their husbands are fishing out at sea, to sit along the shore in the evenings and vociferate these songs, and continue to do so with great violence, till each of them can distinguish the responses of her own husband at a distance.'

The love of music and of poetry distinguishes all classes of Venetians, even amongst the tuneful sons of Italy. The city itself can occasionally furnish respectable audiences for two and even three opera-houses at a time; and there are few events in private life that do not call forth a printed and circulated sonnet. Does a physician or a lawyer take his degree, or a clergyman preach his maiden sermon, has a surgeon performed an operation, would a harlequin announce his departure or his benefit, are you to be congratulated on a marriage, or a birth, or a lawsuit; the Muses are invoked to furnish the same number of syllables, and the individual triumphs blaze abroad in virgin white or party-coloured placards on half the corners of the capital. The last curtsey of a favourite 'prima donna' brings down a shower of these poetical tributes from those upper regions, from which, in our theatres, nothing but cupids and snow storms are accustomed to descend. There is a poetry in the very life of a Venetian, which, in its common course, is varied with those surprises and changes so recommendable in fiction, but so different from the sober monotony of northern existence; amusements are raised into duties, duties are softened into amusements, and every object being considered as equally making a part of the business of life, is announced and performed with the same earnest indifference and gay assiduity. The Venetian gazette constantly closes its columns with the following triple advertisement.

Charade.

Exposition of the most Holy Sacrament in the church
  of St.——

Theatres.

St. Moses, opera
St. Benedict, a comedy of characters.
St. Luke, repose.

When it is recollected what the Catholics believe their consecrated wafer to be, we may perhaps think it worthy of a more respectable niche than between poetry and the playhouse. [H]

95. The lion has lost nothing by his journey to the Invalides, but the gospel which supported the paw that is now on a level with the other foot. The horses also are returned to the ill-chosen spot whence they set out, and are, as before, half hidden under the porch window of St. Mark's church.

Their history, after a desperate struggle, has been satisfactorily explored. The decisions and doubts of Erizzo and Zanetti, and lastly, of the Count Leopold Cicognara, would have given them a Roman extraction, and a pedigree not more ancient than the reign of Nero. But M. de Schlegel stepped in to teach the Venetians the value of their own treasures, and a Greek vindicated, at last and for ever, the pretension of his countrymen to this noble production. Mr. Mustoxidi has not been left without a reply; but, as yet, he has received no answer. It should seem that the horses are irrevocably Chian, and were transferred to Constantinople by Theodosius. Lapidary writing is a favourite play of the Italians, and has conferred reputation on more than one of their literary characters. One of the best specimens of Bodoni's typography is a respectable volume of inscriptions, all written by his friend Pacciaudi. Several were prepared for the recovered horses. It is to be hoped the best was not selected, when the following words were ranged in gold letters above the cathedral porch.

QUATUOR . EQUORUM . SIGNA . A . VENETIS . BYZANTIO . CAPTA . AD . TEMP . D . MAR . A . R . S . MCCIV . POSITA . QUAE . HOSTILIS . CUPIDITAS . A . MDCCIIIC . ABSTULERAT . FRANC . I . IMP . PACIS . ORBI . DATAE . TROPHAEUM . A . MDCCCXV . VICTOR . REDUXIT.

Nothing shall be said of the Latin, but it may be permitted to observe, that the injustice of the Venetians in transporting the horses from Constantinople was at least equal to that of the French in carrying them to Paris, and that it would have been more prudent to have avoided all allusions to either robbery. An apostolic prince should, perhaps, have objected to affixing over the principal entrance of a metropolitan church, an inscription having a reference to any other triumphs than those of religion. Nothing less than the pacification of the world can excuse such a solecism. [H]

100. After many vain efforts on the part of the Italians entirely to throw off the yoke of Frederic Barbarossa, and as fruitless attempts of the Emperor to make himself absolute master throughout the whole of his Cisalpine dominions, the bloody struggles of four and twenty years were happily brought to a close in the city of Venice. The articles of a treaty had been previously agreed upon between Pope Alexander III. and Barbarossa, and the former having received a safe conduct, had already arrived at Venice from Ferrara, in company with the ambassadors of the king of Sicily and the consuls of the Lombard league. There still remained, however, many points to adjust, and for several days the peace was believed to be impracticable. At this juncture it was suddenly reported that the Emperor had arrived at Chioza, a town fifteen miles from the capital. The Venetians rose tumultuously, and insisted upon immediately conducting him to the city. The Lombards took the alarm, and departed towards Treviso. The Pope himself was apprehensive of some disaster if Frederic should suddenly advance upon him, but was reassured by the prudence and address of Sebastian Ziani, the doge. Several embassies passed between Chioza and the capital, until, at last, the Emperor relaxing somewhat of his pretensions, 'laid aside his leonine ferocity, and put on the mildness of the lamb'.

On Saturday the 23d of July, in the year 1177, six Venetian galleys transferred Frederic, in great pomp, from Chioza to the island of Lido, a mile from Venice. Early the next morning the Pope, accompanied by the Sicilian ambassadors, and by the envoys of Lombardy, whom he had recalled from the main land, together with a great concourse of people, repaired from the patriarchal palace to Saint Mark's church, and solemnly absolved the Emperor and his partisans from the excommunication pronounced against him. The Chancellor of the Empire, on the part of his master, renounced the antipopes and their schismatic adherents. Immediately the Doge, with a great suite both of the clergy and laity, got on board the galleys, and waiting on Frederic, rowed him in mighty state from the Lido to the capital. The Emperor descended from the galley at the quay of the Piazzetta. The doge, the patriarch, his bishops and clergy, and the people of Venice with their crosses and their standards, marched in solemn procession before him to the church of Saint Mark's. Alexander was seated before the vestibule of the basilica, attended by his bishops and cardinals, by the patriarch of Aquileja, by the archbishops and bishops of Lombardy, all of them in state, and clothed in their church robes. Frederic approached—'moved by the Holy Spirit, venerating the Almighty in the person of Alexander, laying aside his imperial dignity, and throwing off his mantle, he prostrated himself at full length at the feet of the Pope. Alexander, with tears in his eyes, raised him benignantly from the ground, kissed him, blessed him; and immediately the Germans of the train sang, with a loud voice, "We praise thee, O Lord." The Emperor then taking the Pope by the right hand, led him to the church, and having received his benediction, returned to the ducal palace.' The ceremony of humiliation was repeated the next day. The Pope himself, at the request of Frederic, said mass at Saint Mark's. The Emperor again laid aside his imperial mantle, and, taking a wand in his hand, officiated as *verger*, driving the laity from the choir, and preceding the pontiff to the altar. Alexander, after reciting the gospel, preached to the people. The Emperor put himself close to the pulpit in the attitude of listening; and the pontiff, touched by this mark of his attention, for he knew that Frederic did not understand a word he said, commanded the patriarch of Aquileja to translate the Latin discourse into the German tongue. The creed was then chanted. Frederic made his oblation and kissed the Pope's feet, and, mass being over, led him by the hand to his white horse. He held the stirrup, and would have led the horse's rein to the water side, had not the Pope accepted of the inclination for the performance, and affectionately dismissed him with his benediction. Such is the substance of the account left by the archbishop of Salerno, who was present at the ceremony, and whose story is confirmed by every subsequent narration. It would be not worth so minute a record, were it not the triumph of liberty as well as of superstition. The states of Lombardy owed to it the confirmation of their privileges; and Alexander had reason to thank the Almighty, who had enabled an infirm, unarmed old man to subdue a terrible and potent sovereign. [H]

107. The reader will recollect the exclamation of the highlander, *Oh for one hour of Dundee*! Henry Dandolo, when elected Doge, in 1192, was eighty-five years of age. When he commanded the Venetians at the taking of Constantinople, he was consequently ninety-seven years old. At this age he annexed the fourth and a half of the whole empire of Romania, for so the Roman empire was then called, to the title and to the territories of the Venetian Doge. The three-eighths of this empire were preserved in the diplomas until the dukedom of Giovanni Dolfino, who made use of the above designation in the year 1357.

Dandolo led the attack on Constantinople in person: two ships, the Paradise and the Pilgrim, were tied together, and a drawbridge or ladder let down from their higher yards to the walls. The Doge was one of the first to rush into the city. Then was completed, said the Venetians, the prophecy of the

Erythraean sybil. 'A gathering together of the powerful shall be made amidst the waves of the Adriatic, under a blind leader; they shall beset the goat—they shall profane Byzantium—they shall blacken her buildings—her spoils shall be dispersed; a new goat shall bleat until they have measured out and run over fifty-four feet, nine inches, and a half.'

Dandolo died on the first day of June 1205, having reigned thirteen years, six months, and five days, and was buried in the church of St. Sophia, at Constantinople. Strangely enough it must sound, that the name of the rebel apothecary who received the Doge's sword, and annihilated the ancient government in 1796–7, was Dandolo. [H]

III. After the loss of the battle of Pola, and the taking of Chioza on the 16th of August, 1379, by the united armament of the Genoese and Francesco da Carrara, Signor of Padua, the Venetians were reduced to the utmost despair. An embassy was sent to the conquerors with a blank sheet of paper, praying them to prescribe what terms they pleased, and leave to Venice only her independence. The Prince of Padua was inclined to listen to these proposals, but the Genoese, who, after the victory at Pola, had shouted 'to Venice, to Venice, and long live St. George', determined to annihilate their rival, and Peter Doria, their commander in chief, returned this answer to the suppliants: 'On God's faith, gentlemen of Venice, ye shall have no peace from the Signor of Padua, nor from our commune of Genoa, until we have first put a rein upon those unbridled horses of yours, that are upon the Porch of your evangelist St. Mark. Wild as we may find them, we will soon make them stand still. And this is the pleasure of us and of our commune. As for these my brothers of Genoa, that you have brought with you to give up to us, I will not have them: take them back; for, in a few days hence, I shall come and let them out of prison myself, both these and all the others.' In fact, the Genoese did advance as far as Malamocco, within five miles of the capital; but their own dangers and the pride of their enemies gave courage to the Venetians, who made prodigious efforts, and many individual sacrifices, all of them carefully recorded by their historians. Vettor Pisani was put at the head of thirty-four galleys. The Genoese broke up from Malamocco, and retired to Chioza in October; but they again threatened Venice, which was reduced to extremities. At this time, the 1st of January, 1380, arrived Carlo Zeno, who had been cruising on the Genoese coast with fourteen galleys. The Venetians were now strong enough to besiege the Genoese. Doria was killed on the 22d of January by a stone bullet 195 pounds weight, discharged from a bombard called the Trevisan. Chioza was then closely invested: 5000 auxiliaries, amongst whom were some English Condottieri, commanded by one Captain Ceccho, joined the Venetians. The Genoese, in their turn, prayed for conditions, but none were granted, until, at last, they surrendered at discretion; and, on the 24th of June 1380, the Doge Contarini made his triumphal entry into Chioza. Four thousand prisoners, nineteen galleys, many smaller vessels and barks, with all the ammunition and arms, and outfit of the expedition, fell into the hands of the conquerors, who, had it not been for the inexorable answer of Doria, would have gladly reduced their dominion to the city of Venice. An account of these transactions is found in a work called the War of Chioza, written by Daniel Chinazzo, who was in Venice at the time. [H]

134. The population of Venice at the end of the seventeenth century amounted to nearly two hundred thousand souls. At the last census, taken two years ago, it was no more than about one hundred and three thousand, and it diminishes daily. The commerce and the official employments, which were to be the unexhausted source of Venetian grandeur, have both expired. Most of the patrician mansions are deserted, and would gradually disappear, had not the government, alarmed by the demolition of seventy-two, during the last two years, expressly forbidden this sad resource of poverty. Many remnants of the Venetian nobility are now scattered and confounded with the wealthier Jews upon the banks of the Brenta, whose palladian palaces have sunk, or are sinking, in the general decay. Of the 'gentil uomo Veneto', the name is still known, and that is all. He is but the shadow of his former self, but he is polite and kind. It surely may be pardoned to him if he is querulous. Whatever may have been the vices of the republic, and although the natural term of its existence may be thought by foreigners to have arrived in the due course of mortality, only one sentiment can be expected from the Venetians themselves. At no time were the subjects of the republic so unanimous in their resolution to rally round the standard of St. Mark, as when it was for the last time unfurled; and the cowardice and the treachery of the few patricians who recommended the fatal neutrality, were confined to the persons of the traitors themselves. The present race cannot be thought to regret the loss of their aristocratical forms, and too despotic government; they think only on their vanished independence. They pine away at the remembrance, and on this subject suspend for a moment their gay good humour. Venice may be said, in the words of the scripture, 'to die daily'; and so general and so apparent is the decline, as to become painful to a stranger, not reconciled to the sight of a whole nation expiring as it were before his eyes. So artificial a creation having lost that principal which called it into life and supported its existence, must fall to pieces at once, and sink more rapidly than it rose. The abhorrence of slavery which drove the Venetians to the sea, has, since their disaster, forced them to the land, where they may be at least overlooked amongst the crowd of dependants, and not present the humiliating spectacle of a whole nation loaded with recent chains. Their liveliness, their affability, and that happy indifference which constitution alone can give, for philosophy aspires to it in vain, have not sunk under circumstances; but many peculiarities of costume and manner have

by degrees been lost, and the nobles, with a pride common to all Italians who have been masters, have not been persuaded to parade their insignificance. That splendour which was a proof and a portion of their power, they would not degrade into the trappings of their subjection. They retired from the space which they had occupied in the eyes of their fellow citizens; their continuance in which would have been a symptom of acquiescence, and an insult to those who suffered by the common misfortune. Those who remained in the degraded capital, might be said rather to haunt the scenes of their departed power, than to live in them. The reflection, 'who and what enthrals', will hardly bear a comment from one who is, nationally, the friend and the ally of the conqueror. It may, however, be allowed to say thus much, that to those who wish to recover their independence, any masters must be an object of detestation; and it may be safely foretold that this unprofitable aversion will not have been corrected before Venice shall have sunk into the slime of her choked canals. [H]

172. *Tannen* is the plural of *tanne*, a species of fir peculiar to the Alps, which only thrives in very rocky parts, where scarcely soil sufficient for its nourishment can be perceived. On these spots it grows to a greater height than any other tree in those countries. [B, n. in *MS. H, Proofs*]

235–61. The above description may seem fantastical or exaggerated to those who have never seen an Oriental or an Italian sky, yet it is but a literal and hardly sufficient delineation of an August evening (the eighteenth) as contemplated ⟨by/ as I was⟩ during many a ride along the banks of the Brenta near La Mira. [B, n. in. *MS. H, Proofs.*]

269. Thanks to the critical acumen of a Scotchman, we now know as little of Laura as ever. The discoveries of the Abbé de Sade, his triumphs, his sneers, can no longer instruct or amuse. We must not, however, think that these memoirs are as much a romance as Belisarius or the Incas, although we are told so by Dr. Beattie, a great name but a little authority. His 'labour' has not been in vain, notwithstanding his 'love' has, like most other passions, made him ridiculous. The hypothesis which over-powered the struggling Italians, and carried along less interested critics in its current, is run out. We have another proof that we can be never sure that the paradox, the most singular, and therefore having the most agreeable and authentic air, will not give place to the re-established ancient prejudice.

It seems, then, first, that Laura was born, lived, died, and was buried, not in Avignon, but in the country. The fountains of the Sorga, the thickets of Cabrieres may resume their pretensions, and the exploded *de la Bastie* again be heard with complacency. The hypothesis of the Abbé had no stronger props than the parchment sonnet and medal found on the skeleton of the wife of Hugo de Sade, and the manuscript note to the Virgil of Petrarch, now in the Ambrosian library. If these proofs were both incontestable, the poetry was written, the medal composed, cast, and deposited within the space of twelve hours; and these deliberate duties were performed round the carcase of one who died of the plague, and was hurried to the grave on the day of her death. These documents, therefore, are too decisive: they prove not the fact, but the forgery. Either the sonnet or the Virgilian note must be a falsification. The Abbé cites both as incontestably true; the consequent deduction is inevitable—they are both evidently false.

Secondly, Laura was never married, and was a haughty virgin rather than that *tender and prudent* wife who honoured Avignon by making that town the theatre of an honest French passion, and played off for one and twenty years her *little machinery* of alternate favours and refusals upon the first poet of the age. It was, indeed, rather too unfair that a female should be made responsible for eleven children upon the faith of a misinterpreted abbreviation, and the decision of a librarian. It is, however, satisfactory to think that the love of Petrarch was not platonic. The happiness which he prayed to possess but once and for a moment was surely not of the mind, and something so very real as a marriage project, with one who has been idly called a shadowy nymph, may be, perhaps, detected in at least six places of his own sonnets. The love of Petrarch was neither platonic nor poetical; and if in one passage of his works he calls it 'amore veementeissimo ma unico ed onesto', he confesses in a letter to a friend, that it was guilty and perverse, that it absorbed him quite and mastered his heart.

In this case, however, he was perhaps alarmed for the culpability of his wishes; for the Abbé de Sade himself, who certainly would not have been scrupulously delicate if he could have proved his descent from Petrarch as well as Laura, is forced into a stout defence of his virtuous grand-mother. As far as relates to the poet, we have no security for the innocence, except perhaps in the constancy of his pursuit. He assures us in his epistle to posterity that, when arrived at his fortieth year, he not only had in horror, but had lost all recollection and image of any 'irregularity'. But the birth of his natural daughter cannot be assigned earlier than his thirty-ninth year; and either the memory or the morality of the poet must have failed him, when he forgot or was guilty of this *slip*. The weakest argument for the purity of this love has been drawn from the permanence of effects, which survived the object of his passion. The reflection of Mr. de la Bastie, that virtue alone is capable of making impressions which death cannot efface, is one of those which every body applauds, and every body finds not to be true, the moment he examines his own breast or the records of human feeling. Such apothegms can do nothing for Petrarch or for the cause of morality, except with the very weak and the very young. He that has made even a little progress beyond ignorance and pupilage, cannot be edified with any thing but truth. What is called vindicating the honour of an individual or a nation, is the most futile, tedious and uninstructive of all writing; although it will always meet with more applause than that sober criticism, which is attributed to the malicious desire of reducing a great man to the common standard of humanity. It is, after all, not unlikely, that our historian was right in retaining his favorite hypothetic salvo, which secures the author, although it scarcely saves the honour of the still unknown mistress of Petrarch. [H]

271. Petrarch retired to Arquà immediately on his return from the unsuccessful attempt to visit Urban V. at Rome, in the year 1370, and, with the exception of his celebrated visit to Venice in company with Francesco Novello da Carrara, he appears to have passed the four last years of his life between that charming solitude and Padua. For four months previous to his death he was in a state of continual languor, and in the morning of July the 19th, in the year 1374, was found dead in his library chair with his head resting upon a book. The chair is still shown amongst the precious relics of Arquà, which, from the uninterrupted veneration that has been attached to every thing relative to this great man from the moment of his death to the present hour, have, it may be hoped, a better chance of authenticity than the Shakesperian memorials of Stratford upon Avon.

Arquà (for the last syllable is accented in pronunciation, although the analogy of the English language has been observed in the verse) is twelve miles from Padua, and about three miles on the right of the high road to Rovigo, in the bosom of the Euganean hills. After a walk of twenty minutes across a flat well wooded meadow, you come to a little blue lake, clear, but fathomless, and to the foot of a succession of acclivities and hills, clothed with vineyards and orchards, rich with fir and pomegranate trees, and every sunny fruit shrub. From the banks of the lake the road winds into the hills, and the church of Arquà is soon seen between a cleft where two ridges slope towards each other, and nearly inclose the village. The houses are scattered at intervals on the steep sides of these summits; and that of the poet is on the edge of a little knoll overlooking two descents, and commanding a view not only of the glowing gardens in the dales immediately beneath, but of the wide plains, above whose low woods of mulberry and willow thickened into a dark mass by festoons of vines, tall single cypresses, and the spires of towns are seen in the distance, which stretches to the mouths of the Po and the shores of the Adriatic. The climate of these volcanic hills is warmer, and the vintage begins a week sooner than in the plains of Padua. Petrarch is laid, for he cannot be said to be buried, in a sarcophagus of red marble, raised on four pilasters on an elevated base, and preserved from an association with meaner tombs. It stands conspicuously alone, but will be soon overshadowed by four lately planted laurels. Petrarch's fountain, for here every thing is Petrarch's, springs and expands itself beneath an artificial arch, a little below the church, and abounds plentifully, in the driest season, with that soft water which was the ancient wealth of the Euganean hills. It would be more attractive, were it not, in some seasons, beset with hornets and wasps. No other coincidence could assimilate the tombs of Petrarch and Archilochus. The revolutions of centuries have spared these sequestered vallies, and the only violence which has been offered to the ashes of Petrarch was prompted, not by hate, but veneration. An attempt was made to rob the sarcophagus of its treasure, and one of the arms was stolen by a Florentine through a rent which is still visible. The injury is not forgotten, but has served to identify the poet with the country where he was born, but where he would not live. A peasant boy of Arquà being asked who Petrarch was, replied, 'that the people of the parsonage knew all about him, but that he only knew that he was a Florentine'.

Mr. Forsyth was not quite correct in saying that Petrarch never returned to Tuscany after he had once quitted it when a boy. It appears he did pass through Florence on his way from Parma to Rome, and on his return in the year 1350, and remained there long enough to form some acquaintance with its most distinguished inhabitants. A Florentine gentleman, ashamed of the aversion of the poet for his native country, was eager to point out this trivial error in our accomplished traveller, whom he knew and respected for an extraordinary capacity, extensive erudition, and refined taste, joined to that engaging simplicity of manners which has been so frequently recognized as the surest, though it is certainly not an indispensable, trait of superior genius.

Every footstep of Laura's lover has been anxiously traced and recorded. The house in which he lodged is shewn in Venice. The inhabitants of Arezzo, in order to decide the ancient controversy between their city and the neighbouring Ancisa, where Petrarch was carried when seven months old, and remained until his seventh year, have designated by a long inscription the spot where their great fellow citizen was born. A tablet has been raised to him at Parma, in the chapel of St. Agatha, at the cathedral, because he was archdeacon of that society, and was only snatched from his intended sepulture in their church by a *foreign* death. Another tablet with a bust has been erected to him at Pavia, on account of his having passed the autumn of 1368 in that city, with his son in law Brossano. The political condition which has for ages precluded the Italians from the criticism of the living, has concentrated their attention to the illustration of the dead. [H]

298. The struggle is to the full as likely to be with daemons as with our better thoughts. Satan chose the wilderness for the temptation of our Savior. And our unsullied John Locke preferred the presence of a child to complete solitude. [H]

340. It is needless to more than mention the well known attacks on Tasso

by his contemporaries the Cruscans, academicians; and the subsequent flippant stuff of Boileau. [B, n. in *MS. H* and *Proofs*]

Perhaps the couplet in which Boileau depreciates Tasso, may serve as well as any other specimen to justify the opinion given of the harmony of French verse.

> A Malerbe a Racan préférer Theophile
> Et le clinquant du Tasse à tout l'or de Virgile.
>
> Sat. ix. vers. 176.

The biographer Serassi, out of tenderness to the reputation either of the Italian or the French poet, is eager to observe that the satirist recanted or explained away this censure, and subsequently allowed the author of the *Jerusalem* to be a 'genius, sublime, vast, and happily born for the higher flights of poetry'. To this we will add, that the recantation is far from satisfactory, when we examine the whole anecdote as reported by Olivet. The sentence pronounced against him by Bohours, is recorded only to the confusion of the critic, whose *palinodia* the Italian makes no effort to discover, and would not perhaps accept. As to the opposition which the *Jerusalem* encountered from the Cruscan academy, who degraded Tasso from all competition with Ariosto, below Bojardo and Pulci, the disgrace of such opposition must also in some measure be laid to the charge of Alfonso, and the court of Ferrara. For Leonard Salviati, the principal and nearly the sole origin of this attack, was, there can be no doubt, influenced by a hope to acquire the favour of the House of Este: an object which he thought attainable by exalting the reputation of a native poet at the expense of a rival, then a *prisoner of state*. The hopes and efforts of Salviati must serve to show the cotemporary opinion as to the nature of the poet's imprisonment; and will fill up the measure of our indignation at the tyrant jailer. In fact, the antagonist of Tasso was not disappointed in the reception given to his criticism; he was called to the court of Ferrara, where, having endeavoured to heighten his claims to favour, by panegyrics on the family of his sovereign; he was in his turn abandoned, and expired in neglected poverty. The opposition of the Cruscans was brought to a close in six years after the commencement of the controversy; and if the academy owed its first renown to having almost opened with such a paradox, it is probable that, on the other hand, the care of his reputation alleviated rather than aggravated the imprisonment of the injured poet. The defence of his father and of himself, for both were involved in the censure of Salviati, found employment for many of his solitary hours, and the captive could have been but little embarrassed to reply to accusations, where, amongst other delinquencies he was charged with invidiously omitting, in his comparison between France and Italy, to make any mention of the cupola of St. Maria del Fiore at Florence. The late biographer of Ariosto seems as if willing to renew the controversy by doubting the interpretation of Tasso's self-estimation related in Serassi's life of the poet. But Tiraboschi had before laid that rivalry at rest, by showing, that between Ariosto and Tasso it is not a question of comparison, but of preference. [H]

361. Before the remains of Ariosto were removed from the Benedictine church to the library of Ferrara, his bust, which surmounted the tomb, was struck by lightning, and a crown of iron laurels melted away. The event has been recorded by a writer of the last century. The transfer of these sacred ashes on the 6th of June 1801 was one of the most brilliant spectacles of the short-lived Italian Republic, and to consecrate the memory of the ceremony, the once famous fallen *Intrepidi* were revived and re-formed into the Ariostean academy. The large public place through which the procession paraded was then for the first time called Ariosto Square. The author of the Orlando is jealously claimed as the Homer, not of Italy, but Ferrara. The mother of Ariosto was of Reggio, and the house in which he was born is carefully distinguished by a tablet with these words: '*Qui nacque Ludovico Ariosto il giorno 8 di Settembre dell' anno 1474.*' But the Ferrarese make light of the accident by which their poet was born abroad, and claim him exclusively for their own. They possess his bones, they show his arm-chair, and his ink-stand, and his autographs.

> '. . . . . . Hic illius arma
> Hic currus fuit . . . . . .' [*Aeneid* I. 16–17]

The house where he lived, the room where he died, are designated by his own replaced memorial, and by a recent inscription. The Ferrarese are more jealous of their claims since the animosity of Denina, arising from a cause which their apologists mysteriously hint is not unknown to them, ventured to degrade their soil and climate to a Boeotian incapacity for all spiritual productions. A quarto volume has been called forth by the detraction, and this supplement to Barotti's *Memoirs* of the illustrious Ferrarese has been considered a triumphant reply to the 'Quadro Storico Statistico dell' Alta Italia'. [H]

364. The eagle, the sea calf, the laurel, and the white vine, were amongst the most approved preservatives against lightning: Jupiter chose the first, Augustus Caesar the second, and Tiberius never failed to wear a wreath of the third when the sky threatened a thunder storm. These superstitions may be received without a sneer in a country where the magical properties of the hazel twig have not lost all their credit; and perhaps the reader may not be much surprised to find that a commentator on Suetonius has taken upon himself gravely to disprove the imputed virtues of the crown of Tiberius, by mentioning that a few years before he wrote a laurel was actually struck by lightning at Rome. [H]

368. The Curtian lake and the Ruminal fig-tree in the Forum, having been touched by lightning, were held sacred, and the memory of the accident was preserved by a *puteal*, or altar, resembling the mouth of a well, with a little chapel covering the cavity supposed to be made by the thunderbolt. Bodies scathed and persons struck dead were thought to be incorruptible; and a stroke not fatal conferred perpetual dignity upon the man so distinguished by heaven.

Those killed by lightning were wrapped in a white garment, and buried where they fell. The superstition was not confined to the worshippers of Jupiter: the Lombards believed in the omens furnished by lightning, and a Christian priest confesses that, by a diabolical skill in interpreting thunder, a seer foretold to Agilulf, duke of Turin, an event which came to pass, and gave him a queen and a crown. There was, however, something equivocal in this sign, which the ancient inhabitants of Rome did not always consider propitious; and as the fears are likely to last longer than the consolations of superstition, it is not strange that the Romans of the age of Leo X. should have been so much terrified at some misinterpreted storms as to require the exhortations of a scholar who arrayed all the learning on thunder and lightning to prove the omen favourable: beginning with the flash which struck the walls of Velitrae, and including that which played upon a gate at Florence, and foretold the pontificate of one of its citizens. [H]

370. The two stanzas, XLII and XLIII are, with the exception of a line or two, a translation of the famous sonnet of [Vincenzo da] Filicaja [1642–1707]: 'Italia, Italia, O tu coi feo la sorte.' [B, n. in *MS. H, Proofs;* H, n. in *CHP IV*]

388. The celebrated letter of Servius Sulpicius to Cicero on the death of his daughter, describes as it then was, and now is, a path which I often traced in Greece, both by sea and land, in different journeys and voyages.

'On my return from Asia, as I was sailing from Aegina towards Megara, I began to contemplate the prospect of the countries around me: Aegina was behind, Megara before me; Piraeus on the right, Corinth on the left; all which towns, once famous and flourishing, now lie overturned and buried in their ruins. Upon this sight, I could not but think presently within myself, Alas! how do we poor mortals fret and vex ourselves if any of our friends happen to die or be killed, whose life is yet so short, when the carcases of so many noble cities lie here exposed before me in one view.' [B]

413. It is Poggio who, looking from the Capitoline hill upon ruined Rome, breaks forth into the exclamation, 'Ut nunc omni decore nudata, prostrata jacet, instar gigantei cadaveris corrupti atque undique exesi.' [H]

433. The view of the Venus of Medicis instantly suggests the lines in the *Seasons*, and the comparison of the object with the description proves, not only the correctness of the portrait, but the peculiar turn of thought, and, if the term may be used, the sexual imagination of the descriptive poet. The same conclusion may be deduced from another hint in the same episode of Musidora; for Thomson's notion of the privileges of favoured love must have been either very primitive, or rather deficient in delicacy, when he made his grateful nymph inform her discreet Damon that in some happier moment he might perhaps be the companion of her bath:

'The time may come you need not fly.'

The reader will recollect the anecdote told in the life of Dr. Johnson. We will not leave the Florentine gallery without a word on the *Whetter*. It seems strange that the character of that disputed statue should not be entirely decided, at least in the mind of any one who has seen a sarcophagus in the vestibule of the Basilica of St. Paul without the walls, at Rome, where the whole group of the fable of Marsyas is seen in tolerable preservation; and the Scythian slave whetting the knife is represented exactly in the same position as this celebrated masterpiece. The slave is not naked: but it is easier to get rid of this difficulty than to suppose the knife in the hand of the Florentine statue an instrument for shaving, which it must be, if, as Lanzi supposes, the man is no other than the barber of Julius Caesar. Winkelmann, illustrating a bas relief of the same subject, follows the opinion of Leonard Agostini, and his authority might have been thought conclusive, even if the resemblance did not strike the most careless observer.

Amongst the bronzes of the same princely collection, is still to be seen the inscribed tablet copied and commented upon by Mr. Gibbon. Our historian found some difficulties, but did not desist from his illustration: he might be vexed to hear that his criticism has been thrown away on an inscription now generally recognized to be a forgery. [H]

478. This name will recal the memory, not only of those whose tombs have raised the Santa Croce into the centre of pilgrimage, the Mecca of Italy, but of her whose eloquence was poured over the illustrious ashes, and whose voice is now as mute as those she sung. CORINNA is no more; and with her should expire the fear, the flattery, and the envy, which threw too dazzling or too dark a cloud round the march of genius, and forbad the steady gaze of disinterested criticism. We have her picture embellished or distorted, as friendship or detraction has held the pencil: the impartial portrait was hardly to be expected from a cotemporary. The immediate voice of her survivors will, it is probable, be far from affording a just estimate of her singular capacity. The gallantry, the love of wonder, and the hope of associated fame, which blunted the edge of censure, must cease to exist.—The dead have no sex; they can suprise by no new miracles; they can confer no privilege: Corinna has ceased to be a woman—she is only an author: and it may be foreseen that many will repay themselves for former complaisance, by a severity to which the extravagance of previous praises may perhaps give the colour of truth. The latest posterity, for to the latest posterity they will assuredly descend, will have to pronounce upon her various productions; and the longer the vista through which they are seen, the more accurately minute will be the object, the more certain the justice, of the decision. She will enter into that existence in which the great writers of all ages and nations are, as it were, associated in a world of their own, and, from that superior sphere, shed their eternal influence for the control and consolation of mankind. But the individual will gradually disappear as the author is more distinctly seen: some one, there- fore, of all those whom the charms of involuntary wit, and of easy hospitality, attracted within the friendly circles of Coppet, should rescue from oblivion those virtues which, although they are said to love the shade, are, in fact, more frequently chilled than excited by the domestic cares of private life. Some one should be found to pourtray the unaffected graces with which she adorned those dearer relationships, the performance of whose duties is rather discovered amongst the interior secrets, than seen in the outward manage- ment, of family intercourse; and which, indeed, it requires the delicacy of genuine affection to qualify for the eye of an indifferent spectator. Some one should be found, not to celebrate, but to describe, the amiable mistress of an open mansion, the centre of a society, ever varied, and always pleased, the creator of which, divested of the ambition and the arts of public rivalry, shone forth only to give fresh animation to those around her. The mother tenderly affectionate and tenderly beloved, the friend unboundedly generous, but still esteemed, the charitable patroness of all distress, cannot be forgotten by those whom she cherished, and protected, and fed. Her loss will be mourned the most where she was known the best; and, to the sorrows of very many friends and more dependants, may be offered the disinterested regret of a stranger, who, amidst the sublimer scenes of the Leman lake, received his chief satisfaction from contemplating the engaging qualities of the incomparable Corinna. [B]

484. Alfieri is the great name of this age. The Italians, without waiting for the hundred years, consider him as 'a poet good in law'.—His memory is the more dear to them because he is the bard of freedom; and because, as such, his tragedies can receive no countenance from any of their sovereigns. They are but very seldom, and but very few of them, allowed to be acted. It was observed by Cicero, that nowhere were the true opinions and feelings of the Romans so clearly shown as at the theatre. In the autumn of 1816, a cele- brated improvisatore exhibited his talents at the Opera-house of Milan. The reading of the theses handed in for the subjects of his poetry was received by a very numerous audience, for the most part in silence, or with laughter; but when the assistant, unfolding one of the papers, exclaimed, '*The apotheosis of Victor Alfieri*', the whole theatre burst into a shout, and the applause was continued for some moments. The lot did not fall on Alfieri; and the Signor Sgricci had to pour forth his extemporary common-places on the bombardment of Algiers. The choice, indeed, is not left to accident quite so much as might be thought from a first view of the ceremony; and the police not only takes care to look at the papers beforehand, but, in case of any prudential after-thought, steps in to correct the blindness of chance. The proposal for deifying Alfieri was received with immediate enthusiasm, the rather because it was conjectured there would be no opportunity of carrying it into effect. [H]

486. The affectation of simplicity in sepulchral inscriptions, which so often leaves us uncertain whether the structure before us is an actual depository, or a cenotaph, or a simple memorial not of death but life, has given to the tomb of Machiavelli no information as to the place or time of the birth or death, the age or parentage, of the historian.

TANTO NOMINI NVLLVM PAR ELOGIVM
NICCOLAVS MACHIAVELLI.

There seems at least no reason why the name should not have been put above the sentence which alludes to it.

It will readily be imagined that the prejudices which have passed the name of Machiavelli into an epithet proverbial of iniquity, exist no longer at Florence. His memory was persecuted as his life had been for an attachment to liberty, incompatible with the new system of despotism, which succeeded the fall of the free governments of Italy. He was put to the torture for being a '*libertine*', that is, for wishing to restore the republic of Florence; and such are the undying efforts of those who are interested in the perversion not only of the nature of actions, but the meaning of words, that what was once *patriotism*, has by degrees come to signify *debauch*. We have ourselves outlived the old meaning of 'liberality', which is now another word for treason in one country and for infatuation in all. It seems to have been a strange mistake to accuse the author of the Prince, as being a pandar to tyranny; and to think that the inquisition would condemn his work for such a delinquency. The fact is that Machiavelli, as is usual with those against whom no crime can be proved, was suspected of and charged with atheism; and the first and last most violent opposers of the Prince were both Jesuits, one of whom persuaded the Inquisition 'benchè fosse tardo', to prohibit the treatise, and the other qualified the secretary of the Florentine republic as no better than a fool. The father [Antonio] Possevin was proved never to have read the book, and the father [Romoaldo] Lucchesini not to have understood it. It is clear, however, that such critics must have objected not to the slavery of the doctrines, but to the supposed tendency of a lesson which shows how distinct are the interests of a monarch from the happiness of mankind. The Jesuits are re-established in Italy, and the last chapter of the Prince may again call forth a particular refutation, from those who are employed once more in moulding the minds of the rising generation, so as to receive the impressions of despotism. The chapter bears for title, 'Esortazione a liberare la Italia dai Barbari', and concludes with a *libertine* excitement to the future redemption of Italy. '*Non si deve adunque lasciar passare questa occasione, acciocchè la Italia vegga dopo tanto tempo apparire un suo redentore. Nè posso esprimere con qual amore ei fusse ricevuto in tutte quelle provincie, che hanno patito per queste illuvioni esterne, con qual sete di vendetta, con che ostinata fede, con che lacrime. Quali porte se li serrerebeno? Quali popoli li negherebbeno la obbedienza? Quale Italiano li negherebbe l'ossequio?* AD OGNUNO PUZZA QUESTO BARBARO DOMINIO.' [H]

505. Dante was born in Florence in the year 1261. He fought in two battles, was fourteen times ambassador, and once prior of the republic. When the party of Charles of Anjou triumphed over the Bianchi, he was absent on an embassy to Pope Boniface VIII, and was condemned to two years banishment, and to a fine of 8000 lire; on the non-payment of which he was further punished by the sequestration of all his property. The republic, however, was not content with this satisfaction, for in 1772 was discovered in the archives at Florence a sentence in which Dante is the eleventh of a list of fifteen condemned in 1302 to be burnt alive; *Talis perveniens igne comburatur sic quod moriatur.* The pretext for this judgment was a proof of unfair barter, extortions, and illicit gains. *Baracteriarum iniquarum, extorsionum, et illicitorum lucrorum,* and with such an accusation it is not strange that Dante should have always protested his innocence, and the injustice of his fellow-citizens. His appeal to Florence was accompanied by another to the Emperor Henry, and the death of that sovereign in 1313, was the signal for a sentence of irrevocable banishment. He had before lingered near Tuscany with hopes of recal; then travelled into the north of Italy, where Verona had to boast of his longest residence, and he finally settled at Ravenna, which was his ordinary but not constant abode until his death. The refusal of the Venetians to grant him a public audience, on the part of Guido Novello da Polenta his protector, is said to have been the principal cause of this event, which happened in 1321. He was buried ('in sacra minorum aede,') at Ravenna, in a handsome tomb, which was erected by Guido, restored by Bernardo Bembo in 1483, pretor for that republic which had refused to hear him, again restored by Cardinal Corsi in 1692, and replaced by a more magnificent sepulchre, constructed in 1780 at the expense of the Cardinal Luigi Valenti Gonzaga. The offence or misfortune of Dante was an attachment to a defeated party, and, as his best favourable biographers alledge against him, too great a freedom of speech and haughtiness of manner. But the next age paid honours almost divine to the exile. The Florentines, having in vain and frequently attempted to recover his body, crowned his image in a church, and his picture is still one of the idols of their

cathedral. They struck medals, they raised statues to him. The cities of Italy, not being able to dispute about his own birth, contended for that of his great poem, and the Florentines thought it for their honour to prove that he had finished the seventh Canto, before they drove him from his native city. Fifty-one years after his death, they endowed a professorial chair for the expounding of his verses, and Boccaccio was appointed to this patriotic employment. The example was imitated by Bologna and Pisa, and the commentators, if they performed but little service to literature, augmented the veneration which beheld a sacred or moral allegory in all the images of his mystic muse. His birth and his infancy were discovered to have been distinguished above those of ordinary men: the author of the *Decameron*, his earliest biographer, relates that his mother was warned in a dream of the importance of her pregnancy; and it was found, by others, that at ten years of age he had manifested his precocious passion for that wisdom or theology, which, under the name of Beatrice, had been mistaken for a substantial mistress. When the *Divine Comedy* had been recognized as a mere mortal production, and at the distance of two centuries, when criticism and competition had sobered the judgment of Italians, Dante was seriously declared superior to Homer, and though the preference appeared to some casuists 'an heretical blasphemy worthy of the flames', the contest was vigorously maintained for nearly fifty years. In later times it was made a question which of the Lords of Verona could boast of having patronised him, and the jealous scepticism of one writer would not allow Ravenna the undoubted possession of his bones. Even the critical Tiraboschi was inclined to believe that the poet had foreseen and foretold one of the discoveries of Galileo. Like the great originals of other nations, his popularity has not always maintained the same level. The last age seemed inclined to undervalue him as a model and a study; and Bettinelli one day rebuked his pupil Monti, for poring over the harsh, and obsolete extravagances of the *Commedia*. The present generation having recovered from the Gallic idolatries of Cesarotti, has returned to the ancient worship, and the *Danteggiare* of the northern Italians is thought even indiscreet by the more moderate Tuscans.

There is still much curious information relative to the life and writings of this great poet which has not as yet been collected even by the Italians; but the celebrated Ugo Foscolo meditates to supply this defect, and it is not to be regretted that this national work has been reserved for one so devoted to his country and the cause of truth. [H]

506. The elder Scipio Africanus had a tomb if he was not buried at Liternum, whither he had retired to voluntary banishment. The tomb was near the sea-shore, and the story of an inscription upon it, *Ingrata Patria*, having given a name to a modern tower, is, if not true, an agreeable fiction. If he was not buried, he certainly lived there.

In così angusta e solitaria villa
Era 'l grand' uomo che d'Africa s'appella
Perchè prima col ferro al vivo aprilla.

Ingratitude is generally supposed the vice peculiar to republics; and it seems to be forgotten that for one instance of popular inconstancy, we have a hundred examples of the fall of courtly favourites. Besides, a people have often repented—a monarch seldom or never. Leaving apart many familiar proofs of this fact, a short story may show the difference between even an aristocracy and the multitude.

Vettor Pisani, having been defeated in 1354 at Portolongo, and many years afterwards in the more decisive action of Pola, by the Genoese, was recalled by the Venetian government, and thrown into chains. The Avvogadori proposed to behead him, but the supreme tribunal was content with the sentence of imprisonment. Whilst Pisani was suffering this unmerited disgrace, Chioza, in the vicinity of the capital, was, by the assistance of the *Signor of Padua*, delivered into the hands of Pietro Doria. At the intelligence of that disaster, the great bell of St. Mark's tower rolled to arms, and the people and the soldiery of the gallies were summoned to the repulse of the approaching enemy; but they protested they would not move a step, unless Pisani were liberated and placed at their head. The great council was instantly assembled: the prisoner was called before them, and the Doge, Andrea Contarini, informed him of the demands of the people and the necessities of the state, whose only hope of safety was reposed on his efforts, and who implored him to forget the indignities he had endured in her service. 'I have submitted', replied the magnanimous republican, 'I have submitted to your deliberations without complaint; I have supported patiently the pains of imprisonment, for they were inflicted at your command: this is no time to inquire whether I deserved them—the good of the republic may have seemed to require it, and that which the republic resolves is always resolved wisely. Behold me ready to lay down my life for the preservation of my country.' Pisani was appointed generalissimo, and by his exertions, in conjunction with those of Carlo Zeno, the Venetians soon recovered the ascendancy over their maritime rivals.

The Italian communities were no less unjust to their citizens than the Greek republics. Liberty, both with the one and the other, seems to have been a national, not an individual object: and, notwithstanding the boasted *equality before the laws* which an ancient Greek writer considered the great distinctive mark between his countrymen and the barbarians, the mutual rights of fellow-citizens seem never to have been the principal scope of the old democracies. The world may have not yet seen an essay by the author of the Italian Republics, in which the distinction between the liberty of former states, and the signification attached to that word by the happier constitution of England, is ingeniously developed. The Italians, however, when they had ceased to be free, still looked back with a sigh upon those times of turbulence, when every citizen might rise to a share of sovereign power, and have never been taught fully to appreciate the repose of a monarchy. Sperone Speroni, when Francis Maria II. Duke of Rovere, proposed the question, 'which was preferable, the republic or the principality—the perfect and not durable, or the less perfect and not so liable to change', replied, 'that our happiness is to be measured by its quality, not by its duration; and that he preferred to live for one day like a man, than for a hundred years like a brute, a stock, or a stone.' This was thought, and called, a *magnificent answer*, down to the last days of Italian servitude. [H]

510. The Florentines did not take the opportunity of Petrarch's short visit to their city in 1350 to revoke the decree which confiscated the property of his father, who had been banished shortly after the exile of Dante. His crown did not dazzle them; but when in the next year they were in want of his assistance in the formation of their university, they repented of their injustice, and Boccaccio was sent to Padua to intreat the laureate to conclude his wanderings in the bosom of his native country, where he might finish his *immortal Africa*, and enjoy, with his recovered possessions, the esteem of all classes of his fellow-citizens. They gave him the option of the book and the science he might condescend to expound: they called him the glory of his country, who was dear, and would be dearer to them; and they added, that if there was any thing unpleasing in their letter, he ought to return amongst them, were it only to correct their style. Petrarch seemed at first to listen to the flattery and to the intreaties of his friend, but he did not return to Florence, and preferred a pilgrimage to the tomb of Laura and the shades of Vaucluse. [H]

514. Boccaccio was buried in the church of St. Michael and St. James, at Certaldo, a small town in the Valdelsa, which was by some supposed the place of his birth. There he passed the latter part of his life in a course of laborious study, which shortened his existence; and there might his ashes have been secure, if not of honour, at least of repose. But the 'hyaena bigots' of Certaldo tore up the tombstone of Boccaccio, and ejected it from the holy precincts of St. Michael and St. James. The occasion and, it may be hoped, the excuse, of this ejectment was the making of a new floor for the church; but the fact is, that the tomb-stone was taken up and thrown aside at the bottom of the building. Ignorance may share the sin with bigotry. It would be painful to relate such an exception to the devotion of the Italians for their great names, could it not be accompanied by a trait more honourably conformable to the general character of the nation. The principal person of the district, the last branch of the house of Medicis, afforded that protection to the memory of the insulted dead which her best ancestors had dispensed upon all cotemporary merit. The Marchioness Lenzoni rescued the tombstone of Boccaccio from the neglect in which it had sometime lain, and found for it an honourable elevation in her own mansion. She has done more: the house in which the poet lived has been as little respected as his tomb, and is falling to ruin over the head of one indifferent to the name of its former tenant. It consists of two or three little chambers, and a low tower, on which Cosmo II. affixed an inscription. This house she has taken measures to purchase, and proposes to devote to it that care and consideration which are attached to the cradle and to the roof of genius.

This is not the place to undertake the defence of Boccaccio; but the man who exhausted his little patrimony in the acquirement of learning, who was amongst the first, if not the first, to allure the science and the poetry of Greece to the bosom of Italy;—who not only invented a new style, but founded, or certainly fixed, a new language; who, besides the esteem of every polite court of Europe, was thought worthy of employment by the pre-dominant republic of his own country, and, what is more, of the friendship of Petrarch, who lived the life of a philosopher and a freeman, and who died in the pursuit of knowledge,—such a man might have found more consideration than he has met with from the priest of Certaldo, and from a late English traveller, who strikes off his portraits as an odious, contemptible, licentious writer, whose impure remains should be suffered to rot without a record. That English traveller, unfortunately for those who have to deplore the loss of a very amiable person, is beyond all criticism; but the mortality which did not protect Boccaccio from Mr. Eustace, must not defend Mr. Eustace from the impartial judgment of his successors.—Death may canonize his virtues, not his errors; and it may be modestly pronounced that he transgressed, not only as an author, but as a man, when he evoked the shade of Boccaccio in company with that of Aretine, amidst the sepulchres of Santa Croce, merely to dismiss it with indignity. As far as respects

'Il flagello de' Principi,
Il divin Pietro Aretino,'

it is of little import what censure is passed upon a coxcomb who owes his present existence to the above burlesque character given to him by the poet whose amber has preserved many other grubs and worms: but to classify Boccaccio with such a person, and to excommunicate his very ashes, must of itself make us doubt of the qualification of the classical tourist for writing upon Italian, or, indeed, upon any other literature; for ignorance on one point may incapacitate an author merely for that particular topic, but subjection to a professional prejudice must render him an unsafe director on all occasions. Any perversion and injustice may be made what is vulgarly called 'a case of conscience', and this poor excuse is all that can be offered for the priest of Certaldo, or the author of the *Classical Tour*. It would have answered the purpose to confine the censure to the novels of Boccaccio, and gratitude to that source which supplied the muse of Dryden with her last and most harmonious numbers, might perhaps have restricted that censure to the objectionable qualities of the hundred tales. At any rate the repentance of Boccaccio might have arrested his exhumation, and it should have been recollected and told, that in his old age he wrote a letter intreating his friend to discourage the reading of the *Decameron*, for the sake of modesty, and for the sake of the author, who would not have an apologist always at hand to state in his excuse that he wrote it when young, and at the command of his superiors. It is neither the licentiousness of the writer, nor the evil propensities of the reader, which have given to the *Decameron* alone, of all the works of Boccaccio, a perpetual popularity. The establishment of a new and delightful dialect conferred an immortality on the works in which it was first fixed. The sonnets of Petrarch were, for the same reason, fated to survive his self-admired *Africa*, the *'favourite of kings'*. The invariable traits of nature and feeling with which the novels, as well as the verses, abound, have doubtless been the chief source of the foreign celebrity of both authors; but Boccaccio, as a man, is no more to be estimated by that work, than Petrarch is to be regarded in no other light than as the lover of Laura. Even, however, had the father of the Tuscan prose been known only as the author of the *Decameron*, a considerate writer would have been cautious to pronounce a sentence irreconcilable with the unerring voice of many ages and nations. An irrevocable value has never been stamped upon any work solely recommended by impurity.

The true source of the outcry against Boccaccio, which began at a very early period, was the choice of his scandalous personages in the cloisters as well as the courts; but the princes only laughed at the gallant adventures so unjustly charged upon Queen Theodelinda, whilst the priesthood cried shame upon the debauches drawn from the convent and the hermitage; and, most probably for the opposite reason, namely, that the picture was faithful to the life. Two of the novels are allowed to be facts usefully turned into tales, to deride the canonization of rogues and laymen. Ser Ciappelletto and Marcellinus are cited with applause even by the decent Muratori. The great Arnaud, as he is quoted in Bayle, states, that a new edition of the novels was proposed, of which the expurgation consisted in omitting the words 'monk' and 'nun', and tacking the immoralities to other names. The literary history of Italy particularises no such edition; but it was not long before the whole of Europe had but one opinion of the Decameron; and the absolution of the author seems to have been a point settled at least a hundred years ago: 'On se feroit siffler si l'on pretendoit convaincre Boccace de n'avoir pas été honnête homme, puis qu'il a fait le Decameron.' So said one of the best men, and perhaps the best critic, that ever lived—the very martyr to impartiality. But as this information, that in the beginning of the last century one would have been hooted at for pretending that Boccaccio was not a good man, may seem to come from one of those enemies who are to be suspected, even when they make us a present of truth, a more acceptable contrast with the proscription of the body, soul, and muse of Boccaccio may be found in a few words from the virtuous, the patriotic cotemporary, who thought one of the tales of this impure writer worthy a Latin version from his own pen. '*I have remarked elsewhere,*' says Petrarch, writing to Boccaccio, '*that the book itself has been worried by certain dogs, but stoutly defended by your staff and voice. Nor was I astonished, for I have had proof of the vigour of your mind, and I know you have fallen on that unaccommodating incapable race of mortals who, whatever they either like not, or know not, or cannot do, are sure to reprehend in others; and on those occasions only put on a show of learning and eloquence, but otherwise are entirely dumb.*'

It is satisfactory to find that all the priesthood do not resemble those of Certaldo, and that one of them who did not possess the bones of Boccaccio would not lose the opportunity of raising a cenotaph to his memory. Bevius, canon of Padua, at the beginning of the 16th century erected at Arquà, opposite to the tomb of the Laureate, a tablet, in which he associated Boccaccio to the equal honours of Dante and of Petrarch. [H]

532. Our veneration for the Medici begins with Cosmo and expires with his grandson; that stream is pure only at the source; and it is in search of some memorial of the virtuous republicans of the family, that we visit the church of St. Lorenzo at Florence. The tawdry, glaring, unfinished chapel in that church, designed for the mausoleum of the Dukes of Tuscany, set round with crowns and coffins, gives birth to no emotions but those of contempt for the lavish vanity of a race of despots, whilst the pavement slab simply inscribed to the Father of his Country, reconciles us to the name of Medici. It was very natural for Corinna to suppose that the statue raised to the Duke of Urbino in the *capella de' depositi* was intended for his great namesake; but the magnificent Lorenzo is only the sharer of a coffin half hidden in a niche of the sacristy. The decay of Tuscany dates from the sovereignty of the Medici. Of the sepulchral peace which succeeded to the establishment of the reigning families in Italy, our own Sidney has given us a glowing, but a faithful picture. 'Notwithstanding all the seditions of Florence, and other cities of Tuscany, the horrid factions of Guelphs and Ghibelins, Neri and Bianchi, nobles and commons, they continued populous, strong, and exceeding rich; but in the space of less than a hundred and fifty years, the peaceable reign of the Medices is thought to have destroyed nine parts in ten of the people of that province. Amongst other things it is remarkable, that when Philip the Second of Spain gave Sienna to the Duke of Florence, his embassador then at Rome sent him word, that he had given away more than 650,000 subjects; and it is not believed there are now 20,000 souls inhabiting that city and territory. Pisa, Pistoia, Arezzo, Cortona, and other towns, that were then good and populous, are in the like proportion diminished, and Florence more than any. When that city had been long troubled with seditions, tumults, and wars, for the most part unprosperous, they still retained such strength, that when Charles VIII. of France, being admitted as a friend with his whole army, which soon after conquered the kingdom of Naples, thought to master them, the people taking arms, struck such a terror into him, that he was glad to depart upon such conditions as they thought fit to impose. Machiavel reports, that in that time Florence alone, with the Val d'Arno, a small territory belonging to that city, could, in a few hours, by the sound of a bell, bring together 135,000 well-armed men; whereas now that city, with all the others in that province, are brought to such despicable weakness, emptiness, poverty and baseness, that they can neither resist the oppressions of their own prince, nor defend him or themselves if they were assaulted by a foreign enemy. The people are dispersed or destroyed, and the best families sent to seek habitations in Venice, Genoa, Rome, Naples and Lucca. This is not the effect of war or pestilence; they enjoy a perfect peace, and suffer no other plague than the government they are under.' From the usurper Cosmo down to the imbecil Gaston, we look in vain for any of those unmixed qualities which should raise a patriot to the command of his fellow citizens. The Grand Dukes, and particularly the third Cosmo, had operated so entire a change in the Tuscan character, that the candid Florentines in excuse for some imperfections in the philanthropic system of Leopold, are obliged to confess that the sovereign was the only liberal man in his dominions. Yet that excellent prince himself had no other notion of a national assembly, than of a body to represent the wants and wishes, not the will of the people. [H]

563. '*And such was their mutual animosity, so intent were they upon the battle, that the earthquake, which overthrew in great part many of the cities of Italy, which turned the course of rapid streams, poured back the sea upon the rivers, and tore down the very mountains, was not felt by one of the combatants.*' Such is the description of Livy. It may be doubted whether modern tactics would admit of such an abstraction.

The site of the battle of Thrasimene is not to be mistaken. The traveller from the village under Cortona to Casa di Piano, the next stage on the way to Rome, has for the first two or three miles, around him, but more particularly to the right, that flat land which Hannibal laid waste in order to induce the Consul Flaminius to move from Arezzo. On his left, and in front of him, is a ridge of hills, bending down towards the lake of Thrasimene, called by Livy 'montes Cortonenses', and now named the Gualandra. These hills he approaches at Ossaja, a village which the itineraries pretend to have been so denominated from the bones found there: but there have been no bones found there, and the battle was fought on the other side of the hill. From Ossaja the road begins to rise a little, but does not pass into the roots of the mountains until the sixty-seventh mile-stone from Florence. The ascent thence is not steep but perpetual, and continues for twenty minutes. The lake is soon seen below on the right, with Borghetto, a round tower close upon the water; and the undulating hills partially covered with wood, amongst which the road winds, sink by degrees into the marshes near to this tower. Lower than the road, down to the right amidst these woody hillocks, Hannibal placed his horse, in the jaws of or rather above the pass, which was between the lake and the present road, and most probably close to Borghetto, just under the lowest of the 'tumuli'. On a summit to the left, above the road, is an old circular ruin which the peasants call 'the Tower of Hannibal the Carthaginian'. Arrived at the highest point of the road, the traveller has a partial view of the fatal plain which opens fully upon him as he descends the Gualandra. He soon finds himself in a vale inclosed to the left and in front and behind him by the Gualandra hills, bending round in a segment larger than a semicircle, and running down at each end to the lake, which obliques to the right and forms the chord of this mountain arc. The position cannot be guessed at from the plains of Cortona, nor appears to be so completely inclosed unless to one who is fairly within the hills. It then, indeed, appears 'a place made as it were on purpose for a snare', *locus insidiis natus*. 'Borghetto is then found to stand in a narrow marshy pass close to the hill and to the lake, whilst there is no other outlet at the opposite turn of the mountains than through the little town of Passignano, which is pushed into the water by the foot of a high rocky acclivity.' There is a woody eminence branching down from the mountains into the upper end of the plain nearer to the side of Passignano, and on this stands a white village called Torre. Polybius seems to allude to this eminence as the one on which Hannibal encamped and drew out his heavy armed Africans and Spaniards in a conspicuous position. From this spot he dispatched his Balearic and light-armed troops round through the Gualandra heights to the right, so as to arrive unseen and form an ambush amongst the broken acclivities which the road now passes, and to be ready to act upon the left flank and above the enemy, whilst the horse shut up the pass behind. Flaminius came to the lake near Borghetto at sunset; and, without sending any spies before him, marched through the pass the next morning before the day had quite broken, so that he perceived nothing of the horse and light troops above and about him, and saw only the heavy armed Carthaginians in front on the hill of Torre. The Consul began to draw out his army in the flat, and in the mean time the horse in ambush occupied the pass behind him at Borghetto. Thus the Romans were completely inclosed, having the lake on the right, the main army on the hill of Torre in front, the Gualandra hills filled with the light-armed on their left flank, and being prevented from receding by the cavalry, who, the farther they advanced, stopped up all the outlets in the rear. A fog rising from the lake now spread itself over the army of the consul, but the high lands were in the sun-shine, and all the different corps in ambush looked towards the hill of

Torre for the order of attack. Hannibal gave the signal, and moved down from his post on the height. At the same moment all his troops on the eminences behind and in the flank of Flaminius, rushed forwards as it were with one accord into the plain. The Romans, who were forming their array in the mist, suddenly heard the shouts of the enemy amongst them, on every side, and before they could fall into their ranks, or draw their swords, or see by whom they were attacked, felt at once that they were surrounded and lost.

There are two little rivulets which run from the Gualandra into the lake. The traveller crosses the first of these at about a mile after he comes into the plain, and this divides the Tuscan from the Papal territories. The second, about a quarter of a mile further on, is called 'the bloody rivulet', and the peasants point out an open spot to the left between the 'Sanguinetto' and the hills, which, they say, was the principal scene of slaughter. The other part of the plain is covered with thick set olive trees in corn-grounds, and is no where quite level except near the edge of the lake. It is, indeed, most probable that the battle was fought near this end of the valley, for the six thousand Romans, who, at the beginning of the action, broke through the enemy, escaped to the summit of an eminence which must have been in this quarter, otherwise they would have had to traverse the whole plain and to pierce through the main army of Hannibal.

The Romans fought desperately for three hours, but the death of Flaminius was the signal for a general dispersion. The Carthaginian horse then burst in upon the fugitives, and the lake, the marsh about Borghetto, but chiefly the plain of the Sanguinetto and the passes of the Gualandra, were strewed with dead. Near some old walls on a bleak ridge to the left above the rivulet many human bones have been repeatedly found, and this has confirmed the pretensions and the name of the 'stream of blood'.

Every district of Italy has its hero. In the north some painter is the usual genius of the place, and the foreign Julio Romano more than divides Mantua with her native Virgil. To the south we hear of Roman names. Near Thrasimene tradition is still faithful to the fame of an enemy, and Hannibal the Carthaginian is the only ancient name remembered on the banks of the Perugian lake. Flaminius is unknown; but the postilions on that road have been taught to show the very spot where *il Console Romano* was slain. Of all who fought and fell in the battle of Thrasimene, the historian himself has, besides the generals and Maharbal, preserved indeed only a single name. You overtake the Carthaginian again on the same road to Rome. The antiquary, that is, the hostler, of the posthouse at Spoleto, tells you that his town repulsed the victorious enemy, and shows you the gate still called *Porta di Annibale*. It is hardly worth while to remark that a French travel writer, well known by the name of the President Dupaty, saw Thrasimene in the lake of Bolsena, which lay conveniently on his way from Sienna to Rome. [H]

586. No book of travels has omitted to expatiate on the temple of the

Clitumnus, between Foligno and Spoleto; and no site, or scenery, even in Italy, is more worthy a description. For an account of the dilapidation of this temple, the reader is referred to *Historical Illustrations of the Fourth Canto of Childe Harold* [pp. 35–42]. [H]

639. I saw the 'Cascata del marmore' of Terni twice, at different periods; once from the summit of the precipice, and again from the valley below. The lower view is far to be preferred, if the traveller has time for one only; but in any point of view, either from above or below, it is worth all the cascades and torrents of Switzerland put together: the Staubach, Reichenbach, Pisse Vache, fall of Arpenaz, &c. are rills in comparative appeareance. Of the fall of Schaffhausen I cannot speak, not yet having seen it. [B, n. in *MS. H* and *Proofs* and *CHP IV*]

642. Of the time, place, and qualities of this kind of Iris the reader may have seen a short account in a note to *Manfred*. [B, n. in *MS. H* and *Proofs*]

The fall looks so much like 'the hell of waters' that Addison thought the descent alluded to by the gulf in which Alecto plunged into the infernal regions. It is singular enough that two of the finest cascades in Europe should be artificial—this of the Velino and the one at Tivoli. The traveller is strongly recommended to trace the Velino, at least as high as the little lake, called *Pie' di Lup*. The Reatine territory was the Italian Tempe, and the ancient naturalist, amongst other beautiful varieties, remarked the daily rainbows of the lake Velinus. A scholar of great name has devoted a treatise to this district alone. [H]

674. These stanzas may probably remind the reader of *Ensign Northerton's* remarks: 'D—n Homo', &c. but the reasons for our dislike are not exactly the same. I wish to express that we become tired of the task before we can comprehend the beauty; that we learn by rote before we can get by heart; that the freshness is worn away, and the future pleasure and advantage deadened and destroyed, by the didactic anticipation, at an age when we can neither feel nor understand the power of compositions which it requires an acquaintance with life, as well as Latin and Greek, to relish, or to reason upon. For the same reason we never can be aware of the fulness of some of the finest passages of Shakespeare, ('To be or not to be', for instance), from the habit of having them hammered into us at eight years old, as an exercise, not of mind but of memory: so that when we are old enough to enjoy them, the taste is gone, and the appetite palled. In some parts of the Continent, young persons are taught from more common authors, and do not read the best classics till their maturity. I certainly do not speak on this point from any pique or aversion towards the place of my education. I was not a slow, though an idle boy; and I believe no one could, or can be more attached to

Harrow than I have always been, and with reason;—a part of the time passed there was the happiest of my life; and my preceptor, (the Rev. Dr. Joseph Drury), was the best and worthiest friend I ever possessed, whose warnings I have remembered but too well, though too late—when I have erred, and whose counsels I have but followed when I have done well or wisely. If ever this imperfect record of my feelings towards him should reach his eyes, let it remind him of one who never thinks of him but with gratitude and veneration—of one who would more gladly boast of having been his pupil, if, by more closely following his injunctions, he could reflect any honour upon his instructor. [B, n. in *MS. H, Proofs, CHP IV*]

731. Orosius gives three hundred and twenty for the number of triumphs. He is followed by Panvinius; and Panvinius by Mr. Gibbon and the modern writers. [B, n. written into *Proof B; in CHP IV*]

739. Certainly were it not for these two traits in the life of Sylla, alluded to in this stanza, we should regard him as a monster unredeemed by any admirable quality. The *atonement* of his voluntary resignation of empire may perhaps be accepted by us, as it seems to have satisfied the Romans, who if they had not respected must have destroyed him. There could be no mean, no division of opinion; they must have all thought, like Eucrates, that what had appeared ambition was a love of glory, and that what had been mistaken for pride was a real grandeur of soul. [H]

769. On the third of September Cromwell gained the victory of Dunbar [1750]; a year afterwards he obtained 'his crowning mercy' of Worcester; and a few years after, on the same day, which he had ever esteemed the most fortunate for him, died [1658]. [B, n. in *MS. H, CHP IV*]

775. The projected division of the Spada Pompey has already been recorded by the historian of the *Decline and Fall of the Roman Empire*. Mr. Gibbon found it in the memorials of Flaminius Vacca, and it may be added to his mention of it that Pope Julius III. gave the contending owners five hundred crowns for the statue; and presented it to Cardinal Capo di Ferro, who had prevented the judgment of Solomon from being executed upon the image. In a more civilized age this statue was exposed to an actual operation: for the French who acted the *Brutus* of Voltaire in the Coliseum, resolved that their Caesar should fall at the base of that Pompey, which was supposed to have been sprinkled with the blood of the original dictator. The nine foot hero was therefore removed to the Arena of the amphitheatre, and to facilitate its transport suffered the temporary amputation of its right arm. The republican tragedians had to plead that the arm was a restoration: but their accusers do not believe that the integrity of the statue would have protected it. The love of finding every coincidence has discovered the true Caesarean ichor in a stain near the right knee; but colder criticism has rejected not only the blood but the portrait, and assigned the globe of power rather to the first of the emperors than to the last of the republican masters of Rome. Winkelmann is loth to allow an heroic statue of a Roman citizen, but the Grimani Agrippa, a cotemporary almost, is heroic; and naked Roman figures were only very rare, not absolutely forbidden. The face accords much better with the '*homi-nem integrum et castum et gravem*', than with any of the busts of Augustus, and is too stern for him who was beautiful, says Suetonius, at all periods of his life. The pretended likeness to Alexander the Great cannot be discerned, but the traits resemble the medal of Pompey. The objectionable globe may not have been an ill applied flattery to him who found Asia Minor the boundary, and left it the centre of the Roman empire. It seems that Winkelmann has made a mistake in thinking that no proof of the identity of this statue, with that which received the bloody sacrifice, can be derived from the spot where it was discovered. Flaminius Vacca says *sotto una cantina*, and this cantina is known to have been in the Vicolo de' Leutari near the Cancellaria, a position corresponding exactly to that of the Janus before the basilica of Pompey's theatre, to which Augustus transferred the statue after the *curia* was either burnt, or taken down. Part of the Pompeian shade, the portico, existed in the beginning of the XVth century, and the *atrium* was still called *Satrum*. So says Blondus. At all events, so imposing is the stern majesty of the statue, and so memorable is the story, that the play of the imagination leaves no room for the exercise of the judgment, and the fiction, if a fiction it is, operates on the spectator with an effect not less powerful than truth. [H]

784. Ancient Rome, like modern Sienna, abounded most probably with images of the foster-mother of her founder; but there were two she-wolves of whom history makes particular mention. One of these, *of brass in ancient work*, was seen by Dionysius at the temple of Romulus, under the Palatine, and is universally believed to be that mentioned by the Latin historian, as having been made from the money collected by a fine on usurers, and as standing under the Ruminal fig-tree. The other was that which Cicero has celebrated both in prose and verse, and which the historian Dion also records as having suffered the same accident as is alluded to by the orator. The question agitated by the antiquaries is, whether the wolf now in the con-servators' palace is that of Livy and Dionysius, or that of Cicero, or whether it is neither one or the other. The earlier writers differ as much as the moderns: Lucius Faunus says, that it is the one alluded to by both, which is impossible, and also by Virgil, which may be. Fulvius Ursinus calls it the wolf of Dionysius, and Marlianus talks of it as the one mentioned by Cicero. To him Rycquius *tremblingly* assents. Nardini is inclined to suppose it may be one of the many wolves preserved in ancient Rome; but of the two rather

bends to the Ciceronian statue. Montfaucon mentions it as a point without doubt. Of the latter writers the decisive Winkelmann proclaims it as having been found at the church of Saint Theodore, where, or near where, was the temple of Romulus, and consequently makes it the wolf of Dionysius. His authority is Lucius Faunus, who, however, only says that it *was placed*, not *found*, at the Ficus Ruminalis by the Comitium, by which he does not seem to allude to the church of Saint Theodore. Rycquius was the first to make the mistake, and Winkelmann followed Rycquius.

Flaminius Vacca tells quite a different story, and says he had heard the wolf with the twins was found near the arch of Septimius Severus. The commentator on Winkelmann is of the same opinion with that learned person, and is incensed at Nardini for not having remarked that Cicero, in speaking of the wolf struck with lightning in the Capitol, makes use of the past tense. But, with the Abate's leave, Nardini does not positively assert the statue to be that mentioned by Cicero, and, if he had, the assumption would not perhaps have been so exceedingly indiscreet. The Abate himself is obliged to own that there are marks very like the scathing of lightning in the hinder legs of the present wolf; and, to get rid of this, adds, that the wolf seen by Dionysius might have been also struck by lightning, or otherwise injured.

Let us examine the subject by a reference to the words of Cicero. The orator in two places seems to particularize the Romulus and the Remus, especially the first, which his audience remembered to *have been* in the Capitol, as being struck with lightning. In his verses he records that the twins and wolf both fell, and that the latter left behind the marks of her feet. Cicero does not say that the wolf was consumed; and Dion only mentions that it fell down, without alluding, as the Abate has made him, to the force of the blow, or the firmness with which it had been fixed. The whole strength, therefore, of the Abate's argument, hangs upon the past tense; which, however, may be somewhat diminished by remarking that the phrase only shews that the statue was not then standing in its former position. Winkelmann has observed, that the present twins are modern; and it is equally clear that there are marks of gilding on the wolf, which might therefore be supposed to make part of the ancient group. It is known that the sacred images of the Capitol were not destroyed when injured by time or accident, but were put into certain underground depositaries called *favissae*. It may be thought possible that the wolf had been so deposited, and had been replaced in some conspicuous situation when the Capitol was rebuilt by Vespasian. Rycquius, without mentioning his authority, tells that it was transferred from the Comitium to the Lateran, and thence brought to the Capitol. If it was found near the arch of Severus, it may have been one of the images which Orosius says was thrown down in the Forum by lightning when Alaric took the city. That it is of very high antiquity the workmanship is a decisive proof; and that circumstance induced Winkelmann to believe it the wolf of Dionysius.

The Capitoline wolf, however, may have been of the same early date as that at the temple of Romulus. Lactantius asserts that in his time the Romans worshipped a wolf; and it is known that the Lupercalia held out to a very late period after every other observance of the ancient superstition had totally expired. This may account for the preservation of the ancient image longer than the other early symbols of Paganism.

It may be permitted, however, to remark that the wolf was a Roman symbol, but that the worship of that symbol is an inference drawn by the zeal of Lactantius. The early Christian writers are not to be trusted in the charges which they make against the Pagans. Eusebius accused the Romans to their faces of worshipping Simon Magus, and raising a statue to him in the island of the Tyber. The Romans had probably never heard of such a person before, who came, however, to play a considerable, though scandalous part in the church history, and has left several tokens of his aerial combat with St. Peter at Rome; notwithstanding that an inscription found in this very island of the Tyber shewed the Simon Magus of Eusebius to be a certain indigenal god, called Semo Sangus or Fidius.

Even when the worship of the founder of Rome had been abandoned, it was thought expedient to humour the habits of the good matrons of the city by sending them with their sick infants to the church of Saint Theodore, as they had before carried them to the temple of Romulus. The practice is continued to this day; and the site of the above church seems to be thereby identified with that of the temple: so that if the wolf had been really found there, as Winkelmann says, there would be no doubt of the present statue being that seen by Dionysius. But Faunus, in saying that it was at the Ficus Ruminalis by the Comitium, is only talking of its ancient position as recorded by Pliny; and even if he had been remarking where it was found, would not have alluded to the church of Saint Theodore, but to a very different place, near which it was then thought the Ficus Ruminalis had been, and also the Comitium; that is, the three columns by the church of Santa Maria Liberatrice, at the corner of the Palatine looking on the Forum.

It is, in fact, a mere conjecture where the image was actually dug up, and perhaps, on the whole, the marks of the gilding, and of the lightning, are a better argument in favour of its being the Ciceronian wolf than any that can be adduced for the contrary opinion. At any rate, it is reasonably selected in the text of the poem as one of the most interesting relics of the ancient city, and is certainly the figure, if not the very animal to which Virgil alludes in his beautiful verses:

'Geminos huic ubera circum
Ludere pendentes pueros et lambere matrem
Impavidos: illam teriti cervice reflexam
Mulcere alternos, et fingere corpora lingua. [H]

805. It is possible to be a very great man and to be still very inferior to Julius Caesar, the most complete character, so Lord Bacon thought, of all antiquity. Nature seems incapable of such extraordinary combinations as composed his versatile capacity, which was the wonder even of the Romans themselves. The first general—the only triumphant politician—inferior to none in eloquence—comparable to any in the attainments of wisdom, in an age made up of the greatest commanders, statesmen, orators and philoso- phers that ever appeared in the world—an author who composed a perfect specimen of military annals in his travelling carriage—at one time in a con- troversy with Cato, at another writing a treatise on punning, and collecting a set of good sayings—fighting and making love at the same moment, and willing to abandon both his empire and his mistress for a sight of the Foun- tains of the Nile. Such did Julius Caesar appear to his cotemporaries and to those of the subsequent ages, who were the most inclined to deplore and execrate his fatal genius.

But we must not be so much dazzled with his surpassing glory or with his magnanimous, his amiable qualities, as to forget the decision of his impartial countryman:

HE WAS JUSTLY SLAIN. [H]

830. '. . . . omnes pene veteres; qui nihil cognosci, nihil percepi, nihil sciri posse dixerunt; angustos sensus; imbecillos animos, brevia curricula vitae; in profundo veritatem demersam; opinionibus et institutis omnia teneri; nihil veritati relinqui: deinceps omnia tenebris circumfusa esse dixerunt.' The eighteen hundred years which have elapsed since Cicero wrote this, have not removed any of the imperfections of humanity: and the complaints of the ancient philosophers may, without injustice or affectation, be transcribed in a poem written yesterday. [H]

883. Alluding to the tomb of Cecilia Metella, called Capo di Bove, in the Appian Way. See—*Historical Illustrations of the Fourth Canto of Childe Harold* [pp. 202–3]. [H]

963. The Palatine is one mass of ruins, particularly on the side toward the Circus Maximus. The very soil is formed of crumbled brick-work. Nothing has been told, nothing can be told, to satisfy the belief of any but a Roman antiquary.—See *Historical Illustrations*, Page 206. [B]

964. The author of the *Life of Cicero*, speaking of the opinion entertained of Britain by that orator and his cotemporary Romans, has the following eloquent passage: 'From their railleries of this kind, on the barbarity and misery of our island, one cannot help reflecting on the surprising fate and revolutions of kingdoms, how Rome, once the mistress of the world, the seat of arts, empire and glory, now lies sunk in sloth, ignorance and poverty, enslaved to the most cruel as well as to the most contemptible of tyrants, superstition and religious imposture: while this remote country, anciently the jest and contempt of the polite Romans, is become the happy seat of liberty, plenty and letters; flourishing in all the arts and refinements of civil life; yet running perhaps the same course which Rome itself had run before it, from virtuous industry to wealth; from wealth to luxury; from luxury to an impatience of discipline, and corruption of morals: till by a total degeneracy and loss of virtue, being grown ripe for destruction, it fall a prey at last to some hardy oppressor, and, with the loss of liberty, losing every thing that is valuable, sinks gradually again into its original barbarism.' [H]

990. The column of Trajan is surmounted by St. Peter; that of Aurelius by St. Paul. See—*Historical Illustrations* . . . [p. 214]. [H]

999. Trajan was *proverbially* the best of the Roman princes: and it would be easier to find a sovereign uniting exactly the opposite characteristics, than one possessed of all the happy qualities ascribed to this emperor. 'When he mounted the throne,' says the historian Dion, 'he was strong in body, he was vigorous in mind; age had impaired none of his faculties; he was altogether free from envy and from detraction; he honored all the good and he advanced them; and on this account they could not be the objects of his fear, or of his hate; he never listened to informers; he gave not way to his anger; he abstained equally from unfair exactions and unjust punishments; he had rather be loved as a man than honoured as a sovereign; he was affable with his people, respectful to the senate, and universally beloved by both; he inspired none with dread but the enemies of his country.' [H]

1022. The name and exploits of Rienzi [1313–54] must be familiar to the reader of Gibbon. Some details and inedited manuscripts relative to this unhappy hero, will be seen in the [*Historical Illustrations*, 248–60]. [H]

1027. The respectable authority of Flaminius Vacca would incline us to believe in the claims of the Egerian grotto. He assures us that he saw an inscription in the pavement, stating that the fountain was that of Egeria dedicated to the nymphs. The inscription is not there at this day; but Montfaucon quotes two lines of Ovid from a stone in the Villa Giustiniani, which he seems to think had been brought from the same grotto.

This grotto and valley were formerly frequented in summer, and particularly the first Sunday in May, by the modern Romans, who attached a salubrious quality to the fountain which trickles from an orifice at the bottom of the vault, and, overflowing the little pools, creeps down the matted grass into the brook below. The brook is the Ovidian Almo, whose name and qualities are lost in the modern Aquataccio. The valley itself is called Valle di Caffarelli, from the dukes of that name who made over their fountain to the Pallavicini, with sixty *rubbia* of adjoining land.

There can be little doubt that this long dell is the Egerian valley of Juvenal, and the pausing place of Umbritius, notwithstanding the generality of his commentators have supposed the descent of the satirist and his friend to have been into the Arician grove, where the nymph met Hippolitus, and where she was more peculiarly worshipped.

The step from the Porta Capena to the Alban hill, fifteen miles distant, would be too considerable, unless we were to believe in the wild conjecture of Vossius, who makes that gate travel from its present station, where he pretends it was during the reign of the Kings, as far as the Arician grove, and then makes it recede to its old site with the shrinking city. The tufo, or pumice, which the poet prefers to marble, is the substance composing the bank in which the grotto is sunk.

The modern topographers find in the grotto the statue of the nymph and nine niches for the Muses, and a late traveller has discovered that the cave is restored to that simplicity which the poet regretted had been exchanged for injudicious ornament. But the headless statue is palpably rather a male than a nymph, and has none of the attributes ascribed to it at present visible. The nine Muses could hardly have stood in six niches; and Juvenal certainly does not allude to any individual cave. Nothing can be collected from the satirist but that somewhere near the Porta Capena was a spot in which it was supposed Numa held nightly consultations with his nymph, and where there was a grove and a sacred fountain, and fanes once consecrated to the Muses; and that from this spot there was a descent into the valley of Egeria, where were several artificial caves. It is clear that the statues of the Muses made no part of the decoration which the satirist thought misplaced in these caves for he expressly assigns other fanes (delubra) to these divinities above the valley, and moreover tells us that they had been ejected to make room for the Jews. In fact the little temple, now called that of Bacchus, was formerly thought to belong to the Muses, and Nardini places them in a poplar grove, which was in his time above the valley.

It is probable, from the inscription and position, that the cave now shown may be one of the 'artificial caverns', of which, indeed, there is another a little way higher up the valley, under a tuft of alder bushes: but a *single* grotto of Egeria is a mere modern invention, grafted upon the application of the epithet Egerian to these nymphea in general, and which might send us to look for the haunts of Numa upon the banks of the Thames.

Our English Juvenal was not seduced into mistranslation by his acquaintance with Pope: he carefully preserves the correct plural—

> 'Thence slowly winding down the vale, we view
> The Egerian *grots; oh*, how unlike the true!'

The valley abounds with springs, and over these springs, which the Muses might haunt from their neighbouring groves, Egeria presided: hence she was said to supply them with water; and she was the nymph of the grottos through which the fountains were taught to flow.

The whole of the monuments in the vicinity of the Egerian valley have received names at will, which have been changed at will. Venuti owns he can see no traces of the temples of Jove, Saturn, Juno, Venus, and Diana, which Nardini found, or hoped to find. The mutatorium of Caracalla's circus, the temple of Honour and Virtue, the temple of Bacchus, and, above all, the temple of the god Rediculus, are the antiquaries' despair.

The circus of Caracalla depends on a medal of that emperor cited by Fulvius Ursinus, of which the reverse shows a circus, supposed, however, by some to represent the Circus Maximus. It gives a very good idea of that place of exercise. The soil has been but little raised, if we may judge from the small cellular structure at the end of the Spina, which was probably the chapel of the god Consus. This cell is half beneath the soil, as it must have been in the circus itself, for Dionysius could not be persuaded to believe that this divinity was the Roman Neptune, because his altar was underground. [H]

1135. 'At all events,' says the author of the *Academical Questions*, 'I trust, whatever may be the fate of my own speculations, that philosophy will regain that estimation which it ought to possess. The free and philosophic spirit of our nation has been the theme of admiration to the world. This was the proud distinction of Englishmen and the luminous source of all their glory. Shall we then forget the manly and dignified sentiments of our ancestors, to prate in the language of the mother or the nurse about our good old prejudices? This is not the way to defend the cause of truth. It was not thus that our fathers maintained it in the brilliant periods of our history. Prejudice may be trusted to guard the outworks for a short space of time while reason slumbers in the citadel: but if the latter sink into a lethargy, the former will quickly erect a standard for herself. Philosophy, wisdom, and liberty, support each other; he who will not reason, is a bigot; he who cannot, is a fool; and he who dares not, is a slave.' [H]

1181. We read in Suetonius that Augustus, from a warning received in a dream, counterfeited, once a year, the beggar, sitting before the gate of his palace with his hand hollowed and stretched out for charity. A statue formerly in the Villa Borghese, and which should be now at Paris, represents the Emperor in that posture of supplication. The object of this self degradation was the appeasement of Nemesis, the perpetual attendant on good fortune, of whose power the Roman conquerors were also reminded by certain symbols attached to their cars of triumph. The symbols were the whip and the *crotalo*, which were discovered in the Nemesis of the Vatican. The attitude of beggary made the above statue pass for that of Belisarius: and until the criticism of Winkelmann had rectified the mistake, one fiction was called in to support another. It was the same fear of the sudden termination of prosperity that made Amasis king of Egypt warn his friend Polycrates of Samos, that the gods loved those whose lives were chequered with good and evil fortunes. Nemesis was supposed to lie in wait particularly for the prudent: that is, for those whose caution rendered them accessible only to mere accidents: and her first altar was raised on the banks of the Phrygian Aesepus by Adrastus, probably the prince of that name who killed the son of Croesus by mistake. Hence the goddess was called Adrastea.

The Roman Nemesis was *sacred* and *august*: there was a temple to her in the Palatine under the name of Rhamnusia: so great indeed was the propensity of the ancients to trust to the revolution of events, and to believe in the divinity of Fortune, that in the same Palatine there was a temple to the Fortune of the day. This is the last superstition which retains its hold over the human heart; and from concentrating in one object the credulity so natural to man, has always appeared strongest in those unembarrassed by other articles of belief. The antiquaries have supposed this goddess to be synonymous with fortune and with fate: but it was in her vindictive quality that she was worshipped under the name of Nemesis. [H]

1252. Whether the wonderful statue which suggested this image be a laquearian gladiator, which in spite of Winkelmann's criticism has been stoutly maintained, or whether it be a Greek herald, as that great antiquary positively asserted, or whether it is to be thought a Spartan or barbarian shield-bearer, according to the opinion of his Italian editor, it must assuredly seem *a copy* of that masterpiece of Ctesilaus which represented 'a wounded man dying who perfectly expressed what there remained of life in him'. Montfaucon and Maffei thought it the identical statue; but that statue was of bronze. The gladiator was once in the villa Ludovizi, and was bought by Clement XII. The right arm is an entire restoration of Michael Angelo. [H]

1267. Gladiators were of two kinds, compelled and voluntary; and were supplied from several conditions; from slaves sold for that purpose; from culprits; from barbarian captives either taken in war, and, after being led in triumph, set apart for the games, or those seized and condemned as rebels; also from free citizens, some fighting for hire (*auctorati*), others from a depraved ambition: at last even knights and senators were exhibited, a disgrace of which the first tyant was naturally the first inventor. In the end, dwarfs, and even women, fought; an enormity prohibited by Severus. Of these the most to be pitied undoubtedly were the barbarian captives; and to this species a Christian writer justly applies the epithet '*innocent*', to distinguish them from the professional gladiators. Aurelian and Claudius supplied great numbers of these unfortunate victims; the one after his triumph, and the other on the pretext of a rebellion. No war, says Lipsius, was ever so destructive to the human race as these sports. In spite of the laws of Constantine and Constans, gladiatorial shows survived the old established religion more than seventy years; but they owed their final extinction to the courage of a Christian. In the year 404, on the kalends of January, they were exhibiting the shows in the Flavian amphitheatre before the usual immense concourse of people. Almachius or Telemachus, an eastern monk, who had travelled to Rome intent on his holy purpose, rushed into the midst of the area, and endeavoured to separate the combatants. The praetor Alpius, a person incredibly attached to these games, gave instant orders to the gladiators to slay him; and Telemachus gained the crown of maryrdom, and the title of saint, which surely has never either before or since been awarded for a more noble exploit. Honorius immediately abolished the shows, which were never afterwards revived. The story is told by Theodoret and Cassiodorus, and seems worthy of credit notwithstanding its place in the Roman martyrology. Besides the torrents of blood which flowed at the funerals, in the amphitheatres, the circus, the forums, and other public places, gladiators were introduced at feasts, and tore each other to pieces amidst the supper tables, to the great delight and applause of the guests. Yet Lipsius permits himself to suppose the loss of courage, and the evident degeneracy of mankind, to be nearly connected with the abolition of these bloody spectacles. [B]

1275. When one gladiator wounded another, he shouted 'he has it', 'hoc habet', or 'habet'. The wounded combatant dropped his weapon, and advancing to the edge of the arena, supplicated the spectators. If he had fought well, the people saved him; if otherwise, or as they happened to be inclined, they turned down their thumbs, and he was slain. They were occasionally so savage that they were impatient if a combat lasted longer than ordinary without wounds or death. The emperor's presence generally saved the vanquished: and it is recorded as an instance of Caracalla's ferocity, that he sent those who supplicated him for life, in a spectacle at Nicomedia, to ask the people; in other words, handed them over to be slain. A similar ceremony is observed at the Spanish bull-fights. The magistrate presides; and after the horsemen and piccadores have fought the bull, the matadore steps forward and bows to him for permission to kill the animal. If the bull has done his duty by killing two or three horses, or a man, which last is rare, the people interfere with shouts, the ladies wave their handkerchiefs, and the animal is saved. The wounds and death of the horses are accompanied with the loudest acclamations, and many gestures of delight, especially from the female portion of the audience, including those of the gentlest blood. Every thing depends on habit. The author of *Childe Harold*, the writer of this note, and one or two other Englishmen, who have certainly in other days borne the sight of a pitched battle, were, during the summer of 1809, in the governor's box at the great amphitheatre of Santa Maria, opposite to Cadiz. The death of one or two horses completely satisfied their curiosity. A gentleman present, observing them shudder and look pale, noticed that unusual reception of so delightful a sport to some young ladies, who stared and smiled, and continued their applauses as another horse fell bleeding to the ground. One bull killed three horses *off his own horns*. He was saved by acclamations which were redoubled when it was known he belonged to a priest.

An Englishman who can be much pleased with seeing two men beat themselves to pieces, cannot bear to look at a horse galloping round an arena with his bowels trailing on the ground, and turns from the spectacle and the spectators with horror and disgust. [H]

1293. Suetonius informs us that Julius Caesar was particularly gratified by that decree of the senate, which enabled him to wear a wreath of laurel on all occasions. He was anxious, not to show that he was the conqueror of the world, but to hide that he was bald. A stranger at Rome would hardly have guessed at the motive, nor should we without the help of the historian. [H]

1308. 'Though plundered of all its brass, except the ring which was necessary to preserve the aperture above; though exposed to repeated fires, though sometimes flooded by the river, and always open to the rain, no monument of equal antiquity is so well preserved as this rotundo. It passed with little alteration from the Pagan into the present worship; and so convenient were its niches for the Christian altar, that Michael Angelo, ever studious of ancient beauty, introduced their design as a model in the Catholic church.'
Forsyth's *Remarks, &c. on Italy* (1816), p. 136. [H]

1323. The Pantheon has been made a receptacle for the busts of modern great, or, at least, distinguished, men. The flood of light which once fell through the large orb above on the whole circle of divinities, now shines on a numerous assemblage of mortals, some one or two of whom have been almost deified by the veneration of their countrymen. [H]

1324. This and the three next stanzas allude to the story of the Roman daughter, which is recalled to the traveller, by the site or pretended site of that adventure now shewn at the church of St. Nicholas *in carcere*. The difficulties attending the full belief of the tale are stated in *Historical Illustrations* [295–300]. [H]

1369. This and the six next stanzas have a reference to the church of St. Peter's. For a measurement of the comparative length of this basilica, and the other great churches of Europe, see the pavement of St. Peter's, and [Eustace,] *Classical Tour through Italy*, II, chap. 4, pp. 125 ff. [H]

1536. Mary died on the scaffold [1587]; Elizabeth of a broken heart [1603]; Charles V a hermit [1558]; Louis XIV a bankrupt in means and glory [1715]; Cromwell of anxiety; and, 'the greatest is behind', Napoleon lives a prisoner. To these sovereigns a long but superfluous list might be added of names equally illustrious and unhappy. [B, in *MS. H, CHP IV*]

1549. The village of Nemi was near the Arician retreat of Egeria, and, from the shades which embosomed the temple of Diana, has preserved to this day its distinctive appellation of *The Grove*. Nemi is but an evening's ride from the comfortable inn of Albano. [H]

1566. The whole declivity of the Alban hill is of unrivalled beauty, and from the convent on the highest point, which has succeeded to the temple of the Latian Jupiter, the prospect embraces all the objects alluded to in the cited stanza: the Mediterranean; the whole scene of the latter half of the Aeneid, and the coast from beyond the mouth of the Tyber to the headland of Circaeum and the Cape of Terracina.

The site of Cicero's villa may be supposed either at the Grotta Ferrata, or at the Tusculum of Prince Lucien Buonaparte.

The former was thought some years ago the actual site, as may be seen from Middleton's *Life of Cicero*. At present it has lost something of its credit, except for the Domenichinos. Nine monks of the Greek order live there, and the adjoining villa is a cardinal's summer house. The other villa, called Rufinella, is on the summit of the hill above Frascati, and many rich remains of Tusculum have been found there, besides seventy-two statues of different merit and preservation, and seven busts.

From the same eminence are seen the Sabine hills, embosomed in which lies the long valley of Rustica. There are several circumstances which tend to establish the identity of this valley with the '*Ustica*' of Horace; and it seems possible that the mosaic pavement which the peasants uncover by throwing up the earth of a vineyard, may belong to his villa. Rustica is pronounced short, not according to our stress upon—'*Usticae cubantis*'.—It is more rational to think that we are wrong than that the inhabitants of this secluded valley have changed their tone in this word. The addition of the consonant prefixed is nothing: yet it is necessary to be aware that Rustica may be a modern name which the peasants may have caught from the antiquaries.

The villa, or the mosaic, is in a vineyard on a knoll covered with chestnut trees. A stream runs down the valley, and although it is not true, as said in the guide books, that this stream is called Licenza, yet there is a village on a rock at the head of the valley which is so denominated, and which may have taken its name from the Digentia. Licenza contains 700 inhabitants. On a peak a little way beyond is Civitella, containing 300. On the banks of the

Anio, a little before you turn up into Valle Rustica, to the left, about an hour from the *villa*, is a town called Vico-varo, another favourable coincidence with the *Varia* of the poet. At the end of the valley, towards the Anio, there is a bare hill, crowned with a little town called Bardela. At the foot of this hill the rivulet of Licenza flows, and is almost absorbed in a wide sandy bed before it reaches the Anio. Nothing can be more fortunate for the lines of the poet, whether in a metaphorical or direct sense:

'Me quotiens reficit gelidus Digentia rivus,
    Quem Mandela bibit rugosus frigore pagus.'

The stream is clear high up the valley, but before it reaches the hill of Bardela looks green and yellow like a sulphur rivulet.

Rocca Giovane, a ruined village in the hills, half an hour's walk from the vineyard where the pavement is shown, does seem to be the site of the fane of Vacuna, and an inscription found there tells that this temple of the Sabine victory was repaired by Vespasian. With these helps, and a position corresponding exactly to every thing which the poet has told us of his retreat, we may feel tolerably secure of our site.

The hill which should be Lucretilis is called Campanile, and by following up the rivulet to the pretended Bandusia, you come to the roots of the higher mountain Gennaro. Singularly enough the only spot of ploughed land in the whole valley is on the knoll where this Bandusia rises,

'. . . . tu frigus amabile
    Fessis vomere tauris
    Praebes, et pecori vago.'

The peasants show another spring near the mosaic pavement which they call 'Oradina', and which flows down the hills into a tank, or mill dam, and thence trickles over into the Digentia.

But we must not hope
            'To trace the Muses upwards to their spring'
by exploring the windings of the romantic valley in search of the Bandusian fountain. It seems strange that any one should have thought Bandusia a fountain of the Digentia—Horace has not let drop a word of it; and this immortal spring has in fact been discovered in possession of the holders of many good things in Italy, the monks. It was attached to the church of St. Gervais and Protais near Venusia, where it was most likely to be found. We shall not be so lucky as a late traveller in finding the *occasional pine* still pendant on the poetic villa. There is not a pine in the whole valley, but there are two cypresses, which he evidently took, or mistook, for the tree in the ode. The truth is, that the pine is now, as it was in the days of Virgil, a garden tree, and it was not at all likely to be found in the craggy acclivities of the valley of Rustica. Horace probably had one of them in the orchard close above his farm, immediately overshadowing his villa, not on the rocky heights at some distance from his abode. The tourist may have easily

supposed himself to have seen this pine figured in the above cypresses, for the orange and lemon trees which throw such a bloom over his description of the royal gardens at Naples, unless they have been since displaced, were assuredly only acacias and other common garden shrubs. The extreme disappointment experienced by choosing the Classical Tourist as a guide in Italy must be allowed to find vent in a few observations, which, it is asserted without fear of contradiction, will be confirmed by every one who has selected the same conductor through the same country. This author is in fact one of the most inaccurate, unsatisfactory writers that have in our times attained a temporary reputation, and is very seldom to be trusted even when he speaks of objects which he must be presumed to have seen. His errors, from the simple exaggeration to the downright mistatement, are so frequent as to induce a suspicion that he had either never visited the spots described, or had trusted to the fidelity of former writers. Indeed the *Classical Tour* has every characteristic of a mere compilation of former notices, strung together upon a very slender thread of personal observation, and swelled out by those decorations which are so easily supplied by a systematic adoption of all the common places of praise, applied to every thing, and therefore signifying nothing.

The style which one person thinks cloggy and cumbrous, and unsuitable, may be to the taste of others, and such may experience some salutary excitement in ploughing through the periods of the *Classical Tour*. It must be said, however, that polish and weight are apt to beget an expectation of value. It is amongst the pains of the damned to toil up a climax with a huge round *stone*.

The tourist had the choice of his words, but there was no such latitude allowed to that of his sentiments. The love of virtue and of liberty, which must have distinguished the character, certainly adorns the pages of Mr. Eustace, and the gentlemanly spirit, so recommendatory either in an author or his productions, is very conspicuous throughout the *Classical Tour*. But these generous qualities are the foliage of such a performance, and may be spread about it so prominently and profusely, as to embarass those who wish to see and find the fruit at hand. The unction of the divine, and the exhortations of the moralist, may have made this work something more and better than a book of travels, but they have not made it a book of travels; and this observation applies more especially to that enticing method of instruction conveyed by the perpetual introduction of the same Gallic Helot to reel and bluster before the rising generation, and terrify it into decency by the display of all the excesses of the revolution. An animosity against atheists and regicides in general, and Frenchmen specifically, may be honourable, and may be useful, as a record; but that antidote should either be administered in any work rather than a tour, or, at least, should be served up apart, and not so mixed with the whole mass of information and reflection, as to give a bitterness to every page: for who would choose to have the antipathies of any man, however just, for his travelling companions? A tourist, unless he aspires to the credit of prophecy, is not answerable for the changes which may take place in the country which he describes; but his reader may very fairly esteem all his political portraits and deductions as so much waste paper, the moment they cease to assist, and more particularly if they obstruct, his actual survey.

Neither encomium nor accusation of any government, or governors, is meant to be here offered, but it is stated as an incontrovertible fact, that the change operated, either by the address of the late imperial system, or by the disappointment of every expectation by those who have succeeded to the Italian thrones, has been so considerable, and is so apparent, as not only to put Mr. Eustace's Antigallican philippics entirely out of date, but even to throw some suspicion upon the competency and candour of the author himself. A remarkable example may be found in the instance of Bologna, over whose papal attachments, and consequent desolation, the tourist pours forth such strains of condolence and revenge, made louder by the borrowed trumpet of Mr. Burke. Now Bologna is at this moment, and has been for some years, notorious amongst the states of Italy for its attachment to revolutionary principles, and was almost the only city which made any demonstrations in favour of the unfortunate Murat. This change may, however, have been made since Mr. Eustace visited this country; but the traveller whom he has thrilled with horror at the projected stripping of the copper from the cupola of St. Peter's, must be much relieved to find that sacrilege out of the power of the French, or any other plunderers, the cupola being covered with *lead*.

If the conspiring voice of otherwise rival critics had not given considerable currency to the *Classical Tour*, it would have been unnecessary to warn the reader, that however it may adorn his library, it will be of little or no service to him in his carriage; and if the judgment of those critics had hitherto been suspended, no attempt would have been made to anticipate their decision. As it is, those who stand in the relation of posterity to Mr. Eustace, may be permitted to appeal from cotemporary praises, and are perhaps more likely to be just in proportion as the causes of love and hatred are the farther removed. This appeal had, in some measure, been made before the above remarks were written; for one of the most respectable of the Florentine publishers, who had been persuaded by the repeated inquiries of those on their journey southwards, to reprint a cheap edition of the *Classical Tour*, was, by the concurring advice of returning travellers, induced to abandon his design, although he had already arranged his types and paper, and had struck off one or two of the first sheets.

The writer of these notes would wish to part (like Mr. Gibbon) on good terms with the Pope and the Cardinals, but he does not think it necesary to extend the same discreet silence to their humble partisans. [H]

1674. After the frank avowal contained in the prefatory address, it may appear somewhat a presumption to attempt the task which is there formally declined as above the means of the author who writes, and of the friend to whom he addresses, the letter.

In fact it had been the wish of Lord Byron, and of the compiler of the foregoing notes, to say something of the literary and political condition of Italy, and they had made preparation of some materials, the deliberate rejection of which was the origin of the above confession.

Time and opportunity have, however, very much increased those materials in number, and, it is believed, in value, and the consequence has been the appearance of a short memoir on Italian literature, at the end of the Historical Illustrations of the IVth Canto, and the commencement of a longer treatise, which will be published separately in the course of the present year.

This latter work will attempt a survey of the revolutions of Italy, from the French invasion in 1796 to the present day. It is compiled from information on which the author believes he may implicitly rely, and it contains a series of facts and portraits which, he presumes, are for the most part unknown to his countrymen. [H, concluding n. in *CHP IV*]

COMMENTARY

174. *Childe Harold's Pilgrimage. General Introduction.*

Although *CHP* can and should be regarded as a single poetic *unit*—B himself saw it as such—the work neither is nor was a unified *composition*. The first two cantos appeared together in 1812, the third canto was printed in 1816, and the fourth canto came out in 1818. Nevertheless, although each of the separately printed parts was written at different times and under very different circumstances, the third and fourth cantos pick up and carry forward the narrative as it already existed. Furthermore, Cantos III and IV are almost as closely allied to each other as are Cantos I and II. The result of all this is that the poem can be read in three ways: as a single, integral poem, as two loosely related units (Cantos I–II and Cantos III–IV), or as three separate parts of one changing poetic project (Cantos I–II, Canto III, Canto IV).

For obvious reasons, the commentary here must deal with the poem in terms of its three, separately printed parts. None the less, readers of the later cantos should consult the earlier commentaries as well, since a number of subjects recur through the different cantos.

Besides the great collected editions of Coleridge and *1832*, other useful editions of *CHP* include the Édition classique by James Darmesteter (Paris, 1882), and the editions of H. F. Tozer (Oxford, 1885), August Mommsen (Berlin, 1885), E. C. Everard Owen (1897), and Samuel C. Chew's Odyssey Press edition of *Childe Harold's Pilgrimage and Other Romantic Poems* (New York, 1936). Important textual, contextual, and critical studies are: William A. Borst, *Lord Byron's First Pilgrimage* (New Haven, 1948), Robert F. Gleckner, *Byron and the Ruins of Paradise* (Baltimore, 1967), pp. 39–90, 225–50, 267–97; M. K. Joseph, *Byron the Poet* (1964), 15–35, 70–102; Eugen Kölbing, *Zur Textüberlieferung von Byrons Childe Harold, Cantos I, II* (Leipsig, 1896); Hans Maier, *Entstehungsgeschichte von Byrons 'Childe Harold's Pilgrimage', Gesang I und II* (Berlin, 1911); *McGann(1)*, 31–140, 301–18; George Ridenour, 'Byron and the Romantic Pilgrimage' (Ph.D. thesis, Yale Univ., 1955); Georg Roppen and Richard Sommer, *Strangers and Pilgrims* (Oslo, 1964), 209–83; Andrew Rutherford, *Byron, A Critical Study* (1961), pp. 26–35, 48–65, 93–102; Robert L. Zimmerman, 'Manuscript Revision in Byron's Childe Harold's Pilgrimage' (Ph.D. thesis, Duke Univ., 1960).

Cantos I–II

MS. and Publication History. Two complete MSS. of *CHP I–II* survive: B's first fair copy (*MS. M*, location: Murray) and the printer's copy MS. in the hand of R. C. Dallas, with B's own corrections and additions (*MS. D*, location: *BM*). Each MS. can be further distinguished into first and second states.

MS. M. In its first state, Canto I of *MS. M* contained the following material: stanzas 2–7, 8var., 9var., 10–13, Childe Harold's Goodnight lyric, 14–22, 22var., 23–4, 24var.a,b,c,d, 26–42, 44–84, 'The Girl of Cadiz', 87var.a,b,c,d, 93. Total: 91 stanzas plus two lyrics plus a few brief textual notes. No Preface.

On the front cover of the MS. B wrote, apparently in 1810: 'Byron— Joannina in Albania Begun Oct. 31, 1809 Concluded Canto 2nd March 28, 1810. Byron.' Below this he added, in 1812: 'The marginal remarks pencilled occasionally were ⟨written⟩ made by two friends [Hobhouse and Dallas] who saw the thing in M.S. some time prior to publication. 1812.'

The second state of the MS. of Canto I includes the following deletions and additions: 8var., 9var., 22var., and 'The Girl of Cadiz' were removed from the MS. and 8, 9, and 'To Inez' were added. Total stanzas: 90.

B began Canto I on 31 Oct. 1809 and finished it on 30 Dec. (so dated in the MS.). The deletions and additions were certainly made before B returned to England in 1811 and probably all belong to the period between Jan. and Mar. 1811 when B was adding some long prose notes to the poem and when (1 Feb.) he was revising the Vathek stanza (22var.). The MS. of 'To Inez' is dated 25 Jan. 1810 but this may be a mistake for 1811. In any case, whenever the lyric was composed it was probably not added to the Canto until some time after 28 Mar. 1810, for the MS. scrap containing the lyric also contains the three stanzas added to Canto II in its second state.

The first state of Canto II contained the following: 1–7, 8var., 10–14, 14var. a,b, 16–26, 28–52, 54–72, the Suliote Song, 73–6, 84–7, 91–2. Total: 80 stanzas plus the song plus a few brief textual notes.

The second canto must have been begun shortly after B finished the first canto on 30 Dec., for on 3 Jan. 1810 he was writing stanza 12 (see note to that stanza). The stanzas on Albania were being written towards the end of February, and the canto was completed in its first state on 28 Mar.

When revising Canto II before his return to England B added three stanzas (15, 53, 88) plus a few of the longer prose notes. He did not make any deletions. Thus the second state of Canto II in *MS. M* contained 83 stanzas. The dating of the long prose notes to stanza 73 indicates that the canto was revised during the first months of 1811.

MS. D. The whole of *MS. D* in its first state is a copy of the second state of *MS. M*. The revisions made in this MS. brought it to its second state, which was the printer's copy for the first edition of the poem. To Canto I B added stanzas 1, 25, 43, and 85–92 and he deleted stanzas 24var.a,b,c,d and 87var. a,b,c,d. To Canto II he added 8, 9, and 93–8 and he deleted 8var. and 14var. a,b. He also completed the notes for the poem and added the Preface.

The total contents of *MS. D* are somewhat heterogeneous. Some of the

additions are in Dallas's hand (Canto I, stanza 1 and Canto II, stanzas 93–8),
the remainder are in B's. *MS. D* also contains B's second draft of the Preface
(*MS. Da*), a separate holograph addition to the Preface (*MS. Db*), and Dallas's
transcript of the revised Preface with B's revisions (*MS. Dc*). The latter was
the printer's copy. All of the new notes to the cantos are in B's hand. Also,
since *MS. D* was printer's copy for the entire contents of the first edition,
the MS. contains Dallas's fair copies of the short poems included at the back
of the edition. The MS. does not, however, contain any of the Appendix
material, and a few of the shorter poems printed in the first edition of *CHP I–II*
are no longer in *MS. D* (see individual commentaries below). A few scraps
of proof, with B's revisions, are also bound up with *MS. D*.

B's letters to Dallas establish the dates of the revisions to *MS. D*. Stanza 1
of Canto I was the first addition to the poem, sent to Dallas in late July.
B deleted 87var.a,b,c,d and added 87–92 of Canto I around 15 Aug., and at
the same time he deleted 8var. from Canto II and added 8. Stanza 43 of
Canto I may also have been added at this time. Between this period and the
end of September B added most of the new notes as well as the epigraph
and was busy correcting proof. Early in October B deleted 24var.a,b,c,d
from Canto I and added 25, 85–6, and possibly 43. He also added 9 to Canto
II. Late in October he added 93–8 to Canto II. The date of the deletion of
14var.a,b is uncertain. In the second state of *MS. D*, then, Canto I is in its
complete form of 93 stanzas and Canto II contains 88 stanzas, the number
which appeared in editions 1 to 6.

Other MSS. and Proofs

(*a*) In the Murray archives. 1. A bound volume of 'Miscellaneous Manuscripts' contains B's fair copy of 'To Ianthe' (titled here 'To the Lady
Charlotte Harley' (*MS. MI*) and two proofs of the lyric with B's holograph
corrections; an early draft of Canto II, sts. 27 and 77–83 (*MS. MA*); a draft
of Canto II, sts. 95–8 (*MS. MB*). 2. Draft of Canto II, st. 53 (*MS. MC*, bound
up in *MS. LB* of *Hints*). 3. Notes to Canto II, st. 73. The note in *CHP* headed
'Franciscan Convent, Athens, Jan. 23, 1811' is embedded in *MS. M* of *EBSR*
and is there headed 'Note on Thornton' (*MS. MDa*); the note in *CHP* headed
'Athens, Franciscan Convent, March 17, 1811': a first draft is embedded in
MS. LB of *Hints* and a second copy is in *MS. LA* of *Hints*. Both are dated 19
Mar. 1811 (*MSS. MDb* and *MDc*) 4. Amanuensis copy, corrected by B, of
all the notes to Canto II, st. 73 (*MS. DA*). This was printer's copy for
CHP I-II.

(*b*) Canto I, st. 1, with the prose note (*MS. NL*, draft copy: location,
National Archives, Athens).

(*c*) Canto II, st. 9 (B's fair copy, *MS. T*, location: Texas). It is headed by
B: 'Stanza 9th for Canto 2nd somewhat altered to avoid a recurrence in a
former stanza.' At the bottom of the sheet B wrote to Dallas: 'Dear Sir—
I think it proper to state to *you* that this stanza alludes to an event which

has taken place since my arrival here and not to the death of any *male* friend. Yrs. B. Oct. 14th 1811.'

(*d*) The Preface, plus Canto II, st. 73, and the 'Suliote Song' (*MS. Υ*, B's draft MSS.: location, Yale). *MS. Υ* of II. 73 strongly suggests that *MS. M* is a copy of an anterior MS., now lost, of which *MS. Υ* was a part. *MS. Υ* is reproduced in facsimile in *McGann(1)*, frontispiece.

(*e*) In the Huntington Library is an incomplete set of proofs for the seventh edn. of *CHP I–II*, with B's corrections and inserted holograph fair copy MSS. for Canto II, sts. 77–83 and 89–90 (*MS. H*). Printer's copy for seventh edn.

(*f*) 'To Ianthe' (draft MS. lacking stanza 2, untitled) and Canto II sts. 89–90 (draft). Both in the Lovelace papers, Lytton Collection, on deposit in the Bodleian Library (*MS. L*). Also in this collection is 'Il Diavolo Inamorato' (see above) from which B plundered Canto II, sts. 27 and 78–82.

(*g*) Canto II, sts. 93–4 (draft, location: Bibliotheca Bodmeriana, Cologny–Geneva: *MS. G*).

(*h*) A bound volume of various proofs for editions 1–7; including a full proof of the first edition with B's fair copy MS. of Canto II, st. 27, inserted; full sets of proofs for editions 5 and 7, with minor corrections by B (*Proof M*, location: Murray archives).

(*i*) In a series of letters to R. C. Dallas in 1811, B made corrections while the poem was being printed: 10 Sept. (location: Cornell Univ. Library; *BLJ* II. 96); 16 Sept. (MS. not extant; *BLJ* II. 100); 26 Sept. (location: Newstead; *BLJ* II. 106); 16 Oct. (location: Bodleian; *BLJ* II. 117); 25 Oct. (location: Mrs. Doris Rich Stuart; *BLJ* II. 118). These correct, respectively, I. 6; epigraph; I. 82; I. 16; I. 92. (These MSS. are designated *MS. O* in the apparatus.)

Thus, there are essentially four phases in the history of the composition and revision of Cantos I–II. The first form of the poem was written between 31 Oct. 1809 and 28 Mar. 1810. *MS. Υ* seems to be the only fragment to have survived from that original draft. *MS. M* is a heavily reworked copy of the original draft which was probably executed early in 1811 when B was revising and adding to his poem for the first time. *MS. D* is Dallas's copy of the revised *MS. M* which he made in late July and early Aug. 1811, after B returned to England from the East. Between August and November B revised the poem once again, this time quite extensively, and the revised *MS. D* was the printer's copy for the first edition. Finally, B added 'To Ianthe' and ten new stanzas to Canto II in the seventh edition of the poem (1814). These included 27, 77–83, 89–90. The only other substantive changes in the early editions were more minor deletions, additions, and corrections to the text and the notes in the second, third, fifth, and seventh editions.

Acting as B's intermediary, Dallas first tried to interest the publisher William Miller in *CHP*, but he was unsuccessful, mainly because Miller was Lord Elgin's publisher and bookseller and hence naturally objected to the way B had treated Elgin in the poem. Dallas then gave the poem to John Murray, who accepted it for publication after receiving an enthusiastic report of the poem from William Gifford. The agreement with Murray was concluded early in August, and Dallas continued to help B with the poem by supervising its passage through the printers.

The poem was eventually published on 10 Mar. 1812 in an edition of 500 quarto copies and was sold out in three days. Besides *CHP*, the volume also contained fourteen shorter poems. On 17 Apr. a second edition (octavo) was issued which contained six new poems. The fourth edition, issued on 14 Sept., added the 'Addition to the Preface'. In the seventh edition (1814) the final additions were made to *CHP* and nine further poems were added to the volume. The tenth edition added yet one more poem ('On the Death of Sir Peter Parker') and introduced the final substantive changes into the text of *CHP*. (For additional bibliographical information see *Wise*, I. 50–4; *C* II. ix–xx and VII. 180–201; and *McGann* (*1*).)

The copy text for the present edition is the seventh edition, the last edition of the poem which we know B corrected in proof (see *BLJ* III. 201). Existing proof sheets, plus substantive changes in the different editions, show that B corrected press for the first, fifth, and seventh editions.

Literary and Historical Background

B's own trip to the Levant in 1809–11 is the source of the scenes and incidents narrated in the poem. Moreover, B wrote most of *CHP I–II* while he was still on his journey. A brief account of the general historical background of the poem is therefore called for, as well as a more particular description of B's itinerary in 1809–11.

B went to Portugal and Spain while the Peninsular War was still in progress. France's conflict with England (and her Spanish and Portuguese volunteers) provided the initial context for the general political discussion developed through the poem. In Albania B encountered an almost feudal civilization ruled by the ruthless and unpredictable Ali Pacha, who was himself nominally under the control of the Ottoman Empire, then in its final stages of dissolution. But while Ali Pacha was able to assert a degree of real independence, Greece remained in subjection to the Turks. The birthplace of western ideals of freedom, Greece became—in her current condition—B's central (ironic) focus in Cantos I–II, whose general subject is the collapse of civilized values.

B left England for Lisbon on 2 July 1809 in the company of his friend John Cam Hobhouse, his valet William Fletcher, his old servant Joe Murray, and Robert Rushton, the young son of one of B's Newstead tenants. From Lisbon the party proceeded overland and entered Spain on 22 July. On 25 July they arrived in Seville, where they spent three days before leaving for Cadiz. On 3 Aug. they sailed from Cadiz and arrived in Gibraltar the next day.

At Gibraltar Murray and Rushton left for home (the boy was homesick) and the rest of the party sailed for Malta on 19 August. During his stay in

Malta B had a brief affair with Constance Spencer Smith (the 'Sweet Florence' of the poem). But B's tour was not to be permanently interrupted, so after promising to meet Mrs. Spencer Smith back in Malta in a year, B sailed for Albania on 19 Sept. and landed at Prevesa on 28 Sept.

The party journeyed overland to Janina and Tepelini, where they met Ali Pacha. October, November, and most of December were spent on various tours, by both land and sea, to places of interest around Epirus and Acarnania. On 25 Dec. the party arrived in Athens, which became their base for the next few months. They sailed to Smyrna on 5 Mar., and from Smyrna to Tenedos and the Troad on 11 Apr. The first draft of *CHP* was written during this period, having been begun on 31 Oct. in Janina and finished on 28 Mar. in Smyrna.

The party then sailed for Constantinople, where they arrived on 13 May. They left Constantinople on 14 July, and on 17 July B and Hobhouse parted at Zea, Hobhouse sailing back to England and B proceeding on to Athens, where he arrived the next day. The remainder of B's stay in the Levant was spent principally at Athens, except for two brief trips into the Peloponnese between late July and early Oct. 1810. On 21 Apr. 1811 he left Athens and sailed to Malta on 30 Apr., where he remained for a month. He sailed for England on 2 June and, after a tedious voyage, landed at Portsmouth on 11 July.

B's poem, along with its elaborate prose appendages, testifies to his intense interest in the history and topography of the areas he visited, and especially of the Levant. This interest B shared with a great many people of the late eighteenth and early nineteenth centuries, so that the immediate fame of the poem is at least as related to the readiness of B's audience for his subject as it is to the special manner in which he handled it. (Contemporary interest in the Levant and travel books about the area is usefully dealt with in three essays by W. C. Brown: see *PQ* 15 (1936), 70–80; *PQ* 16 (1937), 249–71; *SP* 34 (1937), 55–64; for the specific matter of Romantic Hellenism see Bernard H. Stern, *The Rise of Romantic Hellenism 1732–1786* (Menasha, Wisc., 1940); Terence Spencer, *Fair Greece, Sad Relic* (1954); Stephen Larrabee, *English Bards and Grecian Marbles* (New York, 1943).)

CHP is a highly moralized travelogue very much in the tradition of eighteenth-century topographical poetry. Its most immediate forebears are Waller Rodwell Wright's *Horae Ionicae* (1809), which B acknowledged, and Richard Polwhele's *Grecian Prospects. A Poem. In Two Cantos* (1799), which B never mentions. Robert Aubin's general comment on B's debt to the topographical tradition is exact: the reader, he says, 'will be impressed by the number of old familiar motifs in Byron's poem: invocation, address, order in variety, praise of the women of a district, genre-scenes, water-mirror, storm and calm, and graveyard and ruin sentiment thoroughly digested by the poet, "a ruin amidst ruins" ' (*Topographical Poetry in XVIIIth Century England*

(New York, 1936), 256). Aubin's comment obviously applies to all four cantos of the poem.

But B adopted only to translate radically the form which he borrowed. He accomplished this by personalizing the topographical poem both more completely and more dramatically than had ever been done before. In this respect, his choice of the Spenserian stanza was regulative, for he took its tradition as a sanction for tonal and structural flexibility. As he notes in his Preface, B looked back to the examples of Ariosto, Thomson, and Beattie to guide him in the practice of mixing tones and moods 'in the style and stanza of Spenser'. This tradition seemed to B to offer a model that would foster stylistic spontaneity and sincerity. *CHP*, he said, 'was intended to be a poem on *Ariosto's plan*, that *is* to *say* on *no plan* at all' (letter to William Miller, 30 July 1811).

But this highly Romantic transformation of certain poetic traditions was not to be fully accomplished until B revised the poem into its final form after his return to England. Once again external events had much to do with the result (see Canto I, st. 91 and notes), for a quick series of tragic personal losses fixed B into a mood of deep (and now famous) melancholy. The poem in its earliest form contained a great deal of comic and satiric material mixed in with more sober reflections and observations. The Spenserian diction at the opening of the poem, for example, is clearly invoked to parody the romance form, and while B allowed some of his comic and satiric material to remain in the poem, he removed a good deal of it during his last revision process, and he augmented his early version with a number of passages of a much more reflective and melancholy character. He also arranged the new passages so as to bring out a sense of dramatic movement in the poem.

The effect upon the two cantos was pronounced. The crucial placement of the revisions altered the poem from a series of loosely connected descriptive and reflective set-pieces, which alternate in no particular pattern of moods, into a dramatic personal record of the growth of a poet's mind—to sorrow, even despair. *CHP I–II* interiorizes the topographical poem so drastically that the convention mutates into a drama of personal history. Thereby the background of larger historical contexts, in which the personal record is set, is made to reflect, and even dramatize, a personal and psychological development. That B was well aware of the cause and nature of the changes he was making in his poem is clear from the early drafts of his Preface, written late in the final process of revision in 1811.

For more particular commentary see esp. *Borst, Marchand,* I. 185–326, and *BLJ* I. 205–57 and II. 3–168 *passim.* For a thorough handling of the poem's biblical materials see Travis Looper, *Byron and the Bible* (1978), 35–51, 177–87.

epigraph   These are the opening sentences of *Le Cosmopolite, ou le Citoyen du Monde* (1753), by Louise Charles Fougeret de Monbron. Cf. *BLJ* II. 105.

Preface

1–2. Compare Waller Rodwell Wright's *Horae Ionicae* (1809), 'Preface': 'A considerable number of the following lines were written amidst the scenes which they profess to describe' (v). See also *EBSR* 873–80 and below, 'Papers Referred to by Note . . . III'.

21. *Childe*: a title implying youth and nobility.

26. *Minstrelsy of the Scottish Border* (1802), I. 201.

27. B especially has in mind Scott's *The Vision of Don Roderick* (1811). Others include John Wilson Croker's *The Battle of Talavera* (1809) and Lord George Grenville's *Portugal, a Poem* (1812).

33. Beattie's Letters. [B] See Sir William Forbes, *Life of James Beattie* (1806), I. 89. The text of the letter reads 'manner', not 'measure'.

44. i.e. Beattie's *The Minstrel* (1771–4) whose hero, Edwin, forecasts later Romantic figures of melancholy; James Thomson's *Castle of Indolence* (1748): see below n. to I. 13; Ariosto's *Orlando Furioso*.

55–6. See George Ellis's review in the *Quarterly Review*, VII (Mar. 1812), 180 ff.

60. La Curne de Sainte-Palaye, *Mémoires sur l'ancienne chevalrie* (Paris, 1781).

66. Rolland d'Erceville (1734–1794), *Recherches . . . sur le Cours d'Amours* (Paris, 1787), 18–30, 117.

69. The Rovers. Antijacobin. [B] 'The Rovers, or the Double Arrangement', by John Hookham Frere, *Poetry of the Anti-Jacobin*, ed. Charles Edmonds, 3rd edn. (1890), 233.

71–2. Pierre du Terrail, Chevalier Bayard (*c.* 1474–1524) is proverbially the knight 'sans peur et sans reproche'.

74. *Salisbury*. See Froissart, *Chronicles*, chaps. 162–8 and George F. Beltz, *Memorials of the Most Noble Order of the Garter* (1841), xlii–xlvii.

75–6. *Reflections on the Revolution in France* (1790), 113.

80. B refers to the much lampooned passages relating to the Queen of Tahiti in *Hawkesworth's Voyages . . . from the Papers of Joseph Banks Esq.* (1773), II. 106. Joseph Banks (1743–1820) sailed with Cook on his famous voyage to the South Seas (1772–5).

122–3. *Timon*. Cf. 'Childish Recollections', 1var.

Zeluco: the title and villain-hero of John Moore's novel (1789).

To Ianthe

The lyric is addressed to the Lady Charlotte Harley (1801–80), second daughter of Lord and Lady Oxford, whom B first met in Oct.–Nov. 1812. B and Lady Oxford carried on a sporadic liaison in 1812–14, a fact of some importance for understanding the peculiar melancholy of the poem, as well as its special appositeness as an introduction to *CHP I–II*.

13. See 'Childish Recollections', 412 n. and 'L'Amitié est L'Amour sans Ailes'.

19. *Peri*: Persian fairy descended from fallen angels.

20. B was 27, Lady Charlotte was just over 13, when this dedication was published in 1814.

37. *name*: Ianthe (Flower of the Narcissus).

Canto I

6 and n. B and Hobhouse visited Delphi on 16 Dec. 1809 (see *Borst*, 88–9). Cf. Pausanias, X. 32. 7. *Dews of Castalie*: Horace, *Odes*, III. iv. 68.

10. *Whilome*: Once upon a time (archaic). B's use of archaisms is deliberately ironic throughout the canto.

13. Cf. *King John*, III. iii. 40 and III. iv. 109, and esp. Thomson's *Castle of Indolence* I. 7, ll. 4–5. Nearly all of B's Spenserian archaisms can be found in the first twenty-three stanzas of Canto I of Thomson's *Castle*. B's opening stanzas, and the portrait of Childe Harold, are clearly in debt to the *Castle*, I, sts. 1–7 and 57–68.

14. A mixed echo of Beattie's *The Minstrel*, I. 190 and Burns's 'Author's Earnest Cry and Prayer', X. I.

18. See B's letter to Murray, 19 Nov. 1820, and also the letter of Charles Skinner Matthews to his sister of 22 May 1809 (*LJ* I. 153–5 and V. 121–8); also *Marchand*, I. 173–4.

23. William, fifth Lord Byron (1722–96), killed his kinsman William Chaworth in a duel in January 1865. Chaworth was the father of B's early love, Mary Chaworth. See below, 39–40 and 66–7 and compare 'Stanzas to a Lady, on Leaving England' and 'The Dream'.

28. *As You Like It*, II. vii. 15.

49. Echoing Scott's *The Lay of the Last Minstrel*, I. ix. 9–10.

52. That is, India and Persia, which B intended to visit when he left England. See his letter to Dallas, 7 Sept. 1811 (*BLJ* II. 92), and line 99 below.

55 ff. Recalling Newstead Abbey; see above 18 and n.

77. The word 'lemman' is used by Chaucer in both senses but more frequently in the feminine. [B, *MS. D*]

in the feminine] ⟨to example a female⟩ D

79. Feere, a consort or mate. [B, *MS. D*]

81. Echoing Pope, *Essay on Criticism*, 625.

82–5. Cf. *Marchand*, I. 181n.

100. B sailed from Falmouth on the Lisbon Packet, 2 July 1809. Compare 'Lines to Mr. Hodgson'.

Childe Harold's Good Night (Cf. 'Preface', 26 and n.)

130–3. Echoing Henry Kirke White, 'The Christiad', I. ii.

134. Robert Rushton grew homesick and was sent home from Gibraltar.

158. B's valet, William Fletcher.

158–65var., 174–81var. Originally followed sts. 6 and 8 in *M*.

160. Cf. Commentary above.

167. B has in mind the lake in the grounds of his Newstead estate.

182–9. Cf. Henry Kirke White, 'Solitude'.

182–3. Echoing *The Rime of the Ancient Mariner*, 233 and 598.

188–9. An ironic reversal of Odysseus' experience with Argus. The lines are based on a personal experience of B's: see his letter to Dallas, 23 Sept. 1811 (*BLJ* II. 104–5).

202–4. Cf. *BLJ* I. 218. *Tagus*. See Ovid, *Amores*, I. xv. 34 and Pliny, IV. xxii. 112.

205. *Lusian*: Portuguese.

214–15 Napoleon's forces invaded Portugal in Nov. 1807, and Spain in the spring of 1808; they left the former in 1811 and the latter in 1814. Cf. also Exodus 10: 1–20.

220–4. England landed a force on the Peninsula in Aug. 1808, three months after Spain revolted against the occupying French troops.

241. Cf. *Paradise Lost*, IV. 131 ff.

247. 'The sky-worn robes of tenderest blue'—Collins. [B, *MSS*. *M* and *D*] Cf. William Collins's 'Ode to Pity', 11.

255 and n. B was 'informed' of his error by Scott on 3 July 1812 (see *LJ* II. 133), but since he corrected it in the second edition he evidently had the information from someone else as well, much earlier.

259. *Honorius*. The Capuchin monk died at 95 years of age after living for thirty years in the small pit he dug for himself, about a metre in diameter. His epitaph reads: HIC HONORIUS/VITAM FINIVIT;/ET IDEO CUM DEO./IN COELIS RECIVIT/OBIT 1596. Honorius was not canonized as a saint.

cave: not near the convent of Our Lady, but near the Capuchin Convent some ten miles away (see *Borst*, 142, n. 2).

260. Echoing Beckford's *Vathek*: 'he did not think . . . that it was necessary to make a hell of this world to enjoy paradise in the next' (1786 edn., p. 2).

262. B was mistaken in his interpretation of the crosses. They were erected 'to appeal to the wayfarer's feeling of piety' (*Dalgado*, 37) and perhaps also served as guideposts.

269 and n. B's note has been disputed (see *Dalgado*, 37–43). Whether English soldiers were in fact assassinated is doubtful, but they were frequently assaulted in Feb. 1809 by Portuguese who believed the English were about to evacuate the Peninsula.

adorned a tale: Johnson, 'The Vanity of Human Wishes', 222. The long extension of this note, given below, was suppressed at the urging of Dallas, who later published it in his *Recollections*, 181–5. B and Hobhouse were attacked in 19 July 1809 (see *BLJ* I. 215 n.).

In the year 1809, it is a well-known fact, that the assassinations in the streets of Lisbon and its vicinity were not confined by the Portuguese to their countrymen; but Englishmen were daily butchered, and so far from the survivors obtaining redress, they were requested 'not to interfere' if they perceived their compatriot defending himself against his amiable allies. I was once stopped in the way to the theatre, at eight in the evening, when the streets were not more empty than they generally are, opposite to an *open shop*, and in a carriage with a friend, by three of our *allies;* and had we not fortunately been armed, I have not the least doubt we should have 'adorned a tale', instead of telling it. We have heard wonders of the Portuguese lately, and their gallantry,—pray heaven it continue; yet, 'would it were bed-time, Hal, and all were well!' They must fight a great many hours, by 'Shrewsbury clock,' before the number of their slain equals that of our countrymen butchered by these kind creatures, now metamorphosed into 'Caçadores', and what not. I merely state a fact not confined to Portugal, for in Sicily and Malta we are knocked on the head at a handsome average nightly, and not a Sicilian and Maltese is ever punished! The neglect of protection is disgraceful to our government and governors, for the murders are as notorious as the moon that shines upon them, and the apathy that overlooks them. The Portuguese, it is hoped, are complimented with the 'Forlorn Hope',—if the cowards are become brave, (like the rest of their kind, in a corner,) pray let them display it. But there is a subscription for these 'θρασὺ δειλον', (they need not be ashamed of the epithet once applied to the Spartans,) and all the charitable patronymicks, from ostentatious A. to diffident Z., and 1*l*. 1*s*. 0*d*. from 'an admirer of valour', are in requisition for the lists at Lloyd's, and the honour of British benevolence. Well, we have fought and subscribed, and bestowed peerages, and buried the killed by our friends and foes; and, lo! all this is to be done over again! Like 'young The' (in Goldsmith's *Citizen of the World,*) as we 'grow older, we grow never the better'. It would be pleasant to learn who will subscribe for us, in or about the year 1815, and what nation will send fifty thousand men, first to be decimated in the capital, and then decimated again (in the Irish fashion, *nine* out of *ten,*) in the 'bed of honour', which, as serjeant Kite says, is considerably larger and more commodious than the 'bed of Ware'. Then they must have a poet to write the 'Vision of Don Perceval', and generously bestow the profits of the well and widely-printed quarto to re-build the 'Backwynd' and the 'Canon-gate', or furnish new kilts for the half-roasted Highlanders. Lord Wellington, however, has enacted marvels; and so did his oriental brother, whom I saw charioteering over the French flag, and heard clipping bad Spanish, after listening to the speech of a patriotic cobler of Cadiz, on the event of his own entry into that city, and the exit of some five thousand bold Britons out of this 'best of all possible worlds'. Sorely were we puzzled how to dispose of that victory of Talavera; and a victory it surely was somewhere, for every body claimed it. The Spanish dispatch and mob called it *Cuesta's,* and made no great mention of the Viscount; the French called it *theirs* (to my great discomfiture, for a French consul stopped my mouth in Greece with a pestilent Paris Gazette, just as I had killed Sebastiani 'in buckram', and king Joseph in 'Kendal green',)—and we have not yet determined *what* to call it, or *whose*, for certes it was none of our own. Howbeit, Massena's retreat is a great comfort, and as we have not been in the habit of pursuing for some years past, no wonder we are a little awkward at first. No doubt we shall improve, or if not, we have only to take to our old way of retrograding, and there we are at home.

> *would it were . . . clock*: 1 *Henry IV*, v. i. 122 and v. v. 146.
> *Caçadores*: cavaliers.
> *the epithet*. See Cornelius de Pauw, *Recherches philosophiques sur les Grecs* (1787) II. 292.
> *Like . . . better*: not in *The Citizen of The World*, but in Goldsmith's essay, 'Serious Reflections on the Life and Death of Mr. T—— C—— by the Ordinary of Newgate', *Collected Works*, ed. Arthur Friedman (Oxford, 1966), III. 48.
> *Kite says*: George Farquhar, *The Recruiting Officer* I. i.
> *a poet . . . Perceval*: ironic allusion to Scott and the Tory minister Spenser Perceval (see below, 'On Perceval', no. 278).
> *Lord . . . brother*. See below, st. 87n.
> *best . . . worlds*: *Candide*, chap. 1.
> *Cuesta*: Gen. Don Gregorio García de la Cuesta, the commander of the Spanish forces at Talavera.
> *French Consul*: Fauvel (see below, Canto II. 101n.).
> *Sebastiani*: François Horace Bastian Sebastiani (1772–1851), one of Napoleon's generals, whose corps suffered heavy losses at Talavera.
> *in buckram . . . Kendal green*: 1 *Henry IV*, II. iv. 202 ff.
> *Massena*. General André Massena (1758–1817) evacuated the French forces from Portugal in 1811.

270–3. B seems to be referring to the Moorish Castle, one of the two oldest monuments in Cintra.

270–8var. Appears in *M* after st. 12. On the MS. B wrote: 'If ever published I shall have this stanza omitted. Byron. February 1st, 1811. I would not have this about Beckford.' See note below, st. 23.

274. The National Palace of Cintra.

279–87. William Beckford (1760–1844) spent two years at Quinta da Monserrate, three miles from Cintra. The cancelled stanza was first published, in a mutilated form, in *1832* by Moore as 'To Dives'. Suspected of pederasty with William, Earl of Courtenay, Beckford was driven into exile by the scandal in 1785. B referred to him as 'the great apostle of pederasty' and 'the martyr of prejudice' (see letters to Hodgson, 25 June 1809, and to Dallas, 26 Sept. 1811).

288 and n. After the French defeat at Vimiera, Richard Colley, Lord Wellesley (1760–1842) was replaced in command by Sir Hew Dalrymple

(1750–1830), who closed an agreement (30 Aug. 1808) with the French which permitted them to leave Portugal without any hindrance and which even provided that English ships should carry the French soldiers back home. The uproar in England was considerable and led Wordsworth to write his Miltonic political pamphlet, *Thoughts on the Convention of Cintra*. The furore had died down considerably by the time B wrote on the subject. The agreement was not signed at Cintra in 'Marialva's dome', as B says, but at Tôrres Vedras. It was ratified in Lisbon and later dispatched from Cintra. The stanza is a set piece imitation of Spenserian allegorical *figurae*.

288–96var. *a* 9. Sir Harry Burrard (1755–1813) took command from Sir Arthur Wellesley (later Duke of Wellington) on 21 Aug. and revoked Wellesley's order to pursue the defeated French. On 22 Aug. Dalrymple succeeded Burrard in command. The three together concluded the agreement with the French. Wellesley opposed the arrangements, but, as junior officer, was forced to accede.

288–96var.*c*5. William Cobbett vigorously attacked the convention and the men who concluded it in a series of articles which appeared in successive issues of the *Weekly Political Register* beginning on 24 Sept.

288–96var.*c*9 'Blatant beast.' A figure for the mob. I think first used by Smollett, in his [*The History and*] *Adventures of an Atom* (1769). Horace has the 'bellua multorum capitum'. In England, fortunately enough, the illustrious mobility [*sic*] has not even one. [B, *MS. D*] Spenser is Smollett's source for the figure (*Faerie Queene*, Book VI. III. xxiv and XII. xxvii). Horace: *Odes*, II. xiii. 34.

288–96var.*d*7. By this query it is not meant that our foolish generals should have been shot, but that Byng might have been spared; though the one suffered and the others escaped, probably for Candide's reason 'pour encourager les autres'. [B, *MS. M*]

Byng: Admiral John Byng, executed in 1757.

Candide's reason: Candide, chap. 22.

298. *Marialva's dome*: the mansion of the Marquis of Marialva, Quinta de Seteais.

300. Cf. Job 41: 22.

314. *Othello*, IV. ii. 54–5.

324. B and Hobhouse left Lisbon for Seville on 17 July.

333 and n. The Grand Palace, church, and convent of Mafra were built by John V between 1717 and 1730. Queen Maria I (1734–1816) used it as her chief residence for many years.

334. Her insane majesty went religiously mad. Dr. Willis, who so dexterously cudgelled kingly pericraniums, could make not a thing of hers. [B, *MS. M*]

cudgelled] ⟨handled⟩ *M*

Maria I fell into a deep mental depression in 1792 after a series of personal crises. The Revd. Dr. Francis Willis, who had successfully treated George III during his first mental breakdown in 1788, treated her unsuccessfully in 1792.

338. Revelation 17: 5.

351–9. An accurate description of the province of Alemtejo, which B was passing through on his way to Spain.

363. *Tayo*: the Tagus (Tajo in Spanish, Tejo in Portuguese).

368. The Pyrenees [B, *MS. M*]

369. The Caia, between Elvas and Badajoz.

377. As I found the Portuguese, so I have characterized them. That they are since improved, at least in courage, is evident. [B]

B's note appears as follows in *D*: 'As I found the Portuguese so have I described them—that they are since improved, at least in courage, is evident, but let those who know them refute me if they were not in 1809 what I have written. ⟨The late exploits of Wellington have effaced the follies of Cintra—he has indeed done wonders, what no other could have done—he has changed the character of a people, reconciled rival superstitions, and baffled an enemy which though often beaten (in our Gazettes) never retreated before his predecessors⟩. The Spaniards seem to have changed characters with the Portuguese who may now repay with interest the contempt they so liberally received. ⟨With regard to my observations on armies, however unpopular, I have religion on my side against armies in particular—they are alike incompatible with our independence and our population. If ever we are enslaved it will not be by a foreign invader, but a domestic army, and should our navy fall I see little reason to augur more favourably of a Land Contest⟩.'

381. Cf. B's recension, 'A Very Mournful Ballad on the Siege and Conquest of Alhama'.

384. Ecclesiastes 9: 11.

388. Pelayo, by tradition the first of the Asturian Kings, ruled from *c*. 718 to *c*. 737. He defeated the Moors at Cangas in 718. His standard, which is preserved in the cathedral of Orviedo, was said to have fallen to him from heaven just before the battle. See Southey's *Roderick, The Last of the Goths* (1814), XXXV.

389–90. In 711 Count Julian Caesarini, the Christian governor of Ceuta in north-west Africa, allowed the Moors to enter Spain. It was an act of revenge against Don Roderick, who had violated Count Julian's daughter La Cava (Fiorinda). Landor treats the story in his tragedy *Count Julian* (1812); see also Southey's *Roderick . . .* and Scott's *Vision . . . .*

393. The Moors were expelled by Ferdinand and Isabella in 1492.

401. 2 Samuel 1: 19.

414. The battle of Talavera was fought near Madrid, 27–8 July 1809.

421. The Siroc is the violent hot wind that for weeks together blows

down the Mediterranean from the Archipelago. Its effects are well known to all who have passed the Straits of Gibraltar. [B, *MS. D*]

421–2. Cf. Revelation 6: 4, 8.

428–9. Cf. Daniel 2: 33–42.

432. See B's letter to his mother, 11 Aug. 1809. B was at Seville when the battle took place.

436–40. Recalling *Julius Caesar*, III. i. 295–305.

443. *Macbeth*, I. ii. 61.

451 Collins. [B, *MS. D*] Collins's 'Ode Written in . . . 1746', 9–10.

459. The battle of Albuera (15 May 1811). The English under Sir William Carr Beresford, Viscount Beresford (1768–1854) defeated the French under Gen. Nicolas Jean de Dieu Soult (1769–1851). Both sides suffered terrible losses.

467. B is not referring to Scott's treatment of the battle in his *Vision* but to the many trivial patriotic verses which dealt with the subject at the time (e.g. anon., *The Battle of Albuera, a Poem*, published in Oct. 1811).

468. *Macbeth*, I. ii. 20.

477–85. B reached Seville on 25 July. The city later surrendered to the French, on 31 Jan. 1810.

508 and n. Manuel de Godoy (1767–1851) was the Spanish Prime Minister under Charles IV when France invaded Portugal and Spain as a direct result of Godoy's treaty with France in 1807 (the Treaty of Fontainebleau). Godoy was the Queen's paramour. He left Spain for a permanent exile in 1808.

513–21. The scene is the plain of Andalucia viewed from the heights of the Sierra Morena. The 'Moorish turrets' are the hill-forts of the mountains of Ronda and Granada. The 'wounded ground' is a reference to the French invasion of the Morena in 1808. The 'dragon's nest' is the city of Jaen, which was recaptured from the French in July 1808.

524. The red cockade with 'Fernando Septimo' in the centre. [B]

531. The name of the Sierra Morena does not come from their dusky appearance, as B suggests, but from *Montes Mariani*.

548. Recalling *Iliad*, I. 3–4.

558. Augustina, the Maid of Saragoza (see below, 576–84 and notes).

560. The anlace, a short two-edged dagger, was the national weapon of the Spanish heroines.

560, 563. *Macbeth*, I. v. 42 and V. v. 10.

566. See above, 81 n.

584. See Southey's *History of the Peninsular War* (1823–32), chap. IX. The Junta was the National Resistance Committee, seated at Seville.

594–5. Sigilla [i.e. laculla] in mento impressa Amoris digitulo
   Vestigio demonstrant Mollitudinem. Aul. Gel. [B]
The lines are actually from Varro's 'Papiapapae', IV (*Saturarum Menippearum*, ed. Alexander Riese (1865), 184).

599. *Antony and Cleopatra*, I. v. 25.

603–11. Written in Turkey with the greater part of the poem. [B, *MS. M*]

604–5. In Albania, a province of European Turkey in 1809.

608. Cf. Job 30: 22.

612. These stanzas were written in Castri (Delphos), at the foot of Parnassus, now called Λιακυρα—Liakura. [B] B reached Castri on 16 Dec. 1809. See also *LJ* v. 450.

619. *Echoes*. See Justinus, *Historiarum* . . ., 24, 6.

646. *plant*: the bay tree, an evergreen.

657–8. Cf. Isaiah 23: 7.

658. Seville was the HISPALIS of the Romans. [B]

HISPALIS] Julia *M, D*

659 ff. See B's letter to his mother, 11 Aug. 1809, and to Hodgson, 6 Aug.

667. *queen*: Aphrodite.

673–4. Cf. *Aeneid*, I. 415–17.

675. *Paradise Lost*, I. 742–3.

679. Alluding to *Hamlet*, V. i. 150, B mistakes the meaning of 'kibes', which means 'chilblains' not 'heels'.

697. *whiskey*: a light carriage.

701var. A festive liquor so called. Query why 'Roman'? [B, *MS. M*] Perhaps B has in mind Purl-Royal, an infusion of bitters not in beer or ale, but in wine.

706 and n. B reached Thebes on 22 Dec. 1809. *riddle*: the Sphinx's riddle, solved by Oedipus.

707. B alludes to the custom at Highgate of 'swearing on the horns', a ceremony regularly performed as part of the tavern 'fooleries' at the Gate House, on the top of the hill. See Hone's *Everyday Book* (1826), II. 40–4 and 189.

720–800. The bullfight stanzas are meant as a parody of the rites of chivalry. (See B's 'Preface'.)

731. The *picadores*.

760. The croupe is a particular leap taught in the manège. [B, *MS. M*] *Croupe* refers to the horse's hindquarters. B means *Croupade*, 'a high curvet in which the hind legs are brought up under the belly of the horse' (*OED*).

776. *brast*: broken (Spenserianism).

778. B refers to the cloak-waving *chulos*, not to the single *matadore*.

800. The Spaniards are as revengeful as ever. At Santa Olalla I heard a young peasant threaten to stab a woman (an old one to be sure, which mitigates the offence), and was told on expressing some small surprise, that this ethic was by no means uncommon. [B, *MS. M*]

802. *centinel*: from the Spanish *centinela* (cf. *Macbeth*, II. i. 53).

809. Horace, *Odes*, I. iv. 5.

815. Cf. 'To Ianthe', 13.

818.   Medio de fonte leporum
              Surgit amari aliquid quod in ipsis floribus angat.
                                                    Luc. [B]
Lucretius, *De rerum natura*, IV. 1133–4.

835. Echoing Scott's *The Lay of the Last Minstrel*, 'Introduction', 18 and, through that, back to Thomson (*The Castle of Indolence*, LXVIII) and, of course, to Milton (*Paradise Lost*, IX. 24).

To Inez

These stanzas, dated in MS. 25 Jan. 1810, were probably addressed to Teresa Macri. They were added to *MS. M* in place of 'The Girl of Cadiz' (see below, no. 133) before B returned to England.

857. Horace, *Odes*, II. xvi. 19-20 and La Rochefoucauld, *Maximes*, 534.

860. Echoes Matthew Prior, *Solomon*, III. 87.

874-6. Cadiz came under siege from Feb. 1810 to Aug. 1812. The stanza was added to the original MS. in 1811, before the siege was raised.

879. Alluding to the conduct and death of Solano, the Governor of Cadiz. [B] Don Francisco Solano Ortiz de Rozas, commander of the forces at Cadiz, refused to obey the Junta's order to attack the French fleet anchored off the city and was killed by the people (1808). B's attitude towards him seems justified, however: see Napier's *History of the War in the Peninsula* . . . (1886) I. 20-1.

884. Charles IV abdicated in favour of his son Ferdinand in Mar. 1808, and both abdicated for themselves and their heirs in May 1809 in favour of Napoleon.

890. 'War to the knife.' Palafox's answer to the French General at the siege of Saragoza. [B] When Marshal Lefebvre (1755–1820) demanded the surrender of José de Palafox (1776?–1847) near the end of the first siege of Saragoza, he received the reply: 'Guerra al cuchillo.' Southey attributes the reply to Palafox, but Napier (I. 41-6) is dubious.

891-9var. The four variant stanzas followed st. 84 in *MS. M*; they were replaced by sts. 85-92 in *MS. D*. See commentary.

var.*b*9. *Giralda*: the cathedral tower at Seville.

var.*c*2. Porphyry said that the prophecies of Daniel were written after their completion, and such may be my fate here; but it requires no second sight to foretell a tome; the first glimpse of the knight was enough.— I presume Marquis and Mr. and Pole and Sir. A. are returned by this time, and eke the bewildered Frere whose conduct was canvassed by the Commons. [B, *MS. M*]

    knight: Sir John Carr, *Descriptive Travels . . . in the Year 1809* (1811).

    I presume: B refers to the four Wellesleys who were all in Spain in 1809. They are, in B's order, Richard Colley Wellesley, the Marquis of Wellesley (1760–1842); his brother Henry, first Baron Cowley (1773–1847), who was to be secretary of the Embassy; Henry's nephew, the dandy William Wellesley Pole ('Long Pole') Wellesley, afterwards third Earl of Mornington (1788–1857); and Sir Arthur Wellesley, later Duke of Wellington.

Frere: John Hookham Frere (1769–1846) was the British minister to the Junta.

var.c5. 'The Needy Knife-grinder' in the *Anti-Jacobin* was a joint production of Messrs. Frere and Canning. [B, *MS. M*] Frere and George Canning's 'Sapphics. The Friend of Humanity and the Knife-Grinder' (*Poetry of the Anti-Jacobin*, 23) was a parody of Southey's 'The Widow. Sapphics'.

var.d1. Henry Richard Vassal Fox, second Lord Holland (1773–1840), proposed a constitution to the Junta during his long tour of Spain in 1808–9.

var.d4–9. A rather nasty reference to Lord Holland's wife Elizabeth. She married Sir Godfrey Webster in 1786, but was divorced by him in 1797 after having openly lived with Lord Holland for a number of years. Lord Holland married her three days after her divorce, and later acknowledged the son she bore him in 1796, Charles Richard Fox.

916. *Quito*: a province in Peru, conquered by the notorious Pizarro in the sixteenth century.

919–20. The battles of Barossa (5 Mar. 1811) and Albuera (16 May 1811).

926. During the American and French revolutions, it was customary to plant trees as symbols of growing freedom.

927 and n. B's note specifically mentions the deaths of his Harrow friend John Wingfield (14 May 1811), of his mother (31 July 1811), and of his Cambridge friend Charles Skinner Matthews (3 Aug. 1811). Not mentioned in the note are the deaths of Hargreaves Hanson, the second son of B's solicitor, and John Edleston, the Cambridge choirboy to whom B was so deeply attached. Between July and Oct. 1811 B learned of their deaths as well.

lines of YOUNG: Edward Young, *Night Thoughts*, Night 1.

unavailing woe: Beattie, *The Minstrel*, II. lxiii. 2.

945. ⟨Fytte means⟩ Part. [B, *MS. M*]

Canto II

1. *blue-eyed*: Homeric epithet.

4. Part of the Acropolis was destroyed by the explosion of a magazine during the Venetian siege. [B]

by . . . magazine] gunpowder *M, D*

The Venetian bombardment of the Turks in 1687 blew up several powder magazines (see *Finlay*, V. 185).

6 and n. *The wild foxes . . . Babylon*: Lamentations 5: 18 and Isaiah 13: 21–2.

how . . . fallen: 2 Samuel 1: 19.

paltry Antiquarian: Lord Elgin (see *Curse*, commentary).

Man, vain man: *Measure for Measure*, II. ii. 117 ff.

10. *Ancient of days*: Daniel 7: 9.

15. Recalling Juvenal, x. 166–7.

19. A Levantine (for the expression see Isaiah 14: 12).

27. 2 Kings 18: 21 and Isaiah 36: 6.

B originally wrote a note for stanzas 3–9 which he sent to Dallas in August. Dallas advised that it should not be included, and B assented. Dallas later printed it in his *Recollections*, 171–2. Only the last sentence of this suppressed note is preserved in D. The text below is taken from the *Recollections*.

In this age of bigotry, when the puritan and priest have changed places, and the wretched catholic is visited with the 'sins of his fathers', even unto generations far beyond the pale of the commandment, the cast of opinion in these stanzas will doubtless meet with many a contemptuous anathema. But let it be remembered, that the spirit they breathe is desponding, not sneering, scepticism; that he who has seen the Greek and Moslem superstitions contending for mastery over the former shrines of Polytheism,—who has left in his own country 'Pharisees, thanking God that they are not like Publicans and Sinners', and Spaniards in theirs, abhorring the Heretics, who have holpen them in their need,—will be not a little bewildered, and begin to think, that as only one of them can be right, they may most of them be wrong. With regard to morals, and the effect of religion on mankind, it appears, from all historical testimony, to have had less effect in making them love their neighbours, than inducing that cordial christian abhorrence between sectaries and schismatics. The Turks and Quakers are the most tolerant; if an Infidel pays heratch to the former, he may pray how, when, and where he pleases; and the mild tenets, and devout demeanour of the latter, make their lives the truest commentary on the Sermon of the Mount.

sins of his fathers: Exodus 20: 5.

publicans and sinners: Luke 18: 11.

heratch: poll-tax levied by the Turks on their Christian subjects.

31–2. *Measure for Measure*, III. i. 15. This and the next stanza rework various Shakespearean themes, especially from *Hamlet*.

38 and n. *Ajax*. Cf. Sophocles, *Aias*, 1376 ff.

Achilles. His ashes were said to have been mixed in an urn with those of Patroclus, and placed at Sigaeum.

Brasidas. Cf. Thucydides, v. 11–12.

Antinous. A beautiful slave youth, the favourite of Hadrian. B accepts the (dubious) legend that Antinous died giving his life for the Emperor (*c.* 130).

42. When Miltiades gained the victory at Marathon, it was said that he and the Athenians were aided by several gods and demi-gods, including Theseus, Heracles, and Echetlus. George Grote, *A History of Greece* (1846–56) cites Herodotus and Pausanias (Part II, chap. 36).

44. 2 Corinthians 6: 16.

50. *As You Like It*, II. vii. 21.

55. Socrates. [B, *MSS. M, D*] Throughout this stanza B is recalling Lucretius, *De rerum natura*, III. 830 ff. See also *DJ VII* lines 33–4 and n.

64–72var.7. The Sadducees did not believe in the Resurrection. [B, *MSS. M, D*] Cf. Matthew 22: 23.

72. Zoroaster and Pythagoras.

73. Despite B's letter to Dallas of 14 Oct. 1811, these lines almost certainly refer to Edleston, as do the elegiac stanzas at the end of the canto (95–6). See B's letter to Dallas of 31 Oct. 1811 and *Marchand*, I. 295–9. The passages in *CHP* are related to the cycle of B's 'Thyrza poems'.

84. The temple of Jupiter Olympius, of which sixteen columns entirely of marble yet survive: originally there were 150. These columns, however, are by many supposed to have belonged to the Pantheon. [B]

99. The ship was wrecked in the Archipelago. [B] Lord Elgin's ship the *Mentor* was wrecked off the island of Cerigo in 1803. Its cargo of antiquities was fully recovered by 1805. B's animus against Lord Elgin is most elaborately set forth in *Curse*: see notes and commentary for that poem.

101 and n. *Lusieri*: Giovanni Battista ('Don Tita') Lusieri (d. 1821), Neapolitan painter and topographical draughtsman.

finder of Verres. See Cicero, *In Verrem*, II. iv. 13.

Fauvel: Louis François Sebastian Fauvel (1753–1838), amateur archaeologist and topographical artist as well as the French consul at Athens.

Waywode: the Turkish governor at Athens.

Sunium: Now Cape Colonna. In all Attica, if we except Athens itself and Marathon, there is no scene more interesting than Cape Colonna. To the antiquary and artist, sixteen columns are an inexhaustible source of observation and design; to the philosopher, the supposed scene of some of Plato's conversations will not be unwelcome; and the traveller will be struck with the beauty of the prospect over '*Isles that crown the Aegean deep*': but for an Englishman, Colonna has yet an additional interest, as the actual spot of Falconer's *Shipwreck*. Pallas and Plato are forgotten, in the recollection of Falconer and Campbell.

> 'Here in the dead of night by Lonna's steep,
> The seaman's cry was heard along the deep.'

This temple of Minerva may be seen at sea from a great distance. In two journeys which I made, and one voyage to Cape Colonna, the view from either side, by land, was less striking than the approach from the isles. In our second land excursion, we had a narrow escape from a party of Mainnotes, concealed in the caverns beneath. We were told afterwards, by one of their prisoners subsequently ransomed, that they were deterred from attacking us by the appearance of my two Albanians: conjecturing very sagaciously, but falsely, that we had a complete guard of these Arnaouts at hand, they remained stationary, and thus saved our party, which was too small to have opposed any effectual resistance.

Colonna is no less a resort of painters than of pirates; there

> 'The hireling artist plants his paltry desk,
> And makes degraded Nature picturesque.'
>
> (See Hodgson's *Lady Jane Grey, &c.*)

But there Nature, with the aid of Art, has done that for herself. I was fortunate enough to engage a very superior German artist; and hope to renew my acquaintance with this and many other Levantine scenes, by the arrival of his performances. [B]

all Attica] ⟨the whole European Greece⟩ *D*   view] ⟨approach⟩ *D*   no less . . . than of] as great . . . and *D*   But there] ⟨Here⟩ *D*

Isles . . . deep: Thomas Gray, 'The Progress of Poesy', ll. 3.

Falconer's Shipwreck: William Falconer, *The Shipwreck* (1762).

Here . . . deep: slightly misquoting Thomas Campbell's *The Pleasures of Hope*, ll. 149–50.

two journeys: in Jan. and Dec. 1810.

effectual resistance: the incident occurred in Dec. 1810—see letter to Hobhouse, 5 Dec. 1810.

The hireling . . . picturesque: Francis Hodgson, 'Lines on a Ruined Abbey in a Romantic Country'.

Lady Jane Grey, a tale . . . with miscellaneous poems (1809), 214.

German artist: Jacob Linckh (1787–1841)—see Borst, 136–8.

Another noble Lord: George Hamilton Gordon, fourth Earl of Aberdeen (1784–1860).

all honourable men: *Julius Caesar*, III. ii. 87.

priggism: i.e. thievery; see Fielding's *The History of Jonathan Wild* (1743), I. 3 n.

Gropius: This Sr. Gropius was employed by a noble Lord for the sole purpose of sketching, in which he excels; but I am sorry to say, that he has, through the abused sanction of that most respectable name, been treading at humble distance in the steps of Sr. Lusieri. A shipful of his trophies was detained, and I believe confiscated at Constantinople in 1810. I am most happy to be now enabled to state, that 'this was not in his bond'; that he was employed solely as a painter, and that his noble patron disavows all connection with him, except as an artist. If the error in the first and second edition has given the noble Lord a moment's pain, I am very sorry for it; Sr. Gropius has assumed for years the name of his agent; and though I cannot much condemn myself for sharing in the mistake of so many, I am happy in being one of the first to be undeceived. Indeed, I have as much pleasure in contradicting this as I felt regret in stating it. [B, 3rd edn.] Carl Wilhelm Gropius (1793–1870) was employed by Lord Aberdeen to do topographical sketching.

this . . . bond: *The Merchant of Venice*, IV. i. 262.

107–8 and n. See also Edward Daniel Clarke (1769–1822), *Travels in Various Countries . . .* (1810–14), II. ii. 483.

Disdar: commandant of a fortress or citadel.

112. 2 Samuel 1: 20.

112–17var.4. Attila was horned, if we may trust contemporary legends, and the etchings of his visage in Lavater. [B, *MS. M*] B was soon to raise 'Minerva's voice' in *Curse*.

118–26var.*a*2. *Hamilton*: William Richard Hamilton (1777–1859), Lord Elgin's private secretary and his agent for purchasing and transporting the marbles.

var.*a*8.–*Thomas*: Thomas Hope, Esq., if I mistake not, the man who publishes quartos on furniture and costume. [B, *MS. M*] Thomas Hope (1770–1831), author of *Household Furniture and Interior Decoration* (1807). Hope's novel *Anastasius* (1819) was to be a great favourite with B.

var.*b*1. *Dilettanti*: The Society of Dilettanti, founded in 1732 for the study of antiquities by noblemen who had done the Grand Tour.

var.*b*2. *Gell*: It is rumoured Gell is coming out to dig in Olympia. I wish him more success than he had at Athens. According to Lusieri's account, he began digging most furiously without a firmann but before the resurrection of a single sauce-pan the Painter countermined and the Waywode countermanded and sent him back to bookmaking. [B, *MSS. M, D*] See *EBSR* 1033–4.

118–19. *Zosimus*: Greek historian (fl. 450–500): Cf. *Historiae*, V. 6.

Alaric. He plundered Athens in 395 but did not destroy buildings or works of art.

Chandler: Richard Chandler, archaeologist and traveller—see his *Travels in Greece* (1776).

144. *land*: i.e. Spain. B left Gibraltar for Malta on 19 Aug. 1809.

155. The netting to prevent blocks or splinters from falling on deck during action. [B]

175. An additional 'misery to human life!'—lying-to at sunset for a large convoy till the sternmost pass ahead. Mem.: fine frigate, fair wind likely to change before morning, but enough at present for ten knots! [B, *MSS. M,D*] Stanzas 17–20 refer to the passage from Malta, in late Sept. 1809, on the frigate *Spider* (see Borst, 57).

185 *Arion*: ancient Greek poet (cf. Herodotus, I. 23).

190. *Calpe*: Gibraltar.

197. *Mauritania*: Morocco.

217–25. Cf. Burton's *Anatomy of Melancholy* (1624), I. 224.

235–43. See below, the fragment, 'The Monk of Athos' (no. 148).

252. *Romeo and Juliet*, III. v. 9.

253. Goza is said to have been the island of Calypso. [B] Ogygia was,

said to have been] supposed to be *M*; *cor. in D*

however. For the error see Strabo, I. ii. 57 and VII. iii. 50. B accepts the supposition in order to associate Goza and Malta ('sister tenants') with Calypso, and thereby to associate Mrs. Constance Spencer Smith with his 'new Calypso . . . Sweet Florence' (265–6). B had a brief affair with the beautiful and celebrated Mrs. Spencer Smith during his stay at Malta (see *Marchand*, I. 199–201 and B's letters to his mother, 15 Sept. 1809, and Lady Melbourne, 15 Sept. 1812). B's other poems to Mrs. Spencer Smith include 'To Florence', 'Stanzas Composed During a Thunderstorm', 'Lines Written in an Album at Malta', 'Stanzas Written in Passing the Ambracian Gulf', and 'The Spell is Broke, the Charm is Flown'.

259–61. See Fénelon's *L'Avantures de Télémaque . . .* (1699), Book VI.

312. Echoes Lucretius, *De rerum natura*, IV. 112 ff.

322. *ared*: expounded (OED 'aread').

335. *Troilus and Cressida*, II. ii. 16.

338 and n. *Scanderbeg*. Giorgio Castrioti (1404–67), the youngest son of an Albanian chieftain, led a fierce resistance movement against the Ottoman Empire, mostly through guerrilla warfare.

Gibbon terms him so: *Decline and Fall*, chap. 67.

interior of America: *Decline and Fall*, chap. 67.

into that country: they arrived 28 Sept. 1809.

Major Leake: William Martin Leake (1777–1860), traveller and author of *Researches in Greece* (1814) and *Travels in Northern Greece* (1835).

anticipate him: referring to Hobhouse's *Journey* (1813).

departure of my friend: 17 July 1810.

my recovery. See B's letter to Hodgson, 3 Oct. 1810 and 'My Epitaph'.

Cogia Bashi: the mayor of a village.

Logotheti: Spiridion Logotheti, the British vice-consul at Athens and grandfather of the 'Maid of Athens', Teresa Macri.

a para: Para, about the fourth of a farthing. [B]

Sterne's . . . fish-kettle: *Tristram Shandy*, IV. 44.

to a milliner's: i.e. Lord Carlisle; see Dallas's *Recollections*, 64; *BLJ* I. 196; *EBSR* 719–40.

One day: 17 Dec. 1809. The incident involved B's valet, Fletcher.

343. Ithaca.[B] B sailed past (modern) Ithaca and Cape Ducato (the Leucadian cliff) on 28 Sept. 1809.

347–9. Perhaps echoing Matthew 27: 42.

356 and n. The combined forces of Spain and Venice defeated the Turks.

363. Leucadia, now Santa Maura. From the promontory (the Lover's Leap) Sappho is said to have thrown herself. [B]

371. *Suli's rocks*: the mountainous district to the south of Epirus.

Pindus' inland peak. The Pindos range of mountains is not visible from the sea coast.

397–8. Echoing the title of Dryden's *All for Love, or The World Well Lost*. Compare B's 'Stanzas Written in Passing the Ambracian Gulf'.

400. It is said, that on the day previous to the battle of Actium Anthony had thirteen kings at his levee. [B] See Plutarch's *Life of Antony*, where, however, only twelve are mentioned. Shakespeare (*Antony and Cleopatra*, III. vi) names only ten.

402 and n. Octavian built Nicopolis to commemorate the victory at Actium. B saw the ruins on 12 Nov. 1809 (*BLJ* I. 229).

415. According to Pouqueville the lake of Yanina; but Pouqueville is always out. [B] F. C. H. L. Pouqueville (1770–1838), in his *Voyage en Morée . . .* (Paris, 1805) I. 10. B actually never saw the Pindus range, which was hidden from his view by nearer mountains along the route he took.

Acherusia's lake: the lake of Janina is the ancient Pambotis; the Palus Acherusia is at the mouth of the gorge of Suli.

417. B left Previsa on 1 Oct., arrived in Janina on the 5th; left Janina on 11 Oct., spent the 12th in Zitza, and arrived in Tepelini on the 19th.

418. The celebrated Ali Pacha. Of this extraordinary man there is an incorrect account in Pouqueville's *Travels*. [B]

an incorrect account] an account *M*

Born in 1741, this epitome of the Romantic bandit (and tyrant) was appointed Pasha in 1788 by the Ottoman Empire. He was assassinated in 1822 after he fell out of favour with the Sultan. See B's letter to his mother, 12 Nov. 1809.

423 and n. The Suliotes resisted Ali Pasha from 1788 to 1803, when they were betrayed by their leaders. See *Finlay*, VI. 45–50.

424 and n. *Kalamas*. B is wrong. The Kalamas is the ancient Thyamis; the Acheron is much further south. Compare below, 456 and note. Whatever the source of B's misinformation, he was ready to accept it for poetic purposes, since his whole treatment of the trip to Albania is a serious parody of the conventional epic descent to the underworld.

438. The Greek monks are so called. [B]

452. The Chimariot mountains appear to have been volcanic. [B]

It is said that all mountains are more or less volcanic in their composition *M, D*

B seems to be referring to the Ceraunian mountains north of Janina.

456. Now called Kalamas. [B]

466. Albanese cloke. [B]

469. The site of Dodona was determined in 1876 to be at the foot of Mount Tomaros (Mount Olytsika). B could not have known that he actually saw the place when he and Hobhouse visited the area during their stay in Janina (see *BLJ* II. 134).

487. Anciently Mount Tomarus. [B] B refers not to Mount Tomarit, or Tomohr, but to Mount Olytsika, ancient Tomaros.

488 and n. A slip for the river Aöus, the Viosa or modern Vavousa.

492. During this month of Ramadhan (the ninth month in the Muslim year) the galleries of the minarets are set with lamps. Cf. *Giaour*, 449–52 and see below, st. 60. The Ramadhan is a movable feast commemorating the first revelation of the Koran. Muslims fast during Ramadhan.

496 ff. See B's letter to his mother, 12 Nov. 1809, and compare Scott's description of Branksome Castle, *The Lay of the Last Minstrel*, Canto I.

502. *santon*: a dervish or recluse, regarded as a saint.

518. *Delhi*: a fierce warrior, a title of honour bestowed by the Turks.

520. i.e. eunuchs.

531. The *muezzin*'s call to prayer, made five times each day.

561. *Hafiz*: fourteenth-century Persian poet.

562. *Teian*: Anacreon.

566. *Macbeth*, III. iv. 122.

593. Alluding to the wreckers of Cornwall. [B]
(The wreckers of Cornwall for instance whose infamies it is as needless as painful to recapitulate) *D*

595–648. These six stanzas plus the interpolated song all deal with B's experiences between 4 Nov. 1809, when he and Hobhouse sailed from Janina for Patras, and 14 Nov. when they left Utraikee for Missalonghi.

617–21. Referring to B's trip from Utraikee to Gouria (15–18 Nov.). Achelous is the Aspropotamo.

622–30. Cf. *Aeneid*, I. 159–65 and *Gerusalemme Liberata*, XV. 42–3.

632. The Albanian Musselmans do not abstain from wine, and indeed very few of the others. [B]

637. Palikar, shortened when addressed to a single person, from Παλικαρι, a general name for a soldier amongst the Greeks and Albinese who speak Romaic—it means properly 'a lad'. [B]

649 and n. Gustav Meyer (see below) shows that these Albanian love songs are from a popular tradition of improvised song which was characteristically made up of brief two-line units.

Caliriotes. The Albanese, particularly the women, are frequently termed 'Caliriotes': for what reason I inquired in vain. [B]

they are copied: probably by Dudu Roque, the daughter of a French merchant settled in Athens. She copied out Romaic folk-songs for B.

expressed by Socrates: Xenophon, *Symposium*, IV. 27–8. Socrates spoke with reference to Critobulus.

649–92. 'The song . . . is not a robbers' song but a more national song which he composed from several different versions he heard' (*Borst*, 83). The influence of Albanian folk-song, characterized by repeated end-rhyme, has been emphasized by Karl Treimer in 'Byron und die Albanologie', *Seminar za arbanasku filologiju arkiv za arbanasku starinu*, III, Parts I–II (Belgrade, 1926), 176–204. See also Gustav Meyer, 'Die Albanischen Tanzlieder in Byrons Childe Harold', *Anglia*, XV (1893), 1–8.

649. *Tambourgi*: drummer. [B]

654. *camese*: a white kilt.

665. *Parga*: a seaport opposite Paxos.

677. It was taken by storm from the French. [B] By Ali Pasha, in 1797.

685. *Muchtar*. Mukhtar, Pasha of Berat and Ali's eldest son, had been sent to oppose the Russians, who invaded the provinces across the Danube in 1809.

686. *yellow-hair'd*. Yellow is the epithet given to the Russians. [B]
Giaours: Infidel. [B]
horse-tail. Horse-tails are the insignia of a Pacha. [B]

687. *Delhis*: Horsemen, answering to our forlorn hope. [B] For 'forlorn hope' see below, *Siege*, 236 and n.

689. *Selictar*: Sword-bearer. [B]

693. Some thoughts on this subject will be found in the subjoined papers. [*B*] See above, pp. 199–211.

subjoined papers] following papers written at Athens *1st edn.*

695–6. The allusion, of course, is not Hellenic, but biblical.

701. *Eurotas*: a river in Sparta.
thee: i.e. the Spartans who died at Thermopylae.

703–4 and n. It is a fortress.
view of Athens. B and Hobhouse first saw Athens from this spot on 25 Dec. 1809.
Thrasybulus . . . Thirty. In 403 B.C. Thrasybulus, expelled from Athens by the oligarchy of the Thirty, returned with a band of followers and freed Athens from their despotic rule. See Diodorus Siculus, XIV. 32–3.

729. Constantinople was captured by Mohammed II in 1453.

732. When taken by the Latins, and retained for several years.—See GIBBON. [B] From 1204 to 1261 (*Decline and Fall*, chap. 60).

734. Mecca and Medina were taken some time ago by the Wahabees, a sect yearly increasing. [B] The Wahabee movement began in the eighteenth century under the leadership of Muhammed ibn 'Abdul Wahhab. They were puritanical zealots determined to reform Muslim practice. They sacked Mecca in 1803 and El-Medina in 1804, and were at the height of their power during B's visit to the area.

738–55. B was in Constantinople from 14 May–14 June 1810. A carnival immediately preceded the Lenten season.

776. *searment*. B seems to mean 'cerecloth' or 'cearcloth', a plaster to cover a wound. He may have been recalling, in some confused way, *Hamlet*, I. iv. 48.

809. Horace, *Odes*, IV. ix. 25 ff.

812. *Tritonia*: one of Athena's names, of doubtful origin.

821. Athena's gift of the olive moved the gods to appoint her protectress of Athens.

829. Lucan, *Pharsalia*, IX. 974.

830. Pope, *Essay on Criticism*, 625.

843 and n. François Mercy de Lorraine was killed in 1645 fighting against the Protestants in the Thirty Years War.

Expende . . . invenies: Juvenal, X. 47. Cf. the epigraph for the *Ode to Napoleon Buonaparte*.

878. Echoes Pliny the Elder, *Epistolae*, IX. 24.

883. Cf. Virgil, *Georgics*, IV. 563.

891–908. Cf. above, st. 9 and n.

899. On a proof marked 'fourth revise' bound up with *MS. D*, B wrote to Dallas: 'The "*he*" refers to "Wanderer" and anything is better then *I I I I* always *I.*'

906. Cf. above, Canto I, st. 91.

915. The punctuation has been altered here to clear the sense, i.e. to show that 'they' in 914 refers to 'Smiles' in 916. Cf. William J. Rolfe, ed., *Childe Harold's Pilgrimage* (Boston, 1885), 244–245n.

922–3. The altered punctuation, though not sanctioned by earlier editions, seems clearly called for.

924–5var. If Mr. D[allas] wishes me to adopt the former line [i.e. the received text] so be it. I prefer the other I confess, it has less egotism—the first sounds affected. [B's n. in *D*]

Papers Referred to by Note [to Stanza 73]

I

Miss Owenson: Sidney Owenson, Lady Morgan (1783–1859), published *Woman, or Ida of Athens*, 4 vols. (1812).

larceny: See Hobhouse, *Travels*, I. 233.

damn . . . spleen: Pope, *Imitations of Horace*, Book I, Ep. I, 159–60.

Hesiod: v. 493 ff.

Trophonius: an oracle.

Dirce: See Hobhouse, *Travels*, I. 233.

Dr. Chandler: Richard Chandler, *Travels in Greece* (1776), chap. 67.

Sternitur . . . Argos: *Aeneid*, X. 782.

In mediis . . . campis: Statius, *Thebaid*, I. 335.

celebrated topographer: Sir William Gell, in *Itinerary of Greece* (1810), xi.

Jews . . . Negropont: quoted by Gibbon, *Decline and Fall*, chap. 62.

Mr. Roque: Phokion Roque de Carcassonne, the uncle of Teresa Macri, the Maid of Athens.

Laudator temporis acti: Horace, *Ars Poetica*, 173.

nulla . . . redemptum: Juvenal, I. iv. 2.

five tours: Besides Hobhouse's tour, B was anticipating John Galt's *Letters from the Levant* (1813), William Martin Leake's *Researches in Greece* (1814), Dr. Henry Holland's *Travels in . . . Greece* (1814), and the much delayed *Classical and Topographical Tour Through Greece* (1819), by Edward Dodwell.

Eton . . . Sonnini . . . De Pauw . . . Thornton: William Eton, *A Survey of the Turkish Empire* (1798–1809); Sonnini de Manoncourt, *Voyage en Grèce et en Turquie* (1801); Cornelius de Pauw, *Recherches philosophiques sur les Grecs* (1787); Thomas Thornton, *Present State of Turkey* (1807).

II.

twice . . . abandoned: After going to war with Turkey and supporting the Greeks, Russia abandoned her efforts twice, in 1770 and 1791, and left the Greeks to the vengeance of the Turks.

Corfu excepted: In 1809 and 1810 England took control of all the Ionian islands except Corfu and Paxos.

Mainotes: a fierce and independent people from Maina (see *Finlay*, V. 113 and VI. 26).

Caractacus: The ancient British king resisted the Roman invasion in the first century A.D. (see Tacitus, *Annals*, XII, XXXIII, XXXVII).

Fanal . . . Horn: The Fanal, or Phanár, is to the left of the Golden Horn, 'which flows between the city and the suburbs [and] is a line of separation seldom transgressed by the Frank residents' (Hobhouse, *Travels*, II. 208).

sources: A word, *en passant*, with Mr. Thornton and Dr. Pouqueville; who have been guilty between them of sadly clipping the Sultan's Turkish.

Dr. Pouqueville tells a long story of a Moslem who swallowed corrosive sublimate in such quantities that he acquired the name of '*Suleyman Yeyen*', i.e. quoth the Doctor, '*Suleyman, the eater of corrosive sublimate.*' 'Aha, thinks Mr. Thornton (angry with the Doctor for the fiftieth time) 'have I caught you?' —Then, in a note twice the thickness of the Doctor's anecdote, he questions the Doctor's proficiency in the Turkish tongue, and his veracity in his own. —'For, observes Mr. Thornton (after inflicting on us the tough participle of a Turkish verb) it means nothing more than '*Suleyman the eater*', and quite cashiers the supplementary *sublimate*. Now both are right, and both are wrong. If Mr. Thornton when he next resides 'fourteen years in the factory', will consult his Turkish dictionary, or ask any of his Stamboline acquaintance, he will discover that '*Suleyma'n yeyen*', put together discreetly, mean the '*Swallower of sublimate*', without any '*Suleyman*' in the case; '*Suleyma*' signifying '*corrosive sublimate*', and not being a proper name on this occasion, although it be an orthodox name enough with the addition of *n*. After Mr. Thornton's frequent hints of profound Orientalism, he might have found this out before he sang such paeans over Dr. Pouqueville.

After this, I think 'Travellers *versus* Factors' shall be our motto, though the above Mr. Thornton has condemned 'hoc genus omne', for mistake and misrepresentation. 'Ne Sutor ultra crepidam', 'No merchant beyond his bales.' N.B. For the benefit of Mr. Thornton, 'Sutor' is not a proper name. [B]

participle] tenses *D*; *cor. in DA*   discreetly] ⟨properly⟩ *D*   with . . . *n*] ⟨in others⟩ *D*

Thornton . . . Pouqueville: See Pouqueville's *Voyage en Morée*, II. 126 and Thornton's *Present State of Turkey*, II. 173.

hoc genus omne: Horace, *Satires*, I. ii. 2.

Ne Sutor ultra crepidam: proverbial, derived from Pliny's *Historia Naturalis*, XXXVI. 85.

Spartans were cowards: de Pauw, *Recherches . . .*, I. 155 and 293.

Lismahago: *The Expedition of Sir Humphry Clinker*, letter of Melford to Sir Watkin Phillips, 13 July.

Drummond . . . Walpole: For Hamilton, Aberdeen, Clarke, Leake, Gell, see above; Sir William Drummond (1780–1828) met B's 'requisites' for his *Review of the Government of Athens and Sparta* (1795) and *Heculanensia . . .* (1810), the latter published jointly with Robert Walpole (1781–1856).

III

At one time B had attached this note to *Hints*, 562.

epigraph: *King Lear*, III. iv. 150.

Edinburgh Review . . . French version: See *Edinburgh Review*, XVI (1810), 55–62. The English captain was probably Captain Fergusson, of the *Pylades* (see *Borst*, 107).

Coray: Adamantius Korais (1748–1833), scholar and philhellenist. Korais' remarks appear in the Preface to a French translation of Beccaria Bonesani's *Dei Delitti e della Pene* (1764), published in Paris in 1802.

Scio . . . incorrectly: He was born at Smyrna.

Danish travellers: the archaeologists Peter Oluf Brønsted and George H. C. Koës (see *Borst*, 136–7).

Zolikogloou: I have in my possession an excellent Lexicon 'τρίγλωσσον', which I received in exchange from S. G——, Esq. for a small gem: my antiquarian friends have never forgotten it, or forgiven me. [B] Gregory Zalikaglou, *Dictionnaire français grec* (Paris, 1809). The lexicon in his possession was that by George Vendotis, of Janina (Vienna, 1790). B received it from Sandford Graham (1788–1852), whom B knew from Trinity College before he saw him again in Constantinople.

M. Gail: In Gail's pamphlet against Coray he talks of 'throwing the insolent Helleniste out of the windows'. On this a French critic exclaims: 'Ah, my God! throw an Helleniste out of the window! what sacrilege!' It certainly would be a serious business for those authors who dwell in the attics: but I have quoted the passage merely to prove the similarity of style among the controversialists of all polished countries: London or Edinburgh could hardly parallel this Parisian ebullition. [B] Jean Baptiste Gail (1755–1829), Professor of Greek in the College of France. For the controversy see Gail's *Réclamations . . .* (Paris, 1810).

Dorotheus . . . Miletius: Dorotheus of Mitylene (fl. sixteenth century), archbishop of Monembasia, the author of *Βιβλίον Ἱστορικόν* (Vienna, 1637); Meletios of Janina (1661–1714), archbishop of Athens, best known for his *Μελετιου Γεογραφια* (Vienna, 1728). B quotes from his *Ἐκκλησιαστικη ἱστορια* 4 vols. (Vienna, 1783–95).

Kodrikas . . . Catherine II: Panagiotakes Kodrikas, Professor of Greek at Paris, published a translation of Fontenelle's *Entretiens sur la pluralité des mondes* (Vienna, 1794); John Camarases never published his translation of Ocellus Lucanus *De universi natura*; Christodulus of Acarnania published *περι φιλοσοφον . . .* (Vienna, 1786); Athanasios Peter Psalidas, a schoolmaster at Janina, published his *Ἀληθης Εὐδαιμονία* (Vienna, 1792).

Polyzois . . . Aristaenetus: The reviewer's Polyzois is Demetrios Poluzoë, who published *Γραμματικη περιεχουσα . . .* (Vienna, 1800) and *Αρισταινετου επιστολαι . . .* (Vienna, 1803).

Vlackbey: Cf. below B's note to his translation from the 'Romaic Extracts'.

Riga: the famous Greek patriot-poet, Constantine Rhigas (1753–93), executed by the order of Ali Pasha. He was the author of the original of B's 'Sons of the Greeks, Arise'.

Marmarotouri: B's tutor in Greek while he stayed at Athens, he was 'a leader among the Greek patriots and . . . was attempting at the time to publish his translation of Barthelemy's *Voyage de jeune Anarcharsis* as a means to awakening national feeling' (*Borst*, 141). B printed Marmarotouri's *Prospectus* of this Romaic translation in his original Appendix to *CHP I–II*.

school . . . Sebastiani: For the school see Hobhouse's *Travels*, I. 509–10; François Horace Bastian, Count Sebastiani (1772–1851), ambassador to the *Porte* in 1806–7.

Potemkin: Gregor Alexandrovich Potemkin (1736–91), the paramour of Catherine II.

Mahomet II: In a former number of the Edinburgh Review, 1808, it is observed: 'Lord Byron passed some of his early years in Scotland, where he might have learned that *pibroch* does not mean a *bagpipe*, any more than *duet* means a *fiddle*.' Query, —Was it in Scotland that the young gentlemen of the Edinburgh Review *learned* that *Solyman* means *Mahomet II*. any more than *criticism* means *infallibility*?—but thus it is,

> 'Caedimus inque vicem praebemus crura sagittis.'

The mistake seemed so completely a lapse of the pen (from the great *similarity* of the two words, and the *total absence of error* from the former pages of the literary leviathan) that I should have passed it over as in the text, had I not perceived in the Edinburgh Review much facetious exultation on all such detections, particularly a recent one, where words and syllables are subjects of disquisition and transposition; and the abovementioned parallel passage in my own case irresistibly propelled me to hint how much easier it is to be critical than correct. The *gentlemen*, having enjoyed many a *triumph* on such victories, will hardly begrudge me a slight *ovation* for the present. [B]

B quotes from the notorious review of *HI* by Henry Brougham. See above, editor's introduction to *HI* and *EBSR*. *Caedimus . . . sagittis*: Persius, *Satires*, IV. 42.

Gibbon: *Decline and Fall*, chap. 53.

Comnena: Anna Comnena (1083–1148), author of the *Alexiad*, a history of the reign of her father, Alexis I.

γλωτταν . . . : Joannes Zonaras (12th cent.), *Annals*, VIII. xxvi, quoted from *Decline and Fall*, chap. 53.

Mr. Wright: Cf. 'Preface', 1–2 n.

Caimacam: the deputy of the Grand Vizier.

epistolary style: B printed a facsimile of a letter from the Bey of Corinth to himself in his original Appendix to *CHP I–II*.

Sir Tristrem: alluding to Scott's *Sir Tristrem . . .* (1804).

Additional Note, On the Turks.

'*receive masks*': See *EBSR* 655.

Cadi: the judge of a town or village (*OED*).

D'Ohsson's French: Ignace de Mouradja D'Ohsson, *Tableau général de l'empire Othoman* (1787–90).

Knight of St. Jago: the Spanish Order of St. James of Compostella, founded c.1170.

Nizam Gedidd: the 'New Ordinance' which was to modernize the Turkish army along European lines; promulgated in 1808.

Mufti . . . Mollas . . . Tefterdar: A Mufti was an expounder of Muslim sacred law, a Molla was a judge of that law; the Tefterdar (or defterdar) was in charge of the Vizier's treasury.

Appendix.

The early editions of the first two cantos contained the following items in the Appendix: (*a*) a 'List of Romaic Authors'; (*b*) the original Romaic of Riga's war song, which B rendered as 'Translation of a Greek War Song'; (*c*) two extracts from the Romaic with B's translation of the first; (*d*) a scene from a Goldoni comedy translated into the Romaic by Spiridion Vlanti along with B's English translation; (*e*) 'Familiar Dialogues', which comprise a selection of Romaic phrases useful for everyday occasions to the traveller, with B's translations; (*f*) 'Parallel Passages from St. John's Gospel' in Romaic and ancient Greek; (*g*) 'The Inscriptions at Orchomenus from Meletius'; (*h*) Marmarotouri's 'Prospectus of a Translation of Anacharsis . . . who wished to publish it in England'; (*i*) The Lord's Prayer in Romaic and ancient Greek; (*j*) A facsimile of a letter of apology from the Bey of Corinth to B; (*k*) a Conclusion to the Appendix. Of these items, only (*a*), (*c*), (*d*), and (*k*) have been printed here.

B's transcripts are made from orally delivered texts, a fact which is plainly reflected in the many odd forms which appear in these extracts. The interest in the passages lies in B's amateur scholarship, and hence is a historical interest. The texts printed here, then, are not 'correct' according to the best scholarship, but they are 'accurate', that is, they reflect what B himself heard and originally transmitted. I have emended only the printer's errors; and I am pleased to thank Professor Diskin Clay for helping me understand, and deal with, the problems of these texts.

List of Romaic Authors: It is to be observed that the names given are not in chronological order, but consist of some selected at a venture from amongst those who flourished from the taking of Constantinople to the time of Meletius. [B] For additional information see Émile Louis Legrand's various *Bibliographie hellénique* (1885–1906). In a letter to Dallas sent with the proofs for the Appendix, B wrote: 'I have omitted to observe that in my extract from ⟨Miletius⟩ the List of Romaic Literati in a former note there are some mentioned of very different dates from the taking of Stambol to the present day—I have selected only such as have treated on subjects not theological without specifying their particular era. ⟨This⟩ It must be stated that they are not intended for a list entirely of *living* authors.' [*MS. D*]

most celebrated: These names are not taken from any publication. [B]

Parios: published a number of works between 1784 and 1806; his treatise on rhetoric was issued in 1799.

Athanasius: B's entry (kept through all early editions) is a slip, merely repeating in slightly different form the entry above on Athanasius of Parios.

Damodos . . . Demetrius: I have been unable to trace a record of any writers with these names living in the early nineteenth century.

Vlackbey: Vlackbey, Prince of Wallachia. [B]

'*Oh, Miss Bailey!*': George Colman the younger, *Love Laughs at Locksmiths* (1803).

'*A captain . . . quarters*': ibid.

Rumores fuge: Λόγος λατινικὸς, ὅπου θέλει νὰ εἰπῇ· φεύγε ταῖς σύγχισες [B] (cf. 'Rumorem fuge', Dionysius Cato, *Disticha de Moribus*, I. 12.)

finishes: Σώνελαι—'finishes'—awkwardly enough, but it is the literal translation of the Romaic. The original of this comedy of Goldoni's I never read, but it does not appear one of his best. 'Il Bugiardo' is one of the most lively; but I do not think it has been translated into Romaic: it is much more amusing than our own 'Liar', by Foote. The character of Lelio is better drawn than Young Wilding. Goldoni's comedies amount to fifty; some perhaps the best in Europe, and others the worst. His life is also one of the best specimens of autobiography, and, as Gibbon has observed, 'more dramatic than any of his plays'. The above scene was selected as containing some of the most familiar Romaic idioms, not for any wit which it displays, since there is more done than said, the greater part consisting of stage directions.

The original is one of the few comedies by Goldoni which is without the buffoonery of the speaking Harlequin. [B]

Il Bugiardo: Goldoni wrote this comedy in 1751.

'*Liar*' *by Foote*: *The Liar* (1764), by Samuel Foote (1720–77).

'*more . . . plays*': *The Autobiography of Edward Gibbon*, ed. Oliphant Smeaton (Everyman edn., 1911), 5.

Canto III

MS. and Publishing History. Four integral MSS. of this canto survive.

MS. M (Murray). B's first draft, a collection of separate MS. leaves and small scraps arranged and numbered by B into a completed unit (see *MS. BM* below). *MS. M* contains a sequence numbered 4–96. At some point the first three and last four stanzas were detached from *MS. M*, but they survive elsewhere (see below, *MS. B*). The sequence numbered 4–96 has the following stanzas of the finished poem: 4–32, 34–87, 89–91, 105–9, 111–12, and the Drachenfels lyric. In addition, st. 110 is among the *MS. M* papers, but unnumbered. It is on a single leaf with sts. 77 and 78–81, with a head-note by B: 'These are detached stanzas to be inserted in the process of the poem—May 1816.' The composition sequence of *MS. M* is as follows. It should be noted that the analysis here revises and augments my earlier one (cf. *McGann*(1), 304–10). Sts. 4–25, 27–30 (4 May); sts. 26, 31–2, 34–9, 40, 42–4 (in that order: 5–10 May); Drachenfels lyric (11 May); 41, 45–57 (11–13 May); 58–62 (20–31 May); 63–6, 68–71 (26–31 May); 72–4, 76, 77, 110 (27–31 May); 78–81, 67, 75, (27 May–3 June); 82–7, 89–91, 105–9, 111–12 (4–8 June).

MS. BM (on deposit, British Library). This important MS., which only appeared in 1975, helps to solve some of the analytical problems connected with *MS. M* in particular. *MS. BM* is B's (and the first) fair copy. The poem is copied in 100 numbered pages contained in a notebook bound in red leather. Two folded sheets are inserted between pp. 83 and 84; these contain some later additions. On 2 Sept. B gave this MS. to Scrope Davies with instructions to carry it back to B's publisher in England. Davies's note on the first leaf reads: 'This MS was given by Lord Byron to Scrope Davies at Geneva September 2nd 1816.' B's heading for the text is: 'Childe Harold's Pilgrimage. Copied in Ghent. April 28th 1816. Begun at Sea.' In its first form *MS. BM* was written as a sequence of 96 numbered stanzas (the contents of *MS. M* plus sts. 1–3, but excluding st. 110, which was added to the sequence in *MS. BM* only after the first form was completed). At the end of this first form of the poem B wrote: 'End of Canto Third. Byron. Lecheron—Geneva—June 8th 1816.' The first addition was sts. 115–18, dated by B 'June 9th 1816' and headed in his note: 'Additions. I know not whether to make these part or no as yet. B.' He then added st. 110, and renumbered the poem to a sequence of 101 stanzas. It should be noted that what B had 'Begun at Sea' was sts. 1–3.

MSS. M and *BM* together show that sts. 1–3 were written 'at Sea', i.e. on 25 Apr. B copied these three stanzas fair three days later, and for the rest of his trip from Belgium to Switzerland he apparently would write draft stanzas on whatever pieces of paper were to hand (*MS. M*). He may have copied some of these drafts into *MS. BM* while he was *en route*—in the evening, probably, when he had leisure. He completed the process of copying *MS. M* into *MS. BM* on 8 June. Stanza 110 was copied into *MS. BM* on 9 June, along with sts. 115–18.

MS. BM also has the remaining stanzas of the received poem inserted in the MS. These were added in the following sequence: 92–8 (composed 13 June and inserted into *MS. BM* on a separate sheet headed by B: 'To be inserted p. 83'); 88 (composed 14–16 June, and added on p. 99 with B's head-note: 'Addition to be stanza 87 (to be inserted at p. 81) after the line "Deep into Nature's breast etc." '); 113–14 (written 16 June—see *MS. S* below: 114 is copied on leaf 94 after st. 112, and 113 is copied across sts. 112, 114); 99–104 (written between 23 and 27 June and inserted in *MS. BM* on a separate sheet); 33 (the final addition, written on leaf 100 between 4 and 10 July).

MS. S (Sterling Library, London Univ.). A second fair copy, with the first seven stanzas in B's hand and the remainder in Mary Shelley's; B's corrections throughout. B's head-note is that the MS. was copied 'from the original MS. sent by me to England [i.e. from *MS. BM*]. Byron. Nov. 3rd 1816.' B's note on p. 1 is: '⟨The Original that is the first stanzas were copied in Ghent April 28th 1816⟩ The first stanzas were copied in at Ghent April 1816—Begun at Sea.'

MS. S has all the received stanzas in proper sequence except sts. 33 and 99–104, which are not in the MS. At the end of st. 112 Mary wrote: 'Secheron—Geneva, June 8th 1816.' Then the MS. has her copy of sts. 113–14, after which the date 16 June 1816. Finally, she copied in at the end sts. 115–18 with B's head-note from *MS. BM*. The contents of *MS. S* show that Mary made the copy between 16 and 27 June.

MS. MC (Murray). The third fair copy—and printer's copy—made from *MS. BM* by Claire Clairmont, with B's corrections and additions. B has fair copied into the MS. sts. 33 and 99–104 as well as a few of the notes and the epigraph. B's cover note is: 'This copy to be *printed* from—subject to comparison with the *Original MS.* (from which this is a transcription) in such parts as it may chance to be difficult to decypher in the following. The notes in this copy are more complete and extended than in the former—and there is also *one stanza more* inserted and added in this—viz. the 33rd. Bn.' B's end-note is: 'Byron. July 4th 1816. Diodati.'

MS. B (Berg), B's draft of sts. 1–3 and 115–18 (numbered 1–3 and 97–100). These were originally part of *MS. M*.

MS. ML (Morgan). The first draft of the Drachenfels lyric, with B's head-note: 'May 11th 1816—Written on the banks of the Rhine—to my dearest sister with some flowers.' B sent this copy to his sister in England.

MS. SB. B's copy of *CHP III*, first edn., second issue (in the Sterling Library with *MS. S*). It contains his corrections for line 959 and the note to st. 99.

MS. H (Huntington Library). Two pieces of proof material with B's corrections. (*a*) A proof sheet of sts. 100–3, with B's correction of line 959. (*b*) A proof sheet of pp. 77–8 with B's correction of the note to st. 99. Murray must have sent these proof revises to B in 1817, for B first saw the misprints on 9 May 1817 (*BLJ* v. 220). Murray corrected the text in the *1818* collected edition.

B's draft of st. 88 was once in the Harry B. Smith library. This draft text is noticed and briefly described in Smith's *Sentimental Library* (privately printed, 1914), pp. 29–30. The present location of this MS. (here cited as *Smith*) is not known.

The early printing history of *CHP III* is complex. B sent *MS. MC* to England with Shelley at the end of August, and on 5 Sept. he sent Davies back with *MS. BM*. The printing instructions on *MS. MC* are clear, but B was less clear about who should see the poem through the press (see letter to Murray of 28 Aug., *BLJ* v. 90): Gifford and Shelley are both mentioned, and so is Moore. B saw no proof for the first edition.

Shelley clearly understood that he was authorized to correct the proofs (see *The Letters of Percy Bysshe Shelley*, ed. F. L. Jones (Oxford, 1964), I. 511, 513–14). But Murray wanted Gifford to edit the poem, not Shelley, whose politics he did not care for. So Murray ignored Shelley and relied on Gifford, in the mean time flattering B with his and Gifford's praises of the poem. Thus B was gradually led to accept Gifford as editor (see B's correspondence with Murray from Aug. 1816 to Feb. 1817), and Shelley's position as B's agent was effectively circumvented. The effect of this action is most clearly seen in the notes in *MS. C*, some of which were not printed. Murray and Gifford carefully excised all the more radical political content in the notes, something which they knew Shelley would not have permitted. Gifford also made textual changes from *MS. MC* at lines 198, 216, 219, 542, and 596. When he learned that changes were being made, B was annoyed, but Murray set his mind to rest about the matter, and B eventually acquiesced (see *BLJ* v. 154, 169). *MS. SB* contains B's final corrected copy of the canto. The notes removed by Murray and Gifford are here first printed; but I have accepted, with B, the textual changes, and placed the *MS. MC* readings in the Apparatus. Copy text is *CHP III*, third issue (see *Wise*, I. 54–8), but incorporating the corrections in *MSS. SB* and *H*.

Literary and Historical Background. CHP III is B's expressed attempt to come to terms with the collapse of his marriage and the public response to that event in England. B wrote the poem as a personal self-examination and a public justification. The various historical characters in the poem are all used as *figurae* expressing one or another aspect of B's central attitudes of mind, qualities of character, or circumstances of life. The two key figures are of course Napoleon and Rousseau, and it is part of the brilliance of the poem that B treated both with such pitiless sympathy. In this canto B begins to develop his special variation upon the traditional poetic use of the pilgrimage as a process of renewal (see especially st. 7).

Much has been made of the influence of Wordsworth, Coleridge, and especially Shelley on *CHP III*, and it is true that each made an important impact on the poem, as B himself acknowledged when he later joked about it to Moore (*BLJ* V. 165). Wordsworth's natural religion, or religious naturalism, has been a special focus of attention. Nevertheless, as M. K. Joseph has pointed out (*Byron The Poet* (1964), 76–83), the Wordsworthian/Shelleyan motifs in the poem are more aimed for than convincing, for B was never so alive to the secret ministries of Nature as were the other Romantics. The *paysage moralisé* is always B's most congenial method of dealing with natural phenomena.

When B toured Lake Geneva with Shelley, then, B brought himself into contact with the idea, and perhaps even the experience, of a selfless order of universal benevolence, as his stanzas, and prose note, on Clarens indicates. Yet much of *CHP III* struggles against such beliefs and attitudes. Thus it is true that the journal of his tour of the Bernese Oberland with Hobhouse in September (see also *Manfred* commentary and *BLJ* V. 96–105) explains both the weaknesses of many of the Wordsworthian and Shelleyan passages in the poem, and the strength of those other passages which expose and analyse disharmony and incompleteness.

Besides the general works cited earlier, other useful commentaries are: Heinrich Gillardon, *Shelley's Einwirkung auf Byron* (Karlsruhe, 1898), 37–50; F. H. Pughe, *Studien über Byron und Wordsworth* (Heidelberg, 1902), 64–88; E. M. Everett, 'Byron's Lakist Interlude', *SP* 55 (1958), 62–75; Charles E. Robinson, *Shelley and Byron* (Baltimore, 1976), 14–27.

epigraph   *Oeuvres de Fréderic Le Grand* (Berlin, 1846–57), XXV. 49–50.

2. Augusta Ada Byron (1815–52). She later (1835) married William King Noel, eighth Baron King, created the Earl of Lovelace. B never saw his daughter again after Lady Byron left him in Jan. 1816, when Ada was five weeks old.

6. B wrote the three opening stanzas while sailing from Dover to Ostend.

7. Cf. Isaiah 42: 11.

10. Echoing *Henry V*, III. i. 1.

11–12. Perhaps recalling *The Two Noble Kinsmen*, II. i. 73–6.

19. That is, Childe Harold.

38. Cf. *Manfred*, II. i. 51–2. B perhaps echoes Sheridan's *Pizarro*, IV. i: 'A life spent worthily should be measured by a noble line—by deeds, not years.'

46–54. Cf. 'The Dream', I. 19–22.

60. Echoing Dr. Johnson: 'the other poisons the springs of life' (*Idler*, 42). See also 'The Dream', VIII. 1–10.

64. Echoes *Hamlet*, III. ii. 69.

75. B refers to the journey in the first two cantos to Greece.

78–9. Cf. *Manfred*, I. i. 259.

89. Cf. Exodus 2: 22.

100–26. Cf. *Manfred*, II. ii, 50–72.

109. Cf. 'The Dream', VIII. 12.

118. The Chaldees were Babylonian astronomers, famous as seers.

131. Echoing *Macbeth*, III. iv. 21.

145–6. The first French empire (1804–15) of Napoleon was overthrown at Waterloo. The lines echo Lucan's *Pharsalia*, IX. 976–7.

147–9. The Lion of Waterloo was not erected until 1823.

153. Waterloo 'made' the monarch-restoring Congress of Vienna.

154. Echoes Matthew 27: 33.

158. 'Pride of place' is a term of falconry, and means the highest pitch of flight.—See *Macbeth*, [II. iv. 12] &c.

> 'A Falcon towering in her pride of place
> Was by a mousing Owl hawked at and killed.' [B]

Falcon] Eagle *MS. C*, *1st edn.*, *1st*, *2nd issues*, *1818–1832*

159. Pryse Lockhart Gordon met B in Brussels and they toured Waterloo together. Gordon asked B for an autograph, and B wrote stanzas 17–18 in Gordon's album. There 158–9 read: 'Here his last flight the haughty Eagle flew,/Then tore with bloody beak the fatal plain.' B altered the lines to their present form when he was later reminded of the inaccuracy of his picture of the attacking habits of birds of prey. The story is related in Gordon's *Personal Memoirs* (1830), II. 325–8.

163–71. Cf. no. 276.

169–70. Echoes the pamphlet *Killing No Murder* (*Harleian Miscellany* (1810), IX. 304–5).

171. *prove*: to test the value of something; here, Waterloo and its results.

175. Recalling Isaiah 63: 3.

180. See the famous Song on Harmodius and Aristogiton.—The best English translation is in Bland's Anthology, by Mr. Denham.

> 'With myrtle my sword will I wreathe,' &c. [B]

In 514 B.C. Harmodius and Aristogeiton, their daggers concealed in myrtle branches, attempted the lives of the brothers Hippias and Hipparchus, tyrants of Athens. Only Hipparchus was killed. Thereafter, the sword dressed in myrtle became an emblem of the upholder of liberty, though in fact the assassins were only avenging a private wrong. See Herodotus, Books I, V, and VI, and Thucydides, Books I and VI. B found Denham's translation in *Translations Chiefly from the Greek Anthology* by Robert Bland and J. H. Merivale (1806): see Bland's augmented edition of 1813, pp. 123–4.

188. On the night previous to the action, it is said that a ball was given at Brussels. [B] The stanza memorializes the famous ball given by the Duchess of Richmond on 15 June, the night before the inconclusive battle of Quatre-Bras. Waterloo was fought on 18 June.

198. Wellington discovered the approach of Napoleon not from the sound of cannon but in dispatches sent to him from Gebhard L. Blücher (1742–1819), the commander of the Prussian forces.

200. Frederick Duke of Brunswick (1771–1815), the nephew of George III, was killed at Quatre-Bras. His father, Charles William Ferdinand, was killed in 1806 at Auerstädt.

226–7. '*Cameron's gathering*': the clan-song and rallying-cry of the Camerons.

Lochiel: the title of the chief of the Camerons.

Albyn: the Gaelic name for Scotland.

234. Sir Evan Cameron, and his descendant Donald, the 'gentle Lochiel' of the 'forty-five'. [B] Sir Evan Cameron (1629–1719) resisted Cromwell between 1652 and 1658 and fought at Killiecrankie for James II in 1689. His grandson Donald Cameron (1695–1748) fought to restore the Stuarts in 1745 and was wounded at Culloden in 1746. See also Campbell's well-known poem celebrating his character, 'Lochiel's Warning'.

235. The wood of Soignies is supposed to be a remnant of the 'forest of Ardennes', famous in Boiardo's *Orlando*, and immortal in Shakespeare's 'As you like it'. It is also celebrated in Tacitus as being the spot of successful defence by the Germans against the Roman encroachments.—I have ventured to adopt the name connected with nobler associations than those of mere slaughter. [B] B's note multiplies confusions. Soignies is between Waterloo and Brussels, Ardennes is in Luxemburg. As for Tacitus, B seems to confound two passages from the *Annals* (1.60 and III.42). For Boiardo's Ardennes see *Orlando Innamorato* I. ii. 30. Shakespeare's Arden is, of course, out of the question.

253. A reference to Scott's *The Field of Waterloo* (Edinburgh, 1815).

256, 261. In *EBSR*, 726 B satirized the Earl of Carlisle, his guardian and the father of the Hon. Frederick Howard (1785–1815), B's cousin who died at Waterloo. See B's letters to Moore (7 July 1815) and to his sister (25 Apr. 1816).

270. My guide from Mont St. Jean over the field seemed intelligent and accurate. The place where Major Howard fell was not far from two tall and

solitary trees (there was a third cut down, or shivered in the battle) which
stand a few yards from each other at a pathway's side.—Beneath these he
died and was buried. The body has since been removed to England. A small
hollow for the present marks where it lay, but will probably soon be effaced;
the plough has been upon it, and the grain is.

After pointing out the different spots where Picton and other gallant men
had perished; the guide said, 'here Major Howard lay; I was near him when
wounded'. I told him my relationship, and he seemed then still more anxious to
point out the particular spot and circumstances. The place is one of the most
marked in the field from the peculiarity of the two trees above mentioned.

I went on horseback twice over the field, comparing it with my recollection
of similar scenes. As a plain, Waterloo seems marked out for the scene of
some great action, though this may be mere imagination: I have viewed
with attention those of Platea, Troy, Mantinea, Leuctra, Chaeronea, and
Marathon; and the field around Mont St. Jean and Hougoumont appears to
want little but a better cause, and that undefinable but impressive halo
which the lapse of ages throws around a celebrated spot, to vie in interest
with any or all of these, except perhaps the last mentioned. [B]

seemed . . . and] was intelligent and seemed   there . . . battle] there had been a third lately
cut down   at a] ⟨near to⟩ by ⟨the⟩ a   the plough has been . . . the last mentioned] The
Guide told me that he was near him when he was wounded and pointed out the different
⟨places⟩ spots where Picton and ⟨many⟩ other gallant men had perished. He mentioned
Major Howard's name among the first ⟨as⟩ he having been near him.—And when ⟨he⟩ I
told him that the major was my relative seemed anxious to point out the particular spot and
circumstances—the place is one of the most marked in the field ⟨by⟩ from the peculiarity
of the two trees above mentioned. *M*

B's guide was Major Pryse Lockhart Gordon, a friend of B's mother in
Scotland.

287. See *Macbeth*, I. iii. 47.

288 ff. This famous passage has been said to echo Burton's *Anatomy of
Melancholy*, II. iii. 7, but the more likely source is Donne's 'The Broken
Heart', 24–32. See also Carew's 'The Spark', 23–6.

298–302. Cf. 'The Dream', VIII. 6–11.

303. The (Fabled) apples on the brink of the lake Asphaltes were said
to be fair without, and within ashes.—*Vide* Tacitus, *Histor.* I, 5, 7. [B]

The Lake Asphaltites (this is a fable) was said to have apples fair without and ashes within
growing on its brink. *M*

304 ff. See Psalms, 90: 10.

308. *tale*: a pun, meaning both 'story' and 'counting'.

313–15. Seems to recall Henry V's speech on St. Crispin's day: see *Henry
V*, IV. iii. 44 ff.

316–414. B's attitude towards Napoleon began to take a more critical
turn after the abdication at Fontainebleau. See the *Ode to Napoleon Buonaparte*
and commentary. When these stanzas were written Napoleon was still
secured on St. Helena.

328. Possibly recalling Pope's *Essay on Man*, II. 18.

346. See Lamentations 3: 19.

352–405. Cf. *De rerum natura*, II. 1120–40.

366. *Philip's son*: Alexander the Great.

369. The great error of Napoleon, 'if we have writ our annals true', was a continued obtrusion on mankind of his want of all community of feeling for or with them; perhaps more offensive to human vanity than the active cruelty of more trembling and suspicious tyranny.

Such were his speeches to public assemblies as well as individuals: and the single expression which he is said to have used on returning to Paris after the Russian winter had destroyed his army, rubbing his hands over a fire, 'This is pleasanter than Moscow', would probably alienate more favour from his cause than the destruction and reverses which led to the remark. [B]

 if we . . . annals true: *Coriolanus*, V. vi. 114.

386. Echoing Tacitus, *Annals*, VI. 6.

388–96. At this point the analysis of Napoleon clearly shifts to a simultaneous act of self-analysis. Such a technique, typical of *CHP* throughout, is generally epitomized in the shifting engagement of B the poet with his titular hero.

397–405. The metaphor here has been said to be mixed, but if 'peaks' is a metaphor not of great men but of their situation, then the figure is consistent.

420. *battles*: meaning at once battalions and military engagements.

429.   'What wants that knave
      That a king should have?'

was King James's question on meeting Johnny Armstrong and his followers in full accoutrements.—See the Ballad. [B] In 1532 Johnnie Armstrong, Laird of Gilnockie, surrendered to James V in such splendid attire that the king had him hanged for his insolence. See *Minstrelsy of the Scottish Border*, 4th edn. (1810), I. 127 for the ballad quotation.

435–6. The device was frequently a bleeding heart.

444–50. Cf. *Giaour*, 46–67.

451. *MS. M* shows eleven minor false starts for this line, all various combinations of conjunctions and adverbs.

454. Cf. Lucan, *Pharsalia*, IX. 969 and Tasso's *Gerusalemme Liberata*, XV. 20.

476. Referring to B's sister Augusta. Her remembered presence passes in and out of the rest of this canto. See also B's other short poems written to Augusta from Switzerland.

Drachenfels lyric

The castle of Drachenfels stands on the highest summit of 'the Seven Mountains', over the Rhine banks; it is in ruins, and connected with some singular traditions: it is the first in view on the road from Bonn, but on the opposite side of the river; on this bank, nearly facing it, are the remains of

another called the Jew's castle, and a large cross commemorative of the
murder of a chief by his brother: the number of castles and cities along the
course of the Rhine on both sides is very great, and their situations remarkably beautiful. [B]

stands] is *BM, cor. in MC*

501. Cf. Genesis 27: 28.

553. The monument of the young and lamented General Marceau (killed
by a rifle-ball at Altenkirchen on the last day of the fourth year of the
French republic) still remains as described.

The inscriptions on his monument are rather too long, and not required:
his name was enough; France adored, and her enemies admired; both wept
over him.—His funeral was attended by the generals and detachments from
both armies. In the same grave General Hoche is interred, a gallant man
also in every sense of the word, but though he distinguished himself greatly
in battle, *he* had not the good fortune to die there; his death was attended
by suspicions of poison.

A separate monument (not over his body, which is buried by Marceau's)
is raised for him near Andernach, opposite to which one of his most memorable exploits was performed, in throwing a bridge to an island on the
Rhine. The shape and style are different from that of Marceau's, and the
inscription more simple and pleasing.

> 'The Army of the Sambre and Meuse
> to its Commander in Chief
> Hoche.'

This is all, and as it should be. Hoche was esteemed among the first of
France's earlier generals before Buonaparte monopolized her triumphs.—
He was the destined commander of the invading army of Ireland. [B]

wept over] wept ⟨for⟩   detachments from] detachments ⟨of⟩ had not the good fortune to
⟨did not⟩ *MC*   ⟨he did not die there—'tam Maximis quam Morte'—the *?* which carried
him off is that *?* has always been pleaded to *?* ⟩*BM*   monopolized her triumphs] ⟨blotted
all from her pages⟩ *BM*   of Ireland.] of Ireland ⟨—and had he lived to *?* ⟩ *BM*

François Sévérin Desgravins Marceau (1769–96) died in an engagement with
the forces of the Archduke Charles. The 'tears' of 542 were Austrian as well
as French because the French, retreating from Altenkirchen, had to leave
Marceau behind in the care of the Austrians, who also buried him. General
Lazare Hoche (1768–97), celebrated as the 'pacificateur de la Vendée', died
of consumption, but the rapid deterioration of his health near the end of his
life, and the fact that he was surrounded by political intrigues, led to wide-
spread (though groundless) speculation that he had been poisoned. The
bridge episode mentioned by B occurred 18 Apr. 1797 during the engagement
which eventually resulted in Hoche's defeat of the Austrians at Neuwied.

554. Ehrenbreitstein, i.e. 'the broad Stone of Honour', one of the strongest
fortresses in Europe, was dismantled and blown up by the French at the

truce of Leoben.—It had been and could only be reduced by famine or treachery. It yielded to the former, aided by surprise. After having seen the fortifications of Gibraltar and Malta, it did not much strike by comparison, but the situation is commanding. General Marceau besieged it in vain for some time, and I slept in a room where I was shown a window at which he is said to have been standing observing the progress of the siege by moonlight, when a ball struck immediately below it. [B] He was killed not long afterwards at Altenkirchen by a rifleman—it is rather singular that these narrow escapes have in several instances been followed closely by death— at Nuremberg shortly before the battle of Lutzen Gustavus Adolphus had his horse killed under him. Falconer but escaped one Shipwreck to perish by another.—The Prince of Orange died by the more successful attempt by a *third* assassin and Nelson rarely came out of action without a wound till the most fatal and glorious of all—which instead of a scar bequeathed him immortality.—[B, *MSS. BM, C*]

bequeathed] left *MC*

Marceau unsuccessfully beseiged Ehrenbreitstein in 1795–6. The fortress was finally taken, after a long siege, in 1799. It was blown up not after the Treaty of Leoben (April 1797) but after the Treaty of Lunéville in 1801.

Nuremberg . . . Gustavus Adolphus: Gustavus II Adolphus, king of Sweden, narrowly escaped death at the battle of Nuremberg in August 1632, but was killed in November of the same year in a cavalry charge at the battle of Lützen.

Falconer: William Falconer (1732–69) based his famous poem, *The Shipwreck* (1762), upon his survival of the wreck of the 'Brittania' in 1760. In 1769 he sailed for India and was never heard from again.

Prince of Orange: William I, 'the Silent' (1533–84), was shot to death by an assassin after narrowly escaping death by another assassin in 1582. The third attempt mentioned by B did not occur. B may have had in mind Alençon's plot to overthrow William in 1583.

567. Alluding to Prometheus on the Caucasus. The line is rather interesting textually. B himself never wrote 'ceaseless', but the sequence of early texts which carry this reading, and which B carefully corrected, is too long to suppose that he did not authorize the word. Mary Shelley seems to be the original author of 'ceaseless', but whether she wrote it deliberately or inadvertently is not clear. (She transcribed many of B's MSS. and often made small changes while she was copying; some of these changes B accepted). Simply as poetry, 'ceaseless' is the patently superior reading; but the history of B's textual corrections in *CHP III* also forbids a return to the earliest MS. reading of 'sleepless'.

590 ff. The Alpine scene is a *locus classicus* in Romantic literature. The

first extended presentation of such a scene in English poetry is George Keate's *The Alps* (1763).

607. The chapel is destroyed, and the pyramid of bones diminished to a small number by the Burgundian legion in the service of France, who anxiously effaced this record of their ancestors' less successful invasions. A few still remain notwithstanding the pains taken by the Burgundians for ages, (all who passed that way removing a bone to their own country) and the less justifiable larcenies of the Swiss postillions, who carried them off to sell for knife-handles, a purpose for which the whiteness imbibed by the bleaching of years had rendered them in great request. Of these relics I ventured to bring away as much as may have made the quarter of a hero, for which the sole excuse is, that if I had not, the next passer by might have perverted them to worse uses than the careful preservation which I intend for them. [B]

sole excuse] sole ⟨cause⟩ *MC*

The Swiss successfully defended themselves in 1476 against the invading army of Charles the Bold, Duke of Burgundy. The battle of Morat, fought near the town and the lake of the same name, was the bloodiest of the three battles (Grandson, Morat, Nancy) fought by the Swiss and the French. Charles was killed at Nancy, but he left more than ten thousand of his men dead at Morat. The ossuary in which their bones were collected was destroyed by the invading French forces in 1798, and the bones scattered about were not collected and reburied until 1822. B sent the bones he collected back to Murray in London, where they are still preserved.

Unsepulchred . . . ghost: See *Odyssey*, XI. 42–3, 633 and Ovid's *Fasti*, II. 551–4.

608–9. Morat and Marathon (490 B.C.) were the victories of men fighting for their liberty, whereas Waterloo and Cannae (216 B.C.) were conflicts of states which sought dominion over each other.

616. Draco—the author of the first Red Book on record was an Athenian special pleader in great business.—Hippias—the Athenian Bourbon was in the battle of Marathon and did not keep at the respectful distance from danger of the Ghent refugees—but the English and Prussians resembled the Medes and the Persians as little as Blucher and the British General did Datis and Artaphernes and Buonaparte was still more remote in cause and character from Miltiades—and a parallel 'after the manner of Plutarch' might have still existed in the fortunes of the sons of Pisistratus and the reigning doctors of right-divinity. [B, *MSS. BM, C*]

of the first] of ⟨some⟩ the first *MC*   but the English . . . right-divinity.] but the English ⟨as little⟩ and Prussians resembled the Medes and Persians ⟨as Blucher and the other General ⟨whom it is usual to praise for talent on this occasion⟩ . . . Pisistratus and the ⟨what shall we call them? what words can convey the almost convulsive contempt which is and ever must be felt for the miserable ℙ of this most foulest of dunghills.⟩ reigning doctors ℙ of this most foulest of dunghills.⟩ reigning doctors of right-divinity. *BM*

Draco: author of the notoriously severe penal code for Athens (624 B.C.).

Hippias, etc.: B's note draws an ironic comparison between the principals at Waterloo and those at Marathon. The sons of Pisistratus, Hippias and Hipparchus, both died ingloriously. Hippias died at Marathon fighting for the Persians against his countrymen; for Hipparchus see above, note to 180. Datis and Artaphernes were the generals of the Persian forces at Marathon.

Blucher and the British General: i.e. Wellington and the Prussian Field-Marshal, Gebhard Leberecht von Blücher (1742–1819).

625. Aventicum (near Morat) was the Roman capital of Helvetia, where Avenches now stands. [B]

634. Julia Alpinula, a young Aventian priestess, died soon after a vain endeavour to save her father, condemned to death as a traitor by Aulus Caecina. Her epitaph was discovered many years ago;—it is thus—

Julia Alpinula
Hic jaceo
Infelicis patris, infelix proles
Deae Aventiae Sacerdos;
Exorare patris necem non potui
Male mori in fatis ille erat.
Vixi annos XXIII.

I know of no human composition so affecting as this, nor a history of deeper interest. These are the names and actions which ought not to perish, and to which we turn with a true and healthy tenderness, from the wretched and glittering detail of a confused mass of conquests and battles, with which the mind is roused for a time to a false and feverish sympathy, from whence it recurs at length with all the nausea consequent on such intoxication. [B]

Aulus Caecina captured Aventicum in A.D. 69 and executed a chief named Julius Alpinus (see Tacitus, I. 67). History leaves no record of his having a daughter. Both her history and her epitaph found their way into the collection of epitaphs published in 1707 by Janus Gruterus via the forger Paul Wilhelm. The epitaph in fact seems to be based upon a genuine inscription at Baden about Alpinia Alpinula: see Lord Stanhope's review of Latin inscriptions in the *Quarterly Review*, 78 (June 1846), 61–75. The autobiographical relevance of this story to B's poem needs no emphasis. B's extended treatment of the Caritas Romana story in Canto IV, sts. 148–51, indicates the strength of his response to situations of this sort.

642. This is written in the eye of Mont Blanc (June 3d, 1816) which even at this distance dazzles mine.

(July 20th). I this day observed for some time the distinct reflection of Mont Blanc and Mont Argentiere in the calm of the lake, which I was crossing in my boat; the distance of these mountains from their mirror is 60 miles. [B] On 3 June B was staying at the Hôtel de l'Angleterre in Sécheron. He moved to the Villa Diodati on 10 June. *BM* has only the first sentence of this note.

644. *Leman*. The Lake of Geneva gets its French name from the Latin Lacus Lemanus.

667. Cf. Ecclesiastes 2: 14 and 1 John 2: 11.

668–70. Cf. *CHP IV*, st. 105 and *DJ* X, st. 4. Shelley's characterization of B as the 'Pilgrim of Eternity' (*Adonais*, XXX) stems from this passage.

673. The colour of the Rhone at Geneva is *blue*, to a depth of tint which I have never seen equalled in water, salt or fresh, except in the Mediterranean and Archipelago. [B] Compare *DJ* XIV, st. 87.

680–715. These are the stanzas which show the clearest influence of Shelley and Wordsworth on *CHP III*. See also *Manfrde*, II. ii, *passim*, and *The Island*, I, st. 16.

682. Echoing 'Tintern Abbey', 76–80.

693–4. Cf. Isaiah 40: 31.

697. See Horace, *Odes*, III. ii. 23–4 and *Cymbeline*, V. iv. 28.

698–706. The dualism here is centrally Byronic. B alternately expresses, analyses, and resists such an attitude throughout his career. The Wordsworthian trappings of this stanza and the others here associated with it clearly weaken the entire passage, whose basic approach, if strongly 'idealistic', is anything but benevolent.

719–20. Rousseau was born in Geneva in 1712.

730–3. The reference is to Rousseau's epistolary novel *Julie, ou la Nouvelle Héloïse* (1761), which treats the illicit love of Julie and her tutor Saint–Preux.

739 ff. The literary reference is to the tradition of Dante's Beatrice and Petrarch's Laura. B recurs to the theme throughout his works.

743–51. The literary pattern described here—that an author projects and translates in fictional forms his own passionate experiences—is not only a paradigmatic statement of the Romantic theory of self-expression; it fairly epitomizes B's method with his materials in *CHP*. If Julie is Rousseau's literary surrogate, Rousseau is even more plainly B's. None the less, B resisted comparisons between himself and Rousseau: see his letter to his mother, 7 Oct. 1808, and his 'Detached Thoughts' for 15 Oct. 1821.

751. This refers to the account in his 'Confessions' of his passion for the Comtesse d'Houdetot (the mistress of St. Lambert) and his long walk every morning for the sake of the single kiss which was the common salutation of French acquaintance.—Rousseau's description of his feelings on this occasion may be considered as the most passionate, yet not impure description and expression of love that ever kindled into words; which after all must be felt, from their very force, to be inadequate to the delineation: a painting can give no sufficient idea of the ocean. [B]

This refers to] ⟨see⟩   long walk . . . single kiss] walk . . . kiss   that ever kindled . . . of the ocean] that was ever worded *M*

See Rousseau's *Les Confessions*, II. ix.

752–3. The list is long and includes the famous instances of Madame de

Warens, Madame d'Epinay, Diderot, Grimm, Voltaire, Hume, and Saint-Lambert.

763. *oracles*: referring to the *Discours* of 1750 and 1753 and to *Le Contrat Social* (1762). B then treats in a general way the impact which Rousseau's social writings had upon the French Revolution and its melancholy aftermath up to and including the restoration of the Bourbons.

772–3. See Matthew 27: 51.

777. See—Spain and France etc. etc.—Ferdinand 'the Beloved' Louis 'the Desired' the Stork and the Log—the lovely and the desirable—but the Frogs *would* have kings and must now keep them. [B. *MSS. BM, C*] B refers ironically to Aesop's fable, 'The Frogs Choose a King', which he read in the L'Estrange version. Ferdinand and Louis are, respectively, Ferdinand VII of Spain (1784–1833) and Louis XVIII (1755–1824), restored to their thrones in 1814.

809. *darken'd Jura*: The mountains of the Jura to the north-west of Lake Geneva 'would appear "darkened" in contrast to the afterglow in the western sky' (*C* II. 269 n.).

813. Echoing Wordsworth's 'Remembrance of Collins', 22.

832. See *CHP III*. 95–6 and 342; 'Stanzas to Augusta', 2; Wordsworth's Ode, 'Intimations of Immortality', 59.

833–41. The Wordsworthian tone is noticeable, though specific allusions seem tenuous.

848. The girdle of Aphrodite bestowed upon its wearer the power to attract love.

851. See Herodotus I. 131 and compare Wordsworth, *The Excursion*, IV. 670 ff.

853. It is to be recollected, that the most beautiful and impressive doctrines of the Founder of Christianity were delivered, not in the *Temple*, but on the *Mount*.

To wave the question of devotion, and turn to human eloquence,—the most effectual and splendid specimens were not pronounced within walls. Demosthenes addressed the public and popular assemblies. Cicero spoke in the forum. That this added to their effect on the mind of both orator and hearers, may be conceived from the difference between what we read of the emotions then and there produced, and those we ourselves experience in the perusal in the closet. It is one thing to read the *Iliad* at Sigaeum and on the tumuli, or by the springs with mount Ida above, and the plain and rivers and Archipelago around you: and another to trim your taper over it in a snug library—*this* I know.

Were the early and rapid progress of what is called Methodism to be attributed to any cause beyond the enthusiasm excited by its vehement faith and doctrines (the truth or error of which I presume neither to canvas nor to question) I should venture to ascribe it to the practice of preaching in the *fields*, and the unstudied and extemporaneous effusions of its teachers.

The Mussulmans, whose erroneous devotion (at least in the lower orders) is most sincere, and therefore impressive, are accustomed to repeat their prescribed orisons and prayers where-ever they may be at the stated hours— of course frequently in the open air, kneeling upon a light mat (which they carry for the purpose of a bed or cushion as required); the ceremony lasts some minutes, during which they are totally absorbed, and only living in their supplication; nothing can disturb them. On me the simple and entire sincerity of these men, and the spirit which appeared to be within and upon them, made a far greater impression than any general rite which was ever performed in places of worship, of which I have seen those of almost every persuasion under the sun: including most of our own sectaries, and the Greek, the Catholic, the Armenian, the Lutheran, the Jewish, and the Mahometan. Many of the negroes, of whom there are numbers in the Turkish empire, are idolaters, and have free exercise of their belief and its rites: some of these I had a distant view of at Patras, and from what I could make out of them, they appeared to be of a truly Pagan description, and not very agreeable to a spectator. [B]

    Mount: See Matthew, 6–7.

    This I Know: Cf. *BLJ* I. 236.

    855–6. Cf. Acts 7: 48.

    859. Cf. Cicero, *De Legibus*, II. 10.

    860. The thunder-storms to which these lines refer occurred on the 13th of June, 1816, at midnight. I have seen among the Acroceraunian mountains of Chimari several more terrible, but none more beautiful. [B]

thunder-storms] storms *BM, MC*   several] many *BM, cor. in MC*

    See B's 'Stanzas Composed ... during ... a Thunder-storm ...' (no. 136).

    865 ff. Perhaps recalling Wordsworth's 'To Joanna', 54 ff.

    878–9. Perhaps in the narrow valley at St. Maurice above the lake.

    879 ff. Echoing Coleridge's *Christabel*, II. 408–26. The autobiographical character of B's passage is underscored by the fact that he had used lines from the same section of *Christabel* as an epigraph to 'Fare Thee Well!'. See also Charles Maturin's *Bertram* (1816), IV. ii: 'We met in madness and in guilt we parted.'

    878–976. This passage on Clarens is a celebration of scenes near the village of Clarens (at the upper end of Lake Geneva) which are described in various parts of Rousseau's *Julie* and which are associated in the novel with the love of Julie and Saint-Preux. B's note to 927, where he speaks of love as 'the great principle of the universe', shows the deep influence of Shelley's ideas on this entire passage. In fact, the stanzas were written during B's and Shelley's sailing tour of Lake Geneva at the end of June 1816 (see Commentary above).

    904. Cf. Jeremiah 49: 16.

    927. Rousseau's Heloise, Letter 17, part 4, note. 'Ces montagnes sont si

hautes qu'une demi-heure après le soleil couché, leurs sommets sont encore éclairés de ses rayons; dont le rouge forme sur ces cimes blanches *une belle couleur de rose* qu'on apperçoit de fort loin.'

This applies more particularly to the heights over Meillerie. 'J'allai à Vévay loger à la Clef, et pendant deux jours que j'y restai sans voir personne, je pris pour cette ville un amour qui m'a suivi dans tous mes voyages, et qui m'y a fait établir enfin les héros de mon roman. Je dirois volontiers à ceux qui ont du goût et qui sont sensibles: allez à Vevay—visitez le pays, examinez les sites, promenez-vous sur le lac, et dites si la Nature n'a pas fait ce beau pays pour une Julie, pour une Claire et pour un St. Preux; mais ne les y cherchez pas.' *Les Confessions*, livre iv. page 306. Lyons ed. 1796.

In July, 1816, I made a voyage round the Lake of Geneva; and, as far as my own observations have led me in a not uninterested nor inattentive survey of all the scenes most celebrated by Rousseau in his 'Heloise', I can safely say, that in this there is no exaggeration. It would be difficult to see Clarens (with the scenes around it, Vevay, Chillon, Bôveret, St. Gingo, Meillerie, Evian, and the entrances of the Rhone), without being forcibly struck with its peculiar adaptation to the persons and events with which it has been peopled. But this is not all; the feeling with which all around Clarens, and the opposite rocks of Meillerie is invested, is of a still higher and more comprehensive order than the mere sympathy with individual passion; it is a sense of the existence of love in its most extended and sublime capacity, and of our own participation of its good and of its glory: it is the great principle of the universe, which is there more condensed, but not less manifested; and of which, though knowing ourselves a part, we lose our individuality, and mingle in the beauty of the whole.

If Rousseau had never written, nor lived, the same associations would not less have belonged to such scenes. He has added to the interest of his works by their adoption; he has shewn his sense of their beauty by the selection; but they have done that for him which no human being could do for them.

I had the fortune (good or evil as it might be) to sail from Meillerie (where we landed for some time), to St. Gingo during a lake storm, which added to the magnificence of all around, although occasionally accompanied by danger to the boat, which was small and overloaded. It was over this very part of the lake that Rousseau has driven the boat of St. Preux and Madame Wolmar to Meillerie for shelter during a tempest.

On gaining the shore at St. Gingo, I found that the wind had been sufficiently strong to blow down some fine old chestnut trees on the lower part of the mountains. On the opposite height of Clarens is a chateau.

The hills are covered with vineyards, and interspersed with some small but beautiful woods; one of these was named the 'Bosquet de Julie', and it is remarkable that, though long ago cut down by the brutal selfishness of the monks of St. Bernard, (to whom the land appertained), that the ground might be inclosed into a vineyard for the miserable drones of an execrable superstition, the inhabitants of Clarens still point out the spot where its trees stood, calling it by the name which consecrated and survived them.

Rousseau has not been particularly fortunate in the preservation of the 'local habitations' he has given to 'airy nothings'. The Prior of Great St. Bernard has cut down some of his woods for the sake of a few casks of wine, and Buonaparte has levelled part of the rocks of Meillerie in improving the road to the Simplon. The road is an excellent one, but I cannot quite agree with a remark which I heard made, that 'La route vaut mieux que les souven with a remark which I heard made, that 'La route vaut mieux que les souvenirs'. [B]

have led me] ⟨can go⟩   would be difficult] ⟨is impossible⟩   opposite rocks] opposite ⟨shore⟩   sublime capacity] sublime ⟨being⟩   we lose] we ⟨become⟩ lose   added to] ⟨rather added to than detracted from⟩ *MC*   overloaded . . . It] overloaded. By a coincidence I could not regret, it *1st edn., all issues; corrected in H, SB*   over this] ⟨in⟩ this *MC* I found] we found *1st edn., all issues; corrected in H*   On the . . . a chateau] On the height is a seat called the Chateau de Clarens *1st ed. all issues* On the opposite side of the lake is a Chateau immediately behind Clarens *SB*   small but] small ⟨and⟩   inclosed] ⟨converted⟩ which consecrated] which ⟨has⟩ consecrated *MC*

Claire: Julie's confidante in Rousseau's novel.
July, 1816: actually, late June. B revisited Clarens in September with Hobhouse.
Bôveret, St. Gingo: i.e. Bouveret, St. Gingolph.
during a lake storm: on 25 June (see B's letter to Murray, 27 June 1816, and Shelley's letter to Peacock, 12 July 1816).
during a tempest: Cf. *Julie*, IV. 17.
a chateau: the Chateau des Crêtes. Beneath its walls are the *bosquets de Julie*.
local habitations . . . : *A Midsummer Night's Dream*, V. i. 16.
a remark . . . made: In the margin of *MS. SB* B wrote that 'Rocca made this remark at Coppett to Mme. de Staël and myself'. Rocca was the young French officer who secretly married Mme de Staël in 1811 (cf. *BLJ* v. 86, 94).
BM has only the first three sentences of this note.
941–9. Echoing Rousseau's *Julie*, IV. 17.
959–61. Echoing the refrain of the *Pervigilium Veneris*.
964–6. Perhaps echoing La Rochefoucauld, *Maxime* 75.
968–76. B is saying that the scenes around Clarens were the appropriate places not merely for situating the love episodes of the novel, but for projecting, via the novel, Rousseau's personal feelings for Madame d'Houdetot.
977. Voltaire and Gibbon. [B] From 1783 to 1793 Gibbon lived at Lausanne, where he finished the *Decline and Fall* in 1787. Voltaire lived on his estate at Ferney from 1758 to 1777. B uses both men as figures of heroic

doubt and free-thinking. Voltaire is a Proteus (991) because of the variety of literary forms in which he worked. Gibbon's 'irony' (1000) was directed at traditional, religiously oriented views of the later Roman period. The clearest instances of this irony are in the notorious chapters 15–16. In fact, Gibbon said that his history recorded the triumph of superstition and barbarism over culture and civilization. His work had indeed 'stung his foes to wrath' (1001), for a whole series of attacks were made upon it (see J. E. Norton, *A Bibliography of the Works of Gibbon* (Oxford, 1940), 233–47).

982. Alluding to the Titans and Giants, who piled Pelion upon Ossa in an attempt to gain heaven and overthrow Jupiter (see Virgil's *Georgics*, I. 281).

993. Echoing John 3: 8.

1022–30. The stanza incorporates various allusions: to Hannibal, who almost conquered Rome in the third century B.C.; to Rome's conquest of the Etruscan and Carthaginian civilizations and her incorporation of the Greek and Persian empires; to the fall of Rome and the rise of the kingdoms of the Goths and Lombards, as well as the founding of the Holy Roman Empire. The final line glances at the commonplace of the 'Eternal City', applied to Rome.

1049. Cf. 1 John 2: 15.

1050. Recalling *Coriolanus*, III. i. 66–7.

1054–7.   'If it be thus,
     For Banquo's issue have I *filed* my mind.' *Macbeth*. [B]

See *Macbeth*, III. i. 64. Cf. also Isaiah 55: 8 and *Manfred*, II. ii. 54–7.

1062–3. Allusion to Lady Byron: cf. 'Lines on Hearing that Lady Byron was Ill', 43.

1064. It is said by Rochefoucault that 'there is *always* something in the misfortunes of men's best friends not displeasing to them'. [B] See *Maxime* 583.

1067–8. Perhaps echoing Horace, *Epistles*, I. i. 1. When B first wrote stanzas 115–18 he was unsure whether he would publish them in the canto (see his letter to Murray, 9 Oct. 1816).

1095. Though B did not correct the punctuation of this line in *SB*, *MSS*. *BM* and *C* agree on the present punctuation, which in fact is more sensible.

CHP IV

MS. and Publishing History. The earliest MS. we have (*MS. B*) is B's holograph, part draft and part fair copy. It contains 126 stanzas: 1, 3–11, 15, 18–26, 30–9, 42–6, 48–50, 53, 61–8, 73–7, 69–72 (in that order in *MS. B*), 78–9, 83–4, 87–92, 99–108, 110–11, 115–19, 128–34, 138–51, 153–66, 175–6, 177–8, 181–4. In addition, B appended st. 40 to *MS. B*, which was begun, as the date on the first leaf indicates, 26 June 1817. B completed *MS. B* on 19 July.

His fair copy of *MS. B*, with some additional stanzas, was made in August. This MS. (*MS. H*) is headed by B: 'Venice—and La Mira on the Brenta. Copied August 1817. Byron. June 26th finished July 19th.' In its first form (i.e. as B copied it in August), *MS. H* contains 144 stanzas, including the contents of *MS. B* and the following additions: 27–9, 40, 54–5, 109, 120–4, 135–7 (including here the dropped stanza 'If to forgive be "heaping coals of fire" '), 152, 180.

Between 3 Sept. 1817 and 7 Jan. 1818 B added 40 more stanzas to the poem, and early in Mar. 1818 he sent the final two additions (sts. 177–8: cf. *BLJ* VI. 19). All these additions, except the last two, are copied by B into *MS. H*. In copying *MS. H* in its first form, B had left ample space for additional material: each stanza of *MS. H* first form is written at the top of a single foolscap leaf, and he copied his later additions into the spaces he had left empty. At the end of *MS. H* first form B writes: 'Laus Deo! La Mira— near Venice. Sept. 3rd 1817.'

Some MSS. for B's various additional stanzas survive. *MS. BA*, a miscel- laneous collection of these additions bound up with *MS. B*, contains: 12 (draft, dated 10 Nov. 1817); 13, 14, 47 (fair copy); 16–17 (fair copy); 27–9 (draft); 51–2 (draft); 54–5, 109 (draft); 56–60 (draft); 80–2 (draft): 85–6 (draft); 93–7 (draft); 112–14 (draft); 125–7 (fair copy); 123, 152, 182 (draft); 135–7, 137a (fair copy); 167–72 (draft); 173–4 (fair copy); 177–8 (fair copy); 181 (draft).

MSS. B, *H*, and *BA* are all in the Murray archives. *MS. B* has a draft version of B's Dedication to Hobhouse, *MS. H* has a fair copy; the epigraph is only in *MS. H*. Two other MS. scraps include: st. 1 (sent in a letter to Murray of 1 July 1817: *BLJ* V. 244; *MS. E*, Murray); st. 98 (*MS. N*, fair copy: Berg). B sent *MS. H*, the printer's copy, to London early in Jan. 1818 with Hobhouse.

The Murray archives also have the following proof material.

Proof A. Partial proof, without the Dedication, but with pp. 3–48 of the text (up to st. 82, line 2): with annotations by Hobhouse and corrections and annotations by B.

Proof B. Complete proof with Dedication and 184 stanzas (lacking 177–8, with notes and comments by Gifford, Murray, and Hobhouse, and B's corrections and responses). B's MS. note at the end of the proof is: 'I have attended to most of Mr. G[ifford]'s suggestions, and I am obliged to him for them—others I have left, partly from the passage of time—and partly from unwillingness—or laziness—or what you will—the truth is best.'

Proof C. Complete proof, with two sets of proofs of the Dedication (but one unmarked and incomplete): with printer's corrections at various places (from corrections made in *Proofs A* and *B*) and a note by B for st. 82, line 2. For bibliographical description of the proofs see the *Bibliographical Catalogue of First Editions, Proof Copies, and Manuscripts of Books by Lord Byron* . . . (Printed for The First Edition Club, 1925), pp. 19–20.

B seems to have received *Proof B* on 25 Feb. 1818 (see *BLJ* VI. 15) and to have sent it back—perhaps with *Proof C*—around 1 Mar. On 5 Mar. he apparently received *Proof A* (*BLJ* VI. 20), which he corrected and sent back immediately. This order of receipt and correction would explain why sts. 177–8 are not marked for insertion on the extant complete proofs.

Of the voluminous notes for *CHP IV*, B wrote some himself, and Hobhouse wrote the remainder. B's notes are normally in *MS. H*, but a few which are manifestly his are not in his MS. Hobhouse collaborated with B on these notes from August to December 1817 and finally made a compilation (H's MS. is in the British Library: Add. 36455). From the latter, as well as some of B's own MSS., the notes to *CHP IV* were printed; but Hobhouse augmented his own prose commentary and it was separately published by Murray as *Historical Illustrations to the Fourth Canto of Childe Harold* (1818). In the notes to the present edition, below, Hobhouse's notes are marked [H].

CHP IV was published 28 Apr. 1818. There is some disagreement about whether the first edition (for which 10,000 copies were printed) comprises 'seven states' or 'five issues' (cf. *Wise*, I. 58–66, and W. H. McCarthy, Jr., 'The Printing of Canto IV of Byron's "Childe Harold" ', *Yale Univ. Library Gazette*, I (June 1926), 39–41. For my editorial purposes this controversy is irrelevant and I have used Wise's designation (of five issues) in my references. The second edition of Canto IV, printed from Wise's fifth issue, appeared in Murray's two-volume complete edition of *CHP* in 1819.

Finally, B received and annotated a copy of *CHP IV* in Sept. 1818 (*Text M*, location: Princeton-Taylor). Some of the corrections made in that volume are repeated in B's letter to Murray of 24 Sept. 1818 (*BLJ* VI. 70–1). An exact copy was made of B's annotations and corrections, apparently by Mrs. Hoppner, the wife of the British Consul R. B. Hoppner. This book is in the editor's possession. Some of the corrections in *Text M* have never been incorporated in any text of *CHP IV* prior to this edition.

For a more detailed description of the stages of the poem's composition see *McGann*(1), 122–38, 311–18, and *C* II. 311–19, 327. Lastly, reference must be made to the 'unpublished' stanza of Canto IV published by Medwin in *The Angler in Wales* (1834), I. 106. The authenticity of this stanza, given here, is not supported by any good evidence.

> Aloft the necks of that vile Vulture rear
> The Cap which Kings once bow'd to, and thus seek,
> Lifting that headless crown in empty air,
> To mark their mockery. In each double beak
> Too well do they the insatiate ravening speak
> Of a most craven bird, that drains the blood

Of two abandon'd carcases, that reek
Festering in their corruption—never brood
Gorged its rapacious maw with a more carrion food.

Literary and Historical Background. CHP *IV* replicates, in a finer tone, the manner of the earlier cantos: it is a poem in the loco-descriptive tradition, romantically modified into a narrative dominated by an undercurrent of personal statement and meditation. The poem's historical, artistic, and geographical subjects were almost completely gathered together from B's experiences in Italy in 1817—when he was at Venice, on his trip from Venice to Rome, during his stay at Rome, and again when he returned to Venice. His letters from this period (cf. *BLJ* v. 203–79) contain an indispensable commentary on the canto.

As in Canto III, *CHP IV* is preoccupied with the aftermath of B's marriage separation. The importance of this subject is emphasized from the start, in B's prose Dedication to Hobhouse. Indeed, the very day he began composing Canto IV—19 June 1817—B wrote to his sister on this topic, and his comments distinctly forecast the poem's crucial 'Forgiveness Curse' passage (sts. 130–7: cf. *BLJ* v. 243). The canto draws repeated parallels between 'the ruins of Rome' and the 'ruin' of B's own life at the hands of his detractors and enemies, including his wife. The poem's prophecy of an Italian *risorgimento* is equally a statement of personal determination. The theme is also allied to the various Italian artists celebrated in the poem—the 'spirits who soar from ruin'. *CHP* as a whole, but especially Canto IV, is made into a particular analogue and poetic parallel of Tasso's *Jerusalem Delivered,* as that poem was conceived by B in his Romantic mythology of Tasso's life and work. In this respect, *The Lament of Tasso*—composed just prior to Canto IV—anticipates a central preoccupation of *CHP IV*. For the influence of Milton on the poem see *McGann*(2), 23–50 *passim.*

B later thought of continuing *CHP* into a fifth or sixth canto, but he never acted on the inclination (cf. *LJ* VI. 157).

The Notes by B and H. These extensive prose notes have required some special editorial treatment. They are important not only in themselves, but also for the information they provide about the books which B and H were reading at the time. (For example, the text of Winckelmann they used was *Storia della arti del disegno presso gli Antichi . . .*, aumentata dall' abate C[arlo] Fea (1753–1836) (Rome, 1783–4).)

But the principal importance of the notes has to do with matters that are intrinsic and crucial to the poem itself; for Hobhouse's prose commentaries are decidedly 'republican' in their ideological position. As such, they clearly represent a veiled defence of B before the English nation and its government. The extensive notes—especially those on Tasso, Petrarch, Dante, and Boccaccio—are commentaries on 'the poetical character', and in particular on B, who stands—in relation to England—as these great Italian authors stood in relation to their various homelands and civil authorities. Such, at any rate, is Hobhouse's representation, in which he only follows B's own practise (exemplified most importantly in *CHP III* and *Lament* earlier; see also *Prophecy*).

Of particular interest is Hobhouse's defence of Boccaccio, for the commentary here anticipates many aspects of the controversy which was soon to boil up around *DJ*. Ironically, Hobhouse would—in face of B's masterwork— retreat somewhat from the vigorous position he took towards the *Decameron*.

I have not modified the texts in any way, except to correct typographical errors, but I have occasionally been forced to alter the original form of H's citations. I have done so for purposes of clarity. H's methods of citation are out of date and will often appear rather cryptic to a modern eye. Sometimes his citations are given in shortened forms, and these I have silently expanded; sometimes they carry slight inaccuracies, and these have been silently corrected.

For some further discussion of these notes see Andrew Rutherford, 'The Influence of Hobhouse on *Childe Harold's Pilgrimage, Canto IV*', *RES* N.S. 12 (1961), 391–7.

epigraph   In *CHP IV* B incorrectly cited *Satira*, III.

Dedication

   5. *death*: Would any other word serve?—to prevent ill-natured stupidity from growing witty. [Gifford's note, *Proof B*. Gifford's notes are hereafter cited as *G*.] Let them be witty and be damned—we'll be witty too. B. [B, *Proof B*]

   27. B's marriage (2 Jan. 1815).

   54–5. Cf. Letter XXXIII.

   64. In the deleted passage B is regretting *EBSR* and praising certain people he attacked in the poem, like Moore and Jeffrey. B deleted this passage at the suggestion of Scrope Davies (see *BLJ* VI. 21).

   69–71. 'for the whole of' and 'excepting . . . and these' deleted by Gifford in *Proof B* with a note: 'Erased because the notes are too few to require this acknowledgement.' [G] B answered: 'the truth requires acknowledgement of the *notes*. B.' [*Proof B*]

   79–81. *party . . . it, so*: B's correction, here first published, in his annotated copy of *CHP IV* (*Text M*). See also the Postscript to the rejected Dedication for *Marino Faliero* (*LJ* V. 104).

   83. Unidentified.

   88–90. Antonio Canova (1757–1822), sculptor; Vincenzo Monti (1754– 1828), poet; Ugo Foscolo (1776–1827), poet; Ippolito Pindemonti (1753– 1828), poet; Ennius Visconti (1751–1818), archaeologist ('since dead': B's annotation, *Text M*); Michele Morelli (d. 1821), patriot and propagandist; Leopoldo Cicognara (1767–1834), archaeologist; Countess Albrizzi (1769–

1836), author whose *salon* B frequented; Giuseppe Cardinal Mezzophanti (1774–1849), linguist; Angelo Cardinal Mai (1782–1854), philologist; Andreas Mustoxides (1787–1860), classicist; Francesco Aglietti (1757–1836), physician, archaeologist; Andrea Vacca Berlinghieri, (1772–1826), a physician.

91–2. *Europe . . . Canova*: Mr. Gifford has struck his pencil over these words in the original. [Murray note, *Proof B*]

93–5. A paraphrase of two sentences in Alfieri's *Del Principe e delle lettere* (1795) Book III, chap. 11.

105. Addison, *Cato*, v. i, 3.

108. *era*: It is positively *era*—ask anybody. *era* let it be. You should be able to recollect as well as I when we were together. [B, *Proof B*] The word is queried by Hobhouse in *Proof B*.

111. *Mont . . . betrayal*: Waterloo and the Congress of Vienna.

113. *The Substance of some Letters written by an Englishman* [i.e. Hobhouse] *resident in Paris during the last Reign of the Emperor Napoleon* (1816).

119–20. *and . . . Corpus*: deleted in *Proof B*, 'By Gifford's direction' [H note]. I won't give up 'auld Apias Korfus'—it was not repealed when I wrote—and if it had—it should spoil my periods—Oons! [B, *Proof B*] It was suspended in 1817.

122. Matthew 6: 2.

Text

1. The 'Bridge of Sighs' (il Ponte dei Sospiri) divides the Doge's Palace from the state prison.—It is roofed and ⟨contains⟩ *divided* by a wall into two passages.—By the one—the prisoner was conveyed to judgment—by the other he returned to death, being generally strangled in an adjoining chamber. The City of Venice properly so called is built upon seventy two islands but there are about thirty-six others including Malmocco, the Lido, Palestrina, etc. etc. [B, *MS. H*] The Bridge was built in 1597 by Antonio da Ponte.

4–5. Echoing Ann Radcliffe, *The Mysteries of Udolpho* (1794), Part I, chap. 15.

the enchanter's: Ld. B. desires *the* to be replaced. [Murray's note, *Proof C*; see *BLJ* VI. 20.]

8. The Lion of St. Mark's: see 95 and n. and 120 and n.

10 n. Marcus Sabellicus (1436–1506).

19 and n. In *MS. H* and the *Proofs*, the note ends after the stanza of Venetian dialect, and B corrects *Proof A* from 'has died' to 'has almost died', and adds in the margin: 'I have heard them sing—but was obliged to search for the singers and find entertainment—it is well worth hearing.' The rest of the note, in *CHP IV*, is by H, who quotes from Isaac Disraeli's *Curiosities of Literature* (1807), II. 156 ff. and John Black's *Life of Tasso* (1810), Appendix

XXIX. H has a note on Disraeli's error 'Libo': 'The writer meant *Lido*, which is not a long row of islands, but a long island: *littus*, the shore.'

28. *us*: i.e. the English.

33–4. *Rialto*: the 'High Bank' district where the city began. B alludes to *The Merchant of Venice*, *Othello*, and Otway's *Venice Preserved* (1682), whose hero is Pierre.

37–40. Cf. 'The Dream', 19–22; *Lament*, II. 37–58; *CHP III*, st. 6.

47. Cf. *DJ* XIV, st. 10.

73–6. Cf. *BLJ* VI. 149. *resume*: reclaim a right to.

82. Not Westminster Abbey, but the Temple of Fame.

86. The above was the answer of the mother of Brasidas to the strangers who praised the memory of her son. [B, n. in *MS. H, Proofs*] H's note in *CHP IV* is phrased slightly differently. The apothegm is from Plutarch's *Moralia*.

88. I say *reaped* because they stung *me*. [B, *Proof B*]

91–3. On Ascension Day the Doge would annually throw a ring into the Adriatic from the state barge, the Bucentaur. It was a symbolic marriage of the city to the sea. The barge was destroyed by the French in 1797, but apparently its broken remains were still visible in 1817–18.

95 and n. *a Greek vindicated*: *Sui quattro Cavalli della Basilica di San Marco in Venezia. Lettera di Andrea Mustoxidi Corcirese* (Padua, 1816). [H]

Erizzo, Zanetti, Cicognara, Schlegel: H refers to the following: Niccolo Guido Erizzo (d. 1847), *Memoria sui fiumi veneti* (Milan, 1807); Girolamo Zanetti's *Dell'origine di alcune arti principali appresso i Veneziani* (Venezia, 1758); Count Leopoldo Cicognara's *Storia della scultura dal suo risorgimento in Italia fino al secolo di Canova* (Venezia, 1813–18); August Wilhelm von Schlegel's critical review of Mustoxidi's work which is reprinted in the *Essais litteraires et historiques*, pp. 171–210.

100 and n. The submission of Frederic Barbarossa to the Pope occurred in the place of St. Mark—which is still the finest square in Europe. [B, *MS. H, Proofs*]

Barbarossa was Suabian. The trampling emperor in 101 is Francis I of Austria, who ruled Venice from 1797 to 1805 and again after 1814. In his note H quotes from, and annotates, Romualdo Guarna Salernitano (*fl.* 12th cent.), *Chronicon*, in L. A. Muratori (d. 1750), *Rerum Italicarum Scriptores . . .* (Milan, 1723–51), VII, pp. 229, 231, and adds: 'In a second sermon which Alexander preached, on the first day of August, before the Emperor, he compared Frederic to the prodigal son, and himself to the forgiving father.'

106. *lauwine*: avalanche. B uses the word incorrectly as a singular form (see also 653).

107 and n. *hour of Dundee*: See Scott, *Tales of a Grandfather* (1830), third series, chap. 10.

empire of Romania: Mr. Gibbon has omitted the important æ, and has written Romani instead of Romaniae. *Decline and Fall*, chap. 61 note 9. But the title acquired by Dandalo runs thus in the Chronicle of his namesake, the Doge Andrew Dandolo. *Ducali titulo addidit. 'Quartae partis et dimidiae totius imperii Romaniæ.'* Andrea Dandolo (1307?–54), *Chronicon*, III. 37, in Muratori, op. cit. XII, p. 331. And the Romaniæ is observed in the subsequent acts of the Doges. Indeed the continental possessions of the Greek empire in Europe were then generally known by the name of Romania, and that appellation is still seen in the maps of Turkey as applied to Thrace. [H]

the year 1357: See the continuation of Dandolo's *Chronicle*, ibid. p. 498. Mr. Gibbon appears not to include [Giovanni] Dolfino (1545–1622), following Sanudo, who says, *'il qua titolo si usò fin al Doge Giovanni Dolfino.'* See [Marin Sanudo, the Younger (1466–1536)], *Vite de' Duchi di Venezia*, in Muratori, op. cit. XXII, pp. 530, 641. [H]

prophecy . . . sybil: H quotes from Dandolo's *Chronicle*, XXXIV.

111 n. Doria's speech is probably mythical. H translates, and cites, Daniello Chinazzo, 'Chronaca della guerra di Chioza', in Muratori, op. cit. XV, pp. 699–804.

113–14. Cf. the 'Ode to Venice', 15–16. The islands of the lagoons were first settled in 452.

120. *Plant the Lion*—that is, the Lion of St. Mark, the standard of the republic, which is the origin of the word Pantaloon—Pianta-leone, Pantaleon, Pantaloon. [B, n. in *MS. H, Proofs*] B erroneously accepts the old etymology. The Venetians were nicknamed Pantaloni in honour of St. Pantaleon (originally Pantaleymon, 'all-pitiful'), a martyr whose cult was popular in medieval Venice.

123. Shakespeare is my authority for the word 'Ottomite' for Ottoman. 'Which Heaven forbid the Ottomites.' [B, n. in *MS. H, Proofs*] Cf. *Othello*, II. iii. 161.

124. Candia, the capital of Crete which was under Venetian control, did not fall to the Turks until 1669.

125. Cf. *CHP II*. 356 and n.

134 n. *have both expired:* H cites *De Principatibus Italiae, Tractatus* (1631). *to die daily:* 1 Cor. 15: 31.

138. The story is told in Plutarch's life of Nicias. [B, n. in *MS. H, Proofs*] Cf. the *Life of Nicias*, chap. 29.

142. *scimitar:* an anachronism.

151–2. Venice was returned to Austrian domination by the Treaty of Paris (3 May 1814). Castlereagh was the British delegate.

158. *Venice Preserved; Mysteries of Udolpho;* the *Ghost-seer, or Armenian;* the *Merchant of Venice; Othello*. [B, n. in *MS. H, Proofs*] For the *Ghost-seer* see 'Il Diavolo Inamorato' and nn.

172 n. H is presumably responsible for the slightly altered wording of this note in *CHP IV*.

185. B's source is probably Goldsmith's *History of the Earth* (1774).

190–1. A traditional thought found in, e.g., Cicero *De finibus*, II. 29.

196. Cf. Isaiah 36: 6.

215–16. Scott, *The Lady of the Lake*, I. xxxiii. 21–2 and Charles Maturin, *Bertram*, II. iii.

235–61 and n. H slightly rewords the note in *CHP IV*. See also Hobhouse's *Recollections*, II. 77. The Friulian Alps are sixty miles north-east of Venice. The Rhaetian Alps are north-west of Venice. The Brenta empties into the Venetian lagoons.

259. Cf. P. A. Robin, *Animal Lore in English Literature* (1932), 127.

269 n. *Laura as ever*: See *An Historical and Critical Essay on the Life and Character of Petrarch* [1810]; and *A Dissertation on an Historical Hypothesis of the Abbé de Sade*. The first appeared about the year 1784; the other is inserted in the fourth volume of the *Transactions of the Royal Society of Edinburgh*, and both have been incorporated into a work, published, under the first title, by Ballantyne in 1810. [H] The author was Alexander Fraser Tytler (Lord Woodhouselee).

instruct or amuse: [Jean François Paul, Abbé de Sade (1705–78),] *Mémoires pour la Vie de Pétrarch* [1764]. [H]

little authority: *Life of Beattie* [1806], by Sir W[illiam] Forbes, II. 106. [H]

him ridiculous: Mr. Gibbon called his Memoirs 'a labour of love' (see *Decline and Fall*, chap. 70 note 1), and followed him with confidence and delight. The compiler of a very voluminous work must take much criticism upon trust; Mr. Gibbon has done so, though not so readily as some other authors. [H]

evidently false: The sonnet had before awakened the suspicions of Mr. Horace Walpole. See his letter to [Joseph] Wharton in 1763 [i.e. 16 Mar. 1765]. [H]

favours and refusals: 'Par ce petit manège, cette alternative de faveurs et de rigueurs bien ménagée, une femme tendre et sage amuse, pendant vingt et un ans, le plus grand poëte de son siècle, sans faire la moindre brêche à son honneur.' *Mém. pour la Vie de Pétrarque*, Preface aux Francois. The Italian editor of the London edition of Petrarch, who has translated Lord Woodhouselee, renders the 'femme tendre et sage' 'raffinata civetta'. Abbé de Sade, *Riflessione intorno a Madonna Laura* . . . (1811) III. 234. [H]

of a librarian: In a dialogue with St. Augustin, Petrarch has described Laura as having a body exhausted with repeated *ptubs*. The old editors read and printed *perturbationibus*; but Mr. Capperonier, librarian to the French King in 1762, who saw the MS. in the Paris library, made an attestation that '*on lit et qu'on doit lire, partubus exhaustum*'. De Sade joined the names of Messrs. Boudot and Bejot with Mr. Capperonier, and in the whole discussion on this *ptubs*, showed himself a downright literary rogue. See *Riflessioni*, p. 267. Thomas Aquinas is called in to settle whether Petrarch's mistress was a *chaste* maid or a *continent* wife. [H] *not of the mind*: Pigmalion, quanto lodar ti dei/ Dell' imagine tua, se mille volte/ N' avesti quel ch' i' sol una vorrei. Sonnetto 58, *quando giunse a Simon l'alto concetto. Le Rime del Petrarcha . . .* (Venice, 1756) I. 189. [H]

own sonnets: *Riflessione*, op. cit., p. 291. [H]

his heart: Quella rea e perversa passione che solo tuto mi occupava e mi regnava nel cuore. [H]

'irregularity': *Azion disonesta* are his words. [H]

slip: A questa confessione così sincera diede forse occasione una nuova caduta ch' ei fece. Girolamo Tiraboschi [1731–94], *Storia della Letteratura Italiana* [1772–95], v. iv, part 2, p. 492. [H]

human feeling: Il n'y a que la vertu seule qui soit capable de faire des impressions que la mort n'efface pas. [Joseph] Bimard, Baron de la Bastie [1703–42], in the *Histoire de L'Académie des Inscriptions et Belles Lettres* for 1740 and 1751. See also *Riflessione*, op. cit., p. 295. [H]

mistress of Petrarch: 'And if the virtue or prudence of Laura was inexorable, he enjoyed, and might boast of enjoying the nymph of poetry.' *Decline and Fall*, chap. 70. Perhaps the *if* is here meant for *although*. [H]

In lines. 266–8 B refers to Petrarch's part in establishing Italian as a literary language. Petrarch's political nationalism is expressed in various writings, e.g. the *Canzone all'Italia*. In 269 B alludes to Petrarch's habit of punning on the Italian *lauro*, to refer both to the tree of poetic fame, and Laura.

Mr. Forsyth: [Joseph Forsyth,] *Remarks, &c. on Italy* [1816], p. 95, note. [H]

at the cathedral: In *CHP IV* H gives the text of the inscription in a note.

286. *busy cities*: Venice and Padua.

294. Cf. Thomas Tickell's 'Elegy' on Addison, lines 82–3.

297. Cf. Genesis 32: 24.

298 n. See H. R. Fox-Bourne, *Life of John Locke* (1876), II. 537.

305. Cf. Joel 2: 31 and Revelation 6: 12.

306. Echoes *Macbeth*, V. i. 34.

307–51. See commentary for *Lament*. B's treatment of Tasso, here and in the *Lament*, adheres to the charming inaccuracies of the Romantic legend.

311. *Este*: the House of Este, whose ducal seat was at Ferrara.

316. Echoes Pope, *Essay on Criticism*, 694.

330. *poor malice*: *Macbeth*, III. ii. 25.

339. The Accademia della Crusca, founded in Florence in 1542, had criticized Tasso's great epic.

Serassi: [Pietro A. Serassi (1721–91),] *La Vita del Tasso* (Bergamo, 1790), II. iii. 284. [H]

Olivet: [Pierre Joseph Thoulier] d'Olivet (1682–1768), *Histoire de l'Academie Francoise depuis 1652, jusqu'à 1700*, (Amsterdam, 1730), 181. 'Mais, ensuite, venant à l'usage qu'il a fait de ses talens, j'aurois montré que le bons sens n'est pas toujours ce qui domine chez lui', 182. Boileau said he had not changed his opinion. '*J'en ai si peu change, dit il.*' [H]

Bohours: [Dominique Bouhours (1628–1702),] *La maniere de bien penser dans les ouvrages de l'esprit, Dialogues* (2nd edn., 1692), 89. Philanthes is for Tasso, and says in the outset, 'de tous les beaux esprits que l'Italie a portés, le Tasse est peut être celui qui pense le plus noblement.' But Bohours seems to speak in Eudoxus, who closes with the absurd comparison: 'Faites valoir le Tasse tant qu'il vous plaira, je m'en tiens pour moi à Virgile', ibid. 102. [H]

be no doubt: [Serassi, op. cit.] II. 90. The English reader may see an account of the opposition of the Crusca to Tasso, in Dr. Black, *Life*, ibid. II, chap. 17. [H]

Salviati: Leonardo Salviati (1540–89).

tyrant jailer: For further and, it is hoped, decisive proof, that Tasso was neither more nor less than a *prisoner of state*, the reader is referred to HISTORICAL ILLUSTRATIONS OF THE IVth CANTO OF CHILD HAROLD, p. 5 ff. [H]

family . . . sovereign: Orazioni funebri . . . delle lodi di Don Luigi Cardinal d'Este . . . delle lodi di Donno Alfonso d'Este. See Serassi, op. cit. II. 117. [H]

paradox: It was founded [i.e. reorganized] in 1582, and the Cruscan answer to Pellegrino's *Caraffa* or *epica poesia* was published in 1584. [H] Camillo Pellegrino the Elder (1527–1603) published *Il Carrafa o vero della epica poesia, dialogo* (1584), which was immediately attacked by the Accademia della Crusca in *Degli Accademici . . . Difesa dell' Orlando Furioso . . . contra 'l 'Dialogo dell' Epica Poesia' di C. Pellegrino.*

at Florence: 'Cotanto potè sempre in lui il veleno della sua pessima volontà contra alla nazion Fiorentina.' Serassi, op. cit. II. 96, 98. [H]

self-estimation: Girolamo Baruffaldi the Younger (1740–1816), *La Vita di M. L. Ariosto* (Ferrara, 1807), Book III, p. 262. See *Historical Illustrations*, p. 26. [H]

rivalry at rest: Tiraboschi, op. cit. VII. 1220. [H]

354. Dante and Ariosto.

359–60. Scott; see the Introduction to *Marmion*. See also *BLJ* v. 255.

361 n. *last century*: 'Mi raccontarono que' monaci, ch' essendo caduto un fulmine nella loro chiesa schiantò esso dalle tempie la corona di lauro a quell' immortale poeta.' [Giovanni Lodovico] Bianconi (1717–81), *Opere* (Milan, 1802), III. 176; lettera al Signor Guido Savini Arcifisiocritico, sull' indole di un fulmine caduto in Dresda l'anno 1759. [H]

Homer . . . Ferrara: 'Appassionato ammiratore ed invitto apologista dell' Omero Ferrarese.' The title was first given by Tasso, and is quoted to the confusion of the *Tassisti*. [See Baruffaldi, op. cit.] 262, 265. [H]

replaced memorial: 'Parva sed apta mihi, sed nulli obnoxia, sed non / Sordida, parta meo sed tamen aere domus.' [H]

Denina . . . Barotti: Carlo Giovanni Maria Denina (1731–1813) published *Tableau historique, statistique, et moral de la Haut-Italie* (Paris, 1805). The book's judgements brought several replies. B's reference is to Baruffaldi's *Continua-*

COMMENTARY 325

zione della Memorie istoriche di letterati ferraresi (1807), which is a 'continuation' of Giovanni A. Barotti (1702–72), *Memorie istoriche di letterati ferrares[e]*, *Opera postuma* (Ferrara, 1777).

364 n. *eagle . . . thunder storm*: Aquila, vitulus marinus, et laurus, fulmine non feriuntur. Pliny, *Historia Naturalis*, II. 55; [Lucius Junius Moderatus] Columella, [*De Re Rustica*] x. [532]; Suetonius, *Vita Augusti*, 90 and *Vita Tiberii*, 89. [H]

lightning at Rome: [*C. Suetonius Tranquillus et in eum commentarius* (London, 1667),] p. 409 n. 2. [H] The commentator was Joanne Schildio.

368 n. *incorruptible*: Vid. J[ules] C[esar] Boulanger (1558–1628), *De Terrae* [*Motibus*], v. 11. [H]

by heaven: Οὐδεὶς κεραυνωθεὶς ἄτιμός ἐστι, ὅθεν καὶ ὡς θεὸς τιμᾶται. Artemidorus, *Oneirocritica* (Paris, 1603), ii. 8, p. 91. Plut., *Sympos.*, vid. J. C. Boulanger, *ut sup.* [H]

and a crown: Pauli Diaconi [Warnefridus (740–801),] *De Gestis Langobardorum* (Taurin 1527), III. 14. [H]

pontificate . . . citizens: I. P. Valerianus [Magnus (1586–1661),] *De fulminum significationibus declamatio*, in [Joannes Georgius] Graevius (1632–1703), *Thesaurus Antiquitatum Romanorum* (London, 1694–9), v. 593. The declamation is addressed to Julian of Medicis. [H]

In margin of *Proof A* B writes: 'Dear Hobhouse—I sent you weeks ago the extract from Bianchoni's works (prose) which narrates the fact mentioned in the 41st stanza—have you received it or the duplicate? which I afterwards included a few days ago? Yrs. B.'

370 n. Cf. *Poesie Toscane* (1823), p. 149. In the margin of *Proof A* B writes: 'For the love of the gods keep an eye on the correctness of the Italian and don't let [me be] excruciated in this way.'

388 n. See [Conyers] Middleton, *History of the Life of M. Tullius Cicero* [1741], II, sec. 7, p. 371. [B, n. in *MS. H, Proofs*: H, n. in *CHP IV*] See Cicero, *Epistola ad Familiares*, IV. 5. B's 'journeys and voyages' were made in 1810.

413 n. He cites *De fortunae urbis Romae et de ruinis ejusdem descriptio*, in [Albert Henri de] Sallengre (1694–1723), *Novus Thesaurus Antiquitatum Romanorum* (The Hague, 1716–19), I. 502.

Poggio: Giovanni Francesco Poggio Bracciolini (1380–1459).

415–16. Echoes Milton, Sonnet 22.

420. Matthew 16: 19.

425. Florence.

433 n. *Thomson's notion*: Cf. *The Seasons*, 'Summer', 1344–70. Later B quotes l. 1370; the 'anecdote' from Boswell's *Life of Johnson* is from 28 May 1768.

Lanzi . . . Agostini: Luigi Antonio Lanzi (1732–1810), in his *Storia pittorica della Italia Inferiore* (Florence, 1792); Leonardo Agostini (*fl.* late 17th cent.).

careless observer: [Johann Joachim Winckelmann (1717–68),] *Monumenti antichi inediti* ... (Rome, 1767), I. 17, n. 43, p. 50; and *Storia delle arti*, op. cit. [see Commentary], II. 1, p. 314, Note 13. [H]

Mr. *Gibbon*: Nomina gentesque Antiquae Italiae [Gibbon's *Miscellaneous Works*, 1814], 204. [H]

443. Echoes Edward Young, *The Revenge*, v. ii. 55–8.

452. *Anchises*: the father of Aeneas by Venus.

457.   ʼΟφθαλμοὺς ἐστιᾶν

'Atque oculos pascat uterque suos.'

Ovid, *Amores* [Eleg. II. 6].

[B, n. in *MS. H* and *Proofs*; H, n. in *CHP IV*] B is also alluding to Lucretius, *De rerum natura*, I. 31–49.

478 n. Though B's MS. of this note does not appear to be extant, this passage is undoubtedly his, and not Hobhouse's. Mme de Staël died in July 1817. See *BLJ* V. 256–7. In this stanza B is recalling her *Corinne*, XVIII. 2. See also *BLJ* V. 218.

484 n. *Alfieri*: Vittorio Alfieri (1749–1803), poet and dramatist.

'*a poet good in law*': unidentified.

at the theatre: The free expression of their honest sentiments survived their liberties. Titius, the friend of Anthony, presented them with games in the theatre of Pompey. They did not suffer the brilliancy of the spectacle to efface from their memory that the man who furnished them with the entertainment had murdered the son of Pompey: they drove him from the theatre with curses. The moral sense of a populace, spontaneously expressed, is never wrong. Even the soldiers of the triumvirs joined in the execration of the citizens, by shouting round the chariots of Lepidus and Plancus, who had proscribed their brothers, *De Germanis non de Gallis duo triumphant Consules*, a saying worth a record, were it nothing but a good pun. [Gaius Velleius Paterculus (19 B.C.–c. A.D. 30),] *Marcus Velleius Paterculus: cum* Notis G. Vossi (Elzevir, London, 1639) II, chaps. 77 and 79. [H]

improvisatore: Tommaso Sgricci (1789–1836); see *BLJ* V. 119.

486 n. *birth or death*: Machiavelli's dates are 1469–1527.

DOMINIO: Il Principe di Niccolò Machiavelli ... con la prefazione e le note istoriche e politiche di Mr. Amelot de la Houssaye e l'esame e confutazione dell'opera ... Cosmopoli, 1769. [H]

487–95. This and the previous stanza seem to echo Foscolo's *De Sepolcri*, 151–98.

499. Boccaccio and his *Decameron*.

505 n. *lucrorum*: Tiraboschi, op. cit. v. iii. 2, p. 448. Tiraboschi's date is incorrect. [H in *CHP IV*, issues 1–4] Tiraboschi is incorrect: the dates of the three decrees against Dante are A.D. 1302, 1314, and 1316. [H in *CHP IV*, 5th issue]

in a church: So relates [Marsilio] Ficino (1433–99), but some think his coronation only an allegory. See Tiraboschi, op. cit., p. 453. [H]

Homer: By Varchi in his Ercolano. [Benedetto Varchi (1502–65), *L'Ercolano-dialogo* (1570).] The controversy continued from 1570 to 1616. See Tira, boschi, op. cit. VII. iii. 3, p. 1280. [H]

patronised him: Giovanni Jacopo Dionisi (1704–1808), canonico di Verona. *Serie di Anedotti*, n. 2. See Tiraboschi, op. cit. V. i. 1, p. 24. [H]

Bettinelli . . . Cesarotti: Saverio Bettinelli (1718–1808); Melchiore Cesarotti (1730–1808).

There is still . . . cause of truth.: added in *CHP IV*, 2nd issue. The passage 'reserved for . . . truth' was corrected to the present form in issues 3–5. It originally read 'reserved for the patriotism of the author of the letters of Ortis'. The cancelled passage refers to Foscolo's *Werther*-like novel translated into English (in 1818) as *The Last Letters of Jacopo Ortis.*

506 n. *lived there*: Vitam Literni egit sine desiderio urbis. See Livy, *Annals*, chap. 38. Livy reports that some said he was buried at Liternum, others at Rome. Ibid., chap. 55. [H]

vivo aprilla: [Petrarch,] *Trionfo della Castità*. [H]

vicinity of the capital: See note to stanza 13. [H]

ancient Greek writer: The Greek boasted that he was ἰσόνομος. See—the last chapter of the first book of Dionysius of Halicarnassus [d. *c.* 7 B.C.: *Antiquitum Romanorum*, ed. R. Stephani (1548)]. [H] *Italian servitude*: 'E intorno alla magnifica riposta', in Serassi, op. cit. II. iii, p. 149. [H]

507. Echoes Lucan, *Pharsalia*, I. i.

510 n. *correct their style*: 'Accingiti innoltre, se ci è lecito ancor l'esortarti, a compire l'immortal tua Africa . . . . Se ti avviene d'incontrar nel nostro stile cosa che ti dispiaccia, ciò debb' essere un altro motivo ad esaudire i desiderj della tua patria.' Tiraboschi, op. cit. V. i. 1, p. 76. [H]

514 n. *without a record*: [Revd. John C. Eustace,] *Classical Tour . . .* (1815, 3rd edn.) II. 355. [H]

'Of Boccaccio the modern Petronius, we say nothing; the abuse of genius is more odious and more contemptible than its absence; and it imports little where the impure remains of a licentious author are consigned to their kindred dust. For the same reason the traveller may pass unnoticed the tomb of the malignant Aretino.'

This dubious phrase is hardly enough to save the tourist from the suspicion of another blunder respecting the burial place of Aretine, whose tomb was in the church of St. Luke at Venice, and gave rise to the famous controversy of which some notice is taken in Bayle. Now the words of Mr. Eustace would lead us to think the tomb was at Florence, or at least was to be somewhere recognized. Whether the inscription so much disputed was ever written on the tomb cannot now be decided; for all memorial of this author has disappeared from the Church of St. Luke, which is now changed into a lamp warehouse. [H]

command . . . superiors: 'Non enim ubique est, qui in excusationem meam consurgens dicat, juvenis scripsit, et majoris coactus imperio.' The letter was addressed to Maghinard of Cavalcanti, marshal of the kingdom of Sicily. See Tiraboschi, op. cit. V. ii. 3, p. 525. [H]

    Muratori: Dissertazione sopra le antichità Italiane (1751), III Diss. 58, p. 253. [H]

    martyr to impartiality: [Antoine Arnauld (1612–94),] *Eclaircissement* [*sur quatre questiones importantes . . .*] (Basle, 1741), 638 in the Supplement to Bayle's Dictionary. [H] Pierre Bayle (1647–1706), *Dictionnaire historique et critique* (1697).

    entirely dumb: In a note, H quotes the original Latin and cites *Epistolae Joannis Boccacio, Opera* (Basle, n. d.) I. 540.

    517. Cf. *Beppo*, st. 44.

    525. Cf. *DJ* XV, st. 49 and Tacitus, *Annals*, III. 76.

    528. Ravenna was the capital of the last Roman emperors (after Honorius).

    532 n. *name of Medici*: Cosmus Medices, Decreto Publico. Pater Patriae. [H] *Corinna*: *Corinne*, Book XVIII, chap. 3. [H]

    they are under: *On Government* (1751), chap. 2, p. 208. Sidney is, together with Locke and Hoadley, one of Mr. Hume's '*despicable*' authors. [H]

    542. The Uffizi Palace. But B also visited the Pitti Palace, and may have had it also in mind here: see *BLJ* V. 218.

    550–85. Hannibal defeated the Romans near Lago Trasimeno in 217 B.C. The account here is indebted to Livy, XXII. 4–6.

    563 n. *the combatants*: Here, and elsewhere in this note when H quotes from Livy, he gives the Latin in a series of footnotes, and cites the text. See previous note.

    conspicuous position: Τὸν μὲν κατὰ πρόσωπον τῆς πορείας λόφον αὐτὸς κατελάβετο καὶ τοὺς Λίβυας καὶ τοὺς Ἴβηρας ἔχων ἐπ' αὐτοῦ κατεστρατοπέδευσε. *Annals* III. 83. The account in Polybius is not so easily reconcileable with present appearances as that in Livy: he talks of hills to the right and left of the pass and valley; but when Flaminius entered he had the lake at the right of both. [H]

    bill of Torre: 'A tergo et super caput decepere insidiae.' Livy, [op. cit.]. [H]

    native Virgil: About the middle of the XIIth century the coins of Mantua bore on one side the image and figure of Virgil. [Giulio Pippi Romano (*fl.* 16th cent.),] *Zecca d'Italia*, pl. xvii. i. 6 in Aubin Louis Millin de Grandmaison (1759–1818), *Voyage dans le Milanais* (Paris, 1817), II. 294. [H]

    Dupaty: Charles Dupaty (1746–88), *Lettres sur l'Italie en 1785* (Paris, 1788).

    584. In *Proof A*, B queried 'Sanguinetto': 'Should this be *o* or *a*—I forget.'

    586. In my gratitude to the Clitumnus I ought not to forget the largest and very best trout that ever were seen in a river or a dish; I twice visited the temple and the stream—on my return and on my journey to Rome; but the whole tract of country from Perugia to Foligno as far as Terni is perhaps the most beautiful in Italy. [B, n. cancelled in *MS. H*] See also *BLJ* V. 233.

590. Cf. Pliny, II. 103 and Virgil, *Georgics*, II. 146–7.

604. The classical 'genius loci'.

612. *disgust*: not 'distaste' but the inability to feel enjoyment; 'boredom'.

613–48. In *MS. B* these stanzas were originally placed before stanza 77. B evidently wrote them on his return journey from Rome to Venice. See above, his n. to 586.

616. *foams shaking*: In *Proof A* Gifford wrote: 'Can this be a little strengthened?' (See apparatus.) B changed the phrase to the received text with the note: 'Will *shaking* answer the purpose?'

642 n. *Addison*: Joseph Addison, *Remarks on Several Parts of Italy* (1761), 100–1.
Italian Tempe: 'Reatini me ad sua Tempe duxerunt.' Cicero, *Epistolarum ad Atticum* IV. 15. [H]
lake Velinus: 'In eodem lacu nullo non die apparere arcus.' Pliny, II. 62. [H]
district alone: [Aldo Manuzio, the Younger (1547–97], *De Reatina urbe agroque*, in Sallengre, op. cit. I. 773. [H]

653. In the greater part of Switzerland the avalanches are known by the name lauwine. [H]

657. Cf. *CHP II*, st. 51.

658–61. Cf. *CHP I*, sts. 60–4 and nn.

662. i.e. from Troy's plain.

665. Soracte's ridge, now Santo Oreste, the furthest point of the mountain chain which extends north of Rome.

666. Recalls Horace, *Odes*, I. 9.

674 n. *Ensign Northerton*: Fielding, *Tom Jones*, VII. 12.

693. Cf. the *Historical Illustrations*, 42–6.

694. Ibid. 46–50.

703. When Niobe boasted that she had more children (twelve) than Apollo's mother, Apollo slew the children, and Niobe was turned into a rock, which wept continually.

706. Cf. *Hamlet*, I. i. 155.

707–8 For a comment on this and the following two stanzas, the reader may consult *Historical Illustrations of the Fourth Canto of Childe Harold* [pp. 58–195]. [H] The tomb of the Scipios, on the Appian Way, was discovered in 1780, and was plundered shortly after.

712. B has in mind, e.g., Alaric (409), Genséric (455), Ricimer (472), Théodoric (493), Totila (546), Barbarossa (1167), Charles V (1527), Massena (1798).

716. The *clivus capitolinus*.

722. *wrap*: an ellipsis, with 'doth' to be understood.

730. Cf. Revelation 18: 10.

731 n. See also *Historical Illustrations*, 195–201. B has a marginal note in *Proof B*: 'I don't [know] what to put for *trebly*. three won't do it hath a mean sound and *triply* is no better than *trebly*.'

Orosius: Paul Orose, Christian historian, 5th century.

Panvinius: Onuphre Panvinio (1529–68), *Fasti et triumphi Romanorum* (Venice, 1557).

739 and n. 'Seigneur, vous changez toutes mes idées de la façon dont je vous vois agir. Je croyois que vous aviez de l'ambition, mais aucun amour pour la gloire: je voyois bien que votre ame étoit haute; mais je ne soup-çonnois pas qu'elle fût grande.' 'Dialogue de Sylla et d'Eucrate' in [Charles de Secondat, Baron de Montesquieu (1689–1755), *Considerations . . . de la Grandeur des Romains . . .* (Paris, 1795) II. 219. [H]

B's stanza sums up Sulla's life in certain key events: the overthrow of his party (86 B.C.), his refusal to leave the campaign against Mithridates until it was finished (83 B.C.), his defeat of Marius and appointment as Dictator (81 B.C.), and his abandonment of his appointment (79 B.C.).

759. Cromwell dissolved the Long Parliament in 1653.

775 n. *Flaminius Vacca*: [Flamino Vacca (1538–1605),] *Memorie [di varie antichità trovate in . . . Roma* (1771)], No. 57, p. 9. [Bernard de] Montfaucon (1655–1741), *Diarium Italicum* [1702]. [H]

Winkelmann is loth: *Storia delle arti*, op. cit. II. pp. 321–2, Book IX, chap. 1. [H]

hominem . . . gravem: *Epistolarum at Atticum*, XI. 6. [H]

medal of Pompey: Published by Causeus in his *Romanum Museum* [Rome, 1690]. [H] Michel Ange de la Chausse (*fl.* late 17th, early 18th cent.).

was discovered: *Storia delle arti*, op. cit. [H]

burnt . . . down: Suetonius, *Life of Augustus* and *Life of Julius Caesar*, chaps. 31, 88. Appian says it was burnt down. See a note of Pitiscus to Suetonius, p. 224. [H] Cf. Samuel Pitiscus (1637–1717), *C. Suetonius Tranquilli Opera* (1690).

Pompeian shade: 'Tu modo Pompeia lenta spatiare sub umbra.' Ovid, *Ars Amatoria* [I. 67]. [H]

Blondus: [Flavius Blondus (1392–1463),] *De Roma instaurata* (Venice, 1510), Book III, p. 25. [H] The references in the text and H's notes are to the statue in the Palazzo Spada. It may be of Pompey, but was not the statue at whose base Caesar was killed.

781. Recollect you have Nemesis again. [Gifford, MS. n. in *Proof B*] I *know* it—and if I had her ten times would not alter once—she is my particu-lar belief and acquaintance—and I wont blaspheme against her for any body. [B, MS. n. in *Proof B*] See below sts. 132–8.

784-6. See the contrasting *Caritas Romana*, sts. 148–51.

784 n. *seen by Dionysius*: Graevius, op. cit., Book I Χάλκεα ποιήματα παλαιᾶς ἐργασίας. [H]

Ruminal fig-tree: 'Ad ficum Ruminalem simulacra infantium conditorum urbis sub uberibus lupae posuerunt.' Livy, X. 69. This was the year U.C. [A.D.] 455, or 457. [H]

The other . . . Cicero: 'Tum statua Nattae tum simulacra Deorum, Romulusque et Remus cum altrice bellua vi fulminis icti conciderunt.' *De Divinatione*, II. 20. 'Tactus est ille etiam qui hanc urbem condidit Romulus, quem inauratum in Capitolio parvum atque lactantem, uberibus lupinis inhiantem fuisse meministis.' *In Catilin.* iii. 8.

> 'Hic silvestris erat Romani nominis altrix
> Martia, quae parvos Mavortis semine natos
> Uberibus gravidis vitali rore rigebat
> Quae tum cum pueris flammato fulminis ictu
> Concidit, atque avulsa pedum vestigia liquit.'
> *De suo Consulatu*, II [42–6].

by the orator: Ἐν γὰρ τῷ Καπετωλίῳ ἀνδριάντες τε πολλοὶ ὑπὸ κεραυνῶν συνεχωνεύθησαν, καὶ ἀγάλματα ἄλλα τε καὶ Διός ἐπὶ κίονος ἱδρυμένον, εἰκών τέ τις λυκαίνης σὺν τε τῷ Ῥώμῳ καὶ σὺν τῷ Ῥωμύλῳ ἱδρυμένη ἔπεσε. Dion, op. cit. 37, p. 37. He goes on to mention that the letters of the columns on which the laws were written were liquefied and become ἀμυδρά All that the Romans did was to erect a large statue to Jupiter, looking towards the east: no mention is afterwards made of the wolf. This happened in A. U. C. 689. The Abate Fea, in noticing this passage of Dion (Winkelmann, op. cit. I. 202 n.), says, *Non ostante, aggiunge Dione, che fosse ben fermata*, (the wolf), by which it is clear the Abate translated the Xylandro-Leuclavian version, which puts *quamvis stabilita* for the original ἱδρυμένη, a word that does not mean *ben-fermata*, but only *raised*, as may be distinctly seen from another passage of the same Dion: Ἠβουλήθη μὲν οὖν ὁ Ἀγρίππας καὶ τὸν Αὔγουστον ἐνταῦθα ἱδρῦσαι. (Dion, op. cit. 56.) Dion says that Agrippa 'wished *to raise a statue* of Augustus in the Pantheon'. [H]

Lucius Faunus: 'In eadem porticu aenea lupa, cujus uberibus Romulus ac Remus lactantes inhiant, conspicitur: de hac Cicero et Virgilius semper intellexere. Livius hoc signum ab Aedilibus ex pecuniis quibus mulctati essent foeneratores, positum innuit. Antea in Comitiis ad Ficum Ruminalem, quo loco pueri fuerant expositi locatum pro certo est.' *De antiquitatis urbis Romae*, II. 7, in Sallengre, op. cit. I. 217. In his XVIIth chapter he repeats that the statues were there, but not that they were *found* there. [H]

Fulvius Ursinus: [Famiano] Nardini [d. 1661], *Roma Vetus*, V. 4, in Graevius, op. cit. IV. 1146. [H]

Marlianus: [Joannes Bartholomaeus Marlianus (d. *c.* 1560)], *Urbis Romae Topographia*, II. 9. He mentions another wolf and twins in the Vatican, ibid. V. 21. [H]

Rycquius: 'Non desunt qui hanc ipsam esse putent, quam adpinximus, quae è comitio in Basilicam Lateranam, cum nonnullis aliis antiquitatum reliquiis, atque hinc in Capitolium postea relata sit, quamvis Marlianus antiquam Capitolinam esse maluit a Tullio descriptam, cui ut in re nimis dubia, trepidè adsentimur.' [Justus Rycquius (1587–1627).] *De Capitolio Romano commentarius* (London, 1696), chap. 24, p. 250. [H]

Ciceronian statue: Nardini, op. cit. V. 4. [H]

Montfaucon: 'Lupa hodieque in capitolinus prostat aedibus, cum vestigio fulminis quo ictam narrat Cicero.' Op. cit. I. 174. [H]

Winkelmann proclaims: *Storia delle arti*, op. cit. III. iii, ^{IT} 11, n. 10. Winkelmann has made a strange blunder in the note, by saying the Ciceronian wolf was *not* in the Capitol, and that Dion was wrong in saying so. [H]

Flaminius Vacca tells: 'Intesi dire, che L'Ercolo di bronzo, che oggi si trova nella sala di Campidoglio, fu trovato nel foro Romano appresso l'arco di Settimio; e vi fu trovata anche la lupa di bronzo che allata Romolo e Remo, e stà nella Loggia de' conservatori.' Vacca, op. cit., No. 3, p. 1; Montfaucon, op. cit. I. [H]

favissae: Lucius Faunus, op. cit. [H]

Orosius: See note to stanza LXXX in *Historical Illustrations*. [H]

Lactantius: 'Romuli nutrix Lupa honoribus est affecta divinis, et ferrem si animal ipsum fuisset, cujus figuram gerit.' [Lucius Coelius Firmianus Lactantius (*fl.* 3rd–4th cent.)], *De falsa religione*, in *Opera* (London, 1660), I. 20, p. 101. That is to say, he would rather adore a wolf than a prostitute. His commentator has observed that the opinion of Livy concerning Laurentia being figured in this wolf was not universal. Strabo thought so. Rycquius is wrong in saying that Lactantius mentions the wolf was in the Capitol. [H]

late period: To A.D. 496. 'Quis credere possit,' says [Caesar Cardinal] Baronius (1538–1607), 'viguisse adhuc Romae ad Gelasii tempora, quae fuere ante exordia urbis allata in Italiam Lupercalia?' (*Annales Ecclesiastici*, VIII. 602, for the year 496.) Gelasius wrote a letter which occupies four folio pages to Andromachus, the senator, and others, to shew that the rites should be given up. [H]

Fidius: Eusebius (267–338) has these words; καὶ ἀνδριάντι παρ' ὑμῖν ὡς θεὸς τετίμηται, ἐν τῷ Τίβερι ποταμῷ μεταξὺ τῶν δύο γεφυρῶν, ἔχων ἐπιγραφὴν ῥωμαϊκὴν ταύτην Cίμωνι δέῳ Cάγκτῳ. *Historia Ecclesiastica*, II. 13, p. 40. Justin Martyr had told the story before; but Baronius himself was obliged to detect this fable. See Nardini, op. cit. VII. 12. [H]

temple of Romulus: Nardini, op. cit. V. 11 convicts Pomponius Laetus *crassi erroris*, in putting the Ruminal fig-tree at the church of Saint Theodore: but, as Livy says, the wolf was at the Ficus Ruminalis, and Dionysius at the temple of Romulus, he is obliged, (chap. 4) to own that the two were close together, as well as the Lupercal cave, shaded, as it were, by the fig-tree. [H]

seen by Dionysius: 'In essa gli antichi pontefici per toglier la memoria de' giuochi Lupercali istituiti in onore di Romolo, introdussero l'uso di portarvi Bambini oppressi da infermità occulte, acciò si liberino per l'intercessione di questo Santo, come di continuo si sperimenta.' Ridolfino Venuti (1705–63), *Accurata e succincta descrizione topographica e istorica di Roma moderna* (Rome, 1766), Rione XII. [H]

actually dug up: 'Ad comitium ficus olim Ruminalis germinabat, sub qua lupae rumam, hoc est, mammam, docente Varrone, suxerant olim Romulus et Remus; non procul a templo hodie D. Mariae Liberatricis appellato ubi *forsan* inventa nobilis illa aenea statua lupae geminos puerulos lactantis, quam hodie in capitolio videmus.' Olaus Borrichius (1626–90), *Dissertationes de antiqua urbis Romae*, chaps. 10, 12. Borrichius wrote after Nardini in 1687. See Graevius, op. cit. IV. 1522. [H]

ancient city: [Aelius] Donatus (*fl.* 4th cent. A.D.) gives a medal representing on one side the wolf in the same position as that in the Capitol; and in the reverse the wolf with the head not reverted. It is of the time of Antonius Pius. See *Life of Virgil*, XI. 18. [H]

Geminos . . . lingua: *Aeneid*, VIII. 631[–4]. See Dr. Middleton, in his letter from Rome, who inclines to the Ciceronian wolf, but without examining the subject. [H]

Hobhouse's laborious erudition deals with the famous Capitoline Wolf in the Palazzo dei Conservatori.

800. Napoleon.

805 n. *fighting and making love*: In a long note, mostly of quotations from Lucan's *Pharsalia*, Book X, H illustrates the descriptions in his own text.

Justly slain: 'Jure caesus existimetur,' says Suetonius after a fair estimation of his character, and making use of a phrase which was a formula in Livy's time. 'Melium jure caesum pronuntiavit, etiam si regni crimine insons fuerit:' (Book IV, chap. 48) which was continued in the legal judgments pronounced in justifiable homicides, such as killing housebreakers. See [Samuel Pitiscus (1637–1717), *C. Suetonii Tranquilli Opera* (1690), 184.] [H] In *Text M* B annotates H's 'fair estimation' thus: 'A false estimate. Suetonius was a mere Scandal monger.'

811. Caesar's famous boast was in his Letter to Amantius after the defeat of Pharnaces (47 B.C.).

812. *flee*: to fly *toward*, not *from* (see Psalms 11: 1 and Isaiah 30: 16 for this usage).

820. Aut Caesar aut nihil: cf. *BLJ* III. 217.

830 n. H cites Cicero's *Academica*, I. 13.

831. Cf. Gray's 'Elegy Written in a Country Churchyard', st. 15.

833. *Opinion an omnipotence*: quoting William Godwin's *Political Justice*, I. x.

839. Cf. *As You Like It*, II. vii. 26–8.

844. Cf. below sts. 140–2.

851. An allusion to the principles of the Holy Alliance. Cf. *CHP III*, st. 19.

857. *champion . . . child*: alluding to the widely current expression describing Napoleon, 'the child and champion of Jacobinism'. Cf. *C* II. 400–1n.

865. Cf. Isaiah 49: 26.

871. *base pageant*: the Congress of Vienna (Sept. 1815).

873. *second fall*: perhaps from Augustine's concept of the second death,

in *The City of God*, which B would have been most likely to encounter in Dante, *Epistola*, VI. 29–30.

904. The mother of the Gracchi.

915. 'Whom the Gods love die soon' is I think in Herodotus. [B, n. cancelled in *MS. H*. Cf. Menander, *Florilegium*, 120.]

$$\text{"Ον οἱ θεοὶ φιλοῦσιν ἀποθνῄσκει νέος,}$$
$$\text{Τὸ γὰρ θανεῖν οὐκ αἰσχρὸν ἀλλ' αἰσχρῶς θανεῖν.}$$

Richard F. P. Brunck (1729–1803), *Gnomici Poetae Graeci* (1784), 231. [H]

917. Cf. Shelley's 'Epigram. To Stella.'

925. Cf. *Historical Illustrations*, 200.

927. There were many of the name but of the Cecilia Metella—the wife of Crassus—I can find nor hear nothing—except the monument above alluded to—and her now empty sarcaphagus in the court of a modern Roman palace. [B, n. in *MS. H*, cancelled]

928–36. Cf. sts. 23–4.

963 n. The note is first in *CHP IV*, at the foot of the page. It is probably by B, a late addition.

964 n. *The History of the Life of M. Tullius Cicero*, op. cit. II. 102. The contrast has been reversed in a late extraordinary instance. A gentleman was thrown into Prison at Paris; efforts were made for his release. The French minister continued to detain him, under the pretext that he was not an Englishman but only *a Roman*. See 'Interesting facts relating to Joachim Murat', p. 139. [H]

981. *golden roofs*: Nero's *Domus Aurea*, stretching from the Palatine to the Esquiline. Cf. Suetonius, VI. 31; Tacitus, *Annals*, XV. 42; Martial, *Epigrammata*, 695.

983. The column of Phocas in the Forum. It was 'nameless' until 1813, as B must have known: cf. *Historical Illustrations*, 240–2.

999 n. *Roman princes*: H's n.: 'Hujus tantum memoriae delatum est ut, usque ad nostram aetatem non aliter in Senatu principibus acclamatur, nisi, FELICIOR. AUGUSTO. MELIOR. TRAJANO.' Eutropius (*fl.* 4th cent. A.D.), *Historiae Romanae breviarum*, VIII. 5. [H]

Dion: H's note quotes the original and cites Dionysius, op. cit. LXVIII. 6–7 (vol. II. 1123–4).

B's brief n. in *MS. H* is cancelled there: 'The ashes and urn of Trajan were deposited on the summit of his column—now occupied by a statue of St. Peter.'

1000. The site of the Temple of Jupiter was not known until 1876–7. Cf. *Historical Illustrations*, p. 224.

1002. The Tarpeian was found by German archaeologists in the 1930s. It is on the Capitoline Hill along the Via di Tor de' Specchi.

1007. I don't [know] how the devil *still* came there—an error in the copying. [B, MS. n. in *Proof B*. Cf. Apparatus.]

1012. Recalling Alexander, who wept that he had no more worlds to conquer.

1022 n. After his insurrection against aristocratic tyranny, Rienzi was proclaimed tribune, but he soon fell from power (1347–54): see *Decline and Fall*, chap. 70.

1022–3. Cf. Psalms 1: 3.

1026. *Numa*: legendary king and lawgiver of Rome. He received his inspiration from the nymph Egeria, according to the legend.

1027 n. *Egerian grotto*: 'Poco lontano dal detto luogo si scende ad un casaletto, del quale ne sono Padroni li Cafarelli, che con questo nome è chiamato il luogo; vi è una fontana sotto una gran volta antica, che al presente si gode, e li Romani vi vanno l'estate a ricrearsi; nel pavimento di essa fonte si legge in un epitaffio essere quella la fonte di Egeria, dedicata alle ninfe e questa, dice l'epitaffio, essere la medesima fonte in cui fu convertita.' Nardini, op. cit. 13. He does not give the inscription. [H]

two lines: 'In villa Justiniana extat ingens lapis quadratus solidus in quo sculpta haec duo Ovidii carmina sunt

> Aegeria est quae praebet aquas dea grata Camoenis.
> Illa Numae conjunx consiliumque fuit. [*Fasti*, III. 275–6]

Qui lapis videtur ex eodem Egeriae fonte, aut ejus vicinia isthuc comportatus.' Montfaucon, op. cit. 153. [H]

shrinking city: [Isaac] Vossius (1618–89), *De antiqua urbis Romae magnitudine* in Graevius, op. cit. IV. 1507. [H]

modern topographers: [Francesco] Eschinardi (1623–c.1700), *Descrizione di Roma e dell'agro Romano corretto dall'Abate R. Venuti* (Roma, 1750). They believe in the grotto and nymph. 'Simulacro di questo fonte, essendovi sculpite le acque a pie di esso.' [H]

late traveller: [Eustace,] *Classical Tour*, op. cit. II. chap. 6, p. 217. [H]

individual cave: H, in a note, quotes Juvenal, *Satires*, I. iii. 11–20.

Nardini: Op. cit. III. 3. [H]

Thence . . . true: Gifford's translation of Juvenal's *Satires*, III. 29–30.

with springs: 'Undique e solo aquae scaturiunt.' Nardini, op. cit. [H]

Venuti: Eschinardi, op. cit., pp. 297–8. [H]

Dionysius: Graevius, op. cit. II. 31. [H]

Frederick L. Beaty ('Byron's Imitations of Juvenal and Persius', *SiR* 15) argues that B's treatment of Egeria is influenced by the Revd. Martin Madan's *A New and Literal Translation of Juvenal and Persius* (1789), and especially by Madan's notes (cf. Beaty, pp. 344–5).

1031. *nympholepsy*: ecstatic vision.

1036. B describes the so-called Grotto of Egeria, which is near the Appian Way two miles outside Rome's walls. The actual grotto of the nymph is at the foot of the Caelian Hill.

1040–44. Recalling Juvenal, *Satires*, I. iii. 17–20.

1054. The entire Egeria passage seems to be recalling, and revising, Coleridge's 'Kubla Khan'.

1057. Echoes *Hamlet*, II. ii. 292.

1064. Cf. st. 82.

1081–5. Perhaps recalling La Rochefoucauld, *Maxime 76*.

1099. Proverbial.

1105. Cf. Hosea 8: 7.

1122. Cf. Horace, *Odes*, III. ii. 32.

1129. The Javanese upas tree was fabled to poison the ground for fifteen miles around itself.

1134. Echoes Milton, *Samson Agonistes*, 620.

1135 n. Cf. Sir William Drummond, *Academical Questions* (1805), I. xiv–xv.

1137–8. Cf. Isaiah 4: 6.

1140. Echoes *Macbeth*, III. iv. 24–5.

1143. *couch*: to remove a cataract.

1144 ff. Cf. *Manfred*, III. iv. 8 ff.

1147. Cf. *Corinne*, XV. iv.

1162–1242. This canto's most nakedly autobiographical passage, concerning B's domestic relations.

1179. Echoes Psalms 105: 18.

1181. *Left'st*: B's correction of this line (*Text M*) carries his annotation as well: 'Mr. J. Murray is a careless Blockhead, and forgets that in addressing the Deity a Blunder may become a Blasphemy. Venice Septr 23^d 1818.' See also *BLJ* VI. 70–1.

1181 n. *a dream*: Suetonius, in *Vita Augusti*, chap. 91. Casaubon, in the note, refers to Plutarch's Lives of Camillus and Aemilius Paulus, and also to his apothegms, for the character of this deity. The hollowed hand was reckoned the last degree of degradation: and when the dead body of the praefect Rufinus was borne about in triumph by the people, the indignity was increased by putting his hand in that position. [H]

Winkelmann: *Storia delle arti*, op. cit. XII. 3 (vol. II, p. 422). Visconti calls the statue, however, a Cybele. ([Cf. Giovanni Battista Visconti (1722–84),] *Il Museo Pio-Clementino descritto* (1782), I, par. 40. The Abate Fea (Spiegazione dei Rami, *Storia &c.*, op. cit., vol. III, p. 513) calls it a Chrisippus. [H]

Adrastea: *Dictionnaire de Bayle*, article 'Adrastea'. [H]

Rhamnusia: It is enumerated by the regionary Victor. [H]

Fortune of the day: 'Fortunae hujusce diei.' Cicero mentions her, *De legibus*, II. [H]

fortune and with fate: See *Questiones Romanae* . . ., in Graevius, op. cit., vol. V, p. 942. See also Muratori, op. cit., vol. I, pp. 88–9, where there are three Latin and one Greek inscription to Nemesis, and others to Fate. [H]

1184. Cf. Aeschylus, *Eumenides* and B's 'Lines on Hearing that Lady Byron was Ill', 13–16, 37.

1207. Echoes Coleridge's *Osorio*, v. ii. 252.

1208. Echoes Aeschylus, *Prometheus Bound*, 88–92.

1215. Cf. the Apparatus for the omitted stanza. When B annotated *CHP IV* he wrote after st. 135 (*Text M*): 'There was another stanza which followed the above in the MSS, which was omitted at the request of some of those to whom the work was shewn previous to publication. It began with "If to forgive be heaping coals of fire".' In *MS. H* B's note to the omitted stanza is: 'Omit this stanza—B.—J[anuary] 6th 1818.' The dropped stanza echoes Proverbs 25: 22. The 'Bat' reference in that stanza is to Lady Caroline Lamb.

1221–2. Cf. 'Lines on Hearing that Lady Byron was Ill', 53–5.

1252 n. *stoutly maintained*: By the Abate Bracci [Domenico Augusto Bracci (1717–92)], *Dissertazione supra un clipeo votivo* . . . (Lucca, 1784), Preface, p. 7, who accounts for the cord round the neck, but not for the horn, which it does not appear the gladiators themselves ever used. Note A, *Storia delle arti*, op. cit. II. 205. [H]

positively asserted: Either Polifontes, herald of Laius, killed by Oedipus; or Cepreas, herald of Euritheus, killed by the Athenians when he endeavoured to drag the Heraclidae from the altar of mercy, and in whose honour they instituted annual games, continued to the time of Hadrian; or Anthemocritus, the Athenian herald, killed by the Megarenses, who never recovered the impiety. See *Storia delle arti*, op. cit. 203–7. [H]

Italian editor: *Storia della arti*, op. cit. II. 205. [H]

life in him: Vulneratum deficientem fecit in quo possit intelligi quantum restet animae. Pliny, XXXIV. 8. [H]

Montfaucon and Maffei: Graevius, op. cit. III, par. 2, tab. 155; *Racc. Stat.*, tab. 64. [H] Francesco Scipione Maffei, 1675–1755.

Michael Angelo: [Giovanni Pietro Locatelli (*fl.* late 17th cent.),] *Museo Capitolino* . . . (1755), III. 154. [H] The statue is now universally regarded as a dying Gaul.

1267 n. Though B's MS. of the note is not extant, he certainly wrote it, as the cancelled portion of Hobhouse's first footnote shows.

first inventor: Julius Caesar, who rose from the fall of the aristocracy, brought Furius Leptinus and A. Calenus upon the arena ⟨; but our English poet has adopted a common mistake in saying that he forced a knight upon the stage; the truth is, he made Laberius, who was an actor, a knight, and not a knight an actor.⟩ [H] The cancelled passage was removed in *CHP IV*, third issue.

Christian writer: Tertullian, 'certe quidem et innocentes gladiatores in ludum veniunt, ut publicae voluptatis hostiae fiant.' Justus Lipsius (1547–1606), *Saturnalium sermonum* (1585), II. 3, p. 84. [H] *rebellion*: Flavius Vopiscus (*fl.* 4th. cent. A.D.) in *Vita Aurelii* and *Vita Claudii*, quoted in Lipsius, op. cit. [H]

Lipsius: 'Credo imò scio nullum bellum cladem vastitiemque generi humano intulisse, quam hos ad voluptatem ludos.' Lipsius, op. cit. I, 12. [H]

these games: St. Augustine (*Confessions*, VI. 8), 'Alypium suum gladiatorii spectaculi inhiatu incredibiliter abreptum', quoted in Lipsius, op. cit. [H]

Theodoret and Cassiodorus: [Theodoret (*c.* 390–457),] *Ecclesiasticae Historiae*, V. 36; [Flavius Cassiodorus Senator (*fl.* 6th cent. A.D.),] *Tripartita*, X. 11 [in B. Bildius, ed., *Autores historiae ecclesiasticae* (1535)]. [H]

Roman martyrology: [Caesar Cardinal] Baronius, [*Martyrologium Romanum* (Venice, 1587)], notes and annotations for 1 January. See—Marangoni, *Delle memorie sacre e profane dell'Anfitreo Flavio* (1746), p. 25. [H] Giovanni Marangoni (1673–1753).

bloody spectacles: 'Quod? non tu Lipsi momentum aliquod habuisse censes ad virtutem? Magnum. Tempora nostra, nosque ipsos videamus. Oppidum ecce unum alterumve captum, direptum est; tumultus circa nos, non in nobis; et tamen concidimus et turbamur. Ubi robur, ubi tot per annos meditata sapientiae studia? ubi ille animus qui possit dicere, *si fractus illabatur orbis*?' Lipsius, op. cit. II. 25. The prototype of Mr. Windham's panegyric on bull-baiting. [H]

1275 n. Cf. *CHP I*, sts. 71–80.

1279–1305. Cf. *Manfred*, III. iv. 1–41.

1293 n. Cf. Suetonius, *op. cit.* I. 45.

1297. This is quoted in the *Decline and Fall of the Roman Empire* [chap. 71]; and a notice on the Coliseum may be seen in the *Historical Illustrations* [pp. 263–86]. [H, in *CHP IV*]

1305. Cf. Matthew 21: 13.

1307. The Pantheon ('temple of all gods') was made into a Christian church in 609 by Boniface IV, and consecrated to the martyrs.

1308. Gifford's n. in *Proof B*: '*From Jove to Jesus* may perhaps displease— and the sense is perfect without those words.' B wrote in response: 'This is true—but the Alliteration—I cannot part with it—I like it so—besides its no worse than Pope's "Jehovah—Jove—or Lord".' Cf. Pope's 'The Universal Prayer', 4.

1314. Cf. *Historical Illustrations*, 287–95.

1319–20. The central opening in the dome. Cf. also *Corinne*, IV. II.

1324 and n. The story of the 'Caritas Romana' is told briefly in Pompeius Sextus Festus (*fl.* late 5th cent.), *De Verborum Significatione*, XIV. XX.

1351. According to legend (cf. Eratosthenes, *Catasterismi*, No. 44), when Hera pushed the infant Heracles away from her breast, after Hermes had given the child to the goddess while she slept, her milk spilled out and formed the Milky Way.

1360. The Castle of St. Angelo. See—*Historical Illustrations*, [300–16]. [H]

Originally, the mole, or mausoleum, of Hadrian. B is wrong when he says it was modelled on the pyramids of Egypt.

1369 n. Cf. *Historical Illustrations*, 316–27.

1370–2. B thought that the ruin he saw at Ephesus in 1810 was the Temple of Diana, one of the seven wonders of the world. He was wrong.

1373–4. Cf. *DJ* IX, st. 27.

1375. Cf. *CHP II*, st. 79.

1382. Cf. Tacitus, *Annals*, V. 13.

1395. Cf. Genesis 32: 30.

1399–1400. Cf. *Corinne*, IV. ii.

1405–13. Ibid. IV. iii.

1433. In the Museo Pio-Clementino. The Apollo Belvedere of the next stanza is also there. B's treatment of the Apollo is modelled on the Homeric hymn, 'To Pythian Apollo'.

1451–2. Cf. above, the Egeria passage, and Coleridge's 'woman wailing for her demon lover' in 'Kubla Khan'.

1460. Cf. Horace, *Odes*, I. iii. 29–31.

1468–76. Echoes James Ridley's *The Tales of the Genii* (1765), the conclusion, where Horam, his story told, vanishes into the kingdom of dream.

1494. *fardels*: *Hamlet*, III. i. 76.

1495. B mourns the Princess Charlotte (1796–1817), who died in child-birth while B was finishing his poem. See *BLJ* V. 276.

1531. Cf. *Macbeth*, III. ii. 23.

1532. Cf. *Coriolanus*, III. iii. 121–2.

1536 n. *'the greatest is behind'*: *Macbeth*, I. iii. 117.

1549 and n. Lago di Nemi, formed in the crater of an extinct volcano; hence B's similes later in the stanza.

1562. Cf. *Aeneid*, I. 1.

1566 n. *Life of Cicero*: Sect. xii, p. 328, vol. iii. This opportunity is taken of mentioning that an allusion to Laberius in p. 217 of these notes is a mistatement into which the writer was seduced by putting too implicit a trust in Dr. Middleton's *Life of Cicero*, sect. 8.

He has since consulted Macrobius Book II, chaps. 7 and 11, in whom, as well as Suetonius, (*Life of Julius Caesar*, chap. 39) he has seen the librarian's error and his own. [H]

In *CHP IV*, third issue and thereafter, the last two sentences of this footnote were omitted. Ambrosius Macrobius (*fl.* 4th–5th cent.), *Saturnaliorum*.

Me quotiens . . . pagus: Horace, *Epistles*, I. xviii. 104–5.

repaired by Vespasian: In a note H quotes the inscription.

tu frigus . . . vago: Horace, *Odes*, III. xiii. 10–12.

To trace . . . spring: Pope, *Essay on Criticism*, 127.

to be found: See *Historical Illustrations*, p. 43. [H]

tree in the ode: See—[Eustace,] *Classical Tour . . .*, op. cit. II, chap. 7, p. 250. [H] *garden shrubs*: 'Under our windows, and bordering on the beach, is the royal garden, laid out in parterres, and walks shaded by rows of orange trees.' *Classical Tour*, op. cit. II, chap. 11, p. 365. [H]

covered with lead: 'What, then, will be the astonishment, or rather the horror, of my reader when I inform him . . . the French Committee turned its attention to Saint Peter's, and employed a company of Jews to estimate and purchase the gold, silver, and bronze that adorn the inside of the edifice, as well as the copper that covers the vaults and dome on the outside.' Chap. 4, p. 130, vol. II. The story about the Jews is positively denied at Rome. [H] B, n. in *MS. H*: 'Weary of the "opes strepitumque Romae".' See Horace, *Odes*, III. xxix. 12.

1574. In 1810, when B and Hobhouse sailed from Gibraltar (Calpe's rock) for the East.

1576. *Symplegades*: two islands lying at the juncture of the Bosporus and the Black Sea (the Euxine).

1585–1602. B's n. in *MS. H*: 'After the stanza near the Conclusion of Canto 4th which ends with the line [1584] insert the two following stanzas. Then go on to the stanza beginning [1603]. You will find the place of insertion near the Conclusion—just before the address to the Ocean—These two stanzas will just make up the number of 500 stanzas to the whole poem. Answer when you receive this. I sent back the packets yesterday and hope that they will arrive in safety.' (B added the two stanzas in March 1818: cf. *BLJ* VI. 19.)

1586. Cf. 'Epistle to Augusta', 1 ff. (No. 300).

1594–6. Cf. *CHP II*, st. 25 and *CHP III*, st. 13.

1601. Cf. *CHP III*, st. 72 and 'Epistle to Augusta', st. 11 (No. 300).

1603. Echoes Thomas Campbell's 'On Leaving a Scene in Bavaria', 17.

1603–20. Echoes *Corinne*, I. iv.

1620. *lay*: a famous solecism. In *Proof B* Gifford writes: 'I have a doubt about *lay*.' B wrote back: 'So have I—but the *post* and *indolence* and *illness*!!'

1628. B's n. in *MS. H*: 'Yeasty—the "yeasty waves"—*Macbeth* [IV. i. 53].'

1629. The Gale of wind which succeeded the battle of Trafalgar [1805] destroyed the greater part (if not all) of the prizes—nineteen sail of the line—taken on that memorable day. I should be ashamed to specify particulars which should be known to all—did we not know that in France the people were kept in ignorance of the event of this most glorious victory in modern times, and that in England it is the present fashion to talk of Waterloo as though it were entirely an English triumph, and a thing to be named with Blenheim [1704] and Agincourt [1415]—Trafalgar and Aboukir [1798]. Posterity will decide; but if it be remembered as a skilful or as a wonderful action, it will be like the battle of Zama [202 B.C.], where we think of Hannibal more than Scipio. For assuredly we dwell on this action, not because it was gained by Blucher or Wellington, but because it was lost by Buonaparte—a man who, with all his vices and his faults, never yet found an adversary with a tithe of his talents (as far as the expression can apply to a conqueror) or his good intentions, his clemency or his fortitude.

Look at his successors throughout Europe, whose imitation of the worst parts of his policy is only limited by their comparative impotence, and their positive imbecility. [B, n. in *MS. H, Proofs*. In *Proof B*, B had a marginal note: 'Erase this passage—after the words: lost by Buonaparte.' But the entire note was deleted from the text.]

1631. Possibly recalling Boswell's *Life of Johnson* (11 April 1776).

1632. Gifford wrote in *Proof B*: 'There seems some error in the verse', and he corrected 'washed them power' to 'wasted them'. B let the correction stand in the proofs, but later changed it back (*Text M*) and protested about the change Gifford had made (*BLJ* VI. 70–1). See Apparatus.

1661. Cf. John 19: 22.

1666. Cf. Macbeth, V. v. 25.

1672. Emblems of the pilgrim to the Holy Land (cf. *Hamlet*, IV. v. 23–6).